CONTINUING THE REFORMATION

Continuing the *REFORMATION*

Essays on Modern Religious Thought

B. A. GERRISH

THE UNIVERSITY OF CHICAGO PRESS

Chicago and London

B. A. GERRISH is the John Nuveen Professor and Professor of Historical Theology in the Divinity School, the University of Chicago.

The University of Chicago Press, Chicago 60637
The University of Chicago Press, Ltd., London

Printed in the United States of America
02 01 00 99 98 97 96 95 94 93 1 2 3 4 5
ISBN: 0-226-28870-6 (cloth)
0-226-28871-4 (paper)

Library of Congress Cataloging-in-Publication Data

Gerrish, B. A. (Brian Albert), 1931–
Continuing the Reformation : essays on modern religious thought / B.A. Gerrish.
p. cm.
Includes bibliographical references and index.
1. Theology, Doctrinal—History. 2. Religious thought—Modern
period, 1500– I. Title.
BT27.G47 1993
230'.09'03—dc20 93-1796
CIP

The paper used in this publication meets the minimum requirements of the American National Standard for Information Sciences—Permanence of Paper for Printed Library Materials, ANSI Z39.48-1984.

To My Colleagues and Students
Past and Present
at the University of Chicago

Our constant endeavor, day and night, is not
just to transmit the tradition faithfully, but also to
put it in the form we think will prove best.

—JOHN CALVIN

The Reformation still goes on.

—FRIEDRICH SCHLEIERMACHER

There are only two possibilities here: either
the Gospel is in all respects identical with its earliest form,
in which case it came with its time and has departed
with it; or else it contains something which,
under differing historical forms,
is of permanaent validity.

—ADOLF VON HARNACK

Contents

Preface

This is not quite the book I intended to write, even promised to write, in the decade of the 1980s. The seed was planted in 1975, when I had occasion to teach an introductory course, "The Making of Modern Theology," to graduate students in religious studies—not in Christian theology or history of Christianity alone. The constraints of the schedule obliged me to concentrate solely on what I take to be the truly pivotal changes that make modern religious thought modern. In the two main sections of the course, I tried to present the Reformation as a revision of the Catholic tradition, and Protestant liberalism as a revision of the Reformation, the pivotal changes I had in mind being gathered under these two broad rubrics. The exercise proved educational, to the instructor at any rate, and I resolved to carry over my design into a book, since I dislike the kind of textbook that tries to say a little about everything. Circumstances and second thoughts have changed the intended title and literary form of the project, but not its main design. (The title, "The Making of Modern Theology," has since been appropriated for a whole series of widely used books.) The result is a collection of essays on modern religious thought in the West that might well be described as a sequel to my book *The Old Protestantism and the New: Essays on the Reformation Heritage* (Chicago and Edinburgh, 1982).

Adoption of the essay form brings both gains and losses. I have been able to dig more deeply, but I have also had to leave a great deal untouched that might otherwise have called for exploration even within the limits of my overall design. Still, the essays are not detached monographs. Though they do not tell a continuous story, they are in large measure—more, certainly, than the essays in *The Old Protestantism and the New*—interlocking arguments for a single thesis. Their individual subjects have their own intrinsic interest and worth, but they are held together by the intention to show two things: the revisionary character of modern religious thought in the West and the roots of this defining characteristic in a shift of interest from unchanging dogmas to the phenomenon of believing. Perhaps one could assert that *all* religious thought is, and always has been, revisionary, whether consciously or not. But here it is sufficient to follow just one trajectory (at least in part) without claiming that it has been the only one. I do claim, however, that the Protestant Reformation has its place on the trajectory. Classical and liberal Protestantism are to be understood as successive modifications of the Latin theological tradition, not as interruptions of it. Reformation and revision are one and the same thing. Hence my new title: *Continuing the Reformation*.

All the essays included in this volume were published or written in the 1980s, and they are collected here with only minor changes. Publication of the three studies in part 1, on the Reformation, was originally occasioned by the Luther anniversary of 1983. (Any hasty inference that I must identify the Reformation with Martin Luther will be safely corrected by chapter 8, if not already forestalled by the fact that I have just devoted a whole book to Calvin.) Two of the essays in part 2 were written out of my current research to honor colleagues whose work I have always admired, and the third was an inaugural lecture. The first chapter in part 3 and the last in part 4 began as purely written assignments, but all the remaining chapters (8–11) were originally designed as lectures or papers to be given orally at professional or public gatherings. The individual occasion for each essay is indicated more exactly in the notes to the Introduction. Some inappropriate allusions to the original situations have been suppressed, but I have seen no reason to reduce everything to a single, uniform style.

It is my belief that the resulting collection includes themes that will be of interest to readers whose field is history or philosophy as well as to theologians and students of religious thought. Chapter 4, for instance, is devoted to a German philosopher whose place in the history of philosophy is only just beginning to receive the acknowledgment it deserves. Taken as a whole, I hope, the volume may be found useful in at least upper-level courses in religious thought. I recognize, however, that, although I have always wanted to be as clear as the subject and my own limitations allow, some of these studies are more detailed and demanding than most of what one would expect to read in the kind of introductory course that gave rise to them. Even the one chapter that is most strictly an introduction to its theme, chapter 7 (on Schleiermacher), is probably set, at least in part, at a more technical level than any but the more advanced students will need to attain. Indeed, all of these essays, in varying degrees, are intended as contributions to the existing state of scholarship on their themes and not merely as attempts to communicate generally held interpretations. Indirectly, however, the collection may provide material for a more elementary book on religious thought in the West, whether I write one myself or leave it to others.

Chapters 1 and 3–5 were already published by the University of Chicago Press in their original versions. For permission freely granted to reuse copyright materials in the other chapters, my thanks go to the following publishers: Cambridge University Press (chapter 7), the Crossroad Publishing Company and T. & T. Clark (chapter 11), Walter de Gruyter & Co. (chapter 8), Gütersloher Verlagshaus Gerd Mohn (chapter 10), Oxford University Press (chapter 2), Pickwick Publications (chapter 9), Scholars Press (chapter 12), and Westminster/John Knox Press (chapter 6).

In the work of assembling the parts into a coherent whole, I have been helped immensely by two discerning readers for the University of Chicago Press. They read with evident care, and I have done my best to take account of their suggestions. I was also glad to have their encouragement. The first reader, who remains anonymous to me, commented approvingly that these essays indicate more explicitly than my previous writing the directions I consider "right and good for a constructive Christian theology." Chiefly intended, I am sure, is not my confession (though it is only half-ironical) that I remain an "honest Calvinist," but my open sympathy with the style of doing theology to which I return repeatedly in these pages, from the first chapter to the last. The second reader, my longtime friend Schubert Ogden, characterized the book succinctly as an attempt "to highlight important moments in the evolution of revisionary theology from the Reformation to the twentieth century." In the twentieth century, no one has done more for revisionary theology than Professor Ogden.

There are other debts I am happy to record. I am grateful once again to my assistant, Mary Stimming, not only for cheerful work on the more tedious aspects of book production—including the index—but also for some acute substantive comments. She has been alert to any signs of lingering Protestant blindness on my part to the richness and complexity of the Roman Catholic tradition. My thanks go to Judith Lawrence for speedily and expertly putting these chapters on disk (without instructing me in all the mysteries of the computer age). Finally, there is another—less definite, but no less significant—obligation that I have incurred over the years: to the academic community in which I have thought, taught, and written since 1965. It is, I think, as lively and enlightened a community as one could hope for. My debt to it is acknowledged in the dedication of this book.

Abbreviations

AAR American Academy of Religion.

AJT *American Journal of Theology.*

Apol. Philip Melanchthon, *Apologia confessionis Augustanae* (1531). Cited by article and section.

CA *Confessio Augustana* (the Lutheran Augsburg Confession, 1530).

CR *Corpus Reformatorum.* Works by Melanchthon and Calvin are cited by volume and column (or page); Zwingli's works, by volume, page, and line.

Gl. Schleiermacher's *Glaubenslehre.* Friedrich Schleiermacher, *Der christliche Glaube nach den Grundsätzen der evangelischen Kirche im Zusammenhange dargestellt.* 7th ed., based on the 2d (1830–31). Ed. Martin Redeker. 2 vols. Berlin: Walter de Gruyter, 1960. Cited by section (§) and subsection. Where indicated, I have followed the English translation edited by Mackintosh and Stewart. Schleiermacher, *The Christian Faith.* Ed. H. R. Mackintosh and J. S. Stewart. Edinburgh: T. & T. Clark, 1928. Since 1976, published in the United States by Fortress Press.

Gl.[1] The first edition of *Gl.* (1821–22). The "propositions" (*Leitsätze*) are given in an appendix in Redeker's edition of *Gl.*

GS Ernst Troeltsch, *Gesammelte Schriften.* 4 vols. (1921–25). Reprint, Aalen: Scientia Verlag, 1961–66.

Inst. John Calvin, *Institutio Christianae religionis.* Cited in the 1559 edition by book, chapter, and section.

JR *Journal of Religion.*

JW *Friedrich Heinrich Jacobi's Werke.* Ed. Jacobi, Friedrich Köppen, and Friedrich Roth. 6 vols. (vol. 4 in 3 pts.) (1812–25). Reprint, Darmstadt: Wissenschaftliche Buchgesellschaft, 1980.

KD Friedrich Schleiermacher, *Kurze Darstellung des theologischen*

Studiums zum Behuf einleitender Vorlesungen. 3d, critical ed., based on the 2d (1830). Ed. Heinrich Scholz (1910). Reprint, Darmstadt: Wissenschaftliche Buchgesellschaft, 1961. Cited by section (§).

KD[1] First ed. of *KD* (1811). Scholz notes variations from the first edition in his critical text (see *KD*).

KS Friedrich Schleiermacher, *Kleine Schriften und Predigten.* Ed. Hayo Gerdes and Emanuel Hirsch. 3 vols. Berlin: Walter de Gruyter, 1969–70.

LCC *Library of Christian Classics.* Ed. John Baillie et al. 26 vols. London: SCM Press, Philadelphia: Westminster Press, 1953–66.

LW *Luther's Works* (American edition). Ed. Jaroslav Pelikan and Helmut T. Lehmann. 55 vols. St. Louis, Missouri: Concordia Publishing House, Philadelphia: Fortress Press, 1955–86.

LWZ *Latin Works of Huldreich Zwingli.* Ed. Samuel Macauley Jackson et al. 3 vols. Vol. 1, New York: G. P. Putnam's Sons, 1912. Vols. 2–3, Philadelphia: Heidelberg Press, 1922–29. Vol. 1 carried the title *The Latin Works and the Correspondence of Huldreich Zwingli.* Vols. 2 and 3 have been reprinted with the titles *On Providence and Other Essays* and *Commentary on True and False Religion* (Durham, North Carolina: Labyrinth Press, 1983, 1981).

OS *Johannis Calvini opera selecta.* Ed. Peter Barth, Wilhelm Niesel, and Doris Scheuner. 5 vols. Munich: Chr. Kaiser, 1926–52.

Reden *Friedrich Schleiermacher's Reden über die Religion.* Critical edition by G. Ch. Bernhard Pünjer. Brunswick: C. A. Schwetschke and Son (M. Bruhn), 1879.

RGG *Die Religion in Geschichte und Gegenwart.* Ed. Michael Schiele and Leopold Zscharnack. 5 vols. Tübingen: J. C. B. Mohr (Paul Siebeck), 1909–13.

Sendschr. *Schleiermachers Sendschreiben über seine Glaubenslehre an Lücke* (1829). Ed. Hermann Mulert. Studien zur Geschichte des neueren Protestantismus, Quellenheft 2. Giessen: Alfred Töpelmann (J. Ricker), 1908.

ST Thomas Aquinas, *Summa theologiae.* Cited by part, question, and article.

SW	*Friedrich Schleiermachers sämmtliche Werke.* 31 vols. Berlin: Georg Reimer, 1834–64. Cited by division, volume, and page.
WA	*D. Martin Luthers Werke: Kritische Gesamtausgabe* (Weimarer Ausgabe). Weimar, 1883– .
WAB	*Briefwechsel* (correspondence) in WA.
WAT	*Tischreden* (table talk) in WA.

Introduction

The biblical injunction is "to contend for the faith that was once for all entrusted to the saints" (Jude 3). But modern religious thought in the West has been marked by the inclination, whether tacit or avowed, to be constantly revising the faith it contends for. When they are not rejected, religious beliefs are recast rather than merely reproduced. New language sometimes supplants the old; more often, the old language is filled with fresh meaning. At the same time, the faith that believes becomes itself a primary datum, not only of the newly emerging discipline of the philosophy of religion, but also of a new style of church theology that no longer works with immutable dogmas but takes for its object of inquiry the changing expressions of the religious life. A full articulation of the new concept of theology had to wait until Friedrich Schleiermacher (1768–1834), but its roots go back to Martin Luther (1483–1546) and beyond him to the Middle Ages—the maternal womb, as Ernst Troeltsch (1865–1923) once said, of us all.

The Reformation

The Protestant Reformers of the sixteenth century often spoke as if they were simply recovering the pure doctrine contained in Holy Scripture. But their reading of the Scriptures was inevitably filtered through their own individuality and circumstances. And what subsequent generations have made of their "pure doctrine" has likewise shown the unmistakable marks of new historical situations, as it must if the heritage of the past is to remain a living tradition. Charged with unfaithfulness to tradition, John Calvin (1509–64) replied that the constant endeavor of the Reformers was not just to transmit the tradition faithfully but to put it in the form they thought would prove best. He spoke, we may say, not only for the first generation of Protestant Reformers but also for all those later reformers who followed them.

The Reformation was neither a new religion nor a simple recovery of an older one. It was a revision, not a rejection, of the medieval tradition.

Luther's message of justification by faith brought about far-reaching changes in the old vocabulary of salvation, not least in the meaning given to the cardinal term "grace," and by the very act of making justification by faith their chief article the Lutherans established a new order of theological priorities (which is also a form of change). A distinctive theological *style* began to emerge that pointed toward Schleiermacher's explicit reformulation of the theological task as disciplined reflection on the phenomenon of believing. As for the *content* of the doctrine of justification, theologians in our own day have discovered a continuing vitality in it largely by giving it quite new applications, not merely repeating it; and even in so doing, they have not always endorsed the original Lutheran assumption that justification by faith must remain forever the center of Christian theology.[1]

In his own vocational self-image, Luther was simply a "sworn doctor of Holy Scripture." He defended his reformation as the consequence of faithfulness to his calling, and he wanted to free the word of God from ecclesiastical control. The question repeatedly posed by his Roman Catholic critics, however, is whether the original Protestant communities bore too strongly the stamp of Luther's own subjectivity. Did the Protestants commit the error of universalizing one type of human encounter with God, making the liberating word of justification into a new law, to which everyone's experience is required to conform? And does not the message of justification *by faith,* by its very nature, throw the religious subject back upon itself in fragile self-dependence?

If the old charge of religious subjectivism, brought against Luther, is to be fairly appraised, some careful distinctions need to be drawn. From his viewpoint, there is a false objectivity that must be corrected if it is faith in the word of God, not the priestly performance of the sacraments, that justifies. But, precisely as faith in the word, faith cannot be pure subjectivity: it rests on the certainty of the divine promise. Luther's faith was not, as has been alleged, thrown back upon itself in self-generated anxiety. Luther did, however, open the way to a distinctive style of theologizing in which the believer makes faith the object of reflection.[2]

Protestant theologians have admitted how difficult it is these days to explain what the controversy over justification was all about, which is why

1. "The Chief Article—Then and Now," JR 63 (1983): 355–75 (© 1983 by The University of Chicago). An address at Yale Divinity School (October 1980) commemorating the 450th anniversary of the Augsburg Confession; first published in the year of the 500th anniversary of Martin Luther's birth, as was the study reprinted in chapter 2.

2. "Doctor Martin Luther: Subjectivity and Doctrine in the Lutheran Reformation," in *Seven-Headed Luther: Essays in Commemoration of a Quincentenary, 1483–1983,* ed. Peter Newman Brooks (Oxford: Clarendon Press, 1983), 1–24. Contribution to a commemorative volume designed after the cartoon by Johann Cochlaeus (1529), which portrayed Luther as a monster with seven heads. The first head showed him as "doctor," wearing the doctor's cap.

they think that the old language has to be reminted. The same holds good for other sixteenth-century quarrels. Nothing can seem more remote to the secular modern mind than the arguments thrown endlessly back and forth between the Lutherans and the disciples of Ulrich Zwingli (1484–1531) about the bodily presence of Christ in the Eucharist. But sometimes the thoughts of a generation gone by take on fresh significance when seen under the rubric of another question. At the heart of the debate over the real presence was at least one question that we still find fascinating, whether our interest is in divinity or in aesthetics: What do signs and symbols do?

Both parties in the eucharistic debate believed themselves to be affirming the heritage of Augustine (354–430) with its distinction between sign and reality, but each made something different of it. Zwingli thought of sacramental signs as reminders of events past, and so of a reality that is not strictly present here and now: the death of Christ on the cross, or the rebirth that the Spirit has brought about in a believer's soul. Signs are indicative or declarative, not instrumental, telling us what has happened rather than making it happen. Luther retorted that this was to misunderstand Augustine, for whom the reality was present with the sign. In any case, he insisted, there is no "figure" at all in Christ's words "This is my body"; rather, when the words are uttered, what was once bread becomes literally Christ's body. It is not by symbolizing anything that the Sacrament does what it does.

A causality that is thus taken out of the order of signification is not, however, the only alternative to a sign of an absent reality. A third view held that there are signs that precisely by signifying bring the reality to which they point, as we know by experience. This was Calvin's view (Luther's, too, when he was not speaking of the real presence). It has its roots in Augustine. But it continues to echo in the writings of literary critics, theologians, and philosophers of our own day. Focusing the attention on what seems to be actually experienced (or at least is held to be experienced) in our encounter with various kinds of symbol has put the old coinage back into circulation, albeit not everywhere with quite the same face value. The reformation still goes on.[3]

The Age of Reason

In the Age of Reason, there were voices that called for eradication of the scandal of religion and subjected every inherited religious belief to criti-

3. "Discerning the Body: Sign and Reality in Luther's Controversy with the Swiss," JR 68 (1988): 377–95 (© 1988 by The University of Chicago). This study, too, was occasioned by the Luther anniversary of 1983. Initial versions were read for the Luther Jubilee in Washington, D.C., and the Raphael-Luther Celebration at the University of Chicago.

cism and scorn. Others were willing to defend at least *some* religious beliefs, arguing for a universal religion of reason that Christianity, like every other historical religion, enshrines—along with much else that is merely superstitious. But they differed on the question whether this makes the Christian church superfluous, inimical, or instrumental to the progress of rational religion. Still others undertook to reassess the old ecclesiastical beliefs and to refurbish them, though in strikingly different ways that could not all please everyone.

The prevailing assumption had been that belief is assent to authority, without proof or even personal insight; hence it was something that the new age should do without. Enlightenment, in the words of Immanuel Kant (1724–1804), is release from just such "self-incurred tutelage," and the attraction of the religion of reason was that it seemed to rest belief not on authority but on demonstration. But what if "belief" properly means something else—neither assent to authority nor yet (as justified belief) the assertion of what we are able to back with arguments? And what if the things the church proposes to us for belief are not the sole options for thinking persons who are by no means irreligious? In F. H. Jacobi (1743–1819) and Friedrich Forberg (1770–1848), it is the concept of believing that is subjected to fresh—and largely original—reappraisals; in J. G. von Herder (1744–1803) the focus shifts to the concept of "God," but with momentous consequences for what it means to *believe* in God, or to be religious.

Against the enlightened dismissal of religious belief, Jacobi argued that every department of human life rests in the end on faith, and faith, though it is not mere assent to authority, is conviction without proof. The conviction, for instance, that actual objects exist outside the perceiving mind can never be proved, and yet we hold it, not because we are told to, but because we cannot do without it. If any choose to doubt the evidence of their senses that there is an external world and demand proof of it, there is nothing we can do for them; yet they are just as much bound to presuppose it in practice as we are. Similarly, the assumption that things are interconnected in a causal network is justified by faith alone. In this sense, even the skeptical David Hume (1711–76) was not against "faith," but for it. The appeal to faith is neither fanaticism nor popery; it is simply the recognition that all knowledge derived from proof must necessarily go back to a knowing without proof.

The reappearance in the twentieth century of something like Jacobi's concept of belief or faith makes it a matter of some importance to give his philosophy of faith its rightful place in modern religious thought, which has remained largely unaware of him. Of course, Jacobi did not justify believing in anything we please. But by examining the use of the concept of faith beyond the explicitly religious discourse to which it is often supposed to be confined, he showed that we all hold convictions we cannot prove, whether we consider ourselves religious or not, and that religious faith has an anchorage in these inescapable beliefs. His procedure, in his own words, was simply "to disclose existence": that is, to show the way things are, not to be forever trying to prove what we cannot prove but do not seriously doubt. There are, I think, as I attempt to show, some difficulties with Jacobi's case, but he earns the credit of being the first to open up a fresh line of reflection on the meaning of faith.[4]

Other varieties of revisionary religious thought in the Age of Reason focused more immediately on the concept of God, the principal object of belief; and a changing perception of God brought with it a changing perception of "piety," the corresponding religious disposition. In Heinrich Heine's (1797–1856) provocative—and sometimes mischievous—reading of German intellectual history, a revolution in philosophy had taken place no less momentous than the political revolution in France, and it had brought with it a fundamental shift in the way the intelligentsia, at least, thought of God. The famous Pantheism Controversy evoked a new interest in the philosophy of Benedict de Spinoza (1632–77), the alleged atheist whom Johann Wolfgang von Goethe (1749–1832) hailed as in actual fact a theist and a Christian of the highest order. For many, not God but the old image of God as the divine monarch above and outside the world had died, and they turned back instead to a world that is itself saturated with deity. To Heine's own thinking, the deity was incarnate in the flesh of humanity, and he transformed the new philosophy into a welfare program for the poor, whom the church admonished to await better things in the world to come. To other reflective minds, the "secret religion of Germany," as Heine called it (he named it "pantheism"), meant seeking God in nature. Herder's winsome conversations on God make clear the religious implications of the quest. A deity without ears to hear is not at the beck and call of human beings, whose blessedness lies rather in bending themselves to nature's orderly, creative activity; and that is precisely what one ought to mean by "God."[5]

With Friedrich Forberg the focus of reappraisal moves back again to the concept of belief. It was Forberg who sparked the second great debate about God in eighteenth-century Germany: the Atheism Controversy. Once again the problem was the old anthropomorphic deity—the super-

4. "Faith and Existence in the Philosophy of F. H. Jacobi," in *Witness and Existence: Essays in Honor of Schubert M. Ogden*, ed. Philip E. Devenish and George L. Goodwin (Chicago: University of Chicago Press, 1989), 106–39 (© 1989 by The University of Chicago).

5. "The Secret Religion of Germany: Christian Piety and the Pantheism Controversy," JR 67 (1987): 437–55 (© 1987 by The University of Chicago). Inaugural lecture (20 May 1986) on appointment to the John Nuveen Chair in the Divinity School of the University of Chicago.

natural, personal being who governs the world from above. But Forberg's solution was to refashion the concept not of God, but of belief. The "belief" he came up with was quite different from Jacobi's "faith," and Hans Vaihinger (1852–1933) was later to discover in Forberg (mistakenly, I think) a forerunner of fictionalism. According to Forberg, religious belief is not factual but practical: it does not assert or predict a state of affairs but only announces a commitment. Belief is acting as if there were a moral government over the world, not asserting that in fact there is. And moral commitment (which is true, practical belief) shines brightest when we do what we ought even if we doubt the existence of a moral order or a kingdom of God that is to come (which is only theoretical disbelief).

Nevertheless, Forberg recognized that moral commitment, though not a factual claim, is itself a remarkable fact of human existence and does imply something about ourselves and the kind of world we live in. Hence he gave a different status than Vaihinger was to give to factual beliefs about the existence of a moral world order and a God who governs it. For Vaihinger, the fictionalist, talk about God is known to be false but is retained for the time being because it is useful in organizing certain aspects of our experience. For Forberg, talk about God is generated by our moral experience and may quite possibly be true, although morality has no stake whatever in asserting that it is, in fact, true. Factual beliefs belong to theology; religion, as practical belief, has no interest in them. It is, of course, possible that Forberg was a closet atheist, but the language he employed suggests an agnostic who did not consider theological assertions either false or totally pointless—just irrelevant to religion or (what was for him the same thing) to morality.[6]

Jacobi, Herder, and Forberg all lived in a world dominated by men greater than themselves, a world their writings continually reflect. Jacobi and Herder were already part of the revolt against the Enlightenment, but they could not escape from the shadow cast by Immanuel Kant. Forberg, though last in time, was the closest of the three to the spirit of the Kantian philosophy, and over *him* fell the shadow of J. G. Fichte (1762–1814), the first of the great absolute idealists. This is not to belittle any one of my three representatives of religious thought in the Age of Reason. Herder was a seminal thinker of the first rank, whose misfortune it is always to be measured against the peerless stature of the Olympians, Kant and Goethe. Jacobi's unique role in the evolution of German philosophy is attested by

6. "Practical Belief: Friedrich Karl Forberg (1770–1848) and the Fictionalist View of Religious Language." From *Probing the Reformed Tradition: Historical Studies in Honor of Edward A. Dowey, Jr.*, ed. Elsie Anne McKee and Brian G. Armstrong (© 1989 Westminster/John Knox Press), 367–85. Used by permission. Written in honor of Professor Dowey, this essay was presented orally as a public lecture at Stanford University (5 December 1988).

the new critical edition of his works (begun in 1981). Even Forberg, nearly forgotten in his own day and little remembered since, played the pawn's role in a grand game and deserves credit for the tenacity with which he followed through one of the perennial difficulties in Kant's system. All three started trains of thought that have reappeared in twentieth-century philosophy of religion (or philosophical theology), including the case for a noncognitive interpretation of religious language. And therein lies one important clue to their significance: they were present at the birth, so to say, of a new discipline.

For the age of Protestant orthodoxy in Continental Europe, "religious thought" means, for the most part, Christian theology practiced as a confessional discipline—from inside one of the three dominant ecclesiastical traditions (Roman Catholic, Lutheran, or Reformed). But by the eighteenth century another kind of religious thought had achieved detachment from the faith of the churches: an independent "philosophy of religion" (as we would call it) had learned to be critical of Christian beliefs and to look at Christianity itself from the outside as one manifestation of religiousness among many. The problem was then no longer to continue refining and defending Roman Catholic, Lutheran, or Reformed dogmas, but to understand them generically as instances of a universally human way of thinking and behaving. The question was not, for instance, Is Christ bodily present in the Sacrament of the Altar, and if so, how? but rather: What is religion, and what does it mean to believe? This did not necessarily imply a rejection of church theology (though for some it certainly did). And when a renewal of church theology came, it was a theology transformed by the new philosophical questions and deeply indebted to the new philosophical answers.

Schleiermacher

Friedrich Schleiermacher is commonly named "the father of modern theology." In the aftermath of the philosophical revolution, he took up once more the distinctively theological approach to Christian belief, an enterprise that had languished in the Age of Reason, but made of it something relatively new. He set aside older styles of doing theology, fully aware that many found his thinking not only novel but a dangerous accommodation to the new "pantheism." Yet he was no iconoclast. Far from it. Schleiermacher's theology, as much as Luther's or Calvin's, was a reworking of inherited materials in a new age, and he supposed that what he made of the old beliefs left them immune to Enlightenment criticisms. In his opinion, the dogmatic language inherited from Augustine was rich and deep enough to be serviceable still, if handled with good sense, and he claimed that his novel style of descriptive theologizing ("empirical," as he called it) actually placed him in the succession of Martin Luther. All he did was to exercise the Protestant right of development.

In Schleiermacher's theological masterpiece, *The Christian Faith,* the Christian way of believing, as one way among others, becomes explicitly the object of sustained, systematic, critical inquiry. "Dogmatics" is now the science not of dogmas but of faith. It does not set out to present or demonstrate unchanging truth, but rather to describe the religious affections expressed in Christian doctrines, which are always subject to criticism and improvement. So understood, dogmatics need not fall into conflict with other sciences. It is true that Christians—and even Christian theologians in their doctrines of creation and providence—often speak as if God, having brought the world into being as a craftsman makes an artifact, occasionally intervened in its normal, law-governed operation. But these are merely naive expressions for the way the devout mind experiences the course of nature—poetic images for the conviction that the world investigated by the natural sciences has meaning and value grounded in a continuous divine activity. The divine interventionism of the older theology, left obsolete by the discovery of natural laws, gives way to the confidence that the world *as it is*—a web of law-governed events—is an "absolutely harmonious work of divine art."

To be religious is to combine every thought of any consequence with thoughts of the omnipotent love that makes the world good. This, Schleiermacher believed, is what Christ did as no one before him or after him; therein lies Christ's continuing ability to "redeem" others through the devout community he brought into being. Like the doctrines of creation and providence, correctly reinterpreted, the doctrine of redemption simply tries to thematize experience, and here, too, conflict with science—in this case, historical science—is unnecessary. Christian claims about the Redeemer rest on the community's actual experience of redemption, not on the historical reliability of the Gospels, which is placed in doubt by historical criticism.[7]

Schleiermacher's theology of experience, as he claimed, had its roots in the theology of Martin Luther. But Luther is not the Reformation, and Schleiermacher was not Lutheran. The theme "Schleiermacher and the Reformation" should not, as usually happens, leave out his relation to the Reformers of his own church, Zwingli and especially Calvin. John Calvin, like Schleiermacher, was preeminently a systematic thinker, and Schleiermacher commended him for the very two things he himself strove

7. "Friedrich Schleiermacher," in *Nineteenth Century Religious Thought in the West,* ed. Ninian Smart et al., 3 vols. (Cambridge: Cambridge University Press, 1985), 1:123–53. The bibliographical essay with which this study originally concluded (153–56) is not reproduced in chapter 7 of the present volume.

for in his own dogmatics: a strict connection with the actual religious affections of the believing community and a combination of sharpness with systematic compass. Not surprisingly, there are striking, though hitherto unexplored, parallels between Calvin's *Institutes* and Schleiermacher's *The Christian Faith*. It goes without saying that there are differences as well.

Calvin begins his *Institutes* (in the 1559 edition), for instance, not immediately with Christian religious experience, but with the universal phenomenon of human religiousness. The function of the opening chapters in the arrangement of the whole is disputed. It is arguable that Calvin here shows himself a forerunner not of Schleiermacher alone, but of every theologian who holds that Christian theology must find in common human experience a point of contact that is the condition for the possibility of revelation. But the argument must be qualified. Between Calvin and Schleiermacher an important change had taken place. The totality of human religiousness outside Christianity could no longer be dismissed, in Calvin's style, as idolatry and superstition. Christianity remained for Schleiermacher the highest development of religion; into it, he assumed, all other religions were destined to pass over. But he insisted that other forms of the religious life had their own measure of truth. "Religion" had become a generic term.[8]

There is an apparent structural parallel in the ways Calvin and Schleiermacher saw the relationship between creation and redemption. Whether or not he was consciously developing Calvin's insights, it was the doctrine of creation that occasioned Schleiermacher's most convincing revision of a traditional church doctrine. How could belief that the world was created by God survive the apparent conflict of the Book of Genesis with modern science? The old assumption had been that "creation" refers to the first act in a cosmic drama, acts 2 and 3 being the fall of Adam and the entry of God into human history in Christ. But if the new theology only describes the modalities of the present religious consciousness, "creation" cannot possibly denote an event in the primal past; rather, it will thematize the creature-consciousness, or sense of finitude, that everyone at all times can become aware of by introspection. The beginning of the cosmos is a matter best left to the speculations of scientific theorists.

If the "feeling of absolute dependence" says nothing about the question how the world began, neither does it run into conflict with the scientific concept of nature as a self-contained causal complex of law-governed events. Indeed, since the core of the religious consciousness is total confidence in the natural order that God sustains, any suspension of the regular

8. "From Calvin to Schleiermacher: The Theme and the Shape of Christian Dogmatics," in *Internationaler Schleiermacher-Kongress Berlin 1984, Schleiermacher-Archiv,* vol. 1, ed. Kurt-Victor Selge (Berlin: Walter de Gruyter, 1985), 1033–51. A paper presented at an international congress commemorating the 150th anniversary of Schleiermacher's death.

course of nature by the intervention of its Creator would undermine piety no less than science. And if the world were not in fact as reliable an order as the natural sciences assume, neither could it become, as Christian faith affirms, the theater for the drama of redemption. Schleiermacher admitted that his was not exactly the orthodox doctrine of creation, but he predicted that it would become orthodox in due course.[9]

With Schleiermacher, we arrive at both an explicit statement of the principles of a revisionary theology and a thorough, systematic implementation of them over the full range of traditional dogmatics. He was convinced that his program set him in the line of theological advance that runs back to Luther and the Reformation. Others who claim the same lineage have nonetheless repudiated him. Often enough, he has simply been misunderstood, sometimes because only a fragment of the program has been put to the test, sometimes because alien meanings have been read into his idiosyncratic terms. But plausible criticisms have been brought against him, too, many of them having to do precisely with his attempt to accommodate the Reformation heritage to the philosophical changes of the eighteenth century. He has been accused of imposing a generic concept of religion on his interpretation of the Christian faith, surrendering to the pantheism of the Spinozist revival, and losing the divine object of theology in subjectivism. And, oddly, he has not always been well served by the defenses put forward by his friends, including Troeltsch.

Ernst Troeltsch

Christian theology was by no means Ernst Troeltsch's principal vocation; he was also a philosopher, a historian, and a political commentator. In his Heidelberg years, however, he did hold a theological post, and in theology he saw himself as Schleiermacher's disciple. Troeltsch developed one of the most astute interpretations of the course of Protestant theology and the place of Luther and Schleiermacher in it. But his interest in religion carried his thoughts beyond Protestantism and beyond Christianity: even more fascinated than Schleiermacher by religious pluralism, he earned himself the nickname "Systematic Theologian of the History of Religions School." In the thoroughness with which he explored the implications of historical thinking for theology, Troeltsch left his master behind, and in at least one respect he misrepresented him.

It is through his monumental work titled in English *The Social Teaching of the Christian Churches* that Troeltsch is best known in the English-

9. "Nature and the Theater of Redemption: Schleiermacher on Christian Dogmatics and the Creation Story," *Ex Auditu: Annual of the Frederick Neumann Symposium on Theological Interpretation of Scripture* 3 (1987): 120–36. A paper presented at the second symposium, Princeton Theological Seminary, 16–19 October 1987.

speaking world, a work that invites comparison with the writings of the "socio-historical school" at the University of Chicago. Through *The Social Teaching* his contributions became at least as well known to historians and sociologists as to theologians. But most of the book-length studies of Troeltsch in English have focused on his significance for theology, and in the 1960s he was sharply criticized from the perspective of the neo-orthodox theology that had eclipsed him in Germany. It was declared that in his last years, by his surrender of the church's insistence on the superiority of Christianity to other religions, Troeltsch dismantled his own earlier theological program. This may well be so. But today, when Christian theologians are learning to speak with the leaders of other religions on an equal footing, not as evangelists or missionaries, Troeltsch's abandonment of the absoluteness of Christianity appears less indefensible than the neoorthodox denial that Christianity can even be considered one of the religions of the world. His notion of "polymorphous truth" has a place once more around the theological table, and some of the participants in the dialogue will consider it a plausible revision of Schleiermacher's program.[10]

Troeltsch saw the heart of the program in the change of nomenclature that Schleiermacher had proposed: from *Dogmatik* ("dogmatics") to *Glaubenslehre* ("the doctrine or science of faith"). Historical thinking had dissolved the concept of dogma as a permanently valid definition of the church's teaching, and where there are no dogmas there is (strictly speaking) no more dogmatics. The theological task is to give a disciplined account of the faith that prevails in a particular religious community at a particular time. And yet, the new theology was not simply severed from the old. Troeltsch developed with uncommonly keen insight Schleiermacher's conviction that the new approach had its roots in the Reformation.

By his *sola fide* ("salvation by faith alone"), Luther had proclaimed a new path to the old destination. But the path, Troeltsch argued, became in time more important than the destination. Faith, indeed, as discernment of the character of God, *is* salvation, which is to say, the source of confident living here and now. Religion, as Troeltsch put it, is drawn into the domain of the psychologically transparent: no longer (in itself) something supernatural, it can be understood as a mechanism of the mind without denying that in it there is a relation to the divine.[11] Clearly, theology now

10. "Protestantism and Progress: An Anglo-Saxon View of Troeltsch," in *Protestantismus und Neuzeit, Troeltsch-Studien,* vol. 3, ed. Horst Renz and Friedrich Wilhelm Graf (Gütersloh: Gütersloher Verlagshaus Gerd Mohn, 1984), 35–53. A paper presented at the First Congress of the Ernst-Troeltsch-Gesellschaft, Augsburg, 14–17 March 1983.

11. "From *Dogmatik* to *Glaubenslehre:* A Paradigm Change in Modern Theology?" in *Paradigm Change in Theology: A Symposium for the Future,* ed. Hans Küng and David Tracy (New York: Crossroad, 1989), 161–72. Authorized English translation of *Theologie—wohin?*

hovers on the edge of the so-called scientific study of religion. Surprisingly, however, Troeltsch opened up the gap between the two disciplines in the answer he gave to my final question, and in so doing he misrepresented the heritage of Schleiermacher.

What is the proper home of a modern, revisionary theology? Where should it be pursued? There can no longer be any argument for restoring theology to its medieval throne as queen of the sciences. But many go further and argue that it has no business in a modern university at all, because the theologian's primary loyalty is always to the church, not to the academy. The consequent demand for a strictly scientific study of religion would either leave theology marginalized in the university or else cloister it in church seminaries. Troeltsch believed himself to be following Schleiermacher when, in effect, he took the first alternative, describing dogmatic theology as a practical, nonscientific expression of personal conviction, undertaken solely for the training of clergy. But he was mistaken in his appeal to Schleiermacher, who in actual fact held *Glaubenslehre* to be a "historical science," or, as we would say, a humanistic discipline. And this is a placement of dogmatic theology among the various academic disciplines that has still not been adequately explored.[12]

Retrospect and Prospect

If the varieties of religious thought from Luther to Troeltsch do not yield a single theology, they do nonetheless illustrate one way of understanding theology: as the continual reformation of a religious tradition through revision of its inherited language. In this view, the wisest way to come to terms with religious beliefs lies neither in rejecting nor in merely rehearsing them, but rather in reforming them by criticism. Naturally, there would be little need for this delicate activity if the old language were not found problematic in a new day, and no need for it at all if the language were simply dead. Every one of my reformers, without exception, wrote because the language of the church had become in one respect or another questionable. But the statistics do not yet call for a requiem or a death certificate: the language of Christian faith still has currency because there are

and *Das neue Paradigma von Theologie,* © T. & T. Clark, Ltd., 1989. Reprinted by permission of The Crossroad Publishing Company. A paper presented at an international ecumenical symposium, University of Tübingen, 23–26 May 1983, on paradigm change in theology.

12. "*Ubi theologia, ibi ecclesia?* Schleiermacher, Troeltsch, and the Prospect for an Academic Theology," in *Religious Studies, Theological Studies, and the University-Divinity School,* ed. Joseph Mitsuo Kitagawa, Scholars Press Studies in Theological Education (Atlanta, Georgia: Scholars Press, 1992), 69–94. Written as a contribution to Professor Kitagawa's symposium, this essay was also presented in large part in public lectures at Lancaster University (26 November 1990) and Trinity College, Dublin (29 November 1990).

still, it seems, profound human experiences which it both echoes and nurtures.

Friedrich Schleiermacher's attempt to articulate the program of a revisionary theology remains classic; perhaps, in all its detail, it is still the most instructive such model that we have. It would plainly be a betrayal of the revisionary spirit if one were content merely to repeat it, but to revise it in its turn would require a different book than this one. Still, in the chapters that follow I do try to remove some of the hindrances to hearing the contribution he has to make, and I occasionally note places where I think ambiguities or difficulties remain. It may help to mention three problems in advance.

First, Schleiermacher's use of terms often goes against the prevailing terminology of the present. (To some extent, it went against the usage of his own day.) By "historical theology," for instance, he did not mean the history of theology, although that is certainly included. The fact that he also included dogmatics shows plainly that by "historical theology" he meant, at least in part, exactly what *we* call "revisionary theology": that is, a variety of *systematic* or *constructive* theology that acknowledges the changing, not fixed or permanent, character of its object—not dogma, but a historical and therefore constantly evolving way of believing.

Second, in our contemporary discussion "descriptive" and "normative" are assumed to be exclusive methodological options. But the way Schleiermacher views it, dogmatics (*Glaubenslehre*) describes the religious affections by criticism of the prevailing language of the church, and in this sense it is a descriptive and a normative discipline at the same time. His own dogmatic work, *The Christian Faith,* is accordingly "descriptive" (*empirisch*) in distinction, not from "normative," but from "exegetical" or "deductive." Though each has its own place, exegetical theology, which works from the biblical texts, and rational theology, which works from rational concepts, are distinct disciplines. This, to be sure, is not an unproblematic position. But the main difficulty, as I hint in passing, lies more in Schleiermacher's concept of philosophical theology than in his dogmatics. For the truth of dogmatic assertions, in his scheme, is strictly the correctness with which they set forth the Christian religious affections. But if Christian beliefs are themselves assertions that claim to be true, then there needs to be another forum for the justification of belief. It is not at all clear to me that Schleiermacher provides it. This leads into the final problem.

Third, Schleiermacher expressly understands dogmatic theology as the activity of an insider, and he frequently appeals directly to the experience of his hearer or reader, who is presumed to be likewise an insider. The risk is that dogmatics may then become esoteric and, for this reason, an unwanted discipline in a university. But it should at least be noted that, as

Schleiermacher thinks of the work of the dogmatic theologians, it places them between the primary, symbolic discourse of the religious community and the rational argumentation that we expect from our philosophers of religion. It is a work, in other words, in which *mythos* and *logos,* symbol and argument, are subtly interwoven, and as such it calls for insight and imagination, which are more likely, at least, to come from the insider. But if this is granted, it does not follow that the listener or reader, too, must enjoy the same creative insight and have the same well-stored imagination. Schleiermacher might have done better to argue that because everyone (in his view) is fundamentally religious, though not Christian, the possibility of sufficient understanding is present in all.

There will, of course, always be those for whom the entire enterprise of a continuing reformation is suspect, if not an outright mistake, and they will not be much interested in any attempt to recondition the Schleiermacherian model for the future. They will see in it not so much a reminting of old coinage as a futile struggle to put new wine in old wineskins—with the disastrous result of which the Gospel warns us (Mark 2:22). Candor, they will say, demands either defense or rejection of the old language, and they will perhaps trace the decline of the so-called mainline denominations precisely to the flexibility of their theology. The difficulty with this position, it seems to me, though I cannot argue the point here, is that even the adversaries of a revisionary theology are usually revisionists themselves. (One thinks, for example, of Schleiermacher's greatest critic, Karl Barth [1886–1968].) The problem is where to set the limits. And the limits cannot be set in advance, which is why we always need theologians.

Part One

THE REFORMATION

1

The Chief Article—Then and Now

We ask for this one thing, that they
allow the Gospel to be taught purely.
—THE AUGSBURG CONFESSION

THE INTRIGUING ecumenical issue of 1980 was whether the Roman Church should recognize the Augsburg Confession (1530) as a "catholic" statement of faith.[1] The question lost none of its fascination in 1983, when the first Protestant took the center of the stage from the first Protestant confession. But whatever the final verdict may be, one thing should not be overlooked: the Lutheran movement did not emerge to reaffirm the catholic faith in general, but to register a protest on behalf of a quite specific item in it. One article was designated the "chief article," and its content was identified with the gospel. To take Martin Luther and his Reformation on their own terms is, above all, to reflect on the chief article and its significance for church and theology both in its own day and in ours.

The Gospel of Grace

The initial design of the Wittenbergers at the Diet of Augsburg was not to confess their faith, but to defend their reforms. It was Luther's old adversary John Eck (1486–1543) who made a change of strategy essential, when he published his catalogue of 380 heresies drawn from the Reformers' writings. A defense of Lutheran orthodoxy became imperative, and Philip Melanchthon (1497–1560) undertook to compose it.[2] He claimed that the Lutheran doctrines contained nothing out of harmony with Scripture or

1. For the original texts of *CA* and Melanchthon's defense of it (*Apol.*), I have used the standard edition, *Die Bekenntnisschriften der evangelisch-lutherischen Kirche,* 4th ed. (Göttingen: Vandenhoeck and Ruprecht, 1959), the Latin and German versions being distinguished, where necessary, by the letters *L* or *G* in parentheses. Page numbers are added in parentheses where my quotations follow Theodore G. Tappert, ed., *The Book of Concord: The Confessions of the Evangelical Lutheran Church* (Philadelphia: Fortress Press, 1959).

2. The shift in Saxon strategy is traced by Jared Wicks, "Abuses under Indictment at the Diet of Augsburg 1530," *Theological Studies* 41 (1980): 253–302.

the catholic church—or even the Roman Church, if the ancient church fathers were to be the court of appeal.[3]

The distinctiveness of Melanchthon's approach is readily highlighted by comparison with Luther's personal "Augsburg Confession," his *Exhortation to the Clergy Assembled at the Diet of Augsburg,* which went on sale during the diet. Not only was Luther's tone belligerent and insulting, but he also spoke throughout of "my doctrine" with an assurance that must have struck the unconvinced as arrogance. To the charge of introducing novelties in the church he replied cheerfully that if his critics would wait a few years, his gospel would be as old as their inventions.[4] Clearly, Melanchthon's was a quite different strategy. As Luther admitted, he himself could not tread so softly.[5]

It can hardly be said, however, that Melanchthon's articles of faith and doctrine make up an evenly weighted summary of Christian beliefs. Article 20, on faith and works, is disproportionately long, and its central theme, the "teaching about faith," is singled out as the chief teaching or chief article in the church. The fourth article summarizes the central theme in terms of the Pauline doctrine of justification, and the very next article makes it clear that the teaching of the gospel is nothing other than the teaching of justification by faith. As Melanchthon asserts many times over in his *Apology,* the gospel *is* the promise of justification: it is the gospel of free forgiveness.[6] Moreover, throughout the Confession and the *Apology* the affirmation of forgiveness by grace is accompanied by the repeated denial of forgiveness by our own merits; the righteousness of faith and its perennial conflict with the righteousness of works dominate the Confession, so that, like most statements of Christian belief, it affirms the catholic faith against a present threat to its integrity.[7]

3. *CA,* conclusion to pt. 1 (articles on faith and doctrine). Cf. the introduction to pt. 2 (articles on abuses) and the conclusion to the whole confession.

4. *Vermahnung an die Geistlichen, versammelt auf dem Reichstag zu Augsburg* (1530); WA 30^2.268–356, esp. 302.3ff.; LW 34:9–61, esp. 29.

5. Luther to Elector John, 15 May 1530: WAB 5.319.5 (no. 1568); LW 49:297–98.

6. The gospel is the "Gospel of the free forgiveness of sins" (*Apol.,* 4.110 [123]) or "of the free forgiveness of sins and the righteousness of faith" (4.20 [110]). Sec. 43 contains another definition: "The Gospel is, strictly speaking, the promise of forgiveness of sins and justification because of Christ" (113). Cf. secs. 120, 186, and 274.

7. It is sometimes asserted that the real center of the Augsburg Confession is *Christus pro nobis;* but it is not clear what textual warrants could be advanced in support of the assertion, whereas there are several explicit statements that count against it—unless a distinction is implied between the "center" and the "chief article." It appears to be a theological rather than a historical judgment when Schlink, for instance, remarks that "it would be more appropriate to see the center in the christological article (III) and especially in its account of Jesus Christ's action, in our place and for our sake." But he goes on, in the same address, to assert that "the center of the Augsburg Confession *is* [my emphasis] the *Christus pro nobis.*" Edmund Schlink, "The Ecumenical Character and Claim of the Augsburg Confession," in *The Augsburg Con-*

A tendency to subordinate other themes to the gospel of justification, or to the faith that apprehends justification,[8] is apparent in the articles following the summary statement of article 4. The church's ministry of word and sacrament, we are told (article 5), has been instituted so that we may obtain the faith God reckons as righteousness. The new obedience of the Christian (article 6) is not an attempt to merit justification; it is the good fruit of faith. The church itself (article 7) is nothing other than the assembly of saints or believers in which the gospel is purely taught and the sacraments rightly administered. And the sacraments (article 13) are said to be signs and testimonies of the will of God toward us, instituted for the awakening and confirming of faith. In this manner church, ministry, and sacraments are all defined by reference to the justifying faith that is born of the gospel and believes the promises.[9] Less directly, but still quite clearly, the conflict of faith and works appears also in articles 2 (on original sin), 12 (on repentance), and 18 (on free will).

The distinction between the righteousness of the law and the righteousness of the gospel naturally carries our thoughts back to Luther's celebrated "breakthrough," especially when we are told that the teaching about faith cannot be understood apart from the conflict of the terrified conscience. We are bound to think again of Luther when we hear that some have been driven by their conscience into monasteries, in the hope that there they might merit God's grace. And it is, of course, Luther's so-called discovery of the gospel that the Confession echoes in these words: "The Gospel teaches that we have a gracious God, not by our own merits but by the merit of Christ, when we believe this."[10] The Augsburg Confession is, in effect, the creedal precipitate of what we find in solution in the biography of the young Luther; the Confession, we may say, changing the metaphor, codifies his encounter with God.

Unfortunately, if there is one other theme that has given the Reformation scholars as much trouble as the chief article, it is the related theme of Luther's theological breakthrough. It is ironic that there should be something like a consensus on what the central Reformation doctrine is, but no consensus on what it means. And on the answer to the question of the doctrine's meaning, some would say, depends the answer to yet another question: When did Luther become a Lutheran? One may wish, for instance, to identify the distinctively evangelical insight with a purely forensic view of justification, and then try to find out when Luther attained this insight (if

---

fession in Ecumenical Perspective, ed. Harding Meyer, LWF Report 6/7 (Stuttgart: Kreuz Verlag, 1980), 1–28; see 8, 11.

8. "Nam remissio peccatorum et iustificatio fide apprehenditur" (*CA,* 6.2).

9. ". . . fides, quae concipitur ex evangelio seu absolutione" (*CA,* 12.5).

10. *CA,* 20.17 (L), 20.20, 5.3 (G [31]).

ever). Be that as it may, if we start from the rival view, which Luther was contesting, at least one conclusion can be drawn with reasonable assurance; and it goes close, I would argue, to the heart of the matter.

Brother Martin's undoing in the Augustinian monastery was a form of piety underwritten by the scholastic formula, "God does not deny grace to those who do what they can [*quod in se est*]." It is curious that Luther and Zwingli came to hold quite different estimates of this often-quoted principle. (Calvin's estimate, as we will see, was different again.) In Zwingli's view, everyone always acts according to his or her ability, however trifling it may be, so that anyone, if the principle held good, could be justified by works.[11] Luther, by contrast, was tormented with doubt whether he had in fact done his best. By the time of his *Lectures on Romans* (1515–16), he had discovered that the nominalist purveyors of "doing one's best" were fools and pig-theologians, crypto-Pelagians who had subverted nearly the whole church with their obnoxious formula.[12] And to the end of his days he continued, at every opportunity, to assail the Nominalists and their views on grace and merit. He recognized that the nominalist path could lead to false security, if only in those who overlooked the subtler sins of the heart such as ingratitude, complaining against God, and resisting God's will.[13] But for Luther himself it led to exactly the opposite predicament, which Melanchthon probes with such skill in his *Apology:* that is, a restless, never-ending invention of religious duties that both dishonors Christ (for whose sake grace is given freely) and drags the anxious conscience ever deeper into despair. Neither a single great work nor the multitude of works piled up together can bear the weight that a false piety lays upon them.[14]

The crucial question is this: Who *are* they who are touched by grace? Is it those who, because their resources are finite, can climb no higher, but who expect the addition of grace because they have done all they can? Or is it those who can slip no lower, because they have hit the bottom of despair

11. LWZ 3:103. Calvin comes close to Zwingli's interpretation in *Inst.*, 2.3.10.

12. *Vorlesung über den Römerbrief,* WA 56.274.14, 502.14–503.12; LW 25:261, 496–97. Many years afterward, Luther still recalled his anxious doubts in the monastery whether he had done enough. *In epistolam S. Pauli ad Galatas commentarius* (1535), WA 40^{2}.15.15ff.; LW 27:13.

13. *In epistolam ad Galatas commentarius,* WA 40^{1}.220.4–221.22, 364.29ff.; LW 26:124–25, 230. The possibility of false security was recognized already in the earlier *Vorlesung über den Römerbrief:* "Because they do not understand that God allows the ungodly to sin even in their good works" (WA 56.502.24; LW 25:496).

14. See esp. *Apol.*, 4.9–30, 203–17, 285–91. Cf. *CA,* 26.12–21. As these passages show, Melanchthon, like Luther, believed that the obligation to do one's best might lead to false security, smugness, or presumption. The double theme, constantly recurring in Melanchthon, of the honor of the Lord and the peace of consciences becomes a chapter in Calvin's *Institutes:* "Two Things to Be Noted in Free Justification" (*Inst.*, 3.13).

and expect nothing but judgment? And behind the conflicting answers of Luther and the Nominalists lie two different conceptions of grace, what it is and what it does. Is grace help for the weak, or the promise of new life for the dead? The same issue surfaced again in the great debate between Luther and Desiderius Erasmus (1469?–1536). For the humanist, grace meant help to move persons beyond their present abilities; in Erasmus's own metaphor, grace is the parental boost that helps the child to its feet and enables it to walk. Father's policy, at every moment, is to challenge the child to exert itself and take a few more tottering steps. He holds up the apple of reward, and he reaches out the supporting, guiding hand of grace to save the weak little limbs from collapsing.[15]

In Luther's *Lectures on Romans* and his *Heidelberg Disputation* (1518) we seem to find ourselves in another world of thought, and in essentials it is a world he never left. Grace, to him, was not so much aid to the weak and undeveloped as a creative word that raises the dead; for grace does not find a weak will but a strong, perverted will, vigorously pursuing its egotistical ends—a will that has to die. To urge sinners to do what is in them is ruinous pastoral psychology, since what is in them is self-will, and any new demand upon them can only stir them up to further outward expressions of their inner self-love. The encounter with God must therefore be, at first, under the form of a judgment. The anguish and despair created by a false religiousness are then perceived as the initial stage in God's design, which is to slay the old person and create the new; and where distrust of self is not yet present, the stern voice of God's demands must be applied to induce it. Hence the word of God comes, when it comes, in a manner contrary to our thinking: it announces life hidden under death, salvation under condemnation, heaven under hell.[16] And sinners' only proper response is to bow before the word that both lays them low and lifts them up. As Luther puts it in a pregnant sentence in his work against Erasmus: "Thus when God makes alive he does it by killing."[17]

"We teach," says Melanchthon, "that a man is justified when, with his conscience terrified by the preaching of penitence, he takes heart and believes that he has a gracious God for Christ's sake."[18] The pattern of Luther's theology of the cross is preserved in Melanchthon's notion that faith exists in penitence: "That is," he explains, "[faith] is conceived in the ter-

15. Ernst F. Winter, trans. and ed., *Erasmus-Luther: Discourse on Free Will* (New York: Frederick Ungar Publishing Co., 1961), 86–87.

16. *Vorlesung über den Römerbrief:* WA 56.446.31, 392.28ff.; LW 25:438–39, 382–83. Cf. *Disputatio Heidelbergae habita:* WA 1.353–74, LW 31:39–70.

17. "Sic Deus dum vivificat, facit illud occidendo; dum iustificat, facit illud reos faciendo; dum in coelum vehit, facit id ad infernum ducendo" (*De servo arbitrio:* WA 18.633.9; LW 33:62). This is the sense Luther assigns to 1 Sam. 2:6.

18. *Apol.*, 4.292 (152).

rors of a conscience that feels God's wrath against our sins and looks for forgiveness of sins and deliverance from sin."[19] In sum: Over against the nominalist theologians, the Lutheran gospel affirms that the ones to whom God does not deny grace are those who have recognized, through tribulation, that nothing in them is worthy of grace. Indeed, even this recognition we are to understand as itself a work of grace.

The continued pertinence of the Lutheran gospel in our time may be glimpsed if we recall that the theology of the cross is a theology of crisis. The early Barth built his platform in part on the insights of the early Luther, in whom he discovered the same "strange new world" he found in the Bible.[20] He wrote:

> The thoughts of the Bible touch just those points where the negative factors in life preponderate, casting doubt over life's possibilities—the very points, that is, where on the human side we have the question arising, Is it true? The Bible, with uncanny singleness of interest, omits all the stages of human life where this crisis is not yet acute, where a man in unbroken naïveté can still take comfort in the presence of God in the cherry tree, the symphony, the state, or his daily work; but it does become concerned with him, and with weird intensity, at the stage—shall we call it the highest or the lowest?—where doubt has seized him.[21]

Like Luther, Barth heard in his Bible a "no" that was really "yes," a judgment that was really grace. And that, it seems to me, although there is a great deal more that could be said about it, is the chief article of a protestant reformation—then and now. We must ask next exactly how this gospel is applied to the task of church reform.

The Gospel and Reform of the Church

Melanchthon claimed that the disagreement was not over the catholic faith, but over abuses in the life of the church. The claim has often been dismissed as naive or perhaps devious. But we do not need to inquire more closely into Melanchthon's motives; more important, for our theme of gospel and church, is the *logical* relationship between the two parts of

19. *Apol.*, 4.142 (126). Cf. *CA* 12 (L), where faith is made a part of penitence—a notion that the Roman Catholic *Confutatio* disapproved of (*Apol.*, 4.398). Calvin, by contrast, held that repentance is "born of faith" (*Inst.*, 3.3.1), apparently reversing Melanchthon's order.

20. "His [the young Luther's] theology, which became that of the Reformation and which we claim as the basis of our own, he defined as a *theologia crucis*." Karl Barth, "The Need and Promise of Christian Preaching" (1922), in *The Word of God and the Word of Man*, trans. Douglas Horton (1928; reprint, New York: Harper & Bros., 1957), 130. "The Strange New World within the Bible" is the title of another address in this collection.

21. "Christian Preaching," 116–17.

his confession: the articles on doctrine (1–21) and the articles on reform (22–28).

Especially striking in the second part of the Confession is the standard by which abuses are identified and judged. To be sure, a wide range of norms is invoked: the express commands of God or the order he has created, the words of Christ and the apostles, the statements of Fathers and Schoolmen, the decisions of councils, ancient canons and customs, the imperial law, the opinions of devout and learned men—even the pronouncements of popes. Melanchthon appeals also to the history of the church and the experience of individuals, and he sometimes argues pragmatically from probable consequences. But among the measures of judgment one stands out: the double accusation that certain abuses both trouble the sinner's conscience and obscure the glory of Christ. In other words, abuses in the life of the church are defined and censured by the gospel itself, since it is the gospel that alone gives peace of conscience and proclaims Christ's merits as the only source of confidence before God. Nothing else dare be proposed as the ground on which God's grace is expected.

It is just here that the essential link is to be found between the two parts of the Confession: on the basis of the Christian gospel, as presented in the doctrinal articles, the second part undertakes to sift the then current practice of the Roman Church. Indeed, already in part 1 (article 15) there is a clear formulation of the critical standpoint that governs part 2: "All ordinances and traditions instituted by men for the purpose of propitiating God and earning grace are contrary to the gospel and the teaching about faith in Christ."[22] The gospel, understood as the message of justification by faith, is the standard of criticism, the norm for the rectification (not the eradication) of all human traditions. In part 2 it is applied in a detailed evangelical critique of disputed religious institutions.[23] But the papacy itself is not among them.

It could be argued that to say nothing on the papal primacy was entirely in line with Luther's remark to Erasmus in 1525: the question of the papacy, he had said, was of little consequence.[24] But the Smalcald Articles of 1537, drafted by Luther himself (in 1536) with an eye to the forthcoming council of Mantua, expressly included the deeds of the pope among those features of the Roman Church that conflict with the first and fundamental article—that is, with what Luther held to be of the very *highest* consequence. On the article concerning Christ and faith, he wrote, "rests all that

22. *CA*, 15.3 (G [36–37]).

23. The seven "chief points at issue" are the withholding of the cup from the laity, clerical celibacy, the Mass, confession, dietary regulations, monastic vows, and the power of bishops. "Discreetly passed over" are a number of controversial issues, including indulgences (*CA*, conclusion [95]).

24. *De servo arbitrio:* WA 18.786.26; LW 33:294.

we teach and practice against the pope, the devil, and the world"; and he concluded that "the church must continue to exist without the pope."[25] Similarly Melanchthon, in his *Treatise on the Power and Primacy of the Pope* (1537), declared forthrightly: "The doctrine of the pope conflicts in many ways with the Gospel. . . . Nowhere do they [the pope and his adherents] teach that sins are forgiven freely for Christ's sake and that by . . . faith we obtain the remission of sins." Accordingly, the pope is not to be obeyed, but resisted as Antichrist.[26] Since Melanchthon's treatise was written and adopted as a supplement to the Augsburg Confession, it might be thought to constitute the definitive Lutheran stand on the question of the papacy. But there is more to be said.

At the end of the last article of the Augsburg Confession, Melanchthon explained that the Lutherans did not intend the bishops to surrender their authority, but only to allow the gospel to be taught purely and to relax some few observances.[27] And he took an exactly similar stand on the authority of the bishop of Rome. When he subscribed to the Smalcald Articles, he added the reservation: "Concerning the pope I hold that, if he would allow the Gospel, we, too, may concede to him that superiority over the bishops which he possesses by human right."[28] The selfsame principle was affirmed, both of the bishops in general and of the pope in particular, by Luther. In his *Exhortation to the Clergy,* he proposed that if the bishops refused to do their job—which was to preach the gospel—they should let the Lutherans be free to do it; they could then remain what they were, princes and lords, or could even resume episcopal jurisdiction while others did the preaching.[29] Similarly, although he asserted in the Smalcald Articles that we ought not to kiss the pope's feet,[30] in his *Commentary on Galatians* (1535) he professed his own readiness to kiss the pope's feet, after all, once it had been securely established that "God alone justifies us solely by His grace through Christ."[31] In other words, if the norm of protest against the papacy is the Lutheran gospel, then there appear to be no grounds for a Lutheran not to "recognize" (I use the word

25. [*Schmalkaldische*] *Artikel christlicher Lehre,* pt. 2, art. 1, sec. 5; art. 4, secs. 3, 5. The German version is translated in Tappert (see 292, 298–99). Luther himself, it should be noted, does formulate the chief article in terms of *Christus pro nobis* (see n. 7 above). The council, intended to meet in Mantua, finally met at Trent (1545–63).

26. *De potestate et primatu papae tractatus,* secs. 40, 44, and 57. The Latin version is translated in Tappert (see 327–28, 330).

27. *CA,* 28.77 (L [94]).

28. Tappert, 316.

29. WA 30^2.340–41; LW 34:49–50.

30. *Schmalkaldische Artikel,* pt. 2, art. 4, sec. 16; Tappert, 301.

31. WA 40^1.181.11; LW 26:99.

advisedly)[32] a pope who holds the same gospel. There is, no doubt, a qualification: Lutheran recognition of the pope, as Melanchthon makes clear, would not rest on a theory of divine right but, for the sake of peace and unity, would acquiesce in a papacy by human right.

This conclusion brings us right back, of course, to Melanchthon's claim that even his opponents could not disagree with his articles of faith. Was the Roman Church in actual fact, we must now ask, willing to grant the Lutherans the chief article of all, their gospel of justification by faith? Well, from Luther's own day right down to the present, Roman Catholic critics have found fault with the Lutheran statement of the chief article. Protestantism, it is said, denies or at least fails to affirm that being justified denotes something ontological in the believer—something more, that is, than merely a changed relationship. Further, the critics have held that the exclusive role the Lutherans assign to faith (*sola fide*) stands in sharp contradiction to an explicit statement of the Apostle Paul: Of the three abiding verities—faith, hope, and love—the greatest is love (1 Cor. 13:13). It is this express testimony of the apostle, not a moot interpretation of Galatians 5:6, that seems to warrant something like the scholastic formula *fides caritate formata* ("faith formed by love"). These, certainly, are large issues that call for a closer look. But how do things stand with respect to that other scholastic formula, from which we took our point of departure: "God does not deny grace to those who do what they can"?

It is interesting to notice that by the time of the 1543 edition of his *Institutes,* Calvin, for one, seems to have concluded that the nominalist formula was not the issue. He was able to draw a distinction between "the sounder Schoolmen" and "the more recent sophists," and he judged that on the *beginning* of justification he had no quarrel with the former.[33] The judgment is less surprising than might appear at first sight.

Recent historical scholarship has demonstrated that the reading of the Roman Catholic *Confutation* (on 3 August 1530) was not the end of the Augsburg affair, although the emperor did pronounce the Lutherans defeated. Charles V's (1500–1558) verdict was entirely predictable, and there is evidence that he slept impartially through the reading of both the Confession and its refutation. More important, the document that finally

32. The ambiguities that attend Roman Catholic "recognition" of the Augsburg Confession are likely to reappear, *mutatis mutandis,* when Lutheran recognition of the papacy is under discussion. See n. 62 below.

33. The pertinent passage is carried over into the 1559 edition: *Inst.,* 3.14.11. The expanded comment in the French version makes it clear that Calvin had the nominalist formula in mind. Luther, too, sometimes referred to the older Schoolmen as better, but he nonetheless identified nominalist views on grace as "the dangerous and wicked opinions of the papists" (*In epistolam ad Galatas commentarius,* WA 40^{1}.220.4; LW 26:124).

emerged from the Roman Catholic party, after a less happy initial draft, was in many ways a worthy and balanced response, not a dismissal of the Confession out of hand. Negotiations followed, and they came close to vindicating Melanchthon's claim that the dissension was over abuses, not doctrine. To take note only of the question of justification: the *Confutation* agreed that grace goes before the justification of the sinner, and that, of themselves, our works have no merit but are made worthy of eternal life precisely by God's grace. The subsequent negotiations took these points up again, until both sides were convinced that the agreement was substantive, not merely specious.[34]

Luther commented: "I fear that we will never again come so close together as at Augsburg."[35] He may have been overly pessimistic. A decade after Augsburg, conferences held under imperial auspices issued, at Regensburg in 1541, in extensive agreement between Roman Catholic and Lutheran delegates on the doctrines of sin and justification. Calvin himself, although not at that time one of the leading Protestant spokesmen, attended the conferences as a delegate from Strasbourg.

Differences remained, and ecumenical encounter in the sixteenth century does not seem to have generated much warmth or trust between the delegates on each side. But the possibility of conversation on the chief article did remain open, as it could hardly have done had the Roman Church been identified with nominalist views on grace and merit. And when the official pronouncement finally came, in the sixth session of the Council of Trent (1547), it began not with how much the self can achieve by its own native abilities, but with the fallen self's inability to free itself from bondage to sin. While the Tridentine fathers did speak of a preparation for justification, they considered it, as Thomas Aquinas (ca. 1225–74) did, to be the effect of predisposing or prevenient grace, and not an antecedent claim upon grace.[36]

At first glance, the Council of Trent even appears to have expressly rejected the nominalist position, according to which those who do their

34. See Herbert Immenkötter, *Um die Einheit im Glauben: Die Unionsverhandlungen des Augsburger Reichstages im August und September 1530*, Katholisches Leben und Kirchenreform im Zeitalter der Glaubensspaltung, vol. 33 (Munster: Aschendorff, 1973), 18, 37–39, 96; Vinzenz Pfnür, *Einig in der Rechtfertigungslehre? Die Rechtfertigungslehre der Confessio Augustana (1530) und die Stellungnahme der katholischen Kontroverstheologie zwischen 1530 und 1535*, Veröffentlichungen des Instituts für Europäische Geschichte Mainz, vol. 60 (Wiesbaden: Franz Steiner, 1970), 231–35, 256–64.

35. WAT 4.495.7 (no. 4780). Immenkötter takes this remark as the motto for his study.

36. Session 6, *Decretum de iustificatione*, chaps. 1 and 5: *Canons and Decrees of the Council of Trent: Original Text with English Translation*, trans. H. J. Schroeder (St. Louis, Missouri: B. Herder Book Co., 1941), 29–32 and 308–11. Like Luther, the council defines the *iustitia dei* with which we have to do in justification as *non qua ipse iustus est, sed qua nos iustos facit* (chap. 7: Schroeder, 33 and 312).

best merit, if only imperfectly (by *merita de congruo*), the bestowal of God's grace. The eighth chapter of session six states that nothing that precedes justification, whether faith or works, merits the grace of justification. In an interesting and important essay Heiko Oberman has argued that it was not really the intention of this statement, as it might appear, to condemn the Nominalists. His argument turns in part around the interpretation of a single word in the Latin, and I will not rehearse it here.[37] For *my* argument, it is enough to establish only this: that the Council of Trent did not identify Roman Catholicism with the nominalist theology of grace that Luther and the Lutherans had attacked, even if, as seems likely, it did give the Nominalists the status of one legitimate school among others in the Roman Catholic fold.

No doubt, it would have been an ecumenical boon if the Roman Church had unambiguously anathematized Luther's "fools" and "pig-theologians." But at least the Council of Trent marked a resurgence of Calvin's "sounder Schoolmen"; and subsequent papal pronouncements have weighted Roman Catholic teaching more decisively in favor of Thomism,[38] with which (on the doctrine of grace) it is surely easier for a Protestant to come to terms. Similarly, it may be easier for a Roman Catholic to come to terms with the Augsburg Confession's statement of the gospel than with Luther's. Despite the fundamental agreements between Luther and Melanchthon, one of which I have tried to lift up, the Confession did smooth out the sharper edges of Luther's truculent paradoxes. From reading Luther himself (or at least the papal condemnation of Luther's teaching) Erasmus inferred that the chief Lutheran article was actually the proposition "Everything happens by absolute necessity"; and Luther commended him for attacking the essential issue. In the article on free will in the Confession (article 18) the necessitarian dogma is not even mentioned; it is deliberately avoided. Erasmus slyly suggested that Luther's honorific title should be *doctor hyperbolicus* ("the doctor of overstatement").[39] It is hard to disagree. And there are those who would prefer to take the Augsburg Confession rather than Luther as the norm for determining what is Lutheran, not least because in the Confession they have the primacy of grace without the dogma of absolute necessity. One might

37. Heiko A. Oberman, "The Tridentine Decree on Justification in the Light of Late Medieval Theology," in *Distinctive Protestant and Catholic Themes Reconsidered*, ed. Robert W. Funk, *Journal for Theology and the Church*, vol. 3 (New York: Harper & Row, 1967), 28–54. The opposing view has been argued by Harry McSorley (see n. 41 below).

38. Notably, Leo XIII's encyclical *Aeterni Patris* (1879) and Pius X's *Doctoris Angelici* (1914). Leo recalls the story, perhaps legendary, that during the Council of Trent the *Summa* of St. Thomas lay open on the altar, together with the Scriptures and papal decrees.

39. *Hyperaspistes II* (1527): *Desiderii Erasmi Roterodami opera omnia*, ed. Jean LeClerc, 10 vols. (Leiden, 1703–6), 10:1345D.

even wish to argue that the Confession is the proper norm for sifting out the genuinely Protestant elements in Luther himself.

There is, in short, no more reason to burden the Roman Church with nominalist semi-Pelagianism than there is to bind the Protestant churches to Luther's determinism. History has shown repeatedly, in the twentieth century as in the sixteenth, that once such misapplications are laid aside, essential agreement on the article of justification is entirely possible. The eminent Roman Catholic historian Joseph Lortz hailed "justification by faith alone" as the rediscovery of an old catholic doctrine, and he concluded: "We must take very seriously the fact that today . . . the doctrine of justification is hardly anywhere considered to divide Protestants and Catholics."[40] A more charitable ambience in the churches has made possible, in addition, a Roman Catholic reappraisal of Luther himself. Detailed comparisons have been made between Luther and the "sounder Schoolmen" like Thomas; and one Roman Catholic author, Harry McSorley, has argued in detail that if we set aside Luther's necessitarianism, we can acknowledge him as the champion of a catholic doctrine of grace against the ambiguities of Erasmus.[41] Luther is seen to be catholic in the very heart of his Reformation protest; the catholic heritage is not simply what he departed from.

Can we all agree, then, that Luther and Lutheranism proved themselves catholic because, or insofar as, they asserted that not human merits but the grace of God comes first? Many on each side of the confessional division are ready to answer yes. But to state the matter in this fashion, however alluring to anyone who has the unity of the catholic church at heart, may conceal an important difference between the Protestant understanding of the gospel and the Roman Catholic. Even if we agree that Luther, with the catholic church, rightly insisted on the primacy of grace, we have to ask next: What *is* this that enjoys the primacy? The answer leads to the heart of what is distinctive in Reformation thinking. Melanchthon seems to be making just this point in a report he sent back from Augsburg to Luther. Eck wanted it said that one is justified through *grace and* faith—not, that is, by faith alone. Melanchthon comments: "I did not object. But the fool does not understand the noun 'grace.'"[42] The point is a sound one, and there should be a more civil way of putting it.

Lutheran grace comes as a message, a promise, a story, a word of God—in short, as gospel ("good news"). It takes a sure word of God, as

40. Lortz, "The Basic Elements of Luther's Intellectual Style," trans. in *Catholic Scholars Dialogue with Luther,* ed. Jared Wicks (Chicago: Loyola University Press, 1970), 3–33; see 31.

41. Harry J. McSorley, *Luther: Right or Wrong? An Ecumenical-Theological Study of Luther's Major Work, The Bondage of the Will* (New York: Newman Press and Minneapolis, Minnesota: Augsburg Publishing House, 1969).

42. Melanchthon to Luther, 22 August 1530: WAB 5.555.9 (no. 1691).

Melanchthon insists, to convince a person that God is no longer angry. The sacraments of baptism and the Lord's Supper he understands as outward signs that further confirm the word or, more correctly, confirm weak believers. As long as sinners perceive God as angry, or vengeful, or exacting, they cannot love God. The perception of God as merciful and forgiving is therefore logically prior to the devotion of love. But the perception of God as merciful in Christ is exactly what is meant by the faith that hears and heeds the promise. God's grace as spoken word thus defines the human response as a hearing by faith. We are justified by faith, Melanchthon tirelessly reminds us, because only faith can receive a word or accept a promise; promise and faith belong together. And it is easy to see why he must conclude that while faith in the promise and love for God are inseparable, faith precedes and love follows. Once we have come to the Father through Christ and have become sure that we have a gracious Father who cares for us, we call upon God, give God thanks, fear and love God.[43]

The entire inherited scheme of justification is moved by the Protestant Reformers a step closer to descriptive psychology. There is, of course, no intention to take away the element of mystery from the Spirit's operation, or to reduce the relationship of God and humans to a purely rational or intellectual process. But the language of infusion is no longer adequate to convey the dynamics of faith and love, and there can be no talk of merely not putting any obstacle in the way of grace. There has to be listening, understanding, believing, trusting, obeying—in short, a faith that counts on the word of God. Hence, Melanchthon suggested that it is not infused charity but faith that should be called *gratia gratum faciens,* "the grace that makes us pleasing to God"; love (*dilectio*) is its effect.[44]

In the gospel of the Reformation a linguistic change takes place that calls for reappraisal of inherited categories, a change that may be said to have its axiomatic starting point in Luther's assertion: "I take grace in the proper sense of the favor of God—not a quality of the soul."[45] It is the language of personal relationships that becomes regulative; and the stress shifts accordingly from acts to person, faith itself being less an act than a total orientation of the self. As Melanchthon puts it, "Justification is not the approval of a particular act but of the total person." Similarly, he can say that faith is a "new life."[46] Indeed, we must go further and recognize that what becomes regulative is the analogy of a quite specific personal relationship, an analogy Calvin exploited with particular thoroughness: rec-

43. *Apol.,* 4.262; 4.275–76; 4.43, 50, 67, 84, 112, 174, 264, 295, 304, 324, 337, 383; 4.110, 129, 141.

44. *Apol.,* 4.116.

45. *Rationis Latomianae confutatio* (1521), WA 8.106.10; LW 32:227.

46. *Apol.,* 4.222, 250. Faith is also "obedience," and this is one reason why Melanchthon regards it as "truly righteousness" (ibid., sec. 308).

onciliation (or justification) meant for him, quite simply, that instead of a judge we have in heaven a gracious *father*. It is in terms of this dominant image that Calvin tackles one of the most refractory problems in the negotiations at Augsburg: the question of merits. He grants that the Bible does speak of rewards, but he argues that the word "reward" cannot be so interpreted that the kingdom of heaven becomes the wages of servants and not the inheritance of sons.[47]

Protestant elevation of the gospel itself, or the spoken word, as the definitive form of grace does signal a difference from Roman Catholicism—or at least from medieval scholasticism. But a departure from medieval ways of thinking, even if it requires an extensive overhaul of the inherited language, need not disrupt the unity of the catholic church. There seems to be no good reason *in principle* why one could not seek to appraise it under the rubric of "doctrinal development,"[48] unless of course the old categories are held to be sacrosanct and their interpretation irreformable. And that leads to my final theme: the chief article and the task of Christian theology.

The Continuing Reformation

As long as there are Christian theologians who must wrestle with the meaning of the Christian gospel, the significance of the chief Lutheran article for theology is not likely to diminish. Luther and Melanchthon, to name no others, were skilled physicians of the soul, endowed with a profound insight into the sickness and the healing of the human spirit. Their writings have won the status of Christian classics from which others in our century, besides the theologians of crisis, have drawn wisdom and even their idiom. The continuing vigor of the old message is perhaps still more convincingly displayed in theologians of our time who have *not* always echoed the old idiom, but have understood how to apply and develop its content in fresh ways, moving beyond the limited domain of personal piety. One thinks of Reinhold Niebuhr's (1892–1971) remarkable claim that justification by faith may have relevance to public life, even international affairs, once it is seen to voice the ambiguity of all human achievements

47. *Inst.*, 3.11.1, 18.2.

48. There is all the more reason to understand the linguistic shift in this way if one notes that medieval Scholasticism allowed for Luther's sense of the word *gratia* without making it regulative for the doctrine of justification. See, in particular, Thomas Aquinas, ST I–II, q. 110, art. 1. But, of course, not all doctrinal differences can be placed under the rubric of "development." And while such material agreement as the churches have on the content of the gospel is gratifying, the theme of "gospel and church" can also be stated as an obstinate formal question of dogmatic norms: Can the church both define the gospel and be subject to the authority of the gospel?

and our willingness nonetheless to risk relative judgments.[49] Or one thinks of Paul Tillich's (1886–1965) declaration that the Protestant principle of justification by grace alone "means that no individual and no human group can claim a divine dignity for its moral achievements, for its sacramental power, for its sanctity, or for its doctrine."[50]

There are Lutherans who see the mission of Lutheranism entirely in its witness to the *critical* role of justification by faith only. They suggest that this is to take Lutheranism exactly for what it originally was: a reforming movement in the church as a whole. And it is not claimed that this movement coincides with the Lutheran denomination as such. Robert Jenson writes: "Fundamentally, to recognize the CA must be to recognize that a specific critique of all churchly discourse is a needed activity in the whole Church."[51]

As far as it goes, we need have no quarrel with this point of view. It was precisely the critical force of justification by faith only that was exhibited by Niebuhr and Tillich; with Niebuhr, I see no reason why much the same critique should not be extended and applied, wherever human pretensions require it, to nonchurchly discourse as well. And I suspect that the rest of us do count on the Lutherans to remind us constantly of the Protestant principle, although we are glad there may be others, too, who have not bowed the knee to Baal. But an instrument of criticism cannot be the sole benefit that Christian theology owes to the doctrine of justification, if the chief article is first and foremost a positive affirmation of the gospel and a scourge only by derivation. We should not overlook the significance for Christian theology of the very fact that the Lutherans moved their affirmation of the gospel to the center of theological reflection. By singling out justification by faith as the chief article, they invited changes in the inherited shape and style of Christian theology; and the same gospel that provided them with the norm for an evangelical critique of church usages prescribed the scope of an evangelical church theology. We may say with Jared Wicks that Luther's theology of Christian living gives a profile of the Christian,[52] and with Otto Pesch that Luther's existential theology makes

49. Reinhold Niebuhr, "The Relevance of Reformation Doctrine in Our Day," in *The Heritage of the Reformation: Essays Commemorating the Centennial of Eden Theological Seminary,* ed. Elmer J. F. Arndt (New York: Richard J. Smith, 1950), 249–64.

50. Paul Tillich, *The Protestant Era,* trans. and ed. James Luther Adams (London: Nisbet & Co., 1951), 226.

51. Robert Jenson, "On Recognizing the Augsburg Confession," in *The Role of the Augsburg Confession: Catholic and Lutheran Views,* ed. Joseph A. Burgess (Philadelphia: Fortress Press, 1980), 151–66; see 163.

52. Jared Wicks, *Man Yearning for Grace: Luther's Early Spiritual Teaching* (Washington and Cleveland: Corpus Books, 1968), 6, 69. Wicks shows the insufficiency of viewing Luther's theology simply as a revolt against Scholasticism. Its distinctive style and its preoccupation with spirituality were rooted in "the eclectic, monastic tradition, which is at once Augustinian, Bernardine, devout, and mystical" (267).

thematic (that is, thematizes) our very existence in faith.[53] Justification or the faith that justifies, grasped from the inside, is the point of reference for everything else. To quote Luther himself: "In my heart there rules this one doctrine, namely, faith in Christ. From it, through it, and to it all my theological thought flows and returns, day and night; yet I am aware that all I have grasped of this wisdom in its height, width, and depth are a few poor and insignificant firstfruits and fragments."[54]

Here is an "evangelical theology" in the precise sense that everything in it is thought in relation to the gospel—or to persons addressed by the gospel and answering in faith. Here, too, is an important bridge across the gap between classical and liberal Protestantism. In agreement with Luther, so he believed, Friedrich Schleiermacher held that the task of theology—or, more precisely, dogmatics—is to interrogate the faith common to all devout Christians and to describe it without one-sidedness. Dogmatics is nothing other than the reflection of the intellect on the fact of the Christian way of believing. Schleiermacher's understanding of the dogmatic task did not coincide perfectly with Luther's, since, to mention only the most important difference, he separated more sharply than Luther the dogmatic and the exegetical functions. But the affinity is clear.[55]

It is equally clear that in our own day Schleiermacher's conception of theology, or something like it, is no longer peculiar to liberals or even to Protestants; it has become a much more generally agreed standpoint. There would be less agreement on the question whether a properly scientific account of religious faith presupposes, or excludes, the commitment of the inquirer. Given their similar views on the object of theological reflection, it is easy to see why Luther and Schleiermacher further concurred that theology is itself an exercise of faith—the reflection of the believer on his or her own believing. "Experience," says Luther, " alone makes a theologian." Again: "It is by living—no, rather is it by dying and being damned that a theologian is made, not by understanding, reading, or speculating."[56] Similarly, the experiential nature of theology as Schleiermacher understood it was announced in the Anselmian epigraph affixed to the title page of *The Christian Faith:* "Anyone who has not experienced will not understand." Astonishingly, the English translators left out the epigraph, although it is an obvious clue to what Schleiermacher

53. Otto H. Pesch, "Existential and Sapiential Theology—The Theological Confrontation between Luther and Thomas Aquinas," in *Catholic Scholars Dialogue with Luther,* ed. Wicks, 61–81, esp. 73.

54. *In epistolam ad Galatas commentarius,* WA 40^{1}.33.7; LW 27:145.

55. I develop the comparison of Luther and Schleiermacher in chapter 2, to which I refer for documentation.

56. WAT 1.16.13 (no. 46); *Operationes in Psalmos* (1519–21), WA 5.163.28.

thought he was about, and for this reason was raised like a banner over his entire enterprise. Dogmatics, he thought, has to do with an experience that one could hardly hope to understand if one did not have it.

Neither Luther nor Schleiermacher meant to imply that a unique prerequisite sets theological understanding apart from other branches of knowledge. On the contrary, each of them found analogues in other disciplines to the experience they judged prerequisite for the interpretation of religious meanings. Luther liked to insist on the general hermeneutic rule that understanding words comes from understanding the matter; the rule is not peculiarly theological.[57] And Schleiermacher's concern was not at all to segregate Christian theology. Quite the contrary, in opposition to the rationalists and the speculative theologians he wanted to give dogmatics its correct classification with the empirical sciences, which deal with matters of fact—that is, with what can only be experienced, not somehow established by the activity of reason.[58] In any case, whether or not the personal involvement of the inquiring subject is desirable in the study of theology, and if so in what sense, the point to be stressed here concerns rather the *object* of theological study. By taking the gospel of justification by faith as its chief article, the Lutheran Reformation may be said to have fostered a distinctively experiential style of evangelical theology; and it is a style that points toward Schleiermacher and the modern view of theology as disciplined reflection on the phenomenon of believing.

What may *not* be said, as far as I can see, is that justification by faith is to be equated for all time with the Christian message. If the real treasure of the church is the gospel of the glory and grace of God, as Luther says in his sixty-second thesis on indulgences, then in every generation the church's gospel is, or should be, the subject of the chief article. But if, in addition, we are to pay more than lip service to historical thinking, we must admit that every formulation of the gospel is individual, relative, and transient—adapted, that is, to a particular time and particular circumstances. Luther's confidence that the Augsburg Confession must remain as the true word of God until the Day of Judgment claims more for it than most of us nowadays would care to claim.[59] The pertinence of the Confession to Christian theology is rather this: It achieved, on the foundations of the catholic heritage, an effective formulation of the word of God for Luther's day, and in so doing set Christian theology a model for carrying out the same task in another day. This is not to deny categorically that similar situations or sim-

57. WAT 1.524.39 (no. 1040), 4.608.6 (no. 5002: LW 54:375), 5.168.27 (no. 5468).

58. On the professedly empirical character of Schleiermacher's dogmatics, see chapter 7.

59. See Joseph Lortz, *The Reformation in Germany,* trans. Ronald Walls from the revised German ed. (1949), 2 vols. (New York: Herder & Herder, 1968), 2:67–68.

ilar individuals ever arise to give fresh pertinence to a classic formula. It may even be that in any classic formulation of the gospel something durable in human nature, or in the way God is thought to deal with it, comes into view. But the church may not force one entire world of thought into the mold of another, or it will pay the price of announcing an ineffective, because inappropriate, message. Even when some of the ingredients in a culture are carried over from a previous age, the priorities may change; and the chief article must adapt. In Troeltsch's crisp aphorism: "The historical and the relative are identical."[60] The *Formula of Concord* made much the same point from the very different perspective of the scriptural principle: "Other symbols and other writings are not judges like Holy Scripture, but merely witnesses and expositions of the faith, setting forth how at various times the Holy Scriptures were understood in the church of God."[61]

Acknowledgment of historical particularity appeared, in some degree, to underlie the debate in 1980 about Roman Catholic recognition of the Augsburg Confession. Cautious advocates on the Roman Catholic side did not say that the confession was a timeless statement of the universal Christian faith; and it was explicitly pointed out that recognition of it would not make it a Roman Catholic confession.[62] The question was whether it could be received as a "particular expression of the common Christian faith."[63] An affirmative answer would not call for the old-style invitation to Protestants: Return to the Church! It would lead, rather, to a fuller communion between sister churches in which the particular identity of each would be preserved.[64] Here, too, something like Schleiermacher's viewpoint appears to have won. Long before the ecumenical movement, he proposed that one should think of Roman Catholicism and Protestantism, not simply in terms of the conflict between truth and error, but as individual forms of Christianity. And there is more readiness in our day than there was in his to grant him his point: to recognize that not only his-

60. Ernst Troeltsch, *The Absoluteness of Christianity and the History of Religions*, trans. from the 3d German ed. (1929) by David Reid (Richmond, Virginia: John Knox Press, 1971), 85.

61. *Formula of Concord* (1577), intro. to Epitome: Tappert, 465. The statement on 502 that "thank God, [the Augsburg Confession] has remained . . . unimpregnable until this day" is plainly a misprint. Even the Bible needs to be "impregnated" (!) with the subsequent historical experience of the church, which is why there is a hermeneutical problem.

62. See Walter Kasper, "What Would Catholic Recognition of the *Confessio Augustana* Mean?" in *Role of the Augsburg Confession*, ed. Burgess, 123–29, esp. 124–25.

63. The phrase is quoted from the proceedings of the 1977 General Assembly of the Lutheran World Federation (Dar-es-Salaam) in *Role of the Augsburg Confession*, ed. Burgess, xiii.

64. So Kasper, for one, does not foresee unity without "pluriformity," although he looks toward structural expression of Christian unity in an ecumenical council ("Catholic Recognition," 127–29).

torical documents, but also entire institutions, have the inevitable limitations of their individuality, which is the product of their historical origin and growth.[65]

The historical principle of individuality, as we may call it, needs to be pressed still further. Protestantism and Roman Catholicism are no longer what they were in the sixteenth century. The Reformation is not Protestantism; neither is the Augsburg Confession the Reformation. Even the Augsburg Confession's chief article is not necessarily the happiest version of the Reformation gospel. A better-balanced formula, which might have turned aside some of the Roman Catholic misgivings about justification by faith alone, could be taken from Calvin's notion of a twofold gift or double grace that we receive from Christ: reconciliation and regeneration.[66] But this formula, too, could not be raised to the status of exclusive orthodoxy, not least because Jesus himself came into Galilee preaching the gospel of the kingdom of God (Mark 1:14–15). Calvin, in any case, although he did strongly emphasize justification or the forgiveness of sins, was less inclined than his friend Melanchthon to speak of a "chief article" at all. Perhaps that is the wisest course. But the church's proclamation needs a cutting edge in every generation, and this, surely, is what the chief article is for. The problems arise only when one formulation of the chief article becomes the shibboleth of orthodoxy, and intellectual good works intrude upon faith. Edmund Schlink observes: "We have to bear in mind that there is also a justification by works based on the 'possession' of the doctrine of justification; this happens when justification by faith is replaced by justification through possessing the right dogmatic formula."[67]

A similar irony results whenever the Protestant sermon sets out to reproduce Luther's religious experience in others. Deliverance is offered from a late medieval situation in which we no longer find ourselves, and which the preacher must vainly try to conjure up again. And then, as Tillich insisted, "the doctrine of justification, which represents a breaking-through of every law, [becomes] a law itself as unrealisable as the laws of the Catholic church."[68] Like Troeltsch before him, Tillich held that the dominant religious question changes from one age to another as the religious sensibility changes, whereas Schleiermacher seems to have located the theological task in the quest for fresh expressions of a constant relationship with Christ—a relationship that he believed to be the same in him, in

65. See B. A. Gerrish, *The Old Protestantism and the New: Essays on the Reformation Heritage* (Chicago: University of Chicago Press, Edinburgh: T. & T. Clark, 1982), 186–89.

66. *Inst.*, 3.11.1. The notion of double grace is not unique to Calvin, but it is not always used in his way.

67. Schlink, "Ecumenical Character of the Augsburg Confession," 21.

68. *Protestant Era,* 148.

the less dialectically gifted members of his congregation, and in the apostle Paul.[69]

The problem of individuality appears, in fact, to go deeper than words, to the experiences that words both express and awaken. It can even make a division between contemporaries. Does the conflict between Luther and Erasmus, for instance, confront us with an inescapable choice between two types of encounter with God, only one of which deserves to be called "Christian"? Or has Protestantism unwisely tried to universalize the exceptional? Lortz maintained that Luther speaks in terms of an extreme borderline case.[70] We certainly have every right to claim that Luther's experience affords a special illustration of the grace of God, and that his theology is a classic exposure of merit as a hindrance to grace rather than a preparation for it. It is a theology, so to say, of the prodigal son. The elder brother in Jesus' parable (Luke 15:11–32) did his best (*quod in se erat*), and his father assured him of his unalterable love—whether or not because he did his best. But it was the prodigal, who "was dead and is alive again" (an extreme borderline case!), who uncovered the depths of paternal love. Still, when this is rightly said, it remains the theologian's art to learn from the extreme without universalizing it. And it may be that Protestants have still not listened attentively enough to their Roman Catholic critics, who ask whether Protestantism does not bear too firm an impress from the religious subjectivity of one man.[71]

In the final analysis, however, it is not a historical principle alone that forbids us to identify the chief article, for all time, with justification by faith. A similar conclusion arises out of the Protestant principle itself, in which the Lutheran chief article has begotten a critical instrument that may turn back in judgment on its parent. The denial of every pretended absolute may as soon become an admonition to Protestantism as Protestantism's scourge for chastising others. It forbids the absolutizing of any theological doctrine or sacred experience, including the doctrine and experience of justification by faith. Exclusive addiction to one form of the gospel transforms the gospel into law, and so negates the message it seeks to commend, turning it into a burden to be borne or else an occasion for false security.

69. See, for example, Troeltsch, "The Dogmatics of the 'Religionsgeschichtliche Schule,'" AJT 17 (1913): 1–21, esp. 12–13, 19; Tillich, *The Courage to Be* (London: Nisbet & Co., 1952), 39; Schleiermacher, *Sendschr.*, 39–40 and *Gl.*, § 88.2.

70. "Luther's Style," 18.

71. See further chapter 2. Naturally the Lutherans, for their part, will wish to be convinced that the judgment implicit in the portrait of the older brother has been taken seriously enough. Also apposite is Calvin's remark on the formula, "Grace is denied to no one who does his best": Anyone who thus seeks after grace must already be moved by grace (*Inst.*, 2.3.10).

Recollection of the past does not leave the theologian with final solutions, but with an endless task and some resources for entering into it. The most urgent assignment for ecumenical theology is not to negotiate concerning inherited differences, important as that may be; it is to think collectively—with the varied resources of the individual traditions—on the meaning and application of the gospel, which can never be taken for granted as though it were a secure possession. The collective task is, first and foremost, to reflect in common on the chief article of the catholic church.

2

Doctor Martin Luther: Subjectivity and Doctrine in the Lutheran Reformation

I had to accept the office of doctor and swear a vow to my most beloved Holy Scriptures that I would preach and teach them faithfully and purely. While engaged in this kind of teaching, the papacy crossed my path and wanted to hinder me in it. How it has fared is obvious to all.
—MARTIN LUTHER

AMONG THE PROCEEDINGS at the Diet of Worms (1521) was a ceremonial burning of Luther's books. An anonymous pamphleteer reports that on top of the bonfire was placed an effigy of the heretic with the inscription in French, German, and Latin, "This is Martin Luther, the Doctor of the Gospel." The high priests and the Romanists, he goes on, objected: "Write not, 'A Doctor of evangelical truth,' but that he said, 'I am a Doctor of evangelical truth.'"[1] The clear echoes of another story leave no doubt which side the pamphleteer was on. But the justice of his comparison, to say nothing of its propriety, may very well be doubted. Whether Luther was, or only said he was, a teacher of the plain gospel truth has been a question for "ecumenical theology," as we now call it, from his own day until ours.

It was Philip Melanchthon, not Luther, who was given the nickname *praeceptor Germaniae:* teacher or schoolmaster of Germany. Of course, he earned it. Whatever needs to be said about the effectiveness of Lutheran indoctrination and the understanding of human nature that sustained it, Melanchthon's impact on German secondary and higher education was profound and lasting. If Gerald Strauss is right, an Augustinian estimate of man caused the Lutherans both to adopt a repressive pedagogy and to acquiesce in its failure when opposed by a vigorous subculture of folk religion. But he does not deny that significant educational measures were taken by the Lutherans, who had better success in channeling the religious energies of an intellectual elite; he reaches his conclusions by uncovering the pedagogical principles *behind* the outward institutional and curricular

1. See Roland H. Bainton, *Here I Stand: A Life of Martin Luther* (Nashville, Tennessee: Abingdon Press, 1950), 191. In the present chapter, wherever possible, I have inserted references for my Luther quotations (in parentheses) in the text. The epigraph will be found in LW 34:103.

changes. That the reformations of the sixteenth century do hold an important place in the history of education is the "familiar fact" with which Strauss begins.[2] Melanchthon's place in this history is secure. The title *praeceptor Germaniae* attests the unparalleled achievement of Luther's modest colleague, who declined the title of doctor for himself. "He was the determining educational influence in Protestant Germany."[3]

And yet, in another sense, it is Luther who has been the *praeceptor Germaniae,* or at any rate of Germany's intellectual elite. The instruction sought from him has less to do with the formal principles of education (though he did concern himself with them, too) than with the potency of his ideas and of his personality. Again and again, eminent German thinkers—and not theologians only—have felt bound to come to terms with his intellectual legacy, even if, as one may well suspect, their ideas have shaped the image of Luther at least as much as Luther has inspired their ideas. Indeed, theological differences within Lutheranism have sometimes become debates on the question: Which party has the real Luther?

To begin with, the Roman Church countered the Lutherans' reverence for their teacher by challenging both his credentials as a doctor of the church and the soundness of his doctrine: Luther's teaching, it was repeatedly alleged, was vitiated by his intense religious subjectivity. But the times have changed. One of the most remarkable features of our ecumenical century has been a new willingness among Roman Catholic theologians to affirm that their communion, too, may be instructed by Dr. Martin Luther, although the problem of his subjectivity has not quite been laid to rest. In some ways, Roman Catholics may even be said to have a keener ear for Luther's voice than their Protestant brothers and sisters, whose faith was more radically transformed by the intellectual changes of the eighteenth and nineteenth centuries.

Not all Protestant theologians have approved the course of modern Protestantism. Far from it! Some of them have perceived it as a story of infidelity to the legacy of Luther; and some have been convinced that even the Luther renaissance led by Karl Holl (1866–1926) was still tainted with the presuppositions of liberal Protestant thinking. Here also, within Protestantism, the problem of religious subjectivity has been in the middle of controversy, and it has ranged neoorthodox and liberals against each other. In the period between the two world wars, it was not uncommon for Roman Catholic theologians to endorse the neoorthodox case against liberal subjectivism, but they were naturally more inclined to see the link

2. Gerald Strauss, *Luther's House of Learning: Indoctrination of the Young in the German Reformation* (Baltimore, Maryland: Johns Hopkins University Press, 1978), esp. 1–2, 106, 307.

3. Robert Stupperich, *Melanchthon,* trans. Robert H. Fischer (Philadelphia: Westminster Press, 1965), 151.

between the Reformation and subjectivism as a necessary one—and the Roman Church as the only secure haven of objectivity.

How has it come about that today Roman Catholics in Germany (and elsewhere) are more willing to hear Luther as "doctor of evangelical truth"? And how did it come about that in the previous century there were German Protestants who may not have heard Luther well enough? The first question, which comes close to the center of present-day relations between Roman Catholics and Protestants, is all the more intriguing because an extensive, fascinating, and still growing literature has sprung up in answer to it. The second question is intriguing almost for the opposite reason: though no less important, it needs a much closer scrutiny than it has so far been given.

The title "doctor" or "teacher" probably comes nearer than any other to the heart of Luther's self-understanding, and it was closely tied up, in his own mind, with the actual reception of his doctor's degree. Luther remarked that the Elector of Brandenburg's son, on seeing the seven-headed Luther in Cochlaeus's famous cartoon, exclaimed: "If Dr. Luther has seven heads, he will be invincible, for so far they have not been able to vanquish him though he has but one!" (WAT 2.382.12). Luther does not say so, but we can perhaps infer it for ourselves, that the one authentic Luther head wears the doctor's cap—in his own self-image and in the images others had of him. This, at any rate, will be the place to begin the theme of subjectivity and doctrine in the Lutheran Reformation; how the theme looks from the standpoint of present-day Roman Catholicism, and how it looked to liberal Protestantism in the nineteenth century, can then be explored in turn.

Doctor of Holy Scripture

Shortly before entering the monastery in 1505, Luther had added to his Erfurt bachelor's degree the master of arts from the same university. Some four years later, on 9 March 1509, he received the baccalaureate in Bible from Wittenberg, though an annotation in the university record reports that he had not yet paid the customary fee. Luther himself later added the comment: "And he's not going to either. At the time he was a poor monk and had nothing."[4] The next step was the *sententiarius* degree, which required the holder to lecture on the *Sentences* of Peter Lombard, books one and two. Luther prepared for the degree in Wittenberg, but graduated at Erfurt (1509). And that, so far as he was concerned, was the end of his

4. Quoted (in Latin) by Hermann Steinlein, "Luthers Doktorat: Zum 400jährigen Jubiläum desselben (18./19. Oktober 1912)," *Neue kirchliche Zeitschrift* 23 (1912): 757–843, 767, n. 1. In the remainder of the first section, I have generally omitted documentation that can readily be found in Steinlein.

education; he had no ambition to become a candidate for the doctorate. But he was coerced into taking yet another step up the academic ladder by Johann von Staupitz (ca. 1469–1524), his superior in the order of the Augustinian Eremites. Later, this was to become a fact of some importance to Luther's self-understanding.

The famous conversation with Staupitz, under the pear tree in the garden of the Black Cloister, is one of the most memorable incidents in Luther's entire career. When the news was broken to him that he was to become a doctor of Holy Scripture, Luther replied with a list of fifteen excuses. None of them impressed his superior, who warned him not to be wiser than his elders. Finally, Luther added that he was already worn out and did not have long to live. (He was not yet thirty.) Staupitz replied cheerfully that this would be fine, since the Lord God had many things to do in heaven; if Luther died, he could become God's adviser.

On 4 October 1512 Luther received the *licencia magistrandi*, or permission to apply for the doctorate; and in the Castle Church two weeks later, on 18–19 October, he engaged in the required disputations, took his oath, and was invested with the doctor's insignia of Bible, cap, and ring. (His cap he later offered to place on the head of anyone who could reconcile James and Paul.) The Erfurters were miffed because he took the doctorate at Wittenberg. Since he had never wanted to take the degree at all, he must have found some irony in this consequence of his obedience. But Staupitz's insistence changed the course of his life.

In later years, Luther sometimes styled himself "doctor of theology," sometimes "doctor of Holy Scripture"; frequently also, from his profession rather than his rank, he used the titles "lecturer" and "professor." But perhaps the most expressive of his chosen titles was "sworn doctor of Holy Scripture." In one respect the phrase has been found odd: his doctor's oath did not in fact include an express obligation to the Scriptures, whereas the bachelor's oath (for the *baccalaureus biblicus*) did. Still, a Bible was presented to the doctoral candidate, possibly with some appropriate words, and he was required to give an address in praise of Scripture both at his graduation and in his inaugural lecture. Hence it is not surprising that the new doctors were sometimes called "masters of the sacred page" or "teachers of Holy Scripture."

According to Luther himself, the doctors in his day despised the Bible and always itched after something new (LW 34:27). For himself, however, the reception of the doctorate carried with it an inescapable demand to be a faithful teacher of the written word of God. The fact that he had not wished for the degree only heightened his sense of obligation: a responsibility had been laid upon him even against his will. Time and again, he identified his call to be a reformer with the commission he received on that October day in the year 1512.

Naturally, Luther's opponents could always retort that his doctorate did not authorize him to teach heresy; as a doctor, he remained answerable to the church. The licentiate oath before the chancellor of Wittenberg University included an explicit pledge of obedience to the Roman Church, and the doctoral oath itself promised avoidance of strange doctrines condemned by the church and offensive to devout ears. Be that as it may (we shall have to come back to it), Luther's self-understanding cannot be appreciated unless one first recognizes that in his own eyes he was a man under constraint. Indeed, he saw this constraint as an obligation laid upon him precisely by pope and emperor. But it was more than that: it came not only from a human ceremony, but from the word of God itself. His calling as a sworn doctor of Holy Scripture made it impossible for him to keep silent even if pope and emperor subsequently opposed him.

> I was forced and driven into this position in the first place, when I had to become Doctor of Holy Scripture against my will. Then, as a Doctor in a general free university, I began, at the command of pope and emperor, to do what such a doctor is sworn to do, expounding the Scriptures for all the world and teaching everybody. Once in this position, I have had to stay in it, and I cannot give it up or leave it yet with a good conscience, even though both pope and emperor were to put me under the ban for not doing so. For what I began as a Doctor, made and called at their command, I must truly confess to the end of my life. I cannot keep silent or cease to teach, though I would like to do so and am weary and unhappy because of the great and unendurable ingratitude of the people [LW 13:66].

As Luther perceived the Reformation, then, it was an unforeseen by-product of his faithfulness to a sworn duty: it came about because the pope, by whose authority the duty came to him in the first place, got in his way. No doubt, what he sincerely believed to be a matter of a doctor's duty and courage struck others as the willfulness and arrogance of one paltry monk who presumed to defy the Catholic Church. Luther was clearly troubled by the contemptuous question: Could he alone be right, and all those who came before him fools and know-nothings? Or was he alone the darling of the Holy Spirit, and had God let his own people go wrong for so many years? Luther overcame the taunt by weighing against it Christ and his word (LW 36:134, 43:160). And to this word he was pledged by his doctorate to be faithful, come what may. As he put it in another memorable utterance, he would not trade his doctorate for all the world's riches; it was a remedy for loss of heart, the reassurance that he had not started a reformation as an interloper, without call or command (LW 40:387–88). It gave him the courage to tread on the lion and the adder, to trample the young lion and the serpent under his foot (LW 34:103–4).

The strength Luther derived from his "office" as a doctor of Holy

Scripture has often been remarked upon in the secondary literature. Karl Holl, for instance, in his much-quoted lecture on Luther's judgments about himself, remarks: "His consolation was always that he had planned nothing, but had instead been forced along his way while carrying out his office."[5] A much more elaborate study of Luther's doctorate appeared in 1912, some years after Holl delivered his lecture but before its publication among his collected essays. The author, who signed himself "Pfarrer Steinlein," timed his essay to coincide with the four-hundredth anniversary of Luther's graduation. Anyone who has since written on the subject will have found it difficult to add much to such a thorough investigation; it sets out to be an exhaustive analysis of all the pertinent sources and yet, despite an occasional word of diffidence, manages to work the countless references into a smooth pattern.[6]

Naturally, Steinlein looks into the many passages in which Luther writes directly about the doctoral degree in general, the doctors of his day, and his own doctorate in particular. But he carries the search further: Account is taken also of the way Luther styles himself in his public writings, and even how he introduces and signs himself in the myriad items of his correspondence (not yet available, in 1912, in the definitive Weimar Edition). The first impression, as Steinlein admits, is one of motley diversity. Even the obvious seems to be open to exceptions. We are told, for instance, that Luther tends, as we would expect, to drop his titles in letters to his friends. And yet one notes from Steinlein's own citations that Luther could style himself "doctor" (apparently without intended humor) even in writing to his wife; and "doctor," as the *Table Talk* abundantly shows, is how she in turn commonly addressed him.

Steinlein argues nonetheless that if the mass of material is set in chronological order, a strikingly consistent picture meets the eye. What he calls Luther's *Doktoratsbewusstsein* (his "doctor consciousness") rises and falls in tune with both his external circumstances as a reformer and his corresponding attitude to the entire business of the academic community. Three main periods can be distinguished, if Steinlein's thesis is correct: the "doctor consciousness" emerges (1517–21), recedes (1521 until around the end of the 1520s), and emerges again (from the end of the 1520s to 1546).

The very first extant letter in which Luther signed himself "doctor" was addressed to Archbishop Albert of Mainz on 31 October 1517; the second instance occurred the same year in a letter to the Elector Frederick

5. Karl Holl, "Martin Luther on Luther," trans. H. C. Erik Midelfort, in *Interpreters of Luther: Essays in Honor of Wilhelm Pauck,* ed. Jaroslav Pelikan (Philadelphia: Fortress Press, 1968), 9–34; quotation on 16.

6. See n. 4 above. The essay also appeared separately as an eighty-seven-page book (Leipzig: A. Deichert, 1912). I have seen only the journal printing, to which my page numbers refer.

(ca. 11 November). Although the title did not appear again at the *end* of his letters (as part of his signature) until 1519, the impression is that from the first Luther undertook his reformation on the strength of his doctoral office or calling. The explanation for the temporary disappearance of the title from Luther's signature, Steinlein suggests, is that soon after the beginning of the Reformation he took to styling himself *Eleutherius* ("the free"). And the first impression of the 1517 letters to Albert and Frederick is confirmed by express statements Luther made in 1518 *within* letters to his bishop, Jerome Scultetus (13 February), and Pope Leo X (ca. 30 May), by whose apostolic authority he claimed to hold his doctorate. Two years later, in a letter to George Spalatin (9 July 1520), he defended himself against the charge that ambition was what spurred him on. Anyone who wanted his "offices" was welcome to them; but as long as he was not free from the duty of teaching, he would exercise his office freely. He was already burdened with enough sins and refused to add the unforgivable sin of dereliction of duty. In a similar vein, he assured Elector Frederick the Wise the following year (25 January 1521) that he had written and taught because of his conscience, oath, and duty as a "poor teacher of the Holy Scripture."

The year 1521 marked the climax of academic attacks on Luther, when the University of Paris finally broke its silence and joined Louvain and Cologne in condemning him. Steinlein believes that the frequency and vehemence of Luther's utterances about "the doctors" and "the high schools" can be correlated with the pattern of these attacks upon him. More important, however, he shows that Luther's use of his own title diminishes in the second period, and that he occasionally speaks of his doctorate disparagingly and even seizes upon doctoral graduations at Wittenberg as occasions for expressing aversion to the folly of the entire academic establishment. What can account for this emphatic shift of attitude? The explanation, Steinlein plausibly argues, lies in the Edict of Worms, which placed Luther under the imperial ban.

Following closely upon the papal condemnation, the imperial ban stripped Luther of the office he had received by human hands; in response, he renounced his doctorate and took his stand on the title "preacher," which he held by the grace of God alone. Evidently, it is the Apostle Paul of the Letter to the Galatians, chapter 1, who has now become the model, and Luther appeals expressly to verse 8: he will not have his doctrine judged even by an angel from heaven (LW 39:247–49, 48:390). But remarkable though this change of attitude undoubtedly is, too much weight cannot be placed upon it, I think, as a clue to Luther's self-estimate; the renunciation of his doctorate was an impetuous reaction to the imperial ban, and it was not long before he had good reason to change his mind back again—that is, to revert to his former stress on his legitimate vocation.

The principal new factor in Luther's circumstances, which occasioned his second thoughts, was of course the growing menace of religious radicalism. Some of his best-known utterances about his doctoral office were in fact made as he looked back, from the conflict with unauthorized preachers, to his own early activity as a reformer. And in the new situation he held that an appeal to the prompting of the Spirit is not a sufficient warrant for preaching and teaching in public: one also needs a legitimate call. It must have been particularly galling to Luther when his own colleague Andreas Bodenstein von Carlstadt (ca. 1480–1541) joined the radicals, shed his doctor's degree, and refused to have part in any further doctoral graduations at Wittenberg University. (Carlstadt wanted the people to call him by no other title than "Brother Andreas.") The conflict with "enthusiasm," reinforced (as Steinlein points out) by the renewed conflict with Rome, accounts for Luther's reaffirmation of his doctoral office and calling. In 1535, in a letter to Justus Jonas (17 October), he can report that Katie is preparing a special feast to celebrate the twenty-third anniversary of his graduation.

To correlate Luther's "doctor consciousness" with the changing circumstances of his career, as Steinlein has done, is a clear improvement on the procedure of culling utterances indiscriminately from all over his writings. One must note in particular the impact first of the Edict of Worms, then of the outbreak of radicalism, on his early sense of mission. Thus far we are taken by his own explicit statements. The further evidence Steinlein adduces—even calculating for each period the exact percentage of letters in which Luther signs himself "doctor"—is striking, but precarious. Steinlein is puzzled, for example, to find that *within* the third period there is a temporary decrease, from 1534 to 1541, in the frequency with which Luther uses his doctor's title. Other interesting items of evidence he takes into account in the third period include the actual number of annual graduations (*Doktorpromotionen*) that appear in the university records and the letters of recommendation furnished for holders of the Wittenberg doctorate. All in all, it is a fascinating inquiry on which Steinlein leads us. Only a textual review as thorough as his could afford firm grounds for doubting or endorsing this side of his argument. But for our purposes it is not necessary to attempt it. What I wish to carry over into my own argument is independent of any such approach.

It would be manifestly unfair to judge Luther's self-image by the claims he occasionally models on the first chapter of Galatians; that would place him too close to the radicals, whose pretensions he rejected. But there are problems also with his appeal to his legitimate vocation. Provoked by his adversaries, he proposed that he should be celebrated as "a great doctor over all bishops, priests, and monks" (LW 23:230), and perhaps one may detect—beneath the good fun—echoes of medieval debates on the relative authority of doctors and prelates (including the pope). But Luther could also boast of being "a doctor over all doctors" (LW 35:187); and while that, too, is said partly in jest, his critics could well reverse his rhetorical question, "Are they doctors? So am I" (LW 35:186), and answer in the same spirit: "Is he a doctor? So are we."

Private Interpretation?

Over the years, from his century until ours, Luther's sense of his doctoral vocation has constantly been echoed in the communion named after him. For the authors of the Formula of Concord (1577) he was "*Doctor* Luther, of blessed and holy memory," who on the basis of the word of God had restored sound doctrine. The first editors of the Weimar Edition called their enterprise a critical edition of "*Doctor* Martin Luther's works." A twentieth-century biography identified its subject as "Martin Luther, *doctor* of the Holy Scripture, reformer of the church."[7] And so one might go on. What exactly his progeny have learned, or have believed themselves to have learned, from Dr. Luther has varied astonishingly at different moments of Lutheran history; and a number of studies have attempted to trace, in whole or in part, the story of his never-ending metamorphosis. One such study, by Ernst Walter Zeeden, is of particular interest for our theme; the work of an ecumenically minded Roman Catholic, it goes a long way toward explaining how, in Roman Catholic eyes, Protestantism has become identified with religious subjectivism.

To begin with, as Zeeden shows, it was chiefly the Lutheran dogmaticians who interested themselves in Luther, and more in his doctrine than in his person. But by the eighteenth century Luther had become the object of a much broader party strife within Lutheranism, as pietists and rationalists alike claimed him for themselves; and in the conflict of faith and philosophy he became at once a symbol of faith and a symbol of progress. It even became possible to view him apart from his doctrine, as a forerunner of intellectual freedom. In G. E. Lessing (1729–81), for example, Zeeden finds "the idea of a *formal* Lutheranism," which consists purely in the right to the same freedom that Luther himself exemplified.[8]

Zeeden's thesis is that attitudes to Luther were able to diverge along two distinct lines only because a certain ambiguity was already present in

7. Willem Jan Kooiman, *Maarten Luther: Doctor der Heilige Schrift, reformator der Kerk,* 2d ed. (Amsterdam: W. ten Have, 1948).

8. Ernst Walter Zeeden, *The Legacy of Luther: Martin Luther and the Reformation in the Estimation of the German Lutherans from Luther's Death to the Beginning of the Age of Goethe,* trans. Ruth Mary Bethell (Westminster, Maryland: Newman Press, 1954), xi–xiii, 139 (my emphasis). This is an abridged, somewhat free, and in places inaccurate version of volume 1 of the German work (1950).

Luther himself: He stood at once for a new guiding principle, which was freedom of conscience, and a new form of belief, which was the doctrine of justification by faith alone. Protestant orthodoxy took the doctrine, pietism and rationalism only "the primacy of personal religious experience and freedom from manmade codes." Although the orthodox attitude may have been "nearer to Luther than the whole body of modern research," Zeeden points out the irony in an appeal made to Luther instead of to Luther's own court of appeal, and in the refusal to grant his followers the freedom he had claimed for himself. But on the other side Luther's name was invoked only to support "the right to form one's own idea of Christianity": religion became a private matter, and the world accordingly became secular. As Johann Adam Moehler (1796–1838) said, Protestants found themselves thanking Luther for freedom to believe the exact opposite of what Luther believed. Zeeden concludes that the history of Protestantism has disclosed the incompatibility of Luther's two original principles. "Protestantism contains the seed of its own destruction."[9]

A similar Roman Catholic critique of Luther and Protestantism appears in the work of Joseph Lortz. His two-volume history is commonly viewed as a milestone along the road to a more irenic historiography of the Reformation, but it nevertheless sharply reformulates some old charges. Lortz recognizes that Luther strove for objectivity, seeking it in the Christian congregation, the Sacrament of the Altar, the word of God—ultimately, in Christ himself. Hence the severity of his attack on the fanatics, whose subjectivism made itself master over the word. But Luther's objectivism was self-deception, since there cannot be religious objectivity without an infallible teaching authority; his illogicality is that he was a servant of the word—according to his own very personal understanding. In the end, the decisive point is that he threw the individual back upon him- or herself, alone before the word; whatever objectivity he tried to preserve could only stand in tension with this subjectivism. The individual had won.[10]

By a longer and more circuitous route than was once the rule, Lortz brings us back to a very old Roman Catholic image of Luther: the rebel whose vigorous individualism had its source in pride, and its consequences in a fragmented church and a secular culture. His pride began with a deep need for utter independence—he had to be *Eleutherius,* "the free"—and ended with a repulsive arrogance and a colossal pugnaciousness. The primary token of this proud attitude was his rejection of what the church had taught for one and a half millennia in favor of his private interpretation of

9. Ibid., 8–9, 47, 207, 212. On Luther's two principles see also 80, 86, 98, 209–10.

10. Joseph Lortz, *The Reformation in Germany,* trans. Ronald Walls, 2 vols. (New York: Herder & Herder, 1968), 1:443–51, 2:340–41. On the identification of objectivity with the magisterium of the Roman Church, see further 1:442, 456.

Scripture. A procedure so essentially divisive can only end in a chaos of individual opinions, in uncertainty of what Christianity is, and in the unchristian life of modern culture.[11]

The question of Luther's temperament and its palpable defects may be set aside for the moment. Four comments of another order seem more appropriate in response to Zeeden and Lortz. First, instead of asserting that Luther wavers between two principles—whether freedom of conscience and the doctrine of justification (Zeeden), or subjectivism and objectivity (Lortz)—it would be closer to his intention to say that he builds on a single principle, which is the strict correlation of subject and object.

In one sense, Luther did put a questionable stamp of religious subjectivity on the Lutheran version of Christian faith. This can readily be verified by noting how his experience of God is canonized in the Lutheran confessions. When Melanchthon asserts in his *Apology* that faith is conceived in terrors of conscience,[12] we are bound to ask: Surely not always? Luther proclaimed the good news that there is hope even for those who have drained the last drops of despair. Does it follow that there is no hope for those who have not? Still, the initial one-sidedness of the Lutheran Reformation was at this point something contingent and therefore itself reformable.

In another sense, however, forcefully presented in Luther's *Babylonian Captivity of the Church* (1520), the stamp of religious subjectivity is essential to Protestant understanding of the gospel. Protestant grace comes as a word, a promise, a message—in fact, precisely as "gospel." And the form of God's grace as spoken word determines the form of the human response as the hearing of faith. What is disclosed in the word is the character of God as gracious; the essence of faith is the perception of God in this, God's true character, and a corresponding trust or confidence. In short, word and faith are correlatives (LW 36:42, 67; cf. 3:22); in this sense, the objective and the subjective belong together.[13] The one who believes, has. Neither is there anything "uncatholic" in this principle. To put it in the old Augustinian formula, which Thomas and Calvin both liked to quote: the word is efficacious "not because it is spoken, but because it is believed."[14]

Second, Luther's use of the Bible cannot be disposed of with the cliché "private interpretation"; whatever its shortcomings, it marks an important stage in the evolution of biblical scholarship. Some of Luther's claims for his doctrine do make painful reading, even for many who sympathize

11. Ibid., 1:471–77, 442–44, 455–58; 2:340–41.

12. *The Book of Concord: The Confessions of the Evangelical Lutheran Church,* trans. and ed. Theodore G. Tappert et al. (Philadelphia: Fortress Press, 1959), 126.

13. Cf. Luther's *Large Catechism* (1529): "These two belong together, faith and God" (*Book of Concord,* 365).

14. Augustine, *In Joan.,* lxxx.3.

with it. "Whoever does not accept my teaching," he asserts, "may not be saved—for it is God's and not mine" (LW 39:249). But his assurance (or cocksureness) at least took the form of a claim about the sense of Scripture ("I have the Scriptures on my side" [LW 32:9]); he pointed to an external court of appeal. The intention was not to parade his own ego, but rather to insist that Christ alone was his master and everyone else a fellow pupil (WA 6.587.1).

In other words, Luther has to be appraised as a figure in the history of hermeneutics. The final verdict on his achievement is bound to be mixed, since he refused to consider the interpretation of the Bible as a purely technical matter. Unquestionably, he thought of his doctorate as a qualification, not only a vocation, to interpret the Scriptures (LW 35:186, 194). But the interpreter's task, as he saw it, is not to "play the master of the Word" but to listen to the Christ who speaks in the Scriptures: "You must hear Him and not master Him or prescribe method, goal, or measure to Him" (LW 23:229–30). The *doctor* of Holy Scripture is not the *master* of Holy Scripture. Luther assures us that he did not want the reputation of being more learned (*doctior*) than others; he wanted Scripture to be sovereign—interpreted neither by his own spirit nor by anyone else's, but understood by itself and by its own spirit (WA 7.98.40). The Scripture is *sui ipsius interpres,* its own interpreter (ibid., 97.23). But it can surely be argued that to disclaim technical mastery of a text is in fact one important hermeneutical principle: the principle that one must always listen. Lortz, to be sure, denies that Luther was a good listener: "This," he says, "is the all-important fact: he who desires to surrender himself without reserve to God's word has never been a hearer in the full sense of the word. . . . He did not listen to everything but chose what he wanted."[15] The question is, however, whether this weakness of Luther's, if such it was, calls for a return to a teaching office, supernaturally preserved from error, or rather for moving on with the principles and practice of biblical scholarship, which is certainly fallible but can find the resources for correction and progress only within its own domain.

Luther insisted on confronting the ecclesiastical authorities on the same scriptural grounds on which he stood against individual opponents. He raised above the doctors and councils, he said, not himself but Christ (WA 6.581.14; cf. LW 32:11). And what he announced at the Diet of Worms was not that he trusted his own subjectivity, but that he was bound by the Scriptures, his conscience being captive to the word of God (LW 32:112). Even the church authorities, therefore, could speak with him only as fellow-pupils of the word; he denied them the right to silence him in any other way than by refuting his understanding of Scripture. The signifi-

15. *Reformation in Germany,* 1:184, 456.

cance of Luther's reformation for Protestant use of the Bible thus lies partly in his rejection of *false* objectivity. As Friedrich Schleiermacher put it in a memorable phrase: the Reformation established the basis for an "eternal covenant between the living Christian faith and completely free, independent scientific inquiry."[16]

Lortz, who did not trust doctrine to theologians, found biblical scholars, too, incapable of rising above the babel of private interpretations, and he thought he saw the Protestant legacy in an "arrogant biblical and dogmatic criticism, constantly revising its position."[17] But it is difficult to see how an unsound biblical scholarship could be corrected by anything but a sounder biblical scholarship. Whatever legitimate claims a church may make in the discipline of its own community of faith, in the work of biblical scholarship its authority as such must be tacitly or expressly replaced by the text, a method for interpreting it, and a community of scholars. These days, the one community of biblical scholars includes both Protestants and Roman Catholics. Much the same holds true of historical and theological scholarship, including Luther research.

Third, then, since the time when the major studies by Zeeden and Lortz first appeared, transconfessional Luther research has made immense strides. Lortz was ready to admit that Roman Catholics could learn from Luther. But he continued to think of a Protestant as a prodigal son whom "the Church" would be glad to forgive and welcome home: "Those returning home," he wrote, "lose nothing, but rather are enriched; they in turn enrich those to whom they return, namely 'in all that of positive value which they have embraced and cherished with particular love.'"[18] Luther was, after all, a heretic, and something of the old ecclesiastical motto lingered on in Lortz's mind: *Oportet haereses esse*—there must be heresies if the church is to clarify her teachings. Hence the most that Lortz and his school were able to do for Luther, as Otto Pesch wrote in 1966, was to excuse him. Announcing that Lortz's method of dealing with Luther had been superseded, Pesch maintained that Roman Catholic theology had learned to study Luther "*as a real possibility for its own theological thought and life*."[19] Remarkably enough, Luther has become a "doctor," we may say, even for German Catholicism. And parallel to this change of theological approach to Luther there has been a change of institutional attitude: among German Catholics, there is greater readiness today to think in terms of sister

16. Schleiermacher, *Sendschr.*, 40.

17. *Reformation in Germany*, 2:341; cf. 1:443, 455.

18. Translated from Lortz's *Die Reformation: Thesen als Handreichung bei ökumenischen Gesprächen* by Leonard Swidler, "Catholic Reformation Scholarship in Germany," *Journal of Ecumenical Studies* 2 (1965): 189–204, 201.

19. Otto H. Pesch, "Twenty Years of Catholic Luther Research," *Lutheran World* 13 (1966): 303–16, esp. 307, 311, 316 (emphasis Pesch's).

churches rather than of "the Church" and an obstinate rebel. And this is my fourth and last comment on Zeeden and Lortz.[20]

Only for a few years, at most, did Rome confront a solitary rebel. Luther, it must be admitted, continued to imagine himself the lonely prophet of Yahweh long after it had ceased to be true (if it ever was). The truth is that in a very short time his protest became a schism, and the Roman Church was faced by a Lutheran church, which developed its own "magisterium." The seeds of this new growth were already sown by Luther himself: in his treatise *On the Councils and the Church* (1539), for example, which contains one of his most defiant assertions of individual interpretation (LW 41:119), there are the beginnings of a Protestant theory of church authority. The individualism even of his belief in his doctorate must not be exaggerated; it should be appraised in relation to the new doctoral oath, instituted at Wittenberg in 1533, which bound the doctor not only to maintain the ecumenical creeds and the Augsburg Confession (1530), but also to preserve fellowship with other leaders of the church:

> I promise the eternal God . . . that with God's help I shall faithfully serve the church in teaching the gospel without any corruptions and shall constantly defend the Apostles', Nicene, and Athanasian Creeds; and that I shall maintain accord with the doctrine comprised in the Augsburg Confession. . . . And when difficult and intricate controversies arise, I shall make no pronouncement on my own, but only after deliberation with some of the elders who teach churches holding the doctrine of the Augsburg Confession.[21]

In short, the ecumenical problem is totally misconceived if it is taken to be (still!) the problem: What shall "the Church" do about Luther?

The debate over Dr. Martin Luther's alleged corruption of doctrine with subjectivism has by no means been laid to rest; it will probably stay with us for a long time yet. The reason is obvious: in Luther's theology there really is a new interest in the religious subject, and the problem is how to describe it fairly. The problem is particularly difficult for anyone who works with the kind of religious objectivity that Luther rejected. On the other hand, Protestants cannot assume that Roman Catholic research is getting better the less critical of Luther it becomes. Indeed, the tendency to be more positive toward him is by no means universal; in the same year in which Pesch's article was published, there appeared one of the most searching discussions yet of Luther's subjectivism. Its author, Paul

20. For a recent Roman Catholic perspective on relations with the Lutherans, see Walter Kasper, "What Would Catholic Recognition of the *Confessio Augustana* Mean?" in *The Role of the Augsburg Confession: Catholic and Lutheran Views,* ed. Joseph A. Burgess et al. (Philadelphia: Fortress Press, 1980), 123–29.

21. Quoted in Latin by Steinlein, 762–63, n. 6.

Hacker, describes Luther's faith as "reflexive faith." That is to say, by making salvation depend on believing that one is saved, Luther, according to Hacker, threw the religious subject back upon itself, precluding that self-abandonment to God in which true faith consists. I do not myself believe that this interpretation can do justice to the christocentric character of Luther's *faith,* the heart of which is single-minded contemplation of Christ; the ego does not, in the act of faith, bend back upon itself. But Hacker seems to me correct when he discovers in Luther an early form of anthropocentric *theology.*[22]

In Luther's theological reflection the religious subject does turn back upon itself; it makes its believing the object of thought. By the very fact of singling out justification by faith as his "chief article," Luther fostered a change of theological priorities and theological style in comparison with medieval scholasticism. As he put it: "The proper subject of theology is man guilty of sin and condemned, and God the Justifier and Savior of man the sinner. Whatever is asked or discussed in theology outside this subject, is error and poison" (LW 12:311). Assertions about God and humans in this theology are made strictly as answers to questions about sin and justification; the object of Christian teaching is the life of faith itself, viewed from the inside. And in this respect there is genuine continuity between the Reformation and liberal Protestantism. For Schleiermacher, the task of theology (or, more correctly, dogmatics) was to interrogate and describe the piety of the Christian. In this sense, the content of doctrine is precisely religious subjectivity.[23]

A Theology of Experience

Luther started a reformation, and Schleiermacher a new period in the history of Protestant thought. To inquire about the relationship between them seems natural enough. But less has been written on the subject than one would expect, and what *has* been written is in large part disappointing. Horst Stephan remarks on the absence even in the mature Schleiermacher of a "warm, personal interest" in Luther, though he nevertheless concludes—on the slenderest of evidence—that Schleiermacher of course revered Luther as "the highest authority next to the Bible."[24] This, I suspect, is a statement only of what Stephan thought fitting in Germany's second most eminent theologian. Similarly, Heinrich Bornkamm finds Schleiermacher's few remarks about Luther "wholly colorless"; like Stephan, he

22. Paul Hacker's study was translated into English as *The Ego in Faith: Martin Luther and the Origin of Anthropocentric Religion* (Chicago: Franciscan Herald Press, 1970).

23. *Sendschr.,* 25, 28, 33.

24. Horst Stephan, *Luther in den Wandlungen seiner Kirche,* 2d ed. (Berlin: Alfred Töpelmann, 1951), 69–71.

points out that Schleiermacher thought of history as the work of a "common spirit" and was unwilling to attribute too much to any individual.[25]

Since the "father of modern theology," as he is commonly called, was not a Lutheran, and often came under critical fire from the Lutherans, it is perhaps unreasonable to expect much warmth or color in his remarks about Luther. Still, I would take with a grain of salt the profession he once made of allegiance to Zwingli's doctrine rather than Luther's. In any case, his own Reformed communion, he said, did not hesitate to join in the glorification of Luther's memory—even at the price of leaving their own Zwingli and Calvin in the shade more than they deserved. If one had to make a choice among the three Reformers, it would surely be Calvin whom one would have to single out as Schleiermacher's favorite. For now, however, the question is, What light can we shed on subjectivity and doctrine in Dr. Martin Luther?[26]

Schleiermacher conceived of dogmatics as an "empirical" discipline, in the sense that its object of inquiry was to be the actual phenomena of religious experience. It was not to be a speculative theology of rational proofs, nor a biblical theology that would derive its propositions by exegesis: dogmatic propositions arise "solely out of logically ordered reflection upon the immediate utterances of the religious self-consciousness," and Christian doctrines are "accounts of the Christian religious affections set forth in speech." Schleiermacher believed that he could claim Luther as his forerunner in this theological program because for Luther, too, theology arose as reflection on religious experience; his theology was the daughter of his religion, and not the other way around.[27]

Schleiermacher's belief that he was a legitimate son of the Reformation still lacks a fully satisfactory treatment. But the affinity of his theology with Luther's has not passed unnoticed. Georg Wobbermin (1869–1943), in particular, an almost forgotten captain of the liberal rearguard, protested vigorously against the neoorthodox attacks on Schleiermacher's alleged subjectivism. He granted that the urgent task for Protestant theology in the 1930s was to ward off the peril of subjectivism; but he did not see this as a problem in Luther's theology, and he was convinced that Schleiermacher had directed Protestant theology back into Luther's path. The crucial point, he held, is the togetherness of God and faith: God reveals Godself only to faith. But Luther's turn to the subjective, which it undoubtedly was, excluded both subjectivism and objectivism; it affirmed the strictly correlative character of faith and its object (that is, God). If we

25. Heinrich Bornkamm, *Luther im Spiegel der deutschen Geistesgeschichte,* 2d ed. (Göttigen: Vandenhoeck and Ruprecht, 1970), 78–79.

26. See further chapter 8 below.

27. Schleiermacher, *Gl.,* § 16 (postscript), § 15; *Sendschr.,* 20–21, 16. A fuller account of Schleiermacher's conception of theology is given in chapter 7 below.

insist on pressing the question, Which is finally definitive, God or faith? Wobbermin's answer is: For faith God (of course); but for theology the correlation itself—God and faith together.[28]

A more recent and more extensive study of Luther and liberal Protestantism was published in 1963 by Walther von Loewenich, whose earlier work on Luther's theology of the cross (1929) is a landmark in Reformation research. The influence of the dialectical theology (neoorthodoxy) in his Luther book, von Loewenich admits, was unmistakable; but now, more than three decades later, the word is out that the end of liberalism may have been celebrated prematurely. In Luther's Scripture principle he finds a revolutionary factor that actually links liberalism with the Reformation. Unlike the medieval church and the Council of Trent, Luther permitted Scripture to criticize tradition, not merely to support it; and he asserted the rights of a well-founded personal interpretation of Scripture against the traditional interpretation held by the church. Von Loewenich writes accordingly of Luther's "subjective approach," and he documents it from the famous remark that simple laypersons, if they adduce Scripture, are more to be believed than pope or council if they do not.[29]

Neither the expression "subjective approach" nor the documentation in support of it seems quite to say what von Loewenich intends. He goes on to mention the right and duty of the *scholars* to understand Scripture in accordance with their best knowledge and conscience; and this, I have pointed out, is a different matter from an appeal to subjective conviction. It is, in fact, an appeal to objective standards. Certainly, the establishment of scholarly criteria does have one thing in common with the Reformation "theonomy" that von Loewenich discovers in Luther's stand at Worms: neither one can be attained except by way of *autonomy,* that is, by refusing heteronomous tutelage to a church.[30] It is this common cause of Protestantism and free inquiry that lends plausibility to Schleiermacher's "eternal covenant," established between faith and science by the Reformation. But von Loewenich comes closer to the point of continuity between Luther and Schleiermacher that I myself have chiefly in mind when he turns from the "subjective approach" (in his misleading sense) to what he calls a "theology of experience."

Put in modern terms, he says, the concern of a theology of experience is for the existential character of theological statements: they are not disin-

28. Georg Wobbermin, "Gibt es eine Linie Luther-Schleiermacher?" *Zeitschrift für Theologie und Kirche* 39 [n.s. 12] (1931): 250–60. Wobbermin does not, as I did, argue from Luther's understanding of the word, but from the passage in the *Large Catechism* (see n. 13 above).

29. Walther von Loewenich, *Luther und der Neuprotestantismus* (Witten: Luther Verlag, 1963), 5, 315–18.

30. Ibid., 319–22.

terested statements of objective knowledge, but statements in which the existence of the knower is at stake or on the line. In this sense, Luther's biblical theology was at the same time a theology of experience, and this is what justifies the liberal Protestant appeal to him.[31] I would myself wish only to add that, for Schleiermacher, at least, theological (or dogmatic) statements are not strictly existential utterances, but *about* existential utterances.

The experiential starting point has sometimes been held to represent the distinctive character of Lutheran, in contrast to Reformed (or Calvinistic), theology. The Danish Lutheran Hans Lassen Martensen (1808–84) wrote in his dogmatics: "The Swiss Reformation started primarily from the formal principle, that of the authority of the Scriptures; whereas the Lutheran originated more especially in the material principle, in the depths of the Christian consciousness, in an experience of sin and redemption."[32] The Calvinists have commonly replied that their concern, properly understood, is to correct the anthropocentrism of the Lutherans; and that while the experiential starting point is indeed distinctively Lutheran, their own theocentric starting point lies in the idea of God. An interesting consequence is that Alexander Schweizer (1808–88), the historian of Reformed theology who proclaimed Schleiermacher the reviver of the Reformed school, felt obliged to admit that something of the "empirical-historical-anthropological" approach of the Lutherans had rubbed off on his hero.[33] Be that as it may (it needs to be asked, I think, whether Schweizer took seriously enough the role of *pietas* in Schleiermacher's predecessor Calvin), the notion of a theology of experience does seem to forge a link between Luther and Schleiermacher—and so, a link with the existentialist theologians of our own day.

Schleiermacher's keenest critic, Karl Barth, was well aware of the appeal the existentialist theologians made to Luther, and he said he did not doubt that out of the great Pandora's box of the Weimar Edition one could extract "a theologically existentialist, and thus indirectly Schleiermacherian thread." But he added: "How many other threads one must then leave unconsidered or must even decisively cut off!"[34] The point is well taken. It invites the question of *material* continuity and discontinuity

31. Ibid., 330, 332. However, I am not persuaded by von Loewenich's view that the problem of certainty underlies Schleiermacher's theology of experience.

32. Hans Lassen Martensen, *Christian Dogmatics: A Compendium of the Doctrines of Christianity,* trans. from the German edition by William Urwick (Edinburgh: T. & T. Clark, 1898), 49.

33. Alexander Schweizer, *Die Glaubenslehre der evangelisch-reformirten Kirche dargestellt und an den Quellen belegt,* 2 vols. (Zurich: Orell, Füssli, and Company, 1844–47), 1:90–96.

34. Karl Barth, "Concluding Unscientific Postscript on Schleiermacher," trans. George Hunsinger, *Studies in Religion/Sciences Religieuses* 7 (1978): 117–35; quotations on 127.

between Luther and Schleiermacher: To what extent did the liberal Protestant understand the actual *content* of Christian experience as the Reformer understood it? One of the most sensitive answers was given by Emanuel Hirsch (1888–1972), who showed how close Schleiermacher could come to Luther's faith in Christ, and yet how far from Luther is a faith that is no longer suspended over the abyss of despair but has become a safe possession.[35] But this is another question—and it would require us to ask not only where Schleiermacher may have been unfaithful to the Reformation, but also where his departure from it may rest on legitimate criticism. For now, our conclusion must be left at the formal level of the question: How did Luther and Schleiermacher, as teachers of Christian doctrine, go about their work, and what can be inferred for the theme of doctrine and subjectivity?

No more than Luther did Schleiermacher lose the religious object in subjectivism; like the Reformer, he held that the Christian God is not to be had as an object, but only in piety or believing. More than this, he also made religious subjectivity the actual referent of dogmatic statements, the content of "doctrine." In so doing, he believed himself to be a disciple of Dr. Martin Luther. Schleiermacher, too, held that experience makes a theologian (cf. LW 54:7), venturing to write on the title page of his dogmatics his quotation from Anselm: "Anyone who has not experienced will not understand." I am not myself persuaded that the work of the theologian calls unconditionally for commitment. But it does seem to me that, by focusing theological interest on what it means to live by faith, Luther created a theology of experience that foreshadowed the modern view of theology as an anthropocentric study of a theocentric phenomenon.

35. Emanuel Hirsch, "Fichtes, Schleiermachers und Hegels Verhältnis zur Reformation" (1930), reprinted in Hirsch, *Lutherstudien*, 2 vols. (Gütersloh: C. Bertelsmann, 1954), 2:121–68; see. esp. 140–42, 156–57, 162–63. But whether Schleiermacher's faith was quite as serene as Hirsch assumes, really needs to be shown! See further chapter 8 below.

3

Discerning the Body: Sign and Reality in Luther's Controversy with the Swiss

ERICH HELLER'S *The Disinherited Mind,* in the American edition, has an epilogue titled "The Hazard of Modern Poetry." In it, Heller's thoughts go back to the great debate between Luther and Zwingli at Marburg (1529), and he suggests that, far from being a mere exercise in scholastic hairsplitting, the colloquy signaled a revolution: the reduction of symbols to the *merely* symbolic. "And ever since Zwingli the most common response to the reality of symbols has been a shrugging of shoulders or an edified raising of eyes and brows, or an apologia for poetry, or an aesthetic theory."[1]

It would be absurd to lay all these dreadful consequences wholly at Zwingli's door, as though he alone were responsible. Heller is using words advisedly, I assume, when he says that the theological dispute *signaled* the revolution. But Zwingli would not have minded being thought revolutionary. In his treatise *On Baptism* (1525) he announced, though with regret, so he said ("I would have preferred to keep silence"), that all the doctors of the church since the time of the apostles had been wrong because they had ascribed to the water of baptism a power it does not have.[2] He detected a like error in what had been said for centuries about the bread of the Eucharist, and the tragedy for the Protestant cause was that he detected this error in the writings of Luther.

Feelings ran high. Long before Marburg, Zwingli's friend Johann Oecolampadius (1482–1531) shamelessly ridiculed the Lutherans as drinkers of God's blood and worshipers of a baked God. Equally shamelessly, Luther perceived the Swiss not as Christians but as devils incarnate, who only *said* "Christ died for us" and did not feel it in their hearts.[3] Marburg

1. Erich Heller, *The Disinherited Mind: Essays in Modern German Literature and Thought* (New York: Farrar, Straus and Cudahy, 1957), 261–64, esp. 263.

2. G. W. Bromiley, trans. and ed., *Zwingli and Bullinger,* LCC 24:130.

3. LW 36:336, 344. In keeping with the original intention of this chapter (as an address to general audiences), the primary sources on which my argument rests are given in readily accessible English versions, and I have not attempted to review the extensive secondary literature.

itself—though at the conclusion Luther called it "this friendly colloquy"—was a shouting match, each side vigorously repeating its own favored text: the Lutherans, "This is my body" (Matt. 26:26); the Zwinglians, "the flesh is of no avail" (John 6:63). The controversy and the secondary literature on it turn around endless arguments about the correct exegesis of the words of institution, the properties of human bodies, the different modes of physical presence, the relationship between Christ's two natures, the significance of his bodily ascension, and the eucharistic opinions of Origen, Tertullian, Jerome, Ambrose, Augustine, Hilary, and others.

Modern readers may have fallen by the wayside long before the intricate arguments and counterarguments have reached their goal. It may even be that they will find Zwingli's case superfluous, because it has become a truism that the bread and wine of the Eucharist signify, rather than literally are, the body and blood of Christ, and that a sign cannot *be* what it signifies. But it does not follow that Zwingli was right, though he may have won, nor that the issues have become trivial; only that we may have to look a little harder to discover what the issues were. It would be strange if it were possible for the present-day theologian to leave the matter where Luther and Zwingli left it. But it would be equally strange if a classic debate about the central Christian rite—the rite in which the nature of the church is, or should be, displayed—had nothing whatever to say to us. Heller's point is that Marburg was a revolution in which poetry and art have as big a stake as theology and religion; he is right if Marburg means one can no longer be sure that in handling symbols one touches reality.

I cannot hope to sketch the course of the debate, or even of the Marburg Colloquy; nor can I attempt to list all the issues. Instead, I have taken my cue from Heller and pulled out one issue that seems to be both pivotal in the debate and perennially fascinating to us all: What do signs or symbols do? This, of course, requires us to ask further, in the limited context of the eucharistic debate: What does the sign of the body refer to? And since Zwingli scholarship of fairly recent date has made some fascinating reflections on his answer to this further question, we will also need to ask: Does the new look at Zwingli call for correction, or even surrender, of Luther's attack on him? Anyone who goes back to the great debate looking for insight into the nature of signs is bound to conclude, I believe, that Luther's critique of Zwingli still stands. And yet Luther's own assertions about the real presence do not offer a more persuasive theory of signification. They were not meant to. His profoundest thoughts on signs appear when he relates the eucharistic bread not to the flesh of Christ but to the church. Whenever he does so, he comes close, as we shall see, to one of Zwingli's most characteristic emphases, their difference over the nature of signs notwithstanding.

The Real Presence

"Carlstadt's poison crawls far. Zwingli at Zurich . . . and many others have accepted his opinion, continually asserting that the bread in the sacrament is no different from the bread sold in the market."[4] In his controversy with Zwingli and the Swiss, as these gruff words make clear, Luther saw the renewal of an earlier conflict with his onetime colleague, Andreas Bodenstein von Carlstadt, with whom he had settled accounts in his great treatise, *Against the Heavenly Prophets* (1525).[5] Carlstadt, as Luther put it, was a man who had swallowed the Holy Ghost feathers and all; his followers were up to their boots in spirit. Less picturesquely: Carlstadt had become convinced that medieval sacramentalism distorted the inwardness of true piety. He scorned dependence on the outward elements of water, bread, and wine and strove to get directly to the Spirit. In the Lord's Supper he discovered an act of remembrance, an occasion for fixing one's thoughts on Calvary, not a physical channel of divine grace.

Luther replies that he does not teach a merely literal and bodily eating in the sacrament, but there cannot be a spiritual eating unless the literal is there first. The plain meaning of the words "This is my body" is that Jesus, by a bodily outward act, truly offers his body to those who participate in the Supper, and that all, not only the devout, actually receive it. The Lord's Supper exemplifies the general rule that while God certainly deals with us inwardly through the Holy Spirit, who works faith in our hearts, God does it by the instrumentality of the external word and sacramental signs, through which the blessings won by Christ on the cross are distributed. The outward should and must come first; everything depends on this order. In his eagerness to get to the Spirit, Carlstadt has torn down the bridge by which the Spirit gets to us. Indeed, he has turned the sacrament into a devotional exercise, and so has made it again what it was for the papists: a human work. He has produced a new brood of monks and hypocrites, who trust in their own devotion. The truly "spiritual," however, is what the Holy Spirit works in us, not what we work for ourselves.

The spread of Carlstadt's "poison" brought about a shift in Luther's public statements on the Eucharist. He himself drew attention to the shift in one of his opening salvos against the Swiss, his "sermon" *The Sacrament of the Body and Blood of Christ—Against the Fanatics* (1526),[6] actually an altered version of three sermons, only two of which were on the Lord's Supper. There are two things in the sacrament, Luther explains: the object of faith, or *what* is believed, and the faith itself, which is the *use* of what is

4. Luther to Nicholas von Amsdorf, 2 December 1524 (my translation).

5. LW 40:73–223; see 83, 146–48, 177–80, 203–8, 212–14.

6. LW 36:329–61; see 335–48.

believed. Hitherto, he has preached mainly on the second thing, for the very good reason that the papists never lost the first; they always affirmed the presence of Christ's body and blood in the sacrament. Their error was that they misused the sacrament by treating it as a good work, and it is this that he has attacked in his assault on the Roman Mass.

The delusion of the fanatics, by contrast, is that Christ's flesh and blood are not present. Luther does not hesitate to call it their "heresy." For his part, he does not doubt that in the Sacrament of the Altar he receives the actual or natural body of Christ, which was born of the Virgin Mary, suffered, died, and rose again. Christ does not need to make a hole in the bread when he enters it, any more than he needs to make a hole when he enters the heart through the word and hearing. But as soon as he says, "This is my body," his body is present through the word and the power of the Holy Spirit. If Luther's bodily voice can fill hundreds of ears at once, how much easier must it be for Christ to distribute his glorified body, or enter the bread and wine, which are not so close-textured as a heart! Actually, Luther's preaching is itself one way by which Christ—the whole Christ—enters the heart. Not that he now sits in your heart as one sits on a chair; neither does he get there by descending from heaven on a ladder. But you know for sure he is there. Why may not the same miracle take place through the bread? Christ has put himself into the word, and through the word he puts himself into the bread also.

The real presence of the body and blood of Christ in the Eucharist has become Luther's bulwark against a new version of an old "heresy"—turning the sacrament into a human work. What he offers, however, is a defense of the real presence without anything like the traditional theory of signs. His argument turns around the sheer power of the word, which does what it says. When we say the words over the bread, Christ is really present. Without the word, it is indeed just bread; but as soon as the words are added, they bring what they speak about, as the angel's words brought Christ into the Virgin's womb. No one can gainsay it: the power comes through the word. And what the words "This is my body" say is perfectly clear, just as clear as if someone were to put a roll in front of me and say, "Take, eat, this is white bread." The fanatics knock themselves out struggling for a subtle interpretation of the words. But even a child can understand. True believers simply wrap themselves up in the word and refuse to be turned away from it. It is their duty to believe these and all Christ's words. As in the controversy with Carlstadt, it is the gift character of the sacrament, imparted by the word, that is at stake. The Roman Catholics failed to affirm the eucharistic gift even *with* the real presence; *without* it, the misuse of the sacrament as a work follows inescapably. And this is exactly what is happening in the Zwinglian arguments. The devil is making a supreme effort. The day of judgment cannot be far off.

Word and Sign in Luther

The stance Luther took up in *The Body and Blood of Christ* not only reaffirmed the case against Carlstadt but also marked out the essential lines for the conflict with Zwingli, then only beginning. If you pay attention to the words of institution, you will believe two things: that the body is there, and that it is given to you. The Swiss, however, if they have their way, will leave you only the shell: they come together to commemorate Christ's death, and they say that the sacrament is a mere sign that identifies them as Christians. In other words, if we may paraphrase Luther, the subject of the sacramental action was misconstrued by the Swiss. The true subject is the living, present Lord, who holds out his body as the food of the soul; *we* are passive recipients.

Interestingly, the concept of a sign has played no role in this discussion, except in the arguments of the adversaries. More exactly, the only sign Luther has discovered is not the sacrament but the ascension. To say that Christ has gone up to heaven and sits at the right hand of God means that he is above all creatures—and in all and beyond all. "That he was taken up bodily, however, occurred as a sign of this."[7] It is true that in part 2 of *The Body and Blood of Christ* Luther does find a positive use for the concept of a symbol or figure in the sacrament, and to this we will need to return. But as far as the real presence is concerned, Luther's single-minded purpose is now to exclude sign talk from the interpretation of the words of institution and to stake everything on the efficacy of those words. If the nature of signs becomes increasingly a central issue in the debate, that is because signification was more important to the Swiss than to Luther. It was precisely by their theory of sacramental signs that the Swiss carried the memorialistic understanding of the Eucharist beyond Carlstadt. This becomes clear in Luther's next broadside, *That These Words of Christ, "This Is My Body," etc., Still Stand Firm against the Fanatics* (1527).[8]

The Swiss, as we may more politely call them, supported a memorialistic view of the sacrament, akin to Carlstadt's, by arguing that the words "This is my body" contain a figure of speech. Christ does not literally give us his natural body to eat in the Lord's Supper; the bread represents or signifies his body (Zwingli), or is a sign of his body (Oecolampadius). In support of their interpretation, they appealed to Augustine, who often called the Supper a sign of Christ's body. Luther's response to the invocation of Augustine's name is interesting: the fanatics, he claims, stupidly misinterpret him.

7. LW 36:342. Luther does, to be sure, call the sacrament a "wondrous sign" (340), but he is merely giving it a conventional name, not saying anything about signification.

8. LW 37:3–150; see 18, 104–7, 141.

For Augustine, Luther points out, a sacrament is not a sign of something absent but of something invisibly present. Out of a sign the fanatics make a mere symbol—a badge or token of identification, like the yellow badge by which Jews are identified. But that is not what Augustine meant. In appealing to him, they are only giving us something else to clout them on the head with, as though we did not have enough weapons already. Here, of course, Luther's glee is justified: the Swiss were not really indebted to Augustine for their notion of signs, but to the Dutch theologian Cornelisz Hoen (Honius, d. 1524), whose controversial letter on the Eucharist Zwingli had published at Zurich in 1525. But Luther was not tempted to take up, in defense of the real presence, a more authentically Augustinian understanding of signs. At least since 1520, his thoughts had been moving in a quite different direction. In his *Prelude on the Babylonian Captivity of the Church,* for instance, while he does speak of the sacramental sign in the Eucharist, he actually identifies the sign with the presence of the body and blood, not with the elements of bread and wine.[9] There is a straight line from this relatively early treatise against the papacy to what Luther intended as his final reckoning with the fanatics eight years later, the great *Confession concerning Christ's Supper* (1528).[10]

The discussion of signs in the *Confession* is couched almost entirely in the form of polemic against the Swiss employment of them. If there is a figure of speech in the words "This is my body. . . . This is my blood," then there must, Luther insists, be a resemblance on which the figure rests. But there is in fact no resemblance between the bread and the body, or between the cup and the blood, either with respect to their several natures or with respect to what happens to them. There is a natural resemblance between, say, a wooden rose and a real rose; and there is a resemblance between the paschal lamb of the Old Testament and the body of Christ, in that the lamb was slain. But neither kind of resemblance applies to the bread or the cup.

For the Swiss, the bread of the Eucharist signifies the body of Christ to those who have the faith to pick up the signal. For Luther, on the other hand, the body of Christ is made present in the Supper by Christ's own words, quite regardless of anyone's believing or not believing it; in those who eat without believing, his flesh works like a deadly poison.[11] Indeed, an entire new substance (*Wesen*) has come into existence out of the bread

9. LW 36:44. But Luther immediately goes on to say that "the bread and wine are the sacrament" (cf. also 23). His fundamental thought here is that a sign is a pledge (a "mark" or "memorial") of God's promise.

10. LW 37:151–372; see 238, 262–68, 300–303, 354, 367.

11. This theme and its positive counterpart—the transformation of the flesh of those who partake believingly—is developed more fully in *This Is My Body* (LW 37:71, 86–87, 93–94, 100–101, 132, 191).

and the body. If we ask, What, then, is this powerful eucharistic substance? Luther tells us it is *Fleischbrot,* "fleshbread." (Similarly, the wine and the blood have become *Blutwein,* "bloodwine.") The bread is not a sign of the body; it has coalesced with it into one new substance. We can no longer properly speak of either the bread or the body separately. If there is a figure of speech in the words of institution, Luther concludes, it can only be synecdoche—naming the part for the whole. To say, "This is my body," designating the bread, is entirely correct, because the bread has now become one sacramental substance with the body of Christ. Plainly, the old Augustinian notion of a sacrament as a sign of a sacred thing has been left behind.

Luther seems, moreover, to have left Andreas Bodenstein von Carlstadt as the only honest literalist of the day. Carlstadt assumed that Jesus, after proffering the bread with the invitation, "Take, eat," must have paused for a moment, pointed to *himself,* and said: "*This* is my body." That is a case of literal-identical predication, if ever there was one.[12] Luther, by contrast, though he always claimed to take the words in their plain and literal sense, in effect concludes that Zwingli just got the wrong figure. "This is my body" is not an instance of symbolism, but of synecdoche.

Luther was not, to be sure, wholly averse to discovering symbolism in the Eucharist. He recognized, for instance, that whereas there is no similarity between bread and a body, there may be a similarity between physical and spiritual nourishment. Hence, in a more pastoral work like the *Large Catechism* (1529), he can say of the Lord's Supper that it is fittingly called "the food of the soul" because it nourishes and strengthens the new man.[13] Perhaps he could have found here a point of contact with his opponents, who also suggested this analogy. But in his polemical writings he was more interested in systematically eliminating any basis for a figure of speech in the words "This is my body. . . . This is my blood," and he therefore dismissed the analogy of eating and drinking as irrelevant to the debate, since *these* words say nothing of eating or drinking. "Here, here in the bread, I say, a resemblance must be shown." Similarly, he was reluctant to admit one other possible resemblance proposed by the adversaries: between the breaking of the bread and Jesus' crucifixion. But the details of his sometimes rather strained arguments in the *Confession* cannot detain us. Suffice it to say that the main lines of Luther's eucharistic thinking made the Augustinian definition of a sacrament as a sign of a sacred thing inconvenient; it was of little positive use to him. All hinged on the power of the word, not on the concept of a sign.

12. LW 40:154–65.

13. *The Book of Concord: The Confessions of the Evangelical Lutheran Church,* trans. and ed. Theodore G. Tappert et al. (Philadelphia: Fortress Press, 1959), 449.

SIGNS AND DEEDS IN ZWINGLI

Zwingli's eucharistic thinking, by contrast, does turn around a theory of signs, and Luther thought him as wrong about signs as he was about the real presence. Before agreeing, we had better see what Zwingli actually says on the nature of sacramental signs.[14] To his way of thinking, the primary reference of the signs is to events lying in the past. They do not so much effect something as signal the fact that something has already been effected. They associate visibly with the church those who have already been received into it invisibly. By baptism, nothing is accomplished but marking with a sign someone who is reckoned a member of the church. Similarly, by joining in the celebration of the Eucharist we attest that we belong to the company of the redeemed.

The specific form of the individual sacraments, as distinct from their general use, points still further back into the past—to the deed of God in the Incarnation. They do not absolve from guilt; they indicate that our guilt was done away by Christ. Baptism signifies that Christ has washed us, and the Supper signifies that God's favor has been procured by Christ's death for us. The sacraments are signs of facts or events—real things that once took place and are now, in the signs, represented, recalled, set before our eyes. The signs are thus not so much pledges or confirmation of God's grace and mercy as pointers to the actual pledge of God's grace, which is God's deed in Jesus Christ. They bring this deed to the believer's mind by picturing its benefits: namely, cleansing from sin (baptism) and the nourishment of the soul (the Lord's Supper). Occasionally, it is true, Zwingli can use Luther's language and speak of the sacramental sign as itself the pledge or symbol of God's grace,[15] just as the bride's ring is a token of the bridegroom's love. But this is less characteristic of him. The pledge of God's mercy, strictly speaking, is Jesus Christ; what you do in the Lord's Supper is to thank the Lord for *this* pledge. If we speak of a sacrament as itself a pledge or covenant sign, then it is a pledge not so much of God's mercy as of our commitment to Christ. This seems to be the import of Zwingli's thoughts on baptism, which enlists us as Christ's soldiers, or pledges us to Christ, just as the white cross proclaims that a man is a Swiss Confederate. But the same notion holds good for his thoughts on the Eu-

14. For Zwingli's conception of signs, see his *Commentary on True and False Religion* (1525), LWZ 3:1–343, esp. 179–86, 201–15, 250. My summary also draws from *On Baptism*, LCC 24:131–53, 166, 169; *On Original Sin* (1526), LWZ 2:29; *On the Lord's Supper* (1526), LCC 24:204, 209, 228–29, 234; *Account of the Faith* (1530), LWZ 2:47–48; *On the Insults of Eck* (1530), LWZ 2:107–9, 113–18; and *Exposition of the Faith* (1531/36), LCC 24:248–51, 258–65 (also in LWZ 2:235–93).

15. See n. 9 above. It must be admitted that it is not always clear who, for Zwingli, pledges what.

charist, too, and he rests this interpretation of a sacrament partly on the classical Latin use of *sacramentum* for an oath of loyalty.

It follows that the sacraments do have a secondary time-reference, but to the future rather than to the present. "We teach therefore that the sacraments should be reverenced as holy things because they signify most holy things, both those which have already happened and those which we ourselves are to produce and do." Hence baptism also means that we are to put on Christ; the Supper, that we are to embrace our brothers and sisters in thankfulness with the same love with which Christ has redeemed us. The future reference, plainly, is implicit in the selfsame concept of a pledge, understood as a public commitment of the Christian to the Lord. When the tense is changed in this way, the signification of a sacrament appears to collapse into its function as a pledge. If we ask what the water of baptism signifies, it is perhaps still possible to answer: It signifies cleansing, the cleansing to which the baptized person is committed. But what do the elements in the Eucharist symbolize, if the meaning of this sacrament is simply that we should embrace our brothers and sisters in love? What do the bread and wine refer to? Presumably, they have become symbols of a symbol—that is, of Christ's death as a sacrificial deed.[16]

A sacrament, then, according to Zwingli, simultaneously recalls the past deed of God and promises the future deed of believers; the past and future tenses convey the dominant features of his sacramental theology. It need not be denied, however, that his language sometimes overflows his customary limits and passes over into the present tense. When this happens, the gap between him and Luther narrows. Take, for instance, his presentation in the *Exposition of the Faith* that he addressed to King Francis I of France in 1531.[17] There it is said that the signs of bread and wine set Christ, in a manner of speaking, before our eyes, and we not only hear but see and taste him whom the soul carries within itself and in whom it rejoices. Or again, the bread and wine signify, in his stead, Christ's goodness and favor. In other words, if the accent shifts from the deed to the doer, or to his eternal disposition, then the tense naturally shifts, too, from the past to the present.

A somewhat different thought leads Zwingli, in the same treatise, to a similar conclusion. When he asks what is meant by a spiritual, rather than a natural or literal, eating of the body of Christ, a change of signification takes place. For what the eating, as distinct from the elements, signifies is faith itself. To eat the body spiritually is to trust in the mercy and goodness God has toward us for the sake of God's Son, who gave himself for us. To eat sacramentally is simply to eat spiritually while participating in the sac-

16. Unless, of course, the symbolic referent is the church; see below.
17. See LCC 24:248, 258–60, 264.

rament. As Zwingli's actual language implies (*coniuncto sacramento*), he is now thinking of a conjunction of two events: You do inwardly what you represent outwardly, as you join your brothers and sisters in partaking of the bread and wine. In this way, the tokens of Christ's body and blood attest the faith of the participants.

Clearly, Zwingli intended something more than a bare memorialism, at any rate in this mature confession of his faith, and it has been suggested that his thinking underwent a change in his later years. Indeed, he seems to come within a hairsbreadth of Luther when he concedes that one virtue or power of the sacraments, especially the Lord's Supper, is their ability to arouse, increase, and assist faith (as distinct from giving or creating it). But the explanation of this power, for Zwingli, is psychological in a manner quite inadequate to Luther's thinking, if not wholly foreign to it. The signs, as Zwingli views them, engage the senses, turning them from whatever normally distracts them and employing them to support and strengthen faith. The senses become faith's handmaidens; the sacraments, to change the metaphor, bridle the senses and so may be said to help the contemplation of faith by conjoining it with the strivings of the heart. But there is no hint that an actual bodily presence of Christ, or indeed anything else, might be mediated through the signs. Any such thought is excluded in principle: Signs are indicative and declarative, not instrumental.[18]

A Reformed Doctrine of Transubstantiation?

But is it only to the natural body of Christ that the signs refer? A quite different thought has been found in Zwingli's liturgical writings, and here we are fortunate to have the guidance of a strikingly fresh study by Julius Schweizer that appeared in 1954. In his liturgy, *Action or Use of the Lord's Supper* (Easter 1525), Zwingli moved the center of Christian worship from the chancel to the nave. Instead of a priestly spectacle and a musical performance, both of which reduce the congregation to a passive audience, he wanted a celebration in the main section of the church, where it would become an "act" of the people. The priestly monologue was to be replaced by the exchange of speech not only between the pastor and his assistants, but also between the men and the women divided as antiphonal groups (a daring innovation that the Zurich council refused to permit). The liturgy called for a simple table to be placed in the nave, laid with wooden plates

18. The principle is clearly stated in Zwingli's *Account of the Faith:* "A channel or vehicle is not necessary to the Spirit" (LWZ 2:46). Sometimes sign and reality occur at the same time (this, too, belongs to the divine freedom). But the coincidence is not intrinsic, and it is foreign to Zwingli's way of thinking to represent it in terms of instrumental causality, as though God gave the reality *through* the sign (see, e.g., LCC 24:135–36, 149, 163); sacraments give only *historical* faith (260).

and cups; for the minister, without vestments, to take his stand behind it; and for the faithful, remaining in their places, to receive bread and wine from the servers with their own hands.

Everything in Zwingli's liturgy was calculated to stress one thing: that a "Eucharist" properly so-called is an act of thanksgiving on the part of the entire congregation. The theological underpinning of this novel proposal is that the congregation is the body of Christ. Schweizer comments: "This is the necessary presupposition of Zwingli's *Action:* in the proclamation that takes place in the liturgy of the word, a transformation happens through the operation of the Spirit not just symbolically but *realiter*—an actual transformation of the assembled community of Zurich Christians . . . into the *verum corpus Christi.*" Not the elements but the citizens of Zurich, herded into church by civil decree, are transformed into the true body of Christ, which then offers itself as an oblation to God. Zwingli has transposed the canon of the Roman mass, if Schweizer reads him correctly, into the Reformed understanding of the sacrament.[19]

In a more general study of Zwingli, published almost a decade after Schweizer's book, Jaques Courvoisier maintained that the "ecclesial dimension" of his thought had never been appreciated. Courvoisier's most interesting case in point is precisely Zwingli's doctrine of the Eucharist, from which all individualism is excluded. "Here," according to Courvoisier, "Zwingli says something new in the history of Christian thought which does not seem to have been taken up by the other Reformers." In certain key passages, Zwingli's eucharistic thinking is directed to the ecclesial body, the church, and in fact takes the word "body" to mean "church." In eating the eucharistic bread, we join ourselves together in one body—Christ's own body. Courvoisier infers: "Here Zwingli clearly makes the Lord's Supper constitutive of the visible church." Commenting on Schweizer's study, he adds: "The body, then, is not localized in the bread but in the church gathered about the bread. Precisely here is the doctrine of the real presence in Zwingli's theology." Zwingli does have a doctrine of the real presence, if this interpretation is right, but the real presence of the ecclesial, not the natural, body of Christ.

The reason why Zwingli's Eucharist has been found colorless and shallow, Courvoisier believes, is that others have viewed it through their own individualistic presuppositions. The culprit named is Courvoisier's own Genevan Reformer, John Calvin, who, he says, seems to have been totally unaware of the ecclesial dimension in Zwingli's thought; otherwise, he would have found something more in Zwingli's Eucharist than naked and empty figures. But behind Calvin, Courvoisier sees Luther,

19. Julius Schweizer, *Reformierte Abendmahlsgestaltung in der Schau Zwinglis* (Basel: Friedrich Reinhardt, 1954?), 84–85, 104–6; cf. 10, 58–59, 87, 92. Translation mine.

whose opinion Calvin trusted so uncritically that he failed even to read Zwingli for himself. And generation after generation of Lutherans and Calvinists have repeated Calvin's mistake.[20]

The importance of Schweizer's and Courvoisier's work goes far beyond the problems of Zwingli interpretation; it is highly suggestive both for constructive theology and for liturgics. But is it cogent Zwingli interpretation? And if so, was Luther totally mistaken about Zwingli? Might he even have learned something from the Swiss, had he been a better listener than he was?

If Schweizer is right, Zwingli believed that when the Zurichers gathered for worship, there was not only a real presence of the body of Christ as a marvelous deed of God but also an actual transformation: the Lord became present and changed the worshiping community into his body. In actual fact, as far as I can see, the notion that the risen Christ is present and active in the service is totally absent from Zwingli's liturgy. The service, as the title indicates, is a "memorial or thanksgiving of Christ." The preface specifies that the memorial and thanksgiving are for the benefit God has manifested to us through God's Son (past tense); and the invitation to the table shows that the thanks are given because Christ has suffered death for us and shed his blood (again the past tense). The subject of the present eucharistic action is the congregation, not the Lord. At a secondary level of interpretation—beyond Zwingli's own actual language—we might perhaps speak, as Schweizer often does, of a presence of God's *deed* in the event of the word and in the action of the sacrament; but we can hardly speak, without license, of an active presence of the Lord to change the Zurichers into his body. The liturgy simply addresses the Lord God Almighty as the one who has made them into God's one body.[21]

Neither, it may be added, does Zwingli's liturgy at any point talk expressly of a "transubstantiation" of the people, rather than the elements, into the body of Christ. It does call the Christian community "the body of Christ," and it does talk of God's having made the people into God's body. But Schweizer's Reformed use of the term "transubstantiation" is warranted only indirectly at best: that is, if one assumes that Zwingli was consciously adapting thoughts from the canon of the Roman Mass. Actually, Zwingli writes elsewhere precisely of a conversion of the eucharistic bread rather than of the assembled congregation, and this might well be termed a Reformed transposition of medieval eucharistic language. He means what

20. Jaques Courvoisier, *Zwingli: A Reformed Theologian* (Richmond, Virginia: John Knox Press, 1963), 8, 74–77, 100 (nn. 35, 45). Courvoisier refers in particular to Zwingli's letter to Matthew Alber (1524) and the *Commentary on True and False Religion*.

21. See the translation of Zwingli's liturgy in Bard Thompson, *Liturgies of the Western Church*, Meridian Living Age Books (Cleveland and New York: World Publishing Co., 1961), 149–56.

we might call nowadays a "transignification" by which common bread becomes a sign of the natural body of Christ, or becomes, as Zwingli puts it, Christ's "sacramental body."[22] This, however, has no connection with Schweizer's "transubstantiation of the people" and affords no support for it. His monograph overflows with fruitful insights into the nature of Christian worship, but it takes too many liberties to rank as a satisfactory interpretation of Zwingli. Is Courvoisier's argument perhaps more convincing?

Courvoisier refers to Schweizer's conclusions as similar to his, only derived from a different primary source. But there appears to be in fact an important divergence between them, which he does not point out. According to Schweizer, Zwingli's Eucharist presupposes that the congregation has already been transformed into the body of Christ by the preaching of the word, in the first part of the service. Courvoisier, by contrast, writes of the sacrament as itself constitutive of the visible church. This is an interesting and attractive interpretation, and there are unquestionably passages in Zwingli that at least point toward it. But it could nevertheless prove quite misleading if it led us to reintroduce, by the back door, the notion of efficacious signs that Zwingli explicitly—and even forcefully—repudiated. Indeed, the rather different thesis of Schweizer, that it is the proclaimed word that brings the body into being, must also be judged suspect for a strictly analogous reason: Neither word nor sacramental sign, for Zwingli, has the power to constitute the church.[23] It is precisely his "soft" view of signs and signification that jeopardizes the attempts to rehabilitate him as a theologian of the church.

The Spiritual Body of Christ

Luther's critique of Zwinglian signs was by no means unjust. It convinced not only the Lutherans but the Calvinists, too; and that is one reason why Zwingli's five-hundredth birthday was celebrated in 1984 with much less fanfare than Luther's in 1983. Even in his own Reformed communion, he lost his leadership to others who were much more sympathetic to Luther's side in the great debate. John Calvin, in particular, learned from Luther a profound distaste for the notion of *mere* symbols—a notion he judged "profane." But is it still possible that Luther, for his part, could have learned something from Zwingli about the "ecclesial setting," as Courvoisier terms it, in which Zwingli placed his thoughts on the Eucharist and on almost everything else?

22. *On the Insults of Eck*, LWZ 2:117–18.

23. What constitutes the church, for Zwingli, is the Spirit's gift of faith, and faith does not, strictly speaking, come through hearing (LCC 24:154, 263).

Zwingli's insight at this point is not to be belittled. It was not proof-texting of a preestablished dogma; in large part, it was an honest attempt at historical exegesis, an attempt to understand the actual setting of the Eucharist in the early church. For what was the situation at Corinth to which Paul addressed his First Letter to the Corinthians? The division of the church into cliques was betraying itself even at table fellowship, which should have culminated in the Lord's Supper. The have-nots went hungry while the haves got drunk. Scandalized, Paul admonished the Corinthians to eat their meals at home (1 Cor. 11:17–22). Zwingli drew what is surely the right conclusion: Paul's warning against unworthy participation in the Lord's Supper was directed to Christians who lacked a proper sense of the church, which is the community or body of Christ. Zwingli's entire emphasis in his eucharistic thinking was exactly on this sense of the church. He thus stood poles apart from Carlstadt (at least, as Luther presents him): remembrance was a key notion for both, but for Carlstadt it meant private devotion, whereas for Zwingli it meant corporate celebration.

That there is a contrast here with Luther's emphasis, too, as well as Carlstadt's, seems undeniable. For Luther, the *raison d'être* of the Sacrament of the Altar, as distinct from the public proclamation of the word, is that it individualizes the grace of forgiveness. Luther preaches to all in general who have ears to hear, but he proffers the body and blood of the Lord to one person at a time. The Lutheran communicant says: "Here my Lord has given me his body and blood in the bread and wine, in order that I should eat and drink. And they are to be my very own, so that I may be certain that my sins are forgiven." Not that Luther impaired the "once for all" that was so dear to Zwingli. Neither did he neglect the element of remembrance that Zwingli placed at the center; on the contrary, when he argued against Carlstadt that remembering is not private meditation but public proclamation, he came remarkably close to the spirit of Zwingli's liturgy. Nevertheless, Luther's practical concern in the eucharistic controversy was for individual distribution of what Christ won on the cross *for me,* and for the absolute assurance that only a physical, tangible taking of his body and blood into my mouth can give me.[24]

The question is, however: Had this always been Luther's main practical concern? The answer is no. A powerful interest in the ecclesial body goes back to his earliest eucharistic treatise, *The Blessed Sacrament of the Holy and True Body of Christ* (1519). There he does start from the Augustinian contrast between the external, visible sign and the internal, spiritual significance. The *sign* in the Eucharist is not the bread and wine but the use of them in eating and drinking, just as the sign in baptism is not water but immersion or the pouring of water. The *significance* is communion or

24. LW 36:348–52; 40:207–8.

fellowship—incorporation with Christ and the saints, having all things common with them. Like Zwingli after him, Luther can even compare the sacrament to a certificate of citizenship, a token of belonging. And he can also, like Zwingli, dwell on the surface symbolism of the one loaf made of many grains ground together. The real presence of the natural body and blood of Christ is not denied. But the transformation of the bread and wine into Christ's natural body and blood is mentioned as a kind of analogue to *our* transformation into Christ's spiritual body, which is the church or communion of saints. And this transformation of ourselves is, of course, exactly the "transubstantiation" that Julius Schweizer detects in Zwingli's liturgy. Finally, Luther says expressly: "It is more needful that you discern the spiritual than the natural body of Christ."[25]

Luther's eucharistic thought underwent a striking reorientation shortly after *The Blessed Sacrament* was written. The shift is already betrayed in the title of his *Treatise on the New Testament* published the following year:[26] "testament" steals center stage from "communion." The formal distinction between sign and thing signified is retained, but with a quite new content. The external, sacramental sign is still thought of as containing and expressing something spiritual, so that through the outward we have (or are "drawn into") the spiritual. Now, however, the sign is there to seal the testament, to notarize Christ's will, in which he bequeathed forgiveness of sins. Moreover, the function of signification, so vivid in the earlier treatise, is now obscured by Luther's peculiar notion that the sign is not in the elements as such, but in the presence of Christ's body and blood *under* the elements of bread and wine. Since the presence of the body and blood is not visible, the entire thought of a visible sign is jeopardized, if not discarded; and Luther must argue in later writings that the real presence, so far from being a sensible support to faith in the spoken word, is itself an affirmation of naked faith, which simply clings to the words of Christ, "This is my body," whatever the appearances.

One effect of Luther's encounter with the Swiss, then, was to confirm a mental shift he had already made. By 1521 he had become acquainted with Cornelisz Hoen's symbolic interpretation of the sacrament. Luther's treatise *The Adoration of the Sacrament,* published two years later,[27] shows his anxiety that an ecclesial emphasis, in combination with the new symbolic theories, might actually displace belief in the real presence. Christ said: "This is my body." Here, at least, he cannot possibly have meant incorporation into his spiritual body, because he adds, "which is given for you." Not the spiritual body but the natural body was given for us—for the sake of his spiritual body, which body we are. Communion, therefore,

25. LW 35:45–73; see 49–53, 58–62.
26. LW 35:75–111; see 86.
27. LW 36:269–305; see 282–87.

in the sense of fellowship in one body, is not what the sacrament is, but what it bestows. The fanatics confuse the institution of the sacrament with its use or benefit; otherwise, they would realize that only participation in Christ's natural body can bring about the fellowship of the spiritual body.

What has happened is clear. Luther has no objection to discovering symbolism in the Sacrament of the Altar, as Christian tradition always had. The foundation for a symbolic interpretation is suggested by Scripture itself—by Paul's image of the one bread (1 Cor. 10:17). The many grains that are ground together become a single loaf. But the important thing, in Luther's eyes, is not to attach your symbolism to the wrong point, which is what the fanatics did: they looked for a symbol not only in the words "We who are many are one body," but also in the words "This is my body given for you." They mistook the fruit for the institution of the Supper, and so took away the only means by which the spiritual body of Christ could be established: by physical reception of his natural body, which has become one with the bread. "Take and eat, this is my body which is given for you." Luther says: "Here the words are plain and clear."

It is a disputed question among the scholars just how far Luther manages to preserve the ecclesial perspective as the debate over bodily presence heats up. But it is certain that he never lost it, not even in his polemical writings. It reappears three years later, for instance, in *The Body and Blood of Christ,* where once again (in part 2) the fruit of the sacrament is said to be that communion of which the bread and wine are signs or symbols:

> A loaf is nothing else than many kernels baked into one another. "We who are many" (says Paul in 1 Cor. 10:[17]), "are nevertheless all one loaf and one body." Just as each grain loses its form and takes on a common form with the others, so that you cannot see or distinguish one from the other, and all of them are identical, yet separately present; so too should Christendom be one, without sects, that all may be one, of one heart, mind, and will, just as faith, the gospel, and baptism are one [Eph. 4:5]. . . . A similar picture is portrayed in the wine. Here many grapes are pressed together, and thereby each grape loses its form and a juice emerges. All the grapes are present in the wine, but there is nothing by which we could distinguish one from another; they have all flowed together and become one juice and one drink.[28]

Just how little of that juice seems to have flowed at Marburg is all too painfully evident. But Luther was still talking about it in his *Confession concerning Christ's Supper.* For all the thoroughness of his massive case against the Swiss appeal to signs, he can still say: "The sacrament of the Supper must indeed prefigure and signify something, viz. the unity of Christians in one

28. LW 36:353.

spiritual body of Christ." And in his exegesis of 1 Corinthians 10:17 he writes: "Here 'body' is a true trope in the scriptural sense: not a figurative body . . . but a second, new body, to which a natural body bears a similarity."[29]

An Efficacious Sign

If we return, in conclusion, to Erich Heller's remarks (with which we began), they must strike us as fully warranted in what they say about Zwingli, except insofar as we judge that some of Zwingli's utterances are only polemical hyperboles. Sign and reality do fall apart in Zwinglianism; or if they coincide, the coincidence lies neither in the nature of things nor in any regular commitment on God's part, but solely in God's sovereign choice for this particular occasion. When all the qualifications are made, and the newest Zwingli research is taken into account, Luther does not seem to have been wrong about his adversary's understanding of sacramental signs. Heller's judgment, of course, coincides with Luther's: in Zwingli's thinking, signs have become *mere* symbols.

What is less clear is whether one may infer, or imply, that Luther himself had a more satisfactory theory of signs. For in his opposition to Zwingli on the matter of the real presence, he was less concerned to propose an alternative theory of signification than simply to affirm the presence and efficacy of the body and blood. He does so in a way that collapses the symbolic relationship of sign and reality, *sacramentum* and *res,* and moves sacramental causality out of the order of signification. Strictly speaking, the word "sign," when Luther continues to use it in this context, carries an improper sense, since the sign now does what it does, not by meaning, signifying, or symbolizing anything to faith, but purely as an efficient cause. The presence of the body and blood with the elements of bread and wine is indeed a pledge to those who believe it, but it does not, apparently, impart life to their bodies only because they believe; their belief is rather their awareness of what it does anyway.[30]

If we move out of the question of the real presence and ask what Luther means by the concept of a sign or symbol in the ecclesial context, in which he undoubtedly does use it, then it is arguable that, like Zwingli, he there understands signs in a purely cognitive and didactic sense. In *The Body and Blood of Christ,* he says that the many grains in the one loaf, or the many grapes in the one juice, picture the community of the church. "Here," he infers, "we have a lesson, the study of which is sufficient to occupy us all

29. LW 37:274–75, 355. But Luther points out that 1 Cor. 10:17 actually says "one body" (not "body of Christ"), and he does not give an ecclesiological sense to 1 Cor. 10:16, 11:27, or 11:29 (LW 37:341–51).

30. LW 37:93–94.

our lives." The same didactic interpretation of the sign goes all the way back to the early treatise *The Blessed Sacrament,* in which the figure of the one body and many members is presented as instruction for the unlearned. There, indeed, Luther even uses what was to become Zwingli's favorite notion of a sign as a token that serves as proof of belonging to the community (an "ID," as we say).[31]

Nevertheless, there are traces in *The Blessed Sacrament* of exactly the idea Courvoisier tries to establish in Zwingli's theology. "In the sacrament," Luther writes, "we become united with Christ, and *are made* one body (*eingeleibt*) with all the saints." Again: "For just as the bread is changed into his true natural body and the wine into his natural true blood, so truly are we also drawn and changed into the spiritual body, that is, into the fellowship of Christ and all saints and *by this sacrament* put into possession of all the virtues and mercies of Christ and his saints."[32] In these words, it seems to me, Luther proves that he did not need to learn from Zwingli about the ecclesial dimension in the Lord's Supper. He proves, too, that he could very well conceive of the sacrament as a symbol that was not *merely* symbolical. He could conceive of it, that is, as an efficacious sign of the church, combining, so to say, Zwingli's ecclesial sense with a higher view than Zwingli held about what signs or symbols can do. Such a view not only has its ancient roots in Augustine but also continues to echo in the writings of literary critics, theologians, and philosophers of our own day.

Some of Luther's offspring, it is true, fault him for not making a clean break with the Augustinian definition of a sacrament as a sign of a sacred thing. Augustine, they suspect, lurks in the shadows behind the heresiarch Zwingli, and it would be best to tear up the heresy by its roots. But others will only regret that Luther did not transfer to the problem of the real presence the notion of an efficacious sign that sometimes lingers in his thoughts on the fruit of the Eucharist. A causality that is taken out of the order of signification, on the one hand, and a sign of an absent reality, on the other, are not the only two options, as every Calvinist knows. One could still argue that the eucharistic bread really is a sign, and therefore not the reality itself, but a sign that *precisely by signifying* brings the reality to which it points.[33] Profound difficulties would remain. For what, after all, *is* the reality of the real presence? Luther and Zwingli both spoke as though everyone knew what was meant by the glorified body of Christ, the main

31. LW 36:353; LW 35:51.

32. LW 35:59 (my emphasis).

33. This I take to be exactly the third option that Calvin intended, except that for him what makes the sacramental signs efficacious is not their power of signification alone but also the operation of the Holy Spirit, who freely uses them as instruments. See further B. A. Gerrish, *Grace and Gratitude: The Eucharistic Theology of John Calvin* (Edinburgh: T. & T. Clark, Minneapolis: Fortress Press, 1993).

question being where to find it—in the bread, or seated at the right hand of God the Father.[34] Those of us for whom it is not that simple may be glad of the young Luther's assurance that it is more important to discern the spiritual body than the natural body of Christ. About this, at least, Zwingli could hardly disagree.

34. Zwingli thought of Christ's body as confined, since the ascension, in heaven (see, e.g., LCC 24:186, 206, 212–13, 232). For Luther, Christ's body can nowhere be strictly absent, but in the Eucharist "through the Word he [Christ] binds his body and blood so that they are also received corporeally in the bread and wine" (LW 36:343). Though present everywhere, the body of Christ must be sought where the word makes it available to us in a unique manner.

Part Two

THE AGE OF REASON

4
Faith and Existence in the Philosophy of F. H. Jacobi

The element of all human knowledge and activity is faith.
—F. H. JACOBI

Even to exist as a self is possible only on the basis of "faith."
—SCHUBERT OGDEN

IN PHILOSOPHICAL accounts of religion the term "faith" or "belief" is commonly used, naturally enough, in a restricted sense: it is taken to mean the explicit acceptance of conventional religious claims, such as those embodied in the Christian creeds.[1] The question of faith and reason is then assumed to be whether religious belief, so understood, can survive rational scrutiny or can be harmonized with what is otherwise held to be true, particularly in the natural sciences. But there has been at least a minor strand in modern religious thought in which "faith" refers, or refers also, to a constant state of mind underlying every human activity, including the scientific enterprise itself. Faith, in this sense, is not peculiar to the conventionally religious; it belongs to human existence as such and is therefore common to all, whether they know it or not.

The dominant usage has credentials that are respectable enough. Thomas Aquinas, for instance, understood faith precisely as assent to the divine truth that is summed up in the articles of the creeds. As such, faith (*fides*) occupies a position on the cognitive scale midway between knowledge (*scientia*) and opinion (*opinio*). It differs from *knowledge* because the mysteries of faith are neither self-evident nor demonstrable; the assent of the intellect to them is not brought about by the objects themselves but requires the assistance of an act of will, and that is why believing can qualify as a merit. But faith is not therefore uncertain; it differs from *opinion* exactly because opinion is accompanied by anxiety that the opposite of

1. In English usage, "faith" perhaps suggests a greater degree of assurance than "belief" and is often perceived as having stronger religious overtones. But there seems to be no agreed differentiation between the two terms in the English authors I shall refer to, and German, like Latin, has only one word for them both. Hence I have used "faith" and "belief" interchangeably in this essay.

what is accepted might be true. Faith is founded on divine truth, and nothing is more certain than the word of God. And that it is in fact divine truth that the church proposes to the intellect for its assent can be supported by evidence, though the evidence is not coercive except to the natural intellectual acumen of demons, who consequently deserve no praise for believing.[2]

Thomas's notion of faith is, in essentials, the notion subjected to scorn by freethinkers in the age of enlightenment. Take, for instance, the placement of faith on the cognitive scale suggested by Anthony Collins (1676–1729) in his *Essay Concerning the Use of Reason* (1707). The domain of *science* is confined to propositions perceived to be true either immediately or by necessary proofs. All other propositions (that is, sentences that make truth claims) have to be shown by proof to be probable or improbable. If they can be assessed by our own resources ("internal evidence"), they yield *opinion*. If they can be assessed only by recourse to the testimony of others ("external evidence"), they yield mere *belief.* While Collins is prepared to admit that our knowledge depends heavily on the testimony of others, he is anxious to protect us from being duped, especially by clergymen, whom he regularly perceives as making a living out of deceit and manipulation of the unwary. And no amount of testimony from others must ever be permitted to override our own experience, that is, "what we *know* to be true by the use of our Faculties." Or, as Collins also puts it: "Nothing which we judg [*sic*] repugnant to natural Notions ought to be assented to upon the highest Testimony whatever."[3] In a later work, his *Discourse of Freethinking* (1713), Collins points out that even those who are commended to us as authorities have only their eyes to direct them, and it is more reasonable to trust your own eyesight than to trust anyone else's. For God "can require nothing of Men . . . but that whereof he has given them an opportunity of being convinced by Evidence and Reason." In short, "faith" is the cognitive label Collins applies to propositions accepted secondhand, on the testimony of others.[4] John Locke (1632–1704) had written more restrictively in his *Essay concerning Human Understanding* (1690) that faith is "the Assent to any Proposition, not . . . made out by the Deductions of Reason; but upon the Credit of the Proposer, as coming

2. Thomas's principal discussion of faith appears in ST II–II, qq. 1–16; see esp. q. 1, arts. 1–2, 4, 6–7, 9; q. 2, arts. 1, 9–10; q. 4, art. 8; q. 5, art. 2.

3. Anthony Collins, *An Essay concerning the Use of Reason in Propositions, the Evidence Whereof Depends upon Human Testimony* (London, 1707), 4–11, 15.

4. Anthony Collins, *A Discourse of Free-Thinking, Occasion'd by the Rise and Growth of a Sect Call'd Free-Thinkers* (London, 1713), 16, 37. "Eyesight," in the former passage, is not an expression of a narrow empiricism. Collins's point is that it is absurd to suppress the free exercise of thought or of any human faculty at all; sight is only taken to exemplify the point (see 15, 25).

from GOD, in some extraordinary way of Communication."[5] But this, clearly, is the kind of faith Collins had especially in mind.

Such a notion of faith readily lends itself to the supposition that intellectual progress in the modern world has been impeded by a continual warfare of science with religion. But it is just this pairing of science with evidence, religion with authority, that advocates of the second notion of faith place in question, arguing that a closer look requires us to acknowledge an ineradicable element of faith even in the activity of scientific inquiry. A classic case along these lines was made, for example, with characteristic rhetorical charm, by A. J. Balfour (1848–1930) in his first series of Gifford Lectures (1914). If Balfour was right, there is a commonsense creed, never summed up in formal articles, that is held by all of us in our ordinary waking moments, even by those of us who criticize it in theory. It includes belief in the existence and the regularity of an external world, a belief presupposed by every scientific experiment and every scientific generalization. Belief in God is not itself to be counted among such "inevitable beliefs," as Balfour called them, but it is more supportive of them than is the naturalism that sometimes passes for scientific; and no amount of armchair philosophical skepticism can shake us out of them. "The philosopher admits—in theory—no ground of knowledge but reason. I recognize that, in fact, the whole human race, including the philosopher himself, lives by faith alone. The philosopher asks what creed reason requires him to accept. I ask on what terms the creed which is in fact accepted can most reasonably be held."[6]

It is faith in this second, noncompartmentalized sense that I intend to suggest by the correlation "faith and existence." Of course, the status and content of this "existential faith" (as we may conveniently call it) can be variously understood; I have only tried to contrast it provisionally with "religious faith" in the first, restricted sense. I do not propose to trace the lineage of the concept of existential faith in all its varieties; nor do I wish to imply that there are no other meanings the word "faith" can bear besides the two I have contrasted with each other.[7] The two quotations at the head

5. John Locke, *An Essay concerning Human Understanding*, ed. Peter H. Nidditch (Oxford: Clarendon Press, 1975), IV, xviii, 2, 689.

6. Arthur James Balfour, *Theism and Humanism* (New York: George H. Doran, 1915); quotation on 263. The theme of inevitable belief appeared already in Balfour's first book, *A Defence of Philosophic Doubt, Being an Essay on the Foundations of Belief* (London: Macmillan & Co., 1879), and its sequel, *The Foundations of Belief, Being Notes Introductory to the Study of Theology* (New York: Longmans, Green & Co., 1895). Balfour actually argued for three classes of inevitable belief—aesthetic and ethical as well as intellectual—and defended theism as supportive of all three. The parallel with Jacobi's position is closer than I need to show in detail here.

7. John Hick mentions Origen (ca. 185–ca. 254) and Arnobius (d. ca. 330) as, so to say, forerunners of Balfour: Hick, *Faith and Knowledge*, 2d ed. (Ithaca, New York: Cornell Uni-

of this essay signal my limited goal, which is to invite a comparison between "basic confidence" in the theology of Schubert Ogden and "faith" in the philosophy of F. H. Jacobi, the modern grandfather of those who want to speak of a faith that underlies the whole of human existence. Jacobi's "philosophy of faith" (as it is commonly called) proves Balfour quite mistaken when he wrote: "I regard the belief in an external world as one of a class whose importance has been ignored by philosophy, though all science depends on them."[8]

Jacobi and His Interpreters

Friedrich Heinrich Jacobi, younger brother of the poet Johann Georg Jacobi (1740–1814), has seldom received his due even in his homeland. There is still no critical edition of his works and no definitive biography of him.[9] It is particularly surprising that, with the exception of the theologians of the Catholic Tübingen School, theologians and historians of theology have hardly ever thought him worthy of their attention.[10] A man of diverse talents and interests, he made significant contributions to German literature and philosophy, and he concerned himself, in addition, with social, economic, and political reform. Together with C. M. Wieland (1733–1813), he founded the journal *Der Teutsche Mercur* ("The German Mercury"), and from 1807 until 1812 he was president of the Munich Academy of Sciences. Philosophically, however, he is usually mentioned merely as the foil to greater minds than his own. He was an astute critic

---

versity Press, 1966), 54n. But it is obvious that the notion of existential faith takes on a new dimension in modern times insofar as it is brought into relationship with the scientific concept of nature. Hick makes no mention of Jacobi, and he has little sympathy for the notion of "scientific faith." But his book, first published in 1957, remains an excellent general account of several other approaches to the epistemology of faith that do not concern me here. It will be clear enough, without further comment, that my discussion does not touch the heart of what Luther or Calvin would consider to be "saving faith."

8. Balfour, *Theism and Humanism,* 174–75. The design of the present chapter arose from its original character as a contribution to a festschrift in honor of Schubert Ogden.

9. A critical edition of Jacobi's writings has been launched (*Gesamtausgabe,* Frommann-Holzboog, 1981–). For the time being, however, we are still dependent on the edition begun by Jacobi himself and continued by Friedrich Köppen and Friedrich Roth (cited as JW).

10. Reinhard Lauth commented on the absence of theologians in his opening remarks at the Jacobi conference in Düsseldorf in 1969 (the 150th anniversary of Jacobi's death). See Klaus Hammacher, ed., *Friedrich Heinrich Jacobi: Philosoph und Literat der Goethezeit,* Studien zur Philosophie und Literatur des neunzehnten Jahrhunderts, vol. 11 (Frankfurt am Main: Vittorio Klostermann, 1971), 4. The interest of the Catholic Tübingen School in Jacobi is noted by Franz Wolfinger, *Denken und Transzendenz—Zum Problem ihrer Vermittlung: Der unterschiedliche Weg der Philosophien F. H. Jacobis und F. W. J. Schellings und ihre Konfrontation im Streit um die Göttlichen Dinge* (1811/12), Theologie im Übergang, vol. 7 (Frankfurt am Main: Peter D. Lang, 1981), 3.

who ventured to take on even Immanuel Kant, and his important, if largely indirect, contributions to the emergence of German speculative idealism are commonly acknowledged. But he produced no system; his philosophical reflections were embodied in his early "romances," *Letters of Edward Allwill* (1776) and *Woldemar* (1779), and in subsequent polemical writings. In the harsh verdict of Johann Wolfgang von Goethe, metaphysical speculation became Jacobi's misfortune; he was neither born nor educated for it.[11]

In the twentieth century, it is true, Jacobi's lack of system has been turned into a virtue, and he has been hailed as a precursor of existentialism and of Wilhelm Dilthey's (1833–1911) philosophy of life. There is something to be said for this reappraisal, which we owe particularly to the work of O. F. Bollnow, written under Dilthey's influence. Jacobi held that the true task of the inquirer is to disclose existence in its individuality and concreteness; hence he was suspicious of rationalistic philosophizing that took mathematical reasoning as its ideal in the quest for universal constructs. The idea of a philosophy of life, according to Bollnow, was the original impulse of Jacobi's philosophical concerns, but it became overlaid with traditional questions in his so-called philosophy of faith. Bollnow concentrates on Jacobi as "the philosopher of *Sturm und Drang*," and so as the initiator of the movement that in the twentieth century has blossomed in the philosophy of life or existence.[12] But that still leaves to Jacobi little more than an interesting paragraph or two in somebody else's chapter, and it is hardly surprising that in the English-speaking world he has been lucky to receive as much as a passing mention in a footnote.

There appear to have been hardly any English translations of Jacobi's writings, and few translations of the foreign literature about him. Benedetto Croce's (1866–1952) appreciative essay on Jacobi was made available in English in 1966; a translation of G. W. F. Hegel's (1770–1831) condescending treatment of him in *Faith and Knowledge* appeared a decade later.[13] Native English and American studies of Jacobi are equally hard to

11. Goethe, conversation with F. v. Müller, 26 January 1825: Johann Wolfgang Goethe, *Gedenkausgabe der Werke, Briefe und Gespräche,* vol. 23 (Zurich: Artemis, 1950), 372.

12. Otto Friedrich Bollnow, *Die Lebensphilosophie F. H. Jacobis,* Göttinger Forschungen, vol. 2 (Stuttgart: W. Kohlhammer, 1933), 1.

13. Since the present essay was written, the first English translations of Jacobi (to the best of my knowledge) have appeared: his "Open Letter to Fichte" (1799) and "On Faith and Knowledge in Response to Schelling and Hegel" (1803), trans. Diana I. Behler, in *Philosophy of German Idealism,* ed. Ernst Behler, The German Library, vol. 23 (New York: Continuum, 1987), 119–57. For translations of the foreign secondary literature, see Benedetto Croce, "Considerations on the Philosophy of Jacobi" (1941), reprinted in Cecil Sprigge, trans. and ed., *Philosophy, Poetry, History: An Anthology of Essays by Benedetto Croce* (London: Oxford University Press, 1966), 145–69; G. W. F. Hegel (1770–1831), *Faith and Knowledge,* trans. Walter Cerf and H. S. Harris (Albany: State University of New York Press, 1977). Hegel's

find. Robert H. Worthington hails him (overgenerously) as, next to Kant, the most original thinker of his times; his relationship to Schelling is explored by Lewis Ford, and his relationship to Coleridge by W. Schrickx.[14] More detailed and comprehensive, albeit still quite brief, are two American dissertations on him; both able studies, they merit a closer look for the light they shed on the fundamental problem of his philosophy of faith—and on some of the difficulties of appraising, or even interpreting, him justly.

In his Columbia dissertation, published in 1894, Norman Wilde pictures Jacobi on the dividing line between the first and the second periods of modern philosophy, unable to unite the two. He held tenaciously to God, freedom, and immortality as facts and simply pronounced self-destructive any system that denied them. At the root of Jacobi's life was a mystical sense that defied every attempt at explanation. As he wrote to his friend Johann Georg Hamann (1730–88), there was light in his heart, but when he would bring it to the intellect, it went out.[15]

Wilde cautions us not to seek in Jacobi's writings either precision or system, but he does find there an idea "imperfectly striving for expression." Jacobi's fundamental principle, according to Wilde, can be put like this: "The ultimate standard of truth and falsehood lies outside the concept in the real, which is forever beyond the reach of discursive thought." The epistemology implied in this principle was shaped by Jacobi's religious concerns: he sought the conditions on which alone we can claim a knowledge of God, freedom, and immortality. The theory of knowledge that grew out of this quest Wilde classifies as "natural realism," according to which what is known in cognition is not ideas but things. Jacobi was not a

---

Faith and Knowledge first appeared anonymously as an article in *Kritisches Journal der Philosophie* (July 1802); from the bad style of the article Jacobi inferred correctly that Hegel, not his coeditor F. W. J. Schelling (1775–1854), must have been the author. The editor of the English translation points out, as does Croce, that Hegel was elsewhere more complimentary to Jacobi.

14. Robert H. Worthington, "Jacobi, and the Philosophy of Faith," *Journal of Speculative Philosophy* 12 (1878): 393–402; Lewis S. Ford, "The Controversy between Schelling and Jacobi," *Journal of the History of Philosophy* 3 (1965): 75–89; W. Schrickx, "Coleridge and Friedrich Heinrich Jacobi," *Revue belge de philologie et d'histoire* 36 (1958): 812–50. Jacobi occasionally makes an appearance as second fiddle to his friend Hamann: e.g., in Philip Merlan, "Kant, Hamann-Jacobi and Schelling on Hume," *Rivista critica di storia della filosofia* 22 (1967): 481–94; Isaiah Berlin, "Hume and the Sources of German Anti-Rationalism" (1977), reprinted in Berlin, *Against the Current: Essays in the History of Ideas,* ed. Henry Hardy (New York: Viking Press, 1980), 162–87. Berlin's essay, unfortunately, is mistaken about the thesis of Jacobi's dialogue on Hume, about the date of the first edition, and even about Jacobi's own dates.

15. Norman Wilde, *Friedrich Heinrich Jacobi: A Study in the Origin of German Realism* (New York: Columbia College, 1894), 7, 72. The letter to Hamann, 16 June 1873, is given on 52–53 (JW 1:363–67; quotation on 367).

"crude realist"; he did not maintain that a thing must exist exactly as it appears to us, but only that there really is a "somewhat independent of us which determines an object to be this rather than that." In short, "the fact of existence is what he seeks to establish." And Wilde concludes that what Jacobi meant by "faith" or (as Jacobi later said) by "reason" is the "faculty of ratification" that guarantees the reality of the objects known.[16]

The cardinal point in Wilde's interpretation of Jacobi is that faith (to put it in my terms, not Wilde's or Jacobi's) is not a mode of cognition but the conviction of reality that accompanies cognition: that is, the confidence that, in knowing, our minds make contact with a reality independent of our knowing. Consequently, Wilde regrets that Jacobi shifted in his later writings from "faith" to "reason" as his key term and spoke of reason as a faculty analogous to sensation but differing in the sphere to which it is applied: the world not of sensible, but of supersensible, objects. Had Jacobi remained true to his original insight, he would have continued to think in terms of "a faculty of belief, testifying to the existence of a reality which finds expression in the appearances of the senses." All our ideas come by way of the senses; applied to the idea of God, Jacobi's epistemology does not, in Wilde's view, claim any special source of knowledge but simply affirms the power of faith (the *Glaubenskraft*) that accompanies the idea—the immediate certainty of a corresponding reality that meets Jacobi's moral and religious needs.[17]

The estimate of Jacobi's development proposed by Wilde is reversed by Alexander Crawford, who thinks the shift from "faith" to "reason" was an improvement. Perhaps Crawford labors too hard in his Cornell dissertation (1902, published 1905) to correct his predecessor's study of Jacobi as a realist; Jacobi, he maintains, was not a typical realist at all, but an idealist who affirmed the rationality of the world and the primacy of spirit. This may well be to confuse the epistemological and the metaphysical senses of "idealism." But, in any case, Crawford thinks that the shift from "faith" to "reason" in Jacobi's later writings was a token of his affinity with spiritualistic idealism and, more important, of his claim to be taken seriously as a philosopher.[18]

Crawford's reading of Jacobi presupposes that the terminological shift was a move toward greater appreciation for thought. Jacobi began by try-

16. Wilde, *Jacobi,* 5–8, 42, 57, 60, 63. The expression "natural realism" is borrowed from the Scottish philosopher William Hamilton (1788–1856).

17. Ibid., 64–68, 70–71.

18. Alexander W. Crawford, *The Philosophy of F. H. Jacobi* (New York: Macmillan Company, 1905), 16, 63–64, 85–86. See also the critique of Wilde's book on 46–47. Crawford does concede that Jacobi may be termed a "psychological realist," insofar as he took what he found in psychology to be real and true (57), or even a "spiritualistic realist" (47).

ing to give the religious principle of faith the dignity of a philosophical principle, but he later "substituted an intellectual element for the feeling element which characterized his first presentation." Hence the cardinal point of Crawford's interpretation is this: "Only in so far as he got beyond the standpoint of immediacy did he formulate a philosophy at all."[19] That this is in fact the import of Jacobi's later use of the term "reason" is open to question. However, one consequence of a preference for the later Jacobi is clear: it heightens the epistemological dualism in his thinking. It is precisely in the later writings that he differentiates most sharply between knowledge of sensible objects and knowledge of supersensible objects, assigning the latter to the domain of faith (or reason!). Crawford recognizes that sensibility and faith/reason were both, for Jacobi, forms of intuition (that is, immediate knowledge), differing only in the objects they reveal. But because he takes sensibility and faith/reason for parallel modes of cognition (my expression, not his), he cannot, like Wilde, represent Jacobi as teaching a unified route to knowledge.[20] This is not to say that Crawford is wrong. But the contrast between his exposition and Wilde's, coupled with the undoubted ambiguities occasioned in part by Jacobi's intellectual development, suffice to indicate some of the difficulties of interpretation. A solution, if one is possible at all, must be sought chiefly in Jacobi's dialogue, *David Hume on Belief.*

The Dialogue on Hume

When Jacobi turned from his romances to more formal philosophical prose, he still chose letters and dialogue, not the didactic treatise, as his medium of expression. After the letters on Spinoza (1785) and the dialogue on Hume (1787), his major philosophical writings were polemical, against Kant (1801) and Schelling (1811); and his last philosophical testament, often pointed out as the best account of his thought, took the literary form of an introduction prefixed to the second edition of the dialogue on Hume (1815). "Of writing a formal treatise," Wilde remarks, "Jacobi was incapable."[21] Perhaps. But anyone who turns to *Hume on Belief* expecting truth to emerge from a lively exchange of conflicting viewpoints will be disappointed. The dialogue begins pleasantly enough, but over the long haul

19. Ibid., 3, 47–50. But Crawford nonetheless does not see the shift as a change of principle (35), and he can still say that Jacobi's service was to show that there is an element of immediacy in thought (50).

20. Ibid., 24–25, 27, 32–38. It is not clear how Crawford relates the epistemological dualism of sensibility and reason to Jacobi's "complete opposition between feeling (reason) and thought (understanding)," or how this "opposition" helps the main thesis that Jacobi moved toward a greater appreciation for thought (see 28).

21. Wilde, *Jacobi,* 37.

Jacobi could make a conversation sound very much like a treatise. The visitor's role in the dialogue is mainly passive, to furnish the puzzlement needed for Jacobi to explain his thoughts more perfectly, or else to offer helpful summaries of what Jacobi has said more copiously.

Jacobi's interest in David Hume was probably acquired in part from Hamann.[22] Just how far Hume materially influenced Jacobi's development is hard to judge, and it would have to be measured in relation to other influences, such as that of Thomas Reid (1710–96), the Scottish commonsense philosopher who tried to answer Hume.[23] But what Jacobi discovered in Hume (so he supposed) was a sense of the word "belief" that justified his own use of the German word *Glaube*. Since my purpose is to discover what Jacobi understood by "belief," the dialogue on Hume is plainly a major source. I shall in fact confine myself, in this essay, to an examination of the dialogue and the fresh introduction furnished with the second edition, before I attempt a summary analysis of Jacobi's term *Glaube* and a critical comparison of it with Schubert Ogden's expression "basic confidence." Indeed, as far as the dialogue itself is concerned, only the first part of it is strictly germane—and perhaps the last few pages. Jacobi originally intended to publish three separate dialogues, to be titled respectively, "David Hume on Belief," "Idealism and Realism," and "Leibniz, or Concerning Reason." For reasons he does not explain, he decided to combine them in a single publication titled *David Hume on Belief, or Idealism and Realism: A Dialogue.* But he admits that the "or" in the title was not quite justified.[24] And readers can readily verify for themselves that both Hume and belief are almost forgotten in the second and third parts, until belief, though not Hume, reappears at the very end.

The preface briefly sets out Jacobi's design in writing the dialogue. He concedes that in his letters on Spinoza he had employed the word "belief"

22. Hamann claimed to have studied Hume even before he wrote his *Socratic Memorabilia* (published in 1759). See the editorial comments in *Hamann's Socratic Memorabilia: A Translation and Commentary,* trans. and ed. James C. O'Flaherty (Baltimore: Johns Hopkins University Press, 1967), 200 note c. Cf. Ronald Gregor Smith, *J. G. Hamann 1730–1788: A Study in Christian Existence* (London: Collins, 1960), 50–52.

23. See, e.g., Günther Baum, *Vernunft und Erkenntnis: Die Philosophie F. H. Jacobis,* Mainzer Philosophische Forschungen, vol. 9 (Bonn: H. Bouvier and Co., 1969), 17, 42–49, 80–83.

24. Jacobi, *David Hume über den Glauben, oder Idealismus und Realismus: Ein Gespräch* (Breslau: Gottl. Loewe, 1787), iii–iv. I have made no attempt to discuss the interpretations of the dialogue in the secondary literature, some of which is noted by Baum (*Vernunft und Erkenntnis,* 17–22). It should at least be mentioned, however, that Bollnow gives a sensitive reading of Jacobi's first thoughts on *Glaube* in the early romances, where it appeared as a mood without definite object—an affirmation of life and a general sense of happiness in contrast to the sense of meaninglessness and despair in *Unglaube.* But unfaith, Bollnow points out, is not taken by Jacobi for a parallel possibility so much as for the *modus deficiens* of faith itself (*Die Lebensphilosophie Jacobis,* 83–89).

in an unusual sense. He had wanted to challenge the view that knowledge established by proofs of reason includes certain knowledge of actual existence, of which sense-perception (*sinnliche Erkenntnis*) yields only uncertain belief. His own view is that there are not two kinds of knowledge of existence, one certain and the other uncertain, but only one, and that it comes by way of perception (*Empfindung*); reason (*Vernunft*), by contrast, is confined to the faculty of grasping relationships. Absolute certainty belongs only to the affirmation of purely identical propositions (that is, propositions reducible to instances of the law of identity); the affirmation that something exists in itself, beyond my idea of it, can never approach such certainty. The idealist, accordingly, can no doubt make Jacobi grant that his conviction of the existence of actual things outside himself is only belief. But, as a realist, Jacobi must then reply: "All knowledge can only come from belief [i.e., *this* belief], since *things* must be *given* to me before I am in a position to perceive relationships."[25]

Both the referent of the word "belief," in Jacobi's sense, and the grounds for treating belief as antecedent to reason are thus immediately stated in the short preface. The belief in question is belief in an external world that exists independently of the perceiving mind. There is also at least a hint at what it is that makes "belief" the right word to use in this context: an object of belief cannot be established by rational proofs. On the other hand, there could not be knowledge—or even an activity of reason at all—without it. The dialogue proper, in which the two partners are identified simply as "He" and "I," moves directly into the same circle of epistemological problems.

A visiting friend ("He") discovers Jacobi still in his dressing gown, nursing a cold and chuckling over a book. Jacobi has been reading some thoughts of David Hume on belief. Against belief, then? No, for belief. The theme of the dialogue is Hume as a teacher of belief. Jacobi has been loudly accused of degrading reason and teaching *blind* belief, which is to say, assent based on authority, without proofs or personal insight. And this is to rob Protestantism of its strongest supports—the use of reason and the spirit of free inquiry—and to encourage Catholicism. He is further charged with craftily altering the customary use of the actual word "be-

25. *Hume über den Glauben,* iv–vi. Like the English word "perception," *Empfindung* is not necessarily confined to awareness through sensation (see also the first reference in n. 33 below, on *Sinn*). References to the dialogue will be given hereafter to the second edition in JW 2. The text occupies pages 125–288 and is followed by the original appendix (*Beylage*) "Über den transcendentalen Idealismus" (289–310). The new introduction, "Vorrede, zugleich Einleitung in des Verfassers sämtliche philosophische Schriften," appears on pages 3–123. Occasionally, the second edition incorporates changes Jacobi alleged to be minor. But see n. 33 below.

lief," since he attributes to belief what is in fact a matter of perception: that we have bodies and that there are other bodies and other thinking beings outside us. The suspicion thus arises that a devious attempt is being made to smuggle in specifically religious beliefs.[26]

In reply, Jacobi reveals his "secret"—with obvious glee, since the secret can readily be found in a famous book that has been translated into several languages. He admits that the way he uses the word "belief" departs from *everyday* usage. He means, I take it, that we do commonly use "belief" for "blind belief" (or "blind faith"), assent based on mere authority. In any case, he himself intends a *philosophical* usage, according to which "belief" is a knowing that cannot strictly be proved. And for this usage, as he ironically puts it, he has an "authority" such as his critics, at least, seem to need: he is using the word "belief" as David Hume used it in his *Enquiry concerning Human Understanding*. Jacobi quotes two well-known passages from the *Enquiry*. The first refers to the belief in external objects, a belief that even animals share with humans: "Without any reasoning . . . we always suppose an external universe, which depends not on our perception." The second passage differentiates belief from fiction (that is, from a product of the imagination) by asserting that there is a special sentiment of feeling annexed to belief, a feeling "which depends not on the will, nor can be commanded at pleasure." "Belief" is indeed, according to Hume, the proper name for this feeling, and everyone knows what is meant by it because everyone is conscious of it. Hard to define, it can nevertheless be described. "Belief is nothing but a more vivid, lively, forcible, firm, steady conception of an object, than what the imagination alone is ever able to attain." It is therefore belief, in Hume's opinion, that gives the ideas of judgment, as distinct from the fictions of the imagination, more weight and influence "and renders them the governing principle of our actions."[27]

Jacobi's visitor is convinced. The quotations from Hume confirm not only Jacobi's use of the word "belief" but also his thesis that belief is the element of all knowledge and activity. Jacobi then moves on to justify another term he is charged with abusing: "revelation." Only here, no appeal to Hume or any other authority is required to support what common

26. JW 2:127–29, 137–39, 148.

27. JW 2:129, 143–44, 149–53, 156–63. Jacobi cites section XII, part i, and section V, part ii, of Hume's *Enquiry*, using the 1770 edition and preferring his own translation to the one in common use. Cf. David Hume, *Enquiries concerning Human Understanding and concerning the Principles of Morals*, reprinted from the posthumous edition of 1777, ed. L. A. Selby-Bigge, 3d ed., revised by P. H. Nidditch (Oxford: Clarendon Press, 1975), 15–52, 47–50. The *Enquiry concerning Human Understanding* first appeared in 1748 (as *Philosophical Essays concerning Human Understanding*).

usage already warrants; in everyday discourse—whether in German, French, English, Latin, or several other languages—one says that objects are "revealed" by the senses. Jacobi's belief, we conclude, is not assent without evidence, but assent to the evidence that the senses disclose, which is the evidence of the thing itself. If anyone chooses to doubt this evidence and demands proof, there is nothing we can do for him or her, because no other evidence is forthcoming. On the contrary, any proof we might try to construct would already presuppose belief and revelation.

> The decided realist who without doubting accepts external things on the evidence of his senses, views this certainty as an original conviction and cannot but think that every use of the intellect to acquire knowledge of the external world must be grounded on this fundamental experience. What shall such a decided realist call the means by which he acquires the certainty of external objects as things existing independently of his representation of them? He has nothing on which to support his judgment but the matter itself, nothing but the fact that things really do stand before him. Can he express himself by a more appropriate word than the word *revelation?* Is not the *root* of this word and *the source of its use* to be sought precisely here?[28]

Jacobi did not need to be told that a decided realism was not David Hume's conclusion from the phenomenon of belief. Hume inclined more to skeptical idealism; he did not find in the *conviction* that there is an external reality any guarantee that there *is* an external reality, but left open the question whether we really *perceive* things outside us or simply perceive them *as* outside us. Jacobi was content to take from Hume only the sense of the word "belief." And he held it to be a manifest misconstrual of our experience when other philosophers sought to make the conviction that there are objects corresponding to our ideas an inferential rather than an immediate conviction, as though we first had the ideas and then concluded that there must be corresponding objects. As Jacobi makes this point in the dialogue, the visitor announces that he sees the light: "In the same indivisible moment, I experience that I exist and that there exists something outside me. . . . No idea, no inference mediates this double revelation." Jacobi is pleased and assures his friend that, yes, he has got it. "Even in the most primitive and simple perception, the self and the other (*das Ich und das Du*), consciousness within and object without, must be there immediately

28. JW 2:163–66. All translations of Jacobi in this essay are mine. Jacobi's "thesis," cited as the first epigraph at the beginning of this chapter, was stated in *Über die Lehre des Spinozas, in Briefen an Herrn Moses Mendelssohn* (1785), JW 4,1:223. In the same work, Jacobi wrote: "Wir alle werden im Glauben geboren, und müssen im Glauben bleiben" (JW 4,1:210). *Glaube* is here linked with *unmittelbare Gewissheit,* but also with *Fürwahrhalten.*

in the soul, both in the same instant, in the same indivisible moment, without before and after, without any operation of the intellect."[29]

The conversation moves on to Hume's critique of the concept of causality, and once again Jacobi appeals to belief: "If you can let yourself be troubled by such doubt, I don't know how to help you. But I think your belief overcomes it just as easily as mine does." For Jacobi, the assertion that things are interconnected in a causal network is justified, we may say, like the assertion that there are things in themselves, by faith alone. And from there the dialogue passes over into the second and third parts. Neither Hume nor belief is any longer the center of attention. Pertinent to the theme of belief, at least indirectly, is the discussion of reason, which Jacobi ties closely to experience or sense.[30] But what must surely strike the reader is that Jacobi does not attempt to move the discussion of Hume's thoughts on belief out of the technical-epistemological domain into the domain of religion. The boundaries of the theme of belief are apparently set by the epistemological interests of British empiricism.

When he does, finally, come back to belief, it has indeed become belief in God and immortality. But the connection with Humean belief, if in Jacobi's mind there is one, is not explained. To be sure, the visitor remarks that *all* belief must finally rest on fact, experience, perception; and Jacobi agrees that if God does not let Godself be perceived or experienced in any way, then belief in God should be given up. But Jacobi does not say what experience of God is; he merely asserts that with the precious gift of reason we receive a presentiment of God (*Gottesahndung*). "Thence *freedom* blows upon the soul, and the realms of immortality are opened." The visitor confesses that Jacobi's last discourse has left him all at sea. But Jacobi cuts him off with the announcement that it is late and they must stop. He ends with some choice quotations from J. H. Pestalozzi's (1746–1827) *Leonard and Gertrude* (1781–87), and his friend responds with a couple of allusions to Asmus (Matthias Claudius, 1740–1815). The import of the closing pages appears to be, not that we move from sense perception, through reason, to the idea of God, but rather that in the activity of reason, by virtue of which we distinguish ourselves as persons from the world of mere things, we

29. JW 2:165, 173–76; see also 257–58, where the notion of intuitive knowledge of our own existence is documented from G. W. Leibniz (1646–1716). Jacobi's appeal to Hume, I may add, given his limited purpose, does not strike me as wholly farfetched. Whether deliberately or not, Jacobi echoes Humean language at more points than one; besides the phrases I have cited, Hume also writes "to repose faith in the senses" (Selby-Bigge, 151), and Jacobi must have noticed his distinction between "definition" or "explanation" and "description" (ibid., 48–49).

30. JW 2:204–5, 225–28, 267–71. *Vernunft* appears here as the mental faculty that processes the data of experience, the role Jacobi later reserves for the *Verstand*.

have a presentiment of the Living God who, like us, is spirit or person. "Humans know God," says Pestalozzi, "only insofar as they know humans, that is, themselves." And it is in deeds rather than words that both humanity and God are made known.[31] But if this is so, we must surely ask, are there not after all *two* sources of knowledge—sense experience and moral experience?

The Second Edition of the Dialogue

The second edition of *Hume on Belief* appeared in Jacobi's collected works largely unchanged, except for the addition of some new footnotes. But the original preface was dropped, and the new preface grew into a general introduction to Jacobi's entire philosophical output; running to 123 pages and published just four years before his death, it is the most important source for understanding his final position. Remarkable is the change from "faith" to "reason" as the key term in Jacobi's philosophical vocabulary: *Vernunft* in the introduction now seems to do duty for what the word *Glaube* did in the dialogue itself. It is perhaps arguable that the terminological shift signals a modification of Jacobi's epistemology, although he denied that the change was substantive. In any case, one may well suspect that the old preface was discarded partly because it asserted a single source of knowledge: namely, perception (*Empfindung*).[32] Already in the dialogue itself, Jacobi was stretching the narrow concept of experience he found in British empiricism: he expressly tells us, for example, that he takes the word "sense" (*Sinn*) "in the whole range of its meaning (as the faculty of perception [*Wahrnehmungsvermögen*] in general)."[33]

The new introduction explains again the purpose of the dialogue. In his book on Spinoza, Jacobi had asserted that all human knowledge comes from revelation and faith. The dialogue on Hume was written in response

31. JW 2:279–88; quotations on 285, 287. The dialogue ends with the words that concluded Claudius's short prose piece, "Diogenes von Sinope": "Aber was hilft der bloße Gedanke des Kopfs? *Fußsalbe,* Mann von Sinope!" Claudius, *Sämtliche Werke* (Munich: Winkler, 1968), 44–45.

32. Jacobi translates Hume's term "perception" both by *Empfindung* and by *Wahrnehmung.* "Idea," as distinct from the primary "impression" in Hume's vocabulary, he usually renders as *Vorstellung* (see, e.g., JW 2:152–53). For his claim that "in the depths of his soul" his convictions had remained unchanged, see the important footnote added to the second edition of the dialogue on 221–22.

33. JW 2:270. The explanatory parenthesis did not appear in the first edition (*Hume über den Glauben,* 184). This is one of the changes that make the reader wary of taking Jacobi's word for it when he claims that he made no corrections that would adulterate the original dialogue's character as a historical document (JW 2:5). Compare also JW 2:284 with *Hume über den Glauben,* 201, and see n. 51 below.

to the charges of fanaticism and popery that the assertion evoked. It is to be understood as an appendix to the book on Spinoza and was intended to justify the notion of a firsthand knowing (*Wissen*) that conditions all secondhand science (*Wissenschaft*), a knowing without proofs that necessarily precedes all knowing derived from proofs, grounds it, and continually governs it.[34] But Jacobi admits that in the dialogue he failed to distinguish "reason" (*Vernunft*) clearly enough from "intellect" (*Verstand*), which prevented him from giving a properly philosophical account of his fundamental doctrine—that there is a power of faith transcending the capacity of demonstrative science. A distinction between "reason" and "intellect" is actually presupposed in our common speech, which assigns to animals only an intellect or intelligence. Jacobi infers that the difference between animals and humans must be one of kind and not degree; otherwise, if reason and intellect were two names for the same faculty, the difference between an orangutan and a Californian would be less than the difference between a Californian and a Plato, a Leibniz, or a Newton.[35]

What, then, is this special "attribute of reason," which alone raises humanity above brute beasts? Jacobi explains that it is the organ of supersensible perception (*Vernehmung*), as the organ of sight is the eye. Animals perceive only the sensible, whereas humans, endowed with reason, perceive also the supersensible.

> If what we call "reason" were only the product of a faculty of reflection based solely upon sense experience (*Sinneserfahrung*), all talk of supersensible things would be mere twaddle; reason as such would be *groundless,* an inventive fantasy. But if it is truly revelatory, then it brings into being a *human* intellect that *knows* of God, freedom, and virtue, of the true, the beautiful, and the good, an intellect exalted above animal intelligence.[36]

Jacobi does not mean to make a psychological separation of reason from intellect: the revelations of reason are possible only *in* an intellect or, as he puts it, in an intellect illumined by reason. But the intellect now takes over the duties that in the dialogue he had sometimes assigned, like every other philosopher of the time, to reason. It is the intellect that is the faculty, hovering over sensibility, of forming concepts, judgments, and inferences, and it can reveal or disclose nothing at all. Reason, by contrast, is the faculty of presupposing the true, the good, and the beautiful with full con-

34. JW 2:3–4.

35. JW 2:7–8, 26–28. In English we would be more inclined to speak of animal "intelligence," but "intellect" is usually the best equivalent for the German *Verstand*. Jacobi takes Californians (and the inhabitants of Tierra del Fuego) to exemplify uncultivated peoples.

36. JW 2:9.

fidence (*Zuversicht*) in the validity of this presupposition; and this is exactly what he had ascribed in the dialogue to the power of belief, as though it were a faculty *above* reason. Jacobi regrets the confusion to which he has innocently given rise.[37]

Obviously, these remarks do not entirely clear up the confusion. For one thing, in the dialogue Jacobi had concentrated on knowledge of the material world and had not said much about supersensible realities. He had no choice, if he wanted David Hume on his side. It now appears, from the new introduction, that the power of faith (*Glaubenskraft*) is attached to two distinct mental operations—if, indeed, it can seriously be maintained that the duties now assigned to reason represent one operation and not several. In Jacobi's view, there are two faculties of perception, two eyes of the soul, corresponding to two kinds of object: sensible things and supersensible things.[38] Every claim we make to possess knowledge can be substantiated only if we trace our concepts and judgments back to the primary mode of cognition in whichever of the two domains they belong, which means, if we trace them back to the immediate pronouncements of sense or reason.[39] Jacobi's terminology is alarmingly fluid, and he does not illustrate concretely how either one of these verification processes might work. But, in general, the ideal of justifying cognitive claims by deriving them from basic or protocol sentences is familiar enough, even if its application to supersensible objects is not. And what chiefly interests Jacobi is the status of those initial pronouncements of sense or reason that such a procedure must get back to.

In the opening paragraphs of the introduction, he has already spoken of "firsthand knowing." Further on, he attempts to differentiate the two varieties of firsthand knowing associated respectively with the two faculties of sense and reason.

> The reason creates no concepts, builds no systems, and it makes no judgments, but, *like the outward senses,* it is purely revelatory, making positive pronouncements. . . . As there is a sensible intuition, an *intuition* through *sense,* so there is also a rational intuition through *reason.* The two stand over against each other as actual sources of knowledge; the latter can just as little be derived from the former as the former from the latter. Likewise, each stands in the same relation to the intellect, and to this extent also to demonstration. There can-

37. JW 2:9–11. For reason as a *Voraussetzungsvermögen* (!), cf. JW 2:101. Jacobi similarly speaks of *Glaube* as *Voraussetzung* (20), a notion that might be compared with Hume's construal of belief as "taking for granted." See Hume, *A Treatise of Human Nature,* ed. L. A. Selby-Bigge (Oxford: Clarendon Press, 1888), I, iv, 2 (187) and I, iv, 7 (269).

38. JW 2:74; cf. 105.

39. This is what Jacobi means by contrasting the revelatory operations of sense and reason with the reflective operations of the intellect (JW 2:109–11).

> not be any demonstration of *sensible intuition,* because all demonstration is simply tracing the concept back to the *sensible intuition* (whether empirical or pure) that verifies it: as far as knowledge of nature is concerned, sensible intuition is first and last, the unconditionally valid, the absolute. For the same cause, there cannot be any demonstration of *rational intuition,* or the *intuition of reason,* which gives us knowledge of objects beyond nature, that is, makes us certain of their reality and truth. . . . If anyone says he knows, we rightly ask him how he knows. He must then inevitably appeal in the end to one of these two: either to sense perception (*Sinnes-Empfindung*) or to spiritual feeling (*Geistes-Gefühl*). Of what we know by spiritual feeling, we say that we *believe* it. That is how we all speak. One can only *believe* in virtue, and so in freedom, and so in spirit and God. But the perception that knowing-in-sensible-intuition establishes (so-called knowing in the proper sense) is just as little above the feeling that establishes *knowing-in-belief* as animals are above humanity, the material world above the intellectual, nature above its Creator.[40]

Jacobi has by now come to use the words "reason," "belief," and even "feeling" almost interchangeably; and he maintains that reason is a kind of intuition, or a kind of perception,[41] and that it issues in a presupposition or in knowledge. It is easy to see why his critics have found a Babel of terminological confusion in his writings. Even if we confine ourselves, for now, to his use of the term "belief," it may well be impossible to evade all the ambiguities.

Perhaps the most natural interpretation is that in the new introduction he means us to understand belief as the conviction of reality (the *Zuversicht*) that accompanies both modes of primary cognition, sense and reason, and he in fact speaks of a corresponding double *disbelief* that arises from the misuse of the intellect: disbelief in a material world and disbelief in an immaterial, spiritual world.[42] It is true that in the passages just cited belief seems to move over from the side of sense to the side of reason alone. But Jacobi's position is, I think, best expressed when he writes: "Man believes his senses necessarily, and he believes his reason necessarily; and there is no certainty higher than the certainty of this belief." In neither domain can there be proof of the veracity of our ideas; hence one can only speak of "belief." But in neither domain is any guarantee needed beyond

40. JW 2:58–60.

41. Sometimes, at least, Jacobi appears to connect *Wahrnehmung* with sensible knowing, *Vernehmung* with supersensible (e.g., JW 2:56); both words are usually translated "perception" in English. But he also speaks of reason as *Wahrnehmung* (74, 100)—and, indeed, calls reason "the inner sense (*Sinn*)" (107).

42. JW 2:99–100. On *Glaube* as *Zuversicht* in things seen and unseen, see 11, 56.

the witness of reality to itself.[43] If there is an idea in Jacobi "imperfectly striving for expression" (Wilde), this would seem to be it.

Jacobi developed this fundamental idea in continual debate with Immanuel Kant. His disagreements with Kant were at least as important to his development as his agreement with Hume, who fades into the background in the new introduction.[44] Although such credit as Jacobi has won for himself as a philosopher probably rests chiefly on his astute criticisms of Kant, in some respects he felt an affinity with him, and he came back repeatedly to three cardinal points in the critical philosophy. First, Kant had shown the impossibility of moving deductively from the sensible to the supersensible, or transforming the logic of the intellect into a metaphysics of reality. But, second, his agnosticism about things in themselves was a mere inconsistency in his philosophy: Kant drifts steadily toward subjective idealism, and yet all the while he is making the realistic presupposition that something really appears in the appearances of sense. To resolve the contradiction, Jacobi believed, Kant should have affirmed forthrightly the faith in nature's objectivity that he tacitly presupposed in the first edition of the *Critique of Pure Reason* (1781). For, third, this would be no more philosophically scandalous than the rational faith in God, freedom, and immortality that Kant proposed in the *Critique of Practical Reason* (1788).[45]

The comparison between the critical philosophy and the philosophy of faith cannot be taken any further here. But I think one may justly conclude, without making it a matter of a direct dependence of Jacobi on Kant, that he was trying in effect to strengthen the doctrine of faith or belief that he discovered in the critical philosophy and pronounced "true in spirit." It is particularly instructive to note what he makes of "rational faith" in the Kantian ethics. For Jacobi, as his long discussion of freedom and foresight

43. JW 2:107–8. It should be noted that in this passage feeling too, like belief, is located in both domains. But the long footnote on 221–22 describes reason as *the* faculty of immediate certainty, which, if pressed, would imply that there is no immediate certainty in the sensible domain.

44. Jacobi's relationship to Kant is easily misconstrued, if one does not note that the philosophy of faith was conceived before the first edition of the *Critique of Pure Reason* (1781) appeared. Jacobi himself was firmly convinced that the second edition of the *Critique* (1789) owed something to his own work. He believed, in particular, that his formula *Ohne Du kein Ich* was transformed by Kant into a refutation of idealism—and subsequently converted by J. G. Fichte (1762–1814) into the formula *Alles Du ist Ich* (see JW 2:40–41n.; cf. JW 4,1:211).

45. These are the three main points Jacobi makes in the extended discussion of the critical philosophy in JW 2:14–45. His best-known comment on it was that without *Naturglaube* one cannot get into the system, with it one cannot stay there (JW 2:38; cf. the *Beylage,* JW 2:304). In the preface to the second edition of the *Critique of Pure Reason,* Jacobi points out, Kant admitted that the existence of things outside us must be accepted on faith. But it is surely highly dubious to speak, as Jacobi does, about the "objective validity" of the Kantian ideas of practical reason (JW 2:42).

(both human and divine) makes transparently clear, it was *moral* experience broadly conceived—humans' awareness of themselves as spiritual and personal beings—that opened up the route to supersensible things. It was hard for him to take seriously the Kantian view that the idea of God is not merely indemonstrable but noncognitive. But the heart of Jacobi's faith is disclosed precisely in his fierce insistence that the root of human nature would be a fearful lie if there were no truth in the revelations of the conscience. "Out of man's *willing* springs his truest *knowing*." In the spiritual and, above all, the ethical being of humanity Jacobi claimed to *see* God, though not with the eye of the body.[46]

Jacobi's Concept of Faith

Is there a belief or a faith on which the entire business of being human must ultimately rest? If so, what is it? And in what way is it related to religious faith in general and Christian faith in particular? It would be hard to name any theologian or philosopher who has made these questions more central to his or her thinking than F. H. Jacobi. It is easy enough to sit in the seat of the scornful as one reads him. He seemed repeatedly to take refuge in edifying rhetoric where one would be happier to have cool analysis; he delighted in provocative paradoxes (a "knowing unknowing," "objective feeling," and the like); and on his side there was no reluctance to heap scorn upon the philosophers. He did not hesitate to confess that his own "philosophy" proceeded from feeling, which it acknowledged as the highest authority. Nevertheless, he protested that his intention was not to disparage reason but to restore it, and that he had never ventured an assertion he did not take pains to establish philosophically. Since he fully accepted the duty to defend his faith before the bar of the philosophical intellect, he thought he deserved a more careful reading than he had received.[47] And he was right.

46. JW 2:44, 120. Cf. the *Vorbericht* to the reprint of *Über die Lehre des Spinoza:* "Durch ein göttliches Leben wird der Mensch Gottes inne. Von dieser Seite ist der Weg zur Erkenntnis des übersinnlichen ein praktischer, kein theoretischer, bloss wissenschaftlicher" (JW 4, 1:xxv). The discussion of freedom and foresight in the new introduction to the dialogue on Hume is given largely in the form of a debate with both materialism and speculative idealism, and it takes up what is actually the longest part of the introduction (JW 2:77–123; cf. 45–55). Jacobi discusses the status of the Kantian postulates further in *Über das Unternehmen des Kriticismus die Vernunft zu Verstande zu bringen und der Philosophie überhaupt eine neue Absicht zu geben* (1801), JW 3:101–5; cf. *Von den göttlichen Dingen und ihrer Offenbarung* (1811), JW 3:362–63.

47. JW 2:20, 61, 109; 99–100, 226, 275–76; 61; 11, 31n., 106–7; 47. Jacobi's claim to be the restorer of reason, not its detractor, rests on his persuasion that since Aristotle (384–322 B.C.E.) there has been a persistent tendency of philosophers to subordinate reason to intellect, immediate to mediate knowledge, perception to reflection, so that the true has become synonymous with the demonstrable. Jacobi thinks of himself as a real, not merely nominal, rationalist ("philosopher of feeling" is a malicious nickname invented by others),

But can Jacobi's philosophy of faith even be shown to be coherent? His disturbing tendency was to multiply terms that, if not quite synonymous, seem to mingle and merge with one another. Perhaps it is not possible to get complete consistency out of his language, even at a single stage of his development; and it is not surprising that the Jacobi specialists have failed to agree among themselves about his fundamental concepts.[48] But the picture is by no means one of total chaos. On the contrary, the outlines of Jacobi's position are reasonably clear. He did not think that in the religious domain one had to fall back on blind faith and leave reason to the scientists and the philosophers. His cardinal point was that *all* factual claims whatever, whether about nature or about God, must in the end be traced back to an immediate awareness. "Intuition" and "feeling" (*Anschauung* and *Gefühl*) are his terms for this immediate, nonreflective awareness. Hence he writes: "Real being (*das reale Seyn*) . . . gives itself to be known only in feeling." It makes no sense to talk about *proving* what immediate awareness *reveals*. But there is no need to prove something that carries its own conviction with it. "All actual being (*alle Wirklichkeit*), bodily (revealed to the senses) just as much as spiritual (revealed to reason), verifies itself to humans only through feeling; there is no verification apart from, or above, this verification." Again: "All human knowledge proceeds from revelation and belief." Why say "belief"? Because the conviction that accompanies the revelations of immediate awareness cannot be proved, and what admits of no proof can only be believed. To distinguish the faculty of immediate awareness or feeling in the so-called supersensible domain by the term "reason" is perhaps eccentric. (Jacobi's use of "reason" was apparently influenced by his reading of Plato [427–347 B.C.E.].) More eccentric still was the association of reason with feeling; Jacobi could even say that it is feeling that distinguishes humans from animals, since "feeling" and "reason" mean the same thing. But the terminological oddities do not make the substance incoherent.[49]

The divergent interpretations of Jacobi put forward by Wilde and

---

and he believes that his notion of a spiritual eye, a higher cognitive power than sense perception, allies him with Socrates (469–399 B.C.E.) and Plato (ca. 427–ca. 347 B.C.E.); see 11–12, 70–71, 74–76. In actual fact, Plato classified belief as fallible sense-perception, not as knowledge in the proper sense at all, whereas Jacobi's entire endeavor in the dialogue is to show that knowledge rests on belief. But, of course, Jacobi applies the cognitive labels differently than Plato, not meaning by *Glaube* what Plato meant by *pistis;* and he could perhaps claim a genuine affinity between his later use of *Vernunft* and Plato's use of *noesis* for the faculty that grasps the *archai* or eternal forms (ideas). See esp. Plato, *Republic,* 509D–521B; cf. *Theaetetus,* 184B–186E, 200D–201C.

48. See, e.g., Baum, who takes issue with Bollnow at several points and doubts whether Jacobi himself correctly represents in the 1815 introduction what he had said in the dialogue (*Vernunft und Erkenntnis,* 118–23).

49. JW 2:105; 108–9; 3–4; 144 (cf. 146); 61–63.

Crawford both have evidence in their support. In part, the difference between them lies in Wilde's preference for the earlier Jacobi, Crawford's for the later. But against Wilde it can now be said that there really *are* two sources of cognition in Jacobi and, according to Jacobi himself, *there always were*. Wilde makes Jacobi do what he denied he had ever done: it never occurred to him, Jacobi expressly says, that he might be accused of making all knowledge the same in kind or, like the philosophers of Locke's school, of deriving the entire spiritual life from the senses.[50] It does not follow, however, that Wilde was mistaken about Jacobi's idea of belief, which is not a mode of cognition (though Jacobi sometimes comes close to saying that it is). Belief is rather the confidence that accompanies cognition, or is presupposed in cognition; cognition evokes it, and is in turn sustained and supported by it as immediate awareness passes into reflection. Part of the difficulty arises from the common assumption in the secondary literature that in the later Jacobi "reason" simply replaces "belief" as the word for immediate awareness, at any rate in the supersensible domain. But as Jacobi himself explains it, "reason" replaces one of the meanings of "sense" (*Sinn*), the word wrongly taken for evidence that he must have been an empiricist of the Lockean type.[51] Belief, then, remains as the conviction of reality, the confidence, attached to both kinds of cognition.[52]

Crawford, on the other hand, though he acknowledges two sources of knowledge in the later Jacobi, is clearly mistaken about Jacobi's reinterpretation of the word "reason." Since the effect of the reinterpretation was to detach reason from the intellect and realign it with feeling or intuition, it is hardly possible to seize upon it as evidence of a greater appreciation for thought. Moreover, Crawford speaks as though intuition were not simply a mode of cognition but a method. Jacobi, he says, did not deny the appropriateness of the materialists' methods for dealing with physical phe-

50. JW 2:221n.

51. Ibid. Jacobi's persistent failure to get his terms straight is betrayed by the fact that he *says* that in the original dialogue he had only the word "sense" for what he now calls "reason": namely, "the faculty of immediate certainty, the faculty of revelation." But "reason" actually became only one kind of revelatory faculty, and he retained "sense" for the other kind, in effect turning "sense" over to the empiricists. The new use of "reason" thus had the consequence that reason became in the later Jacobi exactly what the earlier Jacobi said reason and intellect were not: *besondere [aus sich offenbarende] Kräfte* (284). A further complication is that the phrase I have set in brackets was not in the original edition of the dialogue (cf. *Hume über den Glauben*, 201). Jacobi also inserted into the second edition a sentence that identified sense as the actual revealing faculty, the faculty of perception (*Wahrnehmung*) in general, i.e., presumably, perception of both sensible and supersensible objects. Why did he do that? Apparently, he wished to underscore the very terminological infelicity that he now wanted to renounce!

52. Here, too, Jacobi wavers: in one and the same sentence he speaks of belief as coming from, and being identical with, *ein wissendes Nicht-Wissen*, which means, I take it, immediate knowledge (JW 2:20).

nomena but held that "another method, namely, faith, intuition, and not demonstration" is required to deal with supersensible facts.[53] It is true that Jacobi doubted the possibility of a science of the supersensible.[54] But intuition and belief were, to him, just as much the foundation of natural science as they are of assertions about God and human values. If belief is not strictly a mode of cognition, much less is it a method; and if there is anything like "a form of twofold truth" in Jacobi, as Crawford thinks, it is by no means an opposition between science and faith, seeing that science rests upon faith.[55]

What Jacobi offers is, so to say, neither a monistic nor a dualistic epistemology; it is more like two running-lanes on a single track, which are not identical but must measure up to the same standard. He was the very paragon of those religious apologists who renounce both a theology of proofs and a flight into fideism, and proceed to defend religious faith by showing that formally it has a similar structure to the element of belief in all knowing whatever. Indeed, despite the double-track epistemology, Jacobi was in a position to claim not just that religious faith is *like* nonreligious belief, but that "belief" in both domains means exactly the *same* thing. Of course, the epistemological parallel he draws is not missed by either Wilde or Crawford. But neither of them, it seems to me, quite does justice (for different reasons) to the exact nature of the parallel or its crucial role in his apologetic enterprise, which is, to establish that if belief in supersensible realities has no final defense against radical doubt, at least it is in no worse case than belief in a material world independent of our minds.[56]

Jacobi and Ogden

To argue for the coherence of Jacobi's position, at least in its general features, is not to deny that some tidying up of his leading concepts is desirable. Much less is it to assume that if coherent, his position must be right, or even plausible. It is open, in my opinion, to at least four related questions. I propose now to put these questions to Jacobi, then to ask in conclusion whether Schubert Ogden's notion of "basic confidence" can provide a more satisfactory variation on the theme of existential faith, at least to the extent of not being vulnerable where I think Jacobi's philosophy of faith is vulnerable.

First, even if we allow Jacobi the possibility that there may be two dis-

53. Crawford, *Philosophy of Jacobi,* 24.

54. I return to this point below; for documentation, see n. 63.

55. Crawford, *Philosophy of Jacobi,* 28.

56. Occasionally, Jacobi speaks as though a realistic epistemology were a prerequisite to belief in God: no world, no God (JW 2:37n.).

tinct cognitive routes, is the parallel he draws between them a plausible one? His entire case rests upon an alleged, or presumed, analogy between sensing material objects and perceiving spiritual objects. We "see" God, for instance, though not with the bodily eye. Then what exactly is the second, spiritual eye? Jacobi calls it not just a "capacity" or "faculty," but an "organ"—as though, like the organ of literal seeing, it must have a physiological site somewhere on the human body. Yet he calls it an "invisible organ that in no wise presents itself to outward senses."[57] And what kind of organ is that? Of course, it could be replied that reason, in Jacobi's sense, is a function of the brain. In that case, the analogy with the eye would be weakened, but there might still be a valid analogy between two mental *operations,* sensible intuition and rational intuition, and the question of their respective *organs* could be dismissed as philosophically frivolous. We might wish to argue, for example, passing from the psychological to the linguistic mode, that our moral discourse presupposes a basic recognition that there is a difference between good and bad; and we might further argue that this recognition is the sort of operation Jacobi intends by an "intuition" of a supersensible object (in this case, of "the good"). But this then leads to the next question.

Second, granted that there may be something in the spiritual domain analogous to a simple sensation in the material domain, what would the corresponding object be like? Perhaps Jacobi's best candidate for a supersensible intuition is the one just suggested: the simple—that is, irreducible —notion of "good." I do not mean that such a notion is unproblematic (any more than the notions of a simple sensation and a protocol sentence are unproblematic). It is just that Jacobi had a knack for sounding naive, and it is salutary to remember that his questions, even his answers, usually put him in respectable philosophical company. And from the influential work of G. E. Moore (1873–1958) we are at least familiar with the view that "good" is a simple and indefinable property, the presence of which is not seen but intuited. Something like this appears to be what Jacobi had in mind when he spoke of a rational intuition of the good.[58] That we have an immediate intuition of God, however, can hardly be maintained unless Jacobi is ready with a simple definition of the word "God." Apparently he is not. On the contrary, by "God" (*der Gott* as distinct from *das Gott* of the

57. JW 2:74. God has no reason any more than sense, because God needs no organs (10).

58. George Edward Moore, *Principia Ethica* (Cambridge: Cambridge University Press, 1903), esp. 6–8. It would be harder these days to name a philosopher of aesthetics who thinks similarly of "beautiful" as an irreducible quality, but some recent epistemologists have held that *knowing* is a primitive and indefinable concept, and it might be instructive to compare this view with Jacobi's intuition of the true. See the discussion of John Cook Wilson (1849–1915) and H. A. Prichard (1871–1947) in Anthony Quinton, "Knowledge and Belief," *The Encyclopedia of Philosophy,* ed. Paul Edwards, 8 vols. (New York: Macmillan Company and Free Press, 1967), 4:345–52, esp. 348.

speculative philosophers) Jacobi meant a personal creator outside the material world, endowed with freedom and working by design (*Vorsehung*), and such a complex idea can scarcely qualify as the referent of a simple intuition or presentiment of God.[59] Jacobi tends to assume he is home, when he has only taken the first cautious step. What corresponds to a simple intuition would surely have to be, or (more correctly) become in reflection, a simple idea, not the full-blown Christian doctrine of God. And if rational intuition is an actual mode of cognition or experience, like sensible intuition, to speak of "intuiting immortality" (in Jacobi's sense of intuiting a future life after bodily dissolution) is still more incongruous: it sounds like mere bad grammar. For what could it possibly mean to claim one has an intuition of something that is neither present nor an object at all, but an abstract noun referring to an anticipated future condition?

Third, there is the closely connected problem of, so to say, knowing when to stop. If belief is the inescapable conviction of reality, of how many things are we inescapably convinced? In a sense, Jacobi's reply is: just two things, the reality of the material world and the reality of the spiritual world.[60] But he is prepared to itemize the elements of the spiritual world, and he comes back repeatedly (with variations) to the Platonic triad of the true, the good, and the beautiful, and the Kantian triad of God, freedom, and immortality.[61] *Belief* in the reality of the supersensible thereby becomes the *beliefs* in God, goodness, immortality, and so on. And once again we must protest that Jacobi's thoughts run ahead of his argument. It will not do for him to tell us what he is personally convinced of. There is a sting in the malicious comment of Arthur Schopenhauer (1788–1860) that Jacobi's little weakness was to take all he learned and approved before his fifteenth year for innate ideas of the human mind.[62] If belief in the supersensible is to have any communicable meaning, the content of the supersensible must be specified; and if belief is thus divided into beliefs, each must be shown individually to be strictly universal, a prerequisite of being human. To attempt such a demonstration is by no means the same as trying to prove the reality of the object of belief. And this brings me to the final question.

Fourth, was Jacobi too apprehensive of anything that smacked of a "science of spirit"? For him, belief passed quickly over into wonder, and he

59. JW 2:83, 93, 114; 285.

60. Bollnow rightly observes that belief directed to the reality of "a certain sphere of objects as a whole" lacks specific content. But I cannot see that belief has to assume the character of a *Modus des Wissens* for its object to become specific (see Bollnow, *Die Lebensphilosophie Jacobis*, 142–45).

61. See, e.g., JW 2:9–11, 55–56, 76–77.

62. Schopenhauer, *Die Welt als Wille und Vorstellung* (1819), vol. 1, based on the 3d ed. (1859), Bibliothek der Gesamt-Litteratur, nos. 491–96 (Halle: Otto Hendel, n.d.), pref. to the 1st ed., xiii.

feared that to subject the domain of the spirit to the categories of the intellect was to court disaster. The attitude of wonder would be destroyed, he thought, if some future scientific genius were to demonstrate a mechanics of the human person, as Isaac Newton (1642–1727) had displayed the mechanism of the heavens. For Jacobi, this would be catastrophic for the idea of freedom, the supersensible fact that he made the actual hinge of his entire philosophy.[63] In this sense, he could entertain at least the *hypothetical* possibility of a conflict between science and faith. But his main thought was that the spiritual domain simply eludes, rather than opposes, science; and it was here, I think, that a *real* gap, if not exactly a real conflict, between faith and science opened up.[64] Since belief has a place on both sides of the epistemological paradigm, in the domain of nature as well as in the domain of spirit, to this extent there is no opposition between science and belief. The problem is, however, that on the side of the spiritual realities Jacobi does not complete the paradigm; he does not show how philosophy or theology might correspond to natural science as the parallel activities of the intellect in the domain of the supersensible. He does indeed say that the two kinds of intuition, as two sources of knowledge, stand in a similar relationship to the intellect. But this suggests to him only the impossibility of proving what intuition reveals; he does not see the parallel as a warrant, or a challenge, to develop a science of phenomena in the domain of the spirit.[65] Clearly, what troubles him is the thought of a science of the supersensible objects themselves. But why not a science of religious *belief?* This, in effect, is the question Friedrich Schleiermacher put to Jacobi—and answered in the system of dogmatics he wanted to dedicate to him.[66]

How does Schubert Ogden's notion of "basic confidence" fare if it is confronted with the four questions I have addressed to Jacobi's philosophy of faith? No lengthy exposition is required, I assume, to establish that the notion of a basic confidence or existential faith in the worth, final mean-

63. JW 2:105–6, 121; 53–55; 46–47. That there cannot be a science of spirit is the burden of Jacobi's brief essay *Über die Unzertrennlichkeit des Begriffes der Freyheit und Vorsehung von dem Begriffe der Vernunft* (1799), JW 2:311–23.

64. Crawford, of course, notes this gap (see, e.g., *Philosophy of Jacobi,* 28), but I think he confuses it with a distinction of his own making (not Jacobi's) between faith and science as two methods.

65. JW 2:59. Crawford endorses the view (without any documentation from Jacobi himself) that philosophy for Jacobi was "immediate knowledge of the supersensible" (*Philosophy of Jacobi,* 29). But surely philosophy, just as much as science, can only be an activity of the reflective intellect, and it seems to me unlikely that this is something Jacobi could have failed to notice.

66. Schleiermacher to Jacobi, 30 March 1818, reprinted in Martin Cordes, "Der Brief Schleiermachers an Jacobi: Ein Beitrag zu seiner Entstehung und Überlieferung," *Zeitschrift für Theologie und Kirche* 68 (1971): 195–212; Schleiermacher to Berthold Georg Niebuhr, 28 March 1819, in Heinrich Meisner, ed., *Schleiermacher als Mensch: Familien- und Freundesbriefe,* 2 vols. (Gotha: Friedrich Andreas Perthes, 1922–23), 2:297.

ing, or ultimate significance of life[67] does stand in the lineage of Jacobi's philosophy of faith and Balfour's concept of inevitable beliefs, at least insofar as Ogden's theme is a confidence that is "a necessary presupposition not only of religion but of human existence as such." Ogden's conversation partner, it is true, is neither Jacobi nor Balfour but Stephen Toulmin. Very much in the manner of Balfour, however, he wants to show that theism provides the best reflective account of experiences we all inescapably share; and much like Jacobi, he holds that there is a species of faith that provides the foundations of personal existence.[68] The differences between the three positions, it seems, have more to do with the content than with the function of existential faith. Ogden finds the content in the *secular* affirmation of life here and now. To make his apologetic case, he then needs to provide a link between this affirmation and explicit religious faith in God, so that to profess atheism may accordingly be seen, at one level, as a misunderstanding of one's own existence. The link is forged by the suggestion that the religions of the world can all, including Christianity, be viewed as expressions and re-presentations of the original confidence in the meaning and worth of life.[69]

An important consequence of Ogden's approach is that his final appeal is to just one item of primitive faith, whereas Jacobi struggled to maintain a parallel between two, and Balfour had a whole unwritten creed of inevitable beliefs. Ogden does not deny that there are in fact other existential beliefs; his phrase "reflective inventory of the existential beliefs by which we actually live" could almost stand as an unintended description of what Balfour was about. But Ogden's case actually rests on one belief only: basic confidence in the worth of life. Hence, while he too can see a parallel between confidence in life and experience through sense perception, the kind of epistemological analogy that Jacobi sets up between two sources of knowledge is simply not needed to support his argument; he does not even need to distinguish two mental functions, let alone two organs of knowing. This becomes particularly clear in his criticism of William Christian,

67. Ogden develops this theme, with minor variations of wording, chiefly in the second part of the title essay in *The Reality of God and Other Essays* (1966; paperback ed., New York: Harper & Row, 1977), 21–43. Also pertinent are chapter 3, "Myth and Truth" (99–119), and chapter 4, "The Strange Witness of Unbelief" (120–43). The pagination remained the same in the paperback edition except in the new preface, to which my roman numerals refer. See further Ogden, *On Theology* (San Francisco: Harper & Row, 1986), 69–84, 106–9, esp. 72: "The existential faith by which we live neither needs justification nor can ever be justified. Rather, it is the very ground of justification."

68. *Reality of God,* xi, 20, 42, 114 (the passage from which my second epigraph is taken). Ogden discusses Stephen Toulmin, *An Examination of the Place of Reason in Ethics* (Cambridge: Cambridge University Press, 1950), on 27–39.

69. *Reality of God,* 20, 23, 33–34. Ogden thus sees human experience as "always essentially religious" (114).

who, unlike Toulmin, "fails to see that the religious sort of question is not simply parallel or coordinate to the scientific or moral sorts, but . . . is also fundamental to them." For if the function of religious assertions is to provide reassurance about life's meaning, they are plainly relevant both to scientific explanation and to moral thought and action. Taking morality rather than science as his example, Ogden points out the moral relevance of religious assertions: the original confidence they represent is the necessary condition of all our moral action.[70] In short, the first of my objections to Jacobi's "faith" has no pertinence to Ogden's "basic confidence."

If we turn next from the subjective experience of basic confidence to its objective reference, the advantage of Ogden's unitary approach is confirmed. He expressly indicates that all we can mean by the word "God" at this stage of a case for theism is "the objective ground in reality itself of our ineradicable confidence in the final worth of our existence." Again: "The only God whose reality is implied by a secular affirmation is the God who is the ground of confidence in the ultimate worth or significance of our life in the world." As if this were not already clear enough, Ogden reiterates the point (by way of responding to his critics) in the preface to the paperback edition of *The Reality of God:* "To establish 'the reality of God' in the distinctively theistic sense of that phrase logically requires that one establish more than 'the reality of faith' and its objective ground." Unlike Jacobi, Ogden does not assume he is home once he has taken the first step; accordingly, my second objection to Jacobi also has no pertinence to Ogden's argument, except insofar as one endorses his confession that the argument, as originally stated, was insufficiently clear.[71]

My third objection to Jacobi, too, seems to leave Ogden's position unassailed, and I see no need to consider it more closely. Even if Ogden sometimes indicates an interest in other existential beliefs besides basic confidence,[72] the weight of his argument does not depend on them, and it would therefore be immaterial, as far as the argument is concerned, to ask how many existential beliefs there are, and what they are. I turn, then, to the last of my four questions to Jacobi: whether he was right to surrender the possibility of something like a science of religious belief. No one, I think, will accuse Schubert Ogden of moving too quickly from philo-

70. Ibid., 37 (cf. 43), 115, 34 n. 55, 34–37. Although he focuses on the moral relevance of basic confidence, Ogden takes this as only an illustration of a relevance for life generally (40, 43, 114). His critical remarks are addressed to William A. Christian, *Meaning and Truth in Religion* (Princeton: Princeton University Press, 1964).

71. *Reality of God,* 37, 43, xi.

72. In addition to the references already given above, see ibid., 114: "Man lives and acts, finally, only according to certain principles of truth, beauty, and goodness, which he understands to be normative for his existence. Invariably implied in this understanding is the confidence or assurance that these norms have an unconditional validity and that a life lived in accordance with them is truly worth living." Cf. *On Theology,* 75–76, 106.

sophical to hortatory discourse. His trust in the power of the intellect to illuminate existence is already apparent in the tenacity with which he seeks to establish the concept of basic confidence. He is not content to say that if any should doubt the value of life, he does not know how to help them, but argues forcefully for the presence of a hidden faith even in the person who bows out of life by way of suicide or the person who, like Albert Camus (1913–60), summons us to heroic resistance against life's absurdity.[73] But the point I am more concerned to make now, in comparing Ogden with Jacobi, is that the argument for basic confidence is but half the case he is pleading; the other half is his argument for a revision of classical theism. Whereas Jacobi presupposes the inherited Christian doctrine of God, or defends it at all costs (largely by criticism of the speculative alternatives), Ogden's reduced definition of "God" as the "objective ground of our basic confidence" becomes the point of departure for conceptual or doctrinal change. Although atheism may rest on a misconstrual of the existential affirmations by which even the atheist lives, Ogden grants that it may still be justified as a reflective protest against an untenable variety of theism; and "untenable" is exactly his verdict on conventional, supernaturalistic theism. Hence the discussion of "The Reality of Faith" moves on to a section titled "Toward a New Theism," which asks plainly: *What* doctrine of God best answers to existential faith?[74] I certainly do not wish to imply that Jacobi would find such a logical move wholly inappropriate. I simply draw attention to the systematic determination with which Ogden carries it out—untroubled that the light of faith might go out if brought to the intellect.

Naturally, to conclude that Schubert Ogden's approach is immune to weaknesses that (in my opinion) vitiate Jacobi's approach is not to say that further analysis of his leading concepts would not be useful, and it does not guarantee that there will be no other objections to which the notion of basic confidence might itself be vulnerable. On the matter of his leading concepts, one might wish to know more about how he conceives of the nonreflective element in basic confidence, and why he qualifies the object of confidence as the "final" or "ultimate" significance of life. He clearly does not regard basic confidence as necessarily reflective, since he holds that one function of the positive religions is to reaffirm it at the level of conscious belief. At the level of an unreflective taking-for-granted, how does it differ from the confidence that appears to activate animal behavior? Or does it become distinctively human *only* when raised to reflective con-

73. *Reality of God,* 36, 41–42, 138–40. Ogden does not hesitate to call our existence as such not merely "a standing testimony to God's reality," but "the only really essential 'proof of God's existence'" (43).

74. Ibid., x–xi, 24–25, 42, 44–70.

sciousness?[75] And does the qualifier "final" or "ultimate," when attached to the object of basic confidence, perhaps mean no more than the "after all" in the phrase "reassuring us that our life is, after all, worth while"?[76] Indeed, *can* it mean much more than that without jeopardizing the usefulness of the concept of basic confidence to a Christian theologian?

The objection that might be raised against "confidence in the final worth of our existence" from a theological perspective is that it has the appearance of a strongly anthropocentric, even egocentric, notion, and this appearance is heightened by the suggestion that we should so conceive of God as to exhibit him as "the ground of the significance of our life."[77] Now, of course, it could be answered that the notion of the final worth of our existence is purely formal, asserting nothing at all about what the worth of our existing might in fact be; and it would still be possible for a theologian to argue that in actual fact the *final* significance of human existence is a significance *relative* to the actual being of God, which alone has *ultimate* significance.[78] But perhaps a point made initially for theological reasons may occasion another look at the internal logic of basic confidence itself. For, in the first place, confidence of one's individual worth seems to arise from the perception of oneself as a part of a significant whole; and, in the second place, the confidence that our actions "make a difference," though it may be a presupposition of moral behavior,[79] is surely secondary to the inescapable awareness that we *ought* to make a difference.

If these are sound comments on our confidence in the significance of our existence (and I cannot develop them further here), they may lead us back to thinking again about Jacobi, who discovered *two* irreducible beliefs at the root of human existence: belief in the reality of an ordered world "outside" us, and belief in the authenticity of the voice of conscience. One

75. Faith *stricto sensu,* Ogden says, is "existential self-understanding" (ibid., 93), and "to be a self is not merely to exist, but to understand that one exists" (114; cf. 191, 229). But if even unreflective humans perceive their environment in broader terms than survival and reproduction, it may still be asked whether there is not already a difference between "animal faith" (George Santayana's term) and unreflective human faith; indeed, whether it can properly be said at all (see *On Theology,* 70, 106) that the former includes "accepting," as well as "adjusting to," the larger setting of life.

76. *Reality of God,* 34–35.

77. Ibid., 37, 47.

78. "God must be conceived as a reality which is genuinely related to our life in the world and to which, therefore, both we ourselves and our various actions all make a difference as to its actual being" (ibid., 47). Cf. Ogden, *Faith and Freedom: Toward a Theology of Liberation* (Nashville: Abingdon, 1979), 85: " . . . all things exist, finally, not merely for themselves or for one another, but, as the Christian witness has classically affirmed, for the glory of God, as contributions to his unique and all-encompassing life."

79. *Reality of God,* 35–36. It is, however, precisely this presupposition that Friedrich Forberg wished to challenge. See chapter 6 below.

may wonder if it is possible to defend this double faith without falling into the epistemological difficulties I have pointed out. Be that as it may, Ogden seems to me to provide the happiest formulation of his notion of basic confidence when he writes: "We are selves at all only because of our inalienable trust that our own existence and existence generally are somehow justified and made meaningful by the whole to which we know ourselves to belong."[80] Ogden is not likely to disagree if I venture to add that the whole to which we know ourselves to belong has for us the inescapable character of a *moral* order.[81]

80. *Reality of God,* 114; cf. 33, 37, and *On Theology,* 107.

81. The moral character of the whole to which we belong is expressed, for instance, in Ogden's statement that the existence in freedom actualized by faith is "not only trust in God's love but also loyalty to God and, therefore, also to all those to whom he himself is loyal—which means, of course, literally everyone" (*Faith and Freedom,* 56). After the present essay was completed, it was brought to my attention that the original edition of Jacobi's dialogue on Hume and the introduction to the second edition have recently been reprinted in Friedrich Heinrich Jacobi, *David Hume über den Glauben oder Idealismus und Realismus (1787) with the Vorrede to the 1815 Edition,* with an introduction by Hamilton Beck, The Philosophy of David Hume [unnumbered series] (New York: Garland Publishing, 1983). To the secondary literature on Jacobi in English can now be added Dale Evarts Snow, "F. H. Jacobi and the Development of German Idealism," *Journal of the History of Philosophy* 25 (1987): 397–415. New translations of Jacobi himself are given in *The Spinoza Conversations between Lessing and Jacobi: Text with Excerpts from the Ensuing Controversy,* introduced by Gérard Vallée and translated by Vallée, J. B. Lawson, and C. G. Chapple (Lanham, Maryland: University Press of America, 1988).

5

The Secret Religion of Germany: Christian Piety and the Pantheism Controversy

It is the religion of our greatest thinkers, our best artists. . . . Nobody says it, but everyone knows it: pantheism is an open secret in Germany. We have in fact outgrown deism. We are free and want no thundering tyrant. We are grown up and need no fatherly care. And we are not the botchwork of a great mechanic. Deism is a religion for slaves, for children, for Genevans, for watchmakers. Pantheism is the secret religion of Germany.
—HEINRICH HEINE

A "LIBERATED PRUSSIAN" living in Paris, Heinrich Heine wanted to persuade his French hosts that Germany, too, had undergone a revolution. Unlike the social and political upheaval in France, Germany's revolution, at least initially, was of the mind. But Heine found some remarkable parallels between them. By asserting that for eight years Kant's first critique (1781) attracted little attention, he even managed to place the beginnings of both revolutions in exactly the same year (1789). More important, he discovered in the *Critique of Pure Reason* an act of deicide, the counterpart to the act of regicide that sealed the end of the *ancien régime* in France.[1]

What Heine proclaimed was not the death of God, but the death of one image of God and the enthronement of another: the overthrow of deism by pantheism. There are some oddities about his use of both terms, "deism" and "pantheism," and to this we shall need to come back. In general, however, he was surely right: The passage of thought in Germany from the Enlightenment to Romanticism and Idealism was an intellectual revolution, and it did bring about a shift in the way the intelligentsia thought of

1. Heinrich Heine, *Zur Geschichte der Religion und Philosophie in Deutschland* (1835; hereafter cited as *Deutschland*), in *Heinrich Heine: Historisch-kritische Gesamtausgabe der Werke* (Düsseldorfer Ausgabe), ed. Manfred Windfuhr, vol. 8, pt.-vol. 1 (Hamburg: Hoffmann and Campe, 1979), 77, 90, 115. My epigraph will be found in the same work (61–62). All translations in this chapter are mine, unless otherwise stated. Heine describes himself as a *Prussien libéré* in his *Briefe über Deutschland* (1844), letter 1, in Heine, *Sämtliche Schriften,* vol. 5, ed. Klaus Briegleb and Karl Heinz Stahl (Munich: Carl Hanser, 1974), 194.

God, a shift from deism toward pantheism. The German revolution cannot be simply identified with Kant's first critique. Heine did not imagine that it could; Kant, for him, represented the negative, deicidal phase of the revolution. But the story also goes back to a summer's day in 1780, when a casual meeting between Lessing and Jacobi set in motion events leading to the famous Pantheism Controversy. To trace this other, more positive, thread in the story is to witness one of the pivotal moments in Western religious thought, a moment that brought it closer to some of the forms of Far Eastern religious thought.

Merely to relate what happened cannot tell us who was right, or what view of the deity we ourselves should entertain. The church dogmaticians among us will agree with Karl Barth that the true theologian should not dally overmuch with history but head straight for Jerusalem. When two of his associates published dogmatic works heavily laden with historical digressions, Barth wrote that he hid his face in shame that his friends, good people though they were, had not learned from him even this much: You cannot do theology by engaging every position, old and new, in dialogue.[2] He was right. To the theologian, the destination—the object, the truth itself—is everything. But it does not follow that the road to Jerusalem is straight or short. If the language in which truth becomes flesh is given to us by history, then the dialogue with others is something we have to travel *through,* not, as in Barth's image, something to keep *behind* us.[3] Historical understanding of religious beliefs will always strike the foursquare theologian as a contemptible torso if unaccompanied by the kind of "theses"—the forthright assertions of truth—for which Barth said he was hungry. But the most cogent dogmatic arguments for or against a theological thesis can never quite transcend the relativities of its historical genesis and growth. And the Pantheism Controversy reminds us that religious belief, or religious unbelief, is sometimes more forceful when clothed not in a thesis, but in a poem.

The Pantheism Controversy

The controversy turned around the personal relationships among three remarkable men. It began as a difference of opinion between Jacobi and

2. Karl Barth to Helmut Gollwitzer, 31 July 1962, in Barth, *Briefe 1961–68,* ed. Jürgen Fangmeier and Hinrich Stoevesandt, *Karl Barth: Gesamtausgabe,* division 5, vol. 4 (Zurich: Theologischer Verlag, 1975), 82–83 (no. 49); Barth to Walter Kreck, 31 July 1962, ibid., 86–87 (no. 50). The two "friends" were Kreck and Otto Weber.

3. That Barth thought it at least possible to converse with "the fathers and brethren" along the way, and yet to keep one's mind on the heavenly destination, is clearly attested by those remarkable excursions into historical theology that adorn every chapter of his own *Church Dogmatics.*

Moses Mendelssohn (1729–86) about Lessing's beliefs in the closing decade of his life, the time of the "Wolfenbüttel Fragments" and *Nathan the Wise*. Initially, one is inclined to suppose that Mendelssohn, if anyone, must have known what Lessing believed. But Jacobi claimed to be privy to a dark secret about him. The disagreement centered on Lessing's relation to Spinoza; and when the two contenders took their argument before the public in print, it grew into a broad literary debate about the merits of Spinoza's allegedly "pantheistic" conception of God.

Throughout his career, Lessing had taken a public stand for the cause of religious enlightenment. After his appointment as librarian to the Duke of Brunswick in Wolfenbüttel (1770), he was drawn into theological controversy over the notorious Wolfenbüttel Fragments (1774–78), which may be said to have launched the quest for the historical Jesus. A letter from Duke Charles, dated 17 August 1778, forbade him to publish anything further on religious matters without express authorization. But Lessing was incapable of maintaining silence; in his play *Nathan the Wise* (1779), he returned to what he called his "old pulpit, the theater." Taking his inspiration from Giovanni Boccaccio's (1313–75) *Decameron,* he borrowed the tale of the three rings. In Boccaccio's version, Saladin the Saracen asks the Jew Melchisedek a trick question: Which of the three religions—Judaism, Christianity, or Islam—is the true one? The adroit Jew responds with a story. A certain man had three sons, only one of whom could receive the priceless family ring. Loving all three, the father had two perfect replicas made, and on his deathbed he gave one ring to each son. He himself could hardly tell which was the original heirloom, and he carried the secret with him to the grave; to this day, no one knows for sure which of the three sons was the man's true heir. The moral is clear.

Lessing's version introduces an intriguing change. In *Nathan the Wise* we are told that the original ring makes the one who wears it in faith beloved of God and other people; but when it is brought to the father along with the two copies, even he cannot tell it from the others. Since none of the three sons is much loved by the other two, but each loves himself best, is it possible that the real ring has been lost and that three copies are all that is left? Well, maybe. But the point of the story, as Lessing tells it, is that while each son may believe he has the true ring, all should emulate the father's love, who loved all three alike and would not humiliate two of them to favor one.[4]

Although it has sometimes been denied, the prevailing view has always been—from Lessing's own day until ours—that Nathan the Wise was modeled on the character of the Jewish philosopher Moses Mendelssohn, a prominent leader of the Berlin Enlightenment. Born the same year, Less-

4. G. E. Lessing, *Nathan der Weise,* act 3, scene 7.

ing and Mendelssohn had been friends since 1754, when a common love for chess first brought them together. Mendelssohn stood aloof from the theological wrangling into which Lessing was seduced by his publication of the Wolfenbüttel Fragments. But despite their differences, the two friends occupied common territory in their estimate of religion. While not gainsaying the usefulness of a particular historical religion to those to whom it is revealed, they located the core of every faith in the moral content it shared with the others.

Our third protagonist, Jacobi, was a very different man, mistrustful of human reason and burdened with missionary zeal. His relationship with Lessing was not of such long standing as Mendelssohn's; it dates from the publication of Jacobi's novel, *Woldemar* (1779), which must be understood as part of the incipient revolt against the Enlightenment. Goethe was contemptuous of the work. It was all the more important to the author's self-esteem, therefore, when Lessing, though a spokesman for the enlightened, gave him friendly encouragement and sent him a copy of *Nathan* in exchange. The following summer, less than a year before Lessing's death, Jacobi paid him a visit in Wolfenbüttel.[5]

On the second day of the visit (6 July 1780), Jacobi produced an unpublished poem of Goethe's titled *Prometheus,* expecting that Lessing, who had so often given offense, might now take offense at what another had written. The poem reads like this:

Cover your heavens, Jove,
with misty clouds
and practice, like a boy
beheading thistles,
on oaks and mountain peaks!
My earth you must leave me
still standing,
and my cottage, which you did not build,
and my hearth
whose warmth
you envy me.

I know nothing poorer
under the sun than you gods!
Wretchedly you nourish
your majesty
on sacrificial tolls

5. Our sole source of information for the visit is Jacobi's own account of it in a letter to Mendelssohn (4 November 1783) reproduced in Jacobi, *Über die Lehre des Spinoza, in Briefen an Herrn Moses Mendelssohn* (1st ed., 1785), JW 4, 1:47–94.

and flimsy prayers,
and would starve if children
and beggars were not
hopeful fools.

When I was a child,
not knowing my way,
I turned my erring eyes
sunward, as if above there were
an ear to hear my lamentation,
a heart like mine
to care for the distressed.

Who helped me against the Titan's wanton insolence?
Who rescued me from death,
from slavery?
Have you not done all this yourself,
my holy glowing heart?
And young and good, you glowed,
betrayed, with thanks for rescue
to him who slept above.

I honor you? For what?
Have you ever eased the suffering
of the oppressed?
Have you ever stilled the tears
of the frightened?
Was I not welded to manhood
by almighty Time
and eternal Fate,
my master and yours?

Did you fancy perchance
that I should hate life
and fly to the desert
because not all
my blossom dreams ripened?

Here I sit, forming men
in my own image,
a race to be like me,
to suffer, to weep,
to delight and to rejoice,

and to defy you,
as I do.[6]

To Jacobi's surprise, Lessing said he liked the poem, since he no longer subscribed to the orthodox notions of deity but found his own belief summed up in the ancient Greek doctrine that all is one (*hen kai pan*). This sounded to Jacobi like Spinoza. Lessing agreed: "If I am to call myself after anyone, I know of no one else." Jacobi concluded that Lessing, without the knowledge of the public or even of his friends, was no longer the great champion of the Enlightenment but in his riper years had moved on, or fallen back, to a quite different standpoint. Jacobi had little sympathy for Spinozism; the next morning, he testified to Lessing that he himself believed in an intelligent, personal cause of the world. "Oh," said Lessing, "so much the better! There, for sure, I'm going to hear something completely new." Undaunted by this evident sarcasm, the visitor explained that Spinozism leads to determinism, and any system that logically entails the denial of free will has to be mistaken, however flawlessly reasoned. "I love Spinoza," Jacobi said, "because he . . . has led me to perfect assurance that some things cannot be explained." Lessing commented: "I note that you would like to have your will free. I do not crave free will. . . . I remain an honest Lutheran."[7]

Soon after Lessing's death on 15 February 1781, Mendelssohn determined to write an appreciation of his character, of which, he believed, Lessing's writings could give a false impression. The closeness of the personal relationship between them was common knowledge; and if anyone could claim to be a Lessing expert, it would surely have had to be Mendelssohn. Two years later, the promised character study had still not appeared. But Elise Reimarus was able to assure Jacobi (in March 1783) that Mendelssohn's intention remained firm, and in so doing she unwittingly opened the door to the Pantheism Controversy. In his reply, Jacobi confided to her the secret that in his last days Lessing had become a Spinozist; and he added (twice, in case she did not rise to take the bait the first time) that she should feel free, at her discretion, to pass the secret on to Mendelssohn, who may not have been privy to it. "Perhaps," Jacobi intimated, "Lessing spoke his mind as openly to his dear Mendelssohn as he did to me; but perhaps not, since he had not talked with him for a long time and disliked writing letters."[8] Elise Reimarus did exercise her discretion (as planned), and Jacobi furnished his evidence. The Pantheism Controversy was on.

6. The translation is from Walter Kaufmann, trans. and ed., *Twenty German Poets: A Bilingual Collection,* Modern Library (New York: Random House, 1962), 9–11.

7. JW 4,1:51–55, 59–61, 70–71.

8. Jacobi to "Emilie" (Elise Reimarus), 21 July 1783, JW 4,1:39–40.

The original point at issue was whether Lessing's mind, toward the end of his life, had been tainted with Spinozism, but the nature and merits of Spinozism itself quickly became the center of attention. Once the controversy became public (in 1785), it took a surprising turn that neither Jacobi nor Mendelssohn could have wished for. Albeit by different routes, the two contestants both arrived, after all, at the conception of God as an agent who acts upon the world from outside; neither of them had any inclination to embrace Spinoza's alleged pantheism. But many German intellectuals now took another look at the "dead dog" Spinoza (as Lessing called him), and they discovered they liked him better than they liked either Jacobi or Mendelssohn. A "Neo-Spinozism" broke out that was to become one of the main sources of a new philosophy, and so the source of another beginning for Christian theology, which had suffered in the Age of Reason at the hands of friends and foes alike. Even Goethe, who had no interest in a revival of Christian theology, fell into the habit of carrying Spinoza's *Ethics* in his pocket and wrote to Jacobi the famous words: "[Spinoza] does not prove the existence of God; existence is God. And if for this reason others chide him as an atheist, I should like to name him and praise him as *theissimum* and indeed *christianissimum* [a theist and a Christian in the highest degree]."[9]

Two Types of "Spinozism"

What, then, is "Spinozism"? And why did so many of Germany's leading intellectuals find it attractive? No single answer will do for them all. Goethe no doubt touches on the essential point in his letter to Jacobi: For Spinoza, God is not a being but being itself; nature and God constitute an indivisible unity, *deus sive natura*. But in Heine and Herder, to take just two examples, the possibilities of Spinozism follow two very different courses. The one, though Jewish by birth and Christian by a baptism of convenience, was at heart a cheerful pagan, whereas the other (to borrow Lessing's phrase) was an honest Lutheran; and they lived through different phases of the German revolution, Heine in fact appearing on the scene much later than Herder. Small wonder if they arrived at unlike estimates of Spinoza's alleged atheism. Heine was happy to embrace the fundamental Spinozist principle as "pantheism." Herder was unwilling to accept either name, "Spinozist" or "pantheist," and yet he too believed that Spinoza had opened up the philosophy of the future.

Like everyone else, Heine took "pantheism" and "deism" to be mutually defining terms: The God of the pantheists is *in* the world, whereas the

9. Johann Wolfgang von Goethe to Jacobi, 9 June 1785, in *Goethes sämtliche Werke* (Propyläen-Ausgabe), vol. 4 (Munich: Georg Müller, 1910), 392.

God of the deists is *out of,* or *over,* the world, ruling it from above as though it were a separate establishment. But Heine made no distinction, such as we commonly make, between the absentee God of deism and the ever-present God of theism, between the divine watchmaker who has finished the work of creation and the busy, active Lord whose work never ends. Judaism and Christianity he treats as varieties of deism alongside the "school of Geneva," by which he means Jean-Jacques Rousseau (1712–78) and his friends. Rousseau was not quite the typical deist, but the fact that his father, Isaac Rousseau, was a watchmaker was too happy a coincidence for Heine to resist. The deists, Heine says, differ among themselves only with respect to the manner of God's rule: The Hebrews think of God as a thundering tyrant; the Christians, as a loving father; and the Genevan school, as a clever artist who made the world just as papa made watches. The fundamental point, for Heine, is that in all three varieties of "deism" God is pictured as acting upon the world from the outside.[10] But why did this strike him as such an inappropriate idea?

The notion of a Spirit God who is out of, or above, the material world went together, in Heine's mind, with a religiousness that degrades the body. Here, too, Judaism and Christianity belong together, with only a difference of degree between them: Judaism merely belittles the body as the envelope of the spirit, whereas Christianity spurns the body as something bad. Partly under the influence of Manichaeism and Gnosticism, and more remotely of the religions of Persia and India, Catholic Christianity, according to Heine, set body and spirit in enmity to each other. The purest blossom of the Christian idea, which is that all sensuous delight ought to be suppressed, was the monastic life. Everything sweet and lovely was decried by medieval folk as devilish seduction, and the devout crossed themselves anxiously at the song of the nightingale. But the church, having little success in denying the body, settled for a compromise: an ingenious system of satisfactions and indulgences contrived not to abolish sensuality but to tax it instead. Luther, unfortunately, never appreciated the genius of Catholicism. Misunderstanding was fostered by the fact that fewer indulgences are needed in the chilly German climate than under the glowing Italian sky, and the paternal concern of Pope Leo X misled him into dispatching an oversupply of indulgences to the North.[11]

10. Heine, *Deutschland,* 57–58. Heine discovered a special affinity between deism and Judaism, his own ancestral faith: the Jews are the Swiss guard of deism (55), and Moses Mendelssohn cleaved to pure Mosaism as a bulwark of deism (72).

11. Ibid., 58; 14–20; 27–29. On the antithetical systems of spiritualism and sensualism, see also 49. In general, Heine professed admiration for Luther (27, 33–34), and he hailed the Reformation as the advent of that freedom of thought without which the philosophical revolution would have been impossible (36–37, 47). But he admired only the "spirit" of Protestantism and admitted that (institutionally) his own Protestantism consisted solely in having

No one will fail to notice that there was a good deal of cheerful mischief in Heine's thumbnail sketch of Christianity, and it is unnecessary to carry his exposition any further. But there is no reason to doubt that he did look forward to a time when Germany would recover its health and atone for the unnaturalness of Christian spiritualism. And he understood this to mean, in part, a recovery of the ancient religion practiced in northern Europe before the Christian missionaries arrived, which was not deism but pantheism: a form of nature worship in which everything was full of gods. When Christianity encountered the old Germanic religion, it put in the place of a divinized nature a nature infested with devils. Everything sacred became satanic, and Teutonic pan-theism became pan-demonism—until the philosophical revolution restored the contact of the German mind with its ancient sources.[12]

If Heine's understanding of deism was (to us) unusual, his view of pantheism was nothing less than singular. The philosophical pantheism that arose in Germany under the belated influence of Spinoza was partly, in his eyes, a revival of the old Germanic religious heritage. The innate pantheistic instinct of the German soul reasserted itself first, he believed, in German art, even before it became embodied in a philosophical theory; what the early Romantics wrongly felt as nostalgia for medieval catholicism had an older, deeper source. Astonishingly, then, Heine not only collapsed Judaism, Christianity, and deism into a single religious conception but also viewed in one comprehensive glance the ancient Teutonic religion and modern German art, literature, and philosophy. One would have thought it a giant step from the pleasant fantasy that a fairy breathes in every tree to Schelling's and Hegel's heavy philosophies of nature. But, for Heine, the old religion and the new speculation were alike manifestations of pantheism, and he predicted that the refined German philosophy of nature would eventually draw explosive political strength from the "demonic" (*sic!*) energies of the old Germanic cult. A drama would then be played out in Germany in comparison with which the French Revolution would look like an innocuous idyll. The lust for battle would reassert itself, and old Thor would leap to life again to shatter the Gothic cathedrals with his hammer. France, beware![13]

In Heine's mind, the "secret religion of Germany" had a long ped-

---

his name on the rolls of the Lutheran communion (305; from the French version of his work on Germany). See also Heine, *Die romantische Schule* (1835), *Historisch-kritische Gesamtausgabe,* 8,1:143–44. Protestant accommodation to modern thought he considered in some respects suicidal; see his *Briefe über Deutschland,* letter 1, p. 196.

12. *Deutschland,* 17, 58–59; 20, 26, 64.

13. Ibid., 101; 111, 115–16; 118–19. Heine also saw anticipations of "our doctrine" in Giordano Bruno and, further back, in pre-Socratic philosophy (112, 115). For his thoughts on Goethe's pantheism, see 100–101.

igree. But by his own time, it also held out something new. What Heine really wanted to believe was not that a fairy lurks in every tree, but that God is incarnate in the flesh of humanity. For while the deity of the pantheists is manifest in everything that is, in the totality of humankind deity attains to self-consciousness. And here Heine discovered the possibility of political and social revolution in Germany's revolution of the mind. Once brought to awareness of their own divinity, the people will be inspired to publish it abroad; and if true divinity claims even what is material as its domain, then the material welfare of all becomes a religious cause, including the welfare of the suffering whom the church had counseled to bear the cross in this world for the sake of blessedness in the world to come. This, then, is what captivated Heine about the new pantheism: in effect, the apotheosis of humanity. Spinoza's God who is matter as well as spirit (extension as well as thought), the Hegelian concept of the identity of God and humanity, and the practical, protosocialist faith of the Saint-Simonians were all natural allies in the struggle for a better life. But the pantheistic Germans had seen more clearly than the materialistic French that bread is not just the right of the people, but the divine right of humanity. Beneath Heine's eccentricity and his irrepressible frivolousness there hides an earnest social vision.[14]

Quite different from Heine's neopaganism was the wisdom that Herder drew from the Spinozist revival, closer to its source. He put his thoughts into dialogue form in his book *God: Some Conversations* (1787), perhaps the most interesting monument of the Spinozist revival. The intellectual ferment unwittingly occasioned by the quarrel between Jacobi and Mendelssohn is nowhere more strikingly mirrored than in these winsome, but often murky, dialogues. It must be admitted that the dialogue form is somewhat artlessly employed. The rival systems are not permitted to speak, without partiality, for themselves; Theophron (clearly Herder himself) for the most part lectures his docile friend Philolaus, who keeps a notebook handy. A third, female character, Theano, who appears toward the end, is likewise presented as eager for instruction, if more impatient than Philolaus of subtle speculation.[15]

Theophron will not admit that he is a Spinozist. However, his task is to set the record straight: to rectify misapprehensions about Spinoza, whose leading ideas he expounds with evident sympathy. By "God," the one substance of which all things are modifications, Spinoza meant the one self-dependent nature that no logical mind can deny. But this inde-

14. Ibid., 60–61; cf. *Die romantische Schule,* 153–54. On the church's "consolation" of the suffering, see *Deutschland,* 17; cf. *Briefe über Deutschland,* letter 1, p. 197.

15. J. G. Herder, *Gott: Einige Gespräche* (1787; 2d ed., subtitled *Einige Gespräche über Spinozas System,* 1800), in *Herders sämmtliche Werke,* ed. Bernhard Suphan, vol. 16 (Berlin: Weidmann, 1887), 401–580.

pendent being was for him the immanent, not the "transitive," cause of all things: not, that is, a cause that breaks in occasionally from the outside. Philolaus assents: To suppose that God is a transitive cause would imply that at other times there could be such a thing as a creature without God's support, and that God must be subject to location and change. "But," asks Theophron, to test his pupil, "what if God dwells outside the world?" Philolaus: "Where is there a place outside the world?" Theophron: "Excellent, Philolaus." But Philolaus remains puzzled; for what could Spinoza possibly have meant by making extension, along with thought, one of the two attributes of God? This seems hardly compatible with the insight that God "has no place." Does Spinoza, after all, enclose God *within* the world?[16]

Here Theophron admits that Spinoza went wrong; he was misled by René Descartes (1596–1650), who defined matter in terms of extension and distinguished it sharply from spirit. In his drive for a monistic system, Spinoza thus found himself with one divine substance, yet still with two utterly incongruous attributes: thought and extension. He lacked a "unifying intermediate conception." But, Theophron points out, truth marches on; natural science, without which metaphysics builds in the air, and the philosophy of G. W. Leibniz (1646–1716), our *German* philosopher, have now conspired to give us exactly the category we need, that of "substantial force," an indivisible active element. Philolaus grasps the point: Spinoza's system can be given the unity he vainly pursued if we hold thought to be simply the highest grade of organic force known to us. We will also know how to identify God in this panpsychic philosophy of process: God will be the primal force (*Urkraft*) in an organic system of forces, the Soul of every soul.[17]

All things may not be transparently clear in this half-scientific, half-poetic vision of nature, but clear enough. Herder appropriates Spinoza's fundamental insight partly to save the idea of God by reconstructing it. The image of the divine being who sits above the circle of the earth and intervenes, now and then, in human destiny had fallen on hard times once nature had come to be perceived as moving in accord with its own immanent laws. The temptation was then to think of God either as turning away from the world once made, or else as willfully disrupting its machine-like operation. And what kind of choice was that—either to sacrifice the presence of God to the laws of nature, or to jeopardize scientific inquiry by leaving nature open to the arbitrary intervention of God? The Neo-Spinozist resolved the dilemma by abandoning the image of the extra-

16. Ibid., 420, 493–94, 496; 439–44; 446. "Transitive" (German *vorübergehend*) is the usual English rendering of the word *transiens* in Spinoza's *Ethica* (1677), pt. 1, prop. 18: "Deus est omnium rerum causa immanens, non vero transiens."

17. *Gott*, 446–53; cf. 479–80, 545.

mundane deity, the mind outside the machine. According to Herder, we cannot any longer think of God as a being who acts from outside the world on other beings, nor can we represent the divine activity as arbitrary. Rather, God is precisely the luminous, rational necessity that discovers itself within nature to scientific inquiry.[18]

But Herder was not merely interested in a sounder philosophical concept of God. Like Heine afterward, he was also concerned about what he took to be the defects of conventional Christian piety; only, for Herder, the main problem lay not in Christian spiritualism but in a naive egocentrism that wanted a deity at human disposal. In a somewhat patronizing letter to Jacobi, he professed not to understand what "you dear people" mean by an existence of God outside the world; in another letter, he added pointedly: "You want God in human form, as a friend who thinks of you. Bear in mind that he must then also think of you in a human—that is, restrictive—way; and if he is partial to you, it will be against others."[19] Herder's *Conversations* is a Neo-Spinozist antidote to a naive, self-centered piety. The true religious frame of mind unites with the sober devotion of the scientist or natural philosopher to the task of uncovering the nature of things. Piety is to grasp nature as a tissue of law-governed events. Empirical science, Theophron predicts, will one day exclude the last vestiges of divine arbitrariness. But this by no means excludes religion too; it indicates what real religion is:

> To explore Nature, first to divine her lofty laws, then to observe, test and verify them; now to find them confirmed a thousand times and to apply them anew; finally, to perceive everywhere the same wisest rule, the same sacred necessity, to come to love it, to impress it upon oneself—this it is that gives human life its value. For, good Theano, are we merely spectators? Are we not ourselves actors, Nature's coworkers, and her imitators?[20]

The consciousness of divine necessity, we are told, banishes all senseless fear. But there is more to religion than this. Blessedness is attained in the individual's perception of him- or herself as belonging to the whole, shar-

18. Ibid., 486–88, 493, 497, 500, 519. The identification of God as *lichtvolle, denkende Nothwendigkeit* is changed in the second edition to *lichtvolle, wirkende Nothwendigkeit* (481), but in the passages cited Herder continued to speak of God as a "reason" or "intelligence" in things that may be called analogically "wise" and "beneficent" even though it must not be conceived of as strictly a person. Herder insists that Spinoza himself did not turn God into a *gedankenloses Wesen* (474), for blind power (*blinde Macht*) cannot be the highest power (479).

19. Herder to Jacobi, 6 February 1784, in *Aus Herders Nachlass: Ungedruckte Briefe*, ed. Heinrich Düntzer and Ferdinand Gottfried von Herder, vol. 2 (Frankfurt am Main: Meidinger Sohn, 1857), 255; Herder to Jacobi, 20 December 1784, ibid., 264.

20. *Gott*, 490–91, 557–60. Herder clearly has no difficulty in using the language of religious devotion in speaking of his deity (see, e.g., 562–63).

ing in a magnificent, unremitting process in which even death and destruction have their meaning. Philolaus offers the opinion that the old theologies are dying out, and Theophron replies:

> The truth in them will prove itself incomparably more glorious if we no longer snatch after special little purposes in every single little circumstance, but more and more achieve a view of the whole, which, down to its smallest combinations, is but a single system in which the wisest goodness reveals itself in accord with immutable, internal rules.[21]

Anima Mundi

Jacobi has often been dismissed as a sorry, second-rate philosopher (not quite justly, in my opinion). But at least he let a philosophical genie out of the bottle. It does not matter much whether he was right or wrong about Lessing. Heine thought Mendelssohn was right: "Rest easy in the grave, old Moses," he wrote, " . . . your Lessing was no Spinozist, as slander pretends; he died a good deist like you, and Nicolai, and Teller, and the *Allgemeine deutsche Bibliothek*."[22] Be that as it may (and even Heine admitted that Lessing was on the way to Spinozism), Jacobi's "slander" released a spirit that he was unable to control.

The road from Wolfenbüttel could, and did, lead to more destinations than one: among others, to Herder's vision of the harmony of nature and to Heine's vision of a more just society; to admiration for the primal cosmic force and to the divinization of humanity. That pantheism is the secret religion of Germany turns out to be too simple a revelation. But the different destinations did lie in a common direction, which led away from deism and the Enlightenment. Mendelssohn is sometimes proclaimed the victor in the Pantheism Controversy: whereas Jacobi emerges discredited because of his fideism and the dubious tactics with which he defended it, Mendelssohn scores points for his image of unfailing civility and reasonableness. Yet "old Moses," as Heine called him, stood for the waning outlook of the German Enlightenment, which he had never represented with much originality. He wanted the Spinozist revival even less than Jacobi did. The immediate future in German philosophy lay neither with Jacobi's philosophy of faith, nor with Mendelssohn's rational theism, but with the varieties of speculative idealism that emerged, one might say, at the confluence of the Kantian philosophy and "Herderized" Spinozism. Jacobi and Mendelssohn fought over the grave of Spinoza, only to discover that the body was still breathing.

21. Ibid., 472; 562–67; 492–93.
22. *Deutschland*, 75–76.

Historians of German philosophy trace back through the Spinozist revival to Spinoza himself the fundamental speculative principle that God is not the external, transient cause of things, working arbitrarily by free choice, but the internal cause that proceeds necessarily according to its own rational nature, so that the true revelation of God must be sought after in the eternal laws of the world order. Here, in "the fundamental thought of the inviolably regular order of the world," Otto Pfleiderer (1839–1908) discerned the "sure foundation of all subsequent philosophy, and of the whole modern view of the world," needing only to be represented in less static, more teleological terms.[23] We may be inclined these days to regard this verdict as more parochial than Pfleiderer imagined. But the great creators of speculative idealism would themselves have agreed with him. G. W. F. Hegel announced in his lectures on the history of philosophy: "Spinoza is the high point of modern philosophy; either Spinozism or no philosophy."[24] To be sure, Hegel argued that absolute substance in Spinoza's philosophy was not yet conceived of as active, living Spirit, but only as the abstract unity of Spirit in itself. This, however, was in effect a proposal to move the notion of divine substance in the direction Herder had already pointed out.

The resulting concept—or perhaps one might better say, the resulting image—of God approaches the ancient idea of the *anima mundi,* the "World Soul." Herder, like Schleiermacher afterward, expressed reservations about baptizing the originally pagan term, since it could be said still to construe the relationship of God and world dualistically.[25] But Jacobi was not far wrong when he insisted that, despite every disavowal, a World Soul was exactly what Herder made out of Spinoza's God.[26] The result, we may add, is a radical transformation of eighteenth-century theology. Nature is no longer a machine, but an organism; God, accordingly, is not so much its orderer as its order of reason, not its artificer but its creative life and activity. There remains, it is true, an obvious and important point of continuity between the older Newtonian theism (or deism) and Herder's

23. Otto Pfleiderer, *The Philosophy of Religion on the Basis of Its History,* trans. from the 2d German ed. (1883–84), vol. 1, trans. Alexander Stewart and Allan Menzies (London: Williams & Norgate, 1886), 40–46.

24. Georg Wilhelm Friedrich Hegel, *Vorlesungen über die Geschichte der Philosophie,* ed. Karl Ludwig Michelet (1833), vol. 3, in Hegel, *Sämtliche Werke* (Jubiläumsausgabe), ed. Hermann Glockner, vol. 19, 2d ed. (Stuttgart: Fr. Frommann, 1941), 374.

25. Herder, *Gott,* 526–27; Schleiermacher, *Reden,* 140. Although critical of the term *Weltseele,* Schleiermacher (in the passage cited) defends his use of *Weltgeist* as properly Christian because it suggests neither reciprocal action between the world and God nor independence of the world from God.

26. *Über die Lehre des Spinoza,* JW 4,1:78n.; cf. ibid., 4,2:74–80 (*Beylage* 4).

"dynamic pantheism," as it has been called:[27] for both, nature is law-governed. But the anthropomorphic deity outside the law-governed system has now given way to an organic whole, the creative activity of which is what we mean by "God." The proposed shift of perspective not only lays aside the incurable anthropomorphism of the deists but also excludes the perennial temptation of the orthodox to assume that if God made the system, God may reserve the right to interfere with it from time to time. For the Neo-Spinozist, the notion of divine interference is simply impossible, since the course of nature is nothing other than the necessary activity of God; not being outside the system, God can scarcely be thought to intervene in it.

Revolutions of the mind, like revolutions in politics, are not irreversible. In the preface to the second edition of his *Religion and Philosophy in Germany,* Heine disconcertingly forewarned the reader that everything the book said on the great question of God was as false as it was foolhardy. "Deism lives. . . . It is not dead!" Between the first edition and the second, Heine (so he said) had undergone a conversion, which he attributed not to any miraculous divine intervention but simply to renewed study of the Bible. He had mocked at F. W. J. von Schelling's (1775–1854) conversion to the extramundane God of Catholicism. "It proves," he said, "only that a man inclines to Catholicism when he grows tired and old." Yet when he himself was disillusioned and racked with pain, Heine returned to what he cynically called "the old superstition of a personal God," though without taking refuge in any church. He was homesick for the God who, even if no more a dispenser of comfort than the Olympian Zeus, can at least be rebuked for the cruelty and injustice of the world. The God of the pantheists meets neither of these elemental human needs—to be consoled, or at least to be indignant. Heine threw into his fire an unfinished manuscript he was writing on Hegel.[28]

Still, even if a return to prerevolutionary deism (or theism) could not, and cannot, be ruled out, I want to suggest in conclusion that the conceptual possibilities of the *anima mundi* analogy are not yet exhausted; further, that it entails a reformulation of the fundamental religious question worth pondering even by those who decline to take the road to monism. Spinozism was something new in the history of ideas, but the theme of the World Soul was not, although its credentials were less impressive in

27. Frederick H. Burkhardt, in his excellent introduction to Herder, *God, Some Conversations,* trans. and ed. Burkhardt (1940; reprint, Library of Liberal Arts, Indianapolis and New York: Bobbs-Merrill, 1963?), 41.

28. Heine, *Deutschland,* 497–98, 113–14, 499; *Heinrich Heine's Autobiographie: Nach seinen Werken, Briefen und Gesprächen,* ed. Gustav Karpeles (Berlin: Robert Oppenheim, 1888), 524, 544.

Christendom than those of the extramundane deity. In Western thought, Plato's cosmology had in fact allowed for both a Cosmic Artificer and a World Soul, and it is an interesting problem how he intended us to think of the relationship between the two. Similarly, in the religious thought of India the qualified nondualism of Ramanuja represented the physical world and individual souls as together making up the body of Brahman, personalized as Vishnu. And if neither Ramanuja nor even Plato can command the highest authority among Christian theologians, no less a doctor of the church than Thomas Aquinas thought the soul to be in the body as God is in the world, and the Protestant Reformer Ulrich Zwingli could say: "God is in the world what reason is in a human."[29] It is not my wish to collapse important conceptual differences into one vague analogy, but simply to recall, by these few examples, that the *anima mundi* theme had a history before the Pantheism Controversy; it was neither wholly novel nor necessarily heretical. And, of course, other examples of its use could be given.

The first of my two concluding suggestions, that this tradition is not yet exhausted, may be defended for now simply by recalling that one of Charles Hartshorne's early programmatic essays was published under the title "The New Pantheism." He pointed out the advantages of the old pantheism over traditional theism, and then tried to show how the new pantheism could dispose of the disadvantages of the old, which were its inability to secure either human freedom or divine personality and its apparent implication that God must be, on one side of God's nature, material and lifeless. The new pantheism denies an absolute dualism of matter and spirit and proposes that God is related to the world as a human person is related to the *living cells* of her or his own body. God is the whole of things, and the whole is personal.[30]

Over the years, the banner of the process theologians has been wisely changed from "the new pantheism" to "neoclassical theism." But the cardinal points remain the same. In his recent, lusty venture into philosophy of religion for nonspecialists, *Omnipotence and Other Theological Mistakes,* Hartshorne expressly writes of God as the World Soul and continues to recommend the mind-body or person-to-cells analogy over the interpersonal metaphors of God as parent or ruler.[31] A closely similar position is defended in a study published by a British author in the same year as

29. Thomas, ST I, q. 93, art. 3; Zwingli, *De vera et falsa religione commentarius* (1525), chap. 24, CR 90.842.25 (cf. LWZ 3:272).

30. Charles Hartshorne, "The New Pantheism," *Christian Register* 115 (1936): 119–20, 141–43. I am grateful to Schubert Ogden for drawing this article to my attention. As Professor Ogden points out, Hartshorne's "new pantheism" has sought to avoid the substantival monism of Spinoza even while speaking of God as the whole.

31. Hartshorne, *Omnipotence and Other Theological Mistakes* (Albany: State University of New York Press, 1984), 51–63, 78–79, 122–23.

Hartshorne's *Omnipotence.* In *God's World, God's Body,* Grace Jantzen argues that the usual objections to pantheism and the idea of God's embodiment in the world can be overcome, in large part, if theology will follow science and abandon the notion of inert matter as something wholly alien to thought or life. The replacement of the Platonic-Cartesian dualism with a holistic model of human personality calls for a fresh look at the notion of divine personality and divine embodiment. "The model of the universe as God's body," Jantzen concludes, "helps to do justice to the beauty and value of nature, the importance of conservation and ecological responsibility, the significance and dignity of the human body and sexuality." In quite the reverse of Heine's estimate of Christianity, Jantzen maintains that "denigration of the physical is not an option for Christian theology."[32] She may well be right. But the notion of divine embodiment in the world is still strange to most of us; and since Hartshorne does not mention Herder, and Jantzen does not mention either Herder or Hartshorne, there is evidently plenty of room for better communication on the subject.

Finally, what may the speculative turn toward monism imply for the concrete forms of the religious life? Hartshorne and Jantzen both have some interesting insights on the question. But the differences we have had occasion to note between Heine and Herder make it unlikely that we could discover any single religious vision arising out of the Pantheism Controversy, even if the controversy did set diverse thinkers moving along a common metaphysical course toward monism. For my second concluding suggestion, I take my cue only from Herder and return to his conversations on God. Theophron's philosophy—and he no doubt speaks for Herder himself—is "to concern oneself with the inner nature of things as they exist"; what excites him to something like religious wonder is the thought, "Beautiful, beneficent Necessity, under whose all-embracing sway we live! She is a child of highest wisdom, the twin sister of eternal might, the mother of all goodness, blessedness, security, and order." Theano agrees: God's nature, thoughts, activities press upon us as immutable rules in thousand upon thousand proofs of God's order, goodness, and beauty. "He who does not want to follow, must follow. . . . Happy he who follows willingly!"[33]

This is by no means all that Herder has to say about religion, and what he says here, in the *Conversations,* may strike us today as overhasty in identifying order with necessity. But notice, at a somewhat more general level, what his Spinozist inclinations imply for the fundamental religious quest: it is the quest for the place of humanity in the cosmos. Without saying so, Herder moves the religious goal closer to the ancient Chinese ideal

32. Grace Jantzen, *God's World, God's Body* (Philadelphia: Westminster Press, 1984), 122, 148; 4; 156; 9.

33. Herder, *Gott,* 487; 472–73; 563.

of harmony with the forces of nature, or with their underlying principle or way. Although the Taoist sage might find Herder too energetic in searching out the ultimate reality, in their common desire for harmony with nature there is at least a convergence between East and West. The world of sense is no deceptive appearance to be transcended in thought, as in the strict nondualism of the Indian philosopher Sankara; it is a real world, to which we must adjust because it does not exist for our convenience but is simply the product of the Eternal Order.

To find a niche for humanity in the cosmos may sound like an obvious enough formulation of the religious quest. But it was not the quest of the dominant form of piety in Herder's Germany. Protestant Pietism had nurtured an intensely inward, private, emotional religiousness, centered on the ever-repeated experience of guilt and forgiveness. In Herder, at least, to say nothing for now of others, the Spinozist revival was a revolution in spirituality no less than in metaphysics. But might one be able to take the reformulated religious question without the metaphysical monism that suggested it? Even within traditional Protestantism, there had been one reformer for whom the primary religious question was not "How can I get a gracious God?" but "What is the chief end of human life?" Perhaps that other Genevan was led to his answer by his profound sense of awe before the divine "wisdom, justice, goodness, and power" mirrored in created beings. He even thought it possible for a pious mind to say that nature is God, although, as we all know, he was not much inclined to divinize humanity. For him, humanity was not the point at which God came to self-consciousness, but the point at which the creation came to mirror the glory of God in a conscious act of piety.[34] "What is the chief end of human life?" John Calvin answers that God has placed humans in the cosmos to be glorified in them; in this their chief end and their highest good alike consist.[35] And when I read that austere but eloquent answer, I realize that I remain, after all, an honest Calvinist.

34. Calvin, *Inst.*, 1.14.21; 1.5.5. For humanity as the mirror of God's glory, see B. A. Gerrish, *The Old Protestantism and the New: Essays on the Reformation Heritage* (Chicago: University of Chicago Press, Edinburgh: T. & T. Clark, 1982), chap. 9, esp. 154, 159.

35. Calvin, *The Catechism of the Church of Geneva* (1545), qq. 1–3, LCC 22:91.

6

Practical Belief: Friedrich Karl Forberg and the Fictionalist View of Religious Language

It is *not a duty to believe* that a moral world government, or a God as moral governor of the world, exists. It is simply and solely a *duty to act as if you believed it.*

Anthropomorphism is the touchstone of all theology. From the way a theologian deals with it . . . you can confidently deduce whether or not he has his principles straight.
—FRIEDRICH FORBERG

CHRISTIAN THEOLOGIANS have always recognized what John Calvin perceived as a certain "impropriety" in language about God, since nothing at all can be said of the divine majesty except by analogies taken from created things (*nisi similitudine a creaturis mutuo sumpta*).[1] The problem goes back in part to the Bible itself, which, in particular, freely applies *human* characteristics to God while cautioning us that God is God and not a human (Hosea 11:9). Not surprisingly, the way in which the theologians have dealt with the problem of "anthropomorphism," as we call it, has often reflected the prevailing philosophical mentality of their day. Forberg's thoughts on the subject were put together in an atmosphere filled with excitement over the revolutionary ideas of Immanuel Kant. It was an article by Forberg on the concept of religion that sparked the famous Atheism Controversy in 1798, in which, however, he was totally eclipsed by his older colleague and friend Johann Gottlieb Fichte. History has left him in the shadow cast by the greater man. His writings are difficult to obtain, and one scholar who has written on the Atheism Controversy dismisses him as "a philosophical author without philosophical talent" (Fritz Medicus).

More encouraging was the opinion of Hans Vaihinger, who hailed

This essay is from *Probing the Reformed Tradition: Historical Studies in Honor of Edward A. Dowey, Jr.*, ed. Elsie Anne McKee and Brian G. Armstrong (© 1989 Westminster/John Knox Press), 367–85. Used by permission.

1. John Calvin, Comm. Heb. 1:3, CR 83:11–12.

Forberg as a forerunner of fictionalism, or the "philosophy of *as if*." In Vaihinger's view, Forberg was the only person who really understood Kant's as-if doctrine until Vaihinger himself,[2] and on closer inspection, I think, Forberg's application of the as-if formula to religious language can be shown to have philosophical merit. Forberg invoked the formula to shed some light on what he identified as the touchstone of theology: the problem of anthropomorphic language about God. But it will be as well to begin with at least a provisional definition of "fictionalism," and that can perhaps best be done by contrasting "fictionalism" with Calvin's familiar principle of "accommodation."

From Accommodation to Fictionalism

For his solution to biblical anthropomorphism, Calvin turned to an exegetical tradition that went back, beyond medieval scholasticism, at least to Origen of Alexandria (ca. 185–ca. 254). Origen stood in the Platonic line that had already been wedded with the Hebrew Scriptures by Philo Judaeus (ca. 20 B.C.E.–ca. 40 C.E.); he held that the language of the Bible is "accommodated" to our limited human capacities. Calvin adopted the principle of accommodation as a comprehensive understanding of revelation, since revelation can come to us solely by an act of divine condescension that has regard for our human limitations. But I am concerned with the principle here only insofar as it provided him with an easy solution to the problem of anthropomorphism, whenever he encountered it in his biblical texts.

Take, for example, the notion of God's "anger" or "wrath." It is common enough in the Scriptures, and yet we know that we should not attribute human emotions to God. The difficulty is compounded when the Scriptures represent God as angry with the very same persons whom love moves God to save; for here there seems to be a conflict in the mind or heart of God. Calvin disposes of the difficulty (his own confident phrase) by invoking the principle of accommodation. God represents himself to us not as he *is* in himself, but as he *seems* to us. "Anger" is an expression taken from our human experience: when God exercises judgment, he gives the *appearance* of a person whose anger is kindled. And this is how he shows himself even to those for whom Christ died, to impress upon them their desperate need for the redemption Christ provides. God is *perceived as* hostile to them (*quodammodo infestus*), and although this is said by way of accommodation, it is not said falsely.[3]

2. Hans Vaihinger, *Die Philosophie des Als Ob: System der theoretischen, praktischen und religiösen Fiktionen der Menschheit auf Grund eines idealistischen Positivismus*, 9th and 10th eds. (Leipzig: Felix Meiner, 1927), 736, 752 n. 2.

3. Calvin, *Inst.*, 1.17.13, 2.16.2–4.

Calvin goes on to make his point more complicated by agreeing with Augustine that God still loves in us what God has made, but hates what we sinners have made of ourselves. Clearly, this is a quite different way of solving the problem of God's wrath. But we can set it aside and simply conclude that by "accommodation" (in the context of anthropomorphism) is meant God's self-representation in human terms for the sake of practical ends: to control our attitudes and our behavior. And we may add that this hermeneutic device is fully consistent with Calvin's dominant image of God as a devoted parent. Accommodated language—sometimes at least—is a kind of pretending; indeed, revelation in general is childtalk, like the language a nurse uses when playing with a baby.[4]

Now, religious communities are no doubt skilled in making mental adjustments to biblical language without any help from theologians. But one can well imagine the anthropomorphites being troubled even by such modest adjustments as Calvin proposed. For what prevents accommodation from becoming a more or less subtle form of reductionism, which actually loses something that was present in the primary language of faith? Or perhaps the accommodated language still contains *too much,* being in fact no less anthropomorphic than the language it is supposed to interpret. Must it not occur to someone to wonder, sooner or later, whether God is not merely without "body, parts, or passions," but not *properly* a person at all? And will he or she perhaps conclude that the language of faith is not prescribed by God's own authority (as, so to say, authorized childtalk), but rather created, or at least molded, by our infantile human nature, which Calvin himself aptly described as a "factory of idols"?[5] When that happens, "accommodation" passes over into "fictionalism." And it did in fact happen in the wake of the philosophical revolution brought about by Kant.

Perhaps fictionalism could be described as a radicalized accommodation theory; Kant himself expressly appealed to the principle of accommodation.[6] But it is obvious that Kant's attitude to religious language, or religious ideas (as he would say), was quite different from Calvin's in at least two respects. First, Kant's interest was entirely in the way in which the human reason generates the ideas. He was not offering a doctrine of divine revelation, so that, strictly speaking, the term "accommodation" was no longer appropriate. Second, he retained the ideas solely for their practical utility, and not because of their objective referent (if any). The revolutionary theory of knowledge in the *Critique of Pure Reason* (1781) led

4. Ibid., 1.13.1.

5. Ibid., 1.11.8.

6. Immanuel Kant, *Religion within the Limits of Reason Alone,* trans. Theodore M. Greene and Hoyt H. Hudson (1934; reprint, New York: Harper & Brothers, 1960), 58–59n.; cf. 100–105.

him to conclude that the concept of a Supreme Intelligence is a *mere* idea, justified not by its supposed reference to an actual object but by its usefulness to scientific inquiry insofar as it inspires the quest for a single system of empirical knowledge. We should look on every connection in the world *as if* it had its source in a single, all-sufficient, and necessary first cause. Hence Kant was quite happy to consider the idea of God as a purely mental object; and "belief" was his word for entertaining such an idea—that is, acknowledging its practical utility and permitting oneself to be guided by it.[7]

In the *Critique of Practical Reason* (1788) and *Religion within the Limits of Reason Alone* (1793), Kant extended the discussion beyond the domain of science and sought to establish the utility of certain religious ideas, including the idea of God, also to morality and religion itself. But it is not my intention to follow him there. That would require me to take up some of the most hotly contested issues in the renewed Kant scholarship of the present day. I turn instead to Forberg, Kant's lesser German disciple and the supposed forerunner of the fictionalist philosophy that Vaihinger espoused. It is true that Vaihinger's generous compliment to Forberg (the only true interpreter of Kant) was not unqualified. He insisted that he was in no way dependent on Forberg for his understanding of Kant, nor dependent on Kant for the philosophy of as-if, and he said that Forberg's conception of the Kantian as-if doctrine was inconsistent and contradictory. "The appeal to Forberg was, and is, for me," he wrote, "only an incidental chapter in my book. Forberg is for me not an authority but a curiosity."[8] However, undeterred by that slight (the practical utility of which is only too clear), I hope to show that a look at Forberg may help us to sort out some problems that still occupy us. That, I take it, is finally why we read any thinker from the past, not because we seek an authority or a mere historical diversion.

What, then, is the fictionalist theory that Forberg is credited with anticipating? As Vaihinger understands it, the term "fiction" denotes a way of thinking known to be false, or not in accordance with known facts, but retained for the time being because of its usefulness in organizing some aspect of our experience.[9] In other words, if I may venture a paraphrase: To construct a fiction is not to give an imaginative rendering of the way

7. *Immanuel Kant's Critique of Pure Reason,* trans. Norman Kemp Smith (New York: Macmillan, 1933), 549–70, 648–50; cf. 318–20, 614–15.

8. Vaihinger, "Die Philosophie des Als Ob und das Kantische System gegenüber einem Erneuerer des Atheismusstreites," *Kant–Studien* 21 (1917): 1–25; 21.

9. Vaihinger, *Die Philosophie des Als Ob,* 171–75. More exactly, Vaihinger distinguishes two kinds of fiction: "semi-fictions," which deviate from reality, and "real fictions," which are also *self*-contradictory (24, 128–29, 153, 172). A "hypothesis," by contrast, *may* be true and is subject to confirmation or disconfirmation (143–54).

things are, or at least may be, but to create a wholly imaginary object, even an imaginary world, for strictly practical ends. For now, we will take fictionalism in this tough sense, which theologically, of course, is atheistic. My thesis is then twofold: first, that Forberg, although he uses the as-if formula, probably was not a fictionalist at all in Vaihinger's sense; second, that the agnostic position he advocated left him on the threshold of a fresh venture into philosophical theology—that is, a fresh attempt to represent the real world rather than to create another. The way to this double conclusion leads through a brief look at the three most pertinent sources: his autobiography, his article that sparked the Atheism Controversy, and his defense against his accusers.

The Career of a Missing Person

Forberg's autobiography, written when he was approaching his seventieth birthday, is a sprightly document of uncommon personal and historical interest despite its brevity (it is only sixty-one pages long).[10] Charming, witty, and often mischievous, he keeps the reader entertained while opening up one corner of eighteenth-century German society at the time of the French Revolution. The excitement of the intelligentsia over Kant's publications is vividly illustrated in an account of discussions held in the residence of Baron Franz Paul von Herbert (1759–1811). Forberg notes the presence of two young ladies, the sisters von Drer, who were Roman Catholic. Since their parents were bigots (as Forberg candidly puts it), the sisters were not permitted to discuss the critical philosophy at home. Ingeniously, they had copies of Kant's forbidden books specially bound in black and took them to Mass with them instead of their missals. Of one of the two sisters, Babette, the aging Forberg says that he still preserves a silhouette of her in his family album and preserves her memory in his heart.

The information given in the autobiography appears to be meticulously accurate: Forberg recalls minute details, gives exact dates, and reports in quotation marks precisely what (he claims) was said. He must surely have kept a diary. For my purposes, what is important is the context he provides for understanding his alleged atheism. He writes as an eighteenth-century "alienated theologian" (to borrow Van Harvey's expression). Brought up in a clergyman's household and himself destined for the Lutheran ministry, he becomes increasingly indifferent to conventional religion. He is captivated by the new philosophy, becomes embroiled in public controversy, renounces even the vocation of the philosopher, and passes quietly from the academic scene. Forberg titled his autobiography *Career of a Miss-*

10. Friedrich Carl Forberg, *Lebenslauf eines Verschollenen* (Hildburghausen and Meiningen: Kesselring, 1840). All translations from Forberg are mine, unless otherwise indicated.

ing Person. (The German word has the legal sense of "pronounced missing" or even "presumed dead.") Whether there is a trace of bitterness in his chosen title, I am not sure. There seems to have been no special occasion for writing—just the sense, perhaps, that time was running out.

His mother, Forberg tells us, was of the melancholic type and very devout. Steeped in pietistic literature, she worried that she was not sufficiently conscious of her sins. "She thought amazingly highly of the Lord Jesus, as she always called him. He was supposed to help her in every need, and in comparison God receded, so to say, into the background of her heart." The father, by contrast, was choleric: short-tempered, but quickly over it. Basically he was orthodox, yet no bigot. Though he spoke disparagingly of Voltaire (1694–1778) and Jean-Jacques Rousseau, their portraits were displayed prominently in the hall. And in later years, Forberg recalls, his father admitted that he did not accept the orthodox belief in immortality. His popular sermons were biblical and—to arouse attention—humorous, although in those days it did not occur to anyone to laugh.

The burden of Forberg's early education fell mostly on his father, who set great store by memory work. Forberg was required to learn a host of biblical passages without any explanation, albeit many of them would have profited from explanation. He professes to have been puzzled, for instance, by a verse from Psalm 147 that was prayed every day at table: "The Lord has no delight in the strength of the horse, and no pleasure in anyone's legs" (v. 10). But then, in 1782, the father had the happy idea of buying Johann Gottfried Eichhorn's (1752–1827) introduction to the Old Testament—"an event," Forberg says, "that marked an epoch in my life." He had been struggling to understand how the Bible could possibly be a divine revelation. Some of the stories it related—Joshua's commanding the sun to stand still, the Devil's conversation with Jesus, and so on—were simply incredible. "But if I rejected one [such story], then the credibility of them all collapsed, and with it the credibility of the Bible as divine revelation." Eichhorn said nothing about revelation, and Forberg began to reconceive of the Bible as literature—a very remarkable library of ancient writings, in which the cultivated reader can trace the origins of certain influential ideas. To begin with, Forberg continued to believe in a revelation *in* the Bible (as the theologians of the time liked to say). "But soon the sun of philosophy was to eradicate from my soul even this last vestige of the old faith."

His love of philosophy was first sparked when Forberg became a student, four years later (1786), at the University of Leipzig. Still intending an ecclesiastical career, he studied theological subjects and went to church. (He recalls that later he himself preached occasionally in Jena.) But the skeptical philosopher Ernst Platner (1744–1818) turned his interest to philosophy, and when Forberg moved on to the University of Jena (1788) he discovered Kant in the classroom of Karl Leonhard Reinhold (1758–1823). "Actually," he says, "I had no desire to study Kantian philosophy. As a pupil of Platner's, I was a strict determinist and eudaemonist, and I was downright shocked when in that class Reinhold spoke of the moral law."

The vividness with which Forberg writes of his relationship with Reinhold is one of the most intriguing features of his narrative. He remembers as though it were yesterday the day when a contemptuous review of one of Reinhold's publications arrived in Jena. With tears in his eyes and speaking in a subdued tone that was quite unlike him, Reinhold gathered his students around him and produced letters in which other scholars had praised his writings; and Forberg was directed to read aloud from them to the embarrassed company. But I must be content to draw attention to just two points in Forberg's reminiscences about Reinhold. First, he represents himself as becoming—in contrast to Reinhold—a genuine Kantian, or at least an authentic interpreter of Kant. Second, he tells of a day in 1792 when Reinhold asked him bluntly: "Are you still a Christian?" Forberg replied that if Christianity is taken to be "nothing but a kind of philosophical morality," he had never stopped being Christian, but he did not feel any need for a Christian revelation. And Reinhold was silent.

By this time, Forberg had become Reinhold's junior colleague: he had begun his first course of lectures in philosophy the previous autumn (on 24 October 1791, as he records with his usual precision). But in 1794 Reinhold left Jena, and amid high expectations Fichte arrived as his successor. Another series of fascinating reminiscences begins in Forberg's autobiography. Once again, only the essentials (for my present purpose) can be noted. Forberg had shown no very deep respect for Reinhold, whose attempts to correct Kant struck him as muddleheaded. Reinhold was not even capable of explaining the difficulties in his own thought, let alone Kant's, and in response to persistent questions he became grouchy. Fichte, by contrast, was a philosophical genius of the highest order—and an immensely powerful personality. He made something original out of Kant's transcendental idealism and proclaimed it with an eloquence that was hard to resist. Forberg was overwhelmed, though I assume no humor is intended when he says that he argued constantly about Fichte's absolute ego. He tired of hearing his students recite the jargon of the latest philosophy; with the modicum of philosophical talent that nature had bestowed on him, he says, he was no match for these transcendental heroes. His classroom was emptied by the genius and eloquence of the greater man, and Forberg decided to move on.

He did try to put together some critical reflections on "the most recent philosophy" (i.e., Fichte's) and asked Fichte what he thought of them. The reply was: "A waste of good paper." But Forberg took no offense. "Fichte," he says, "was an open, straightforward man, who said everything in such a way and with such a look and tone that it was impossible to be angry with him." From Saalfeld, where in 1797 he had been elected assistant superintendent of a high school, he sent Fichte a token of his undeterred interest in philosophy: it was the article that precipitated the Atheism Controversy, "Development of the Concept of Religion" (1798). The content of the article will occupy my next section; the history of the Atheism Controversy belongs elsewhere. But there are at least two points made in the autobiography that should be stressed here.

First, Forberg tells us expressly what he was trying to do in the article: "My purpose was actually to give a more admissible sense to Kant's practical belief, which had long ceased to satisfy me." Unfortunately, we are left to guess for ourselves *why* he found Kant's notion of practical belief unsatisfactory. But I think we can do so from the article itself and from the subsequent apology.

Second, Forberg is perfectly candid in admitting the implications of his argument:

> If by "God" one means the usual notion of an extramundane, substantial, personal being that created and governs the world by understanding and will, then our doctrine was certainly atheistic, and our accusers were perfectly right. Against the accusation, we could only reply in our defense that we took the concept of God in a totally different sense, which the public at large could not comprehend, and in this sense acknowledged a God. And that is what we did. But we convinced no one of our innocence, and once there was talk of indictment, we could not really expect anything else.[11]

The "we" in this passage is intended to include Fichte. But Fichte's position was different from Forberg's, and so was his personality. Forberg thought the official censure fair enough and accepted it without complaint. Fichte warned in advance that if the state ventured to reprimand him, he would resign.

> This [Forberg comments] was not taken kindly in Weimar. With the censure, Fichte was given his dismissal at the same time. "Why did you do that?" I asked him when I spoke with him soon after in Jena. "You could have remained as quietly in your post as I in mine." "If I were Parmenio," he replied [i.e., if *he* were the second-rate man], "that is what I would have done. But because I am Alexander [Alexander the Great], I could not." "You are right," I said, "and basically I am happy with that. Germany will never forget you." Since then, I never saw him again.[12]

11. Ibid., 54–55. In actual fact, Forberg's position had less to do with the concept of God than with the logical status of the concept.

12. Ibid., 55.

The forgotten member of the team was unhappy at Saalfeld, even though he was promoted to the senior position of superintendent. He felt isolated, and teaching youngsters did not press him intellectually. Enrollment declined, as word of his unorthodoxy spread. But he could not give up his ideas, he said, even if he wanted to: they were his existence. In 1801 he moved to Coburg, where he became curator of the ducal library and did the one thing for which he is not *quite* forgotten: he gathered an extensive collection of erotic texts from Latin, Greek, and other literatures, and furnished it with illustrations. In the preface he explains: "These trifles engaged our attention first as a mere pastime. We were led to them accidentally, as we roamed from subject to subject, for Philosophy, the garden we had hoped to set up our tent in for life, lies desolate."[13]

There I must leave Forberg's autobiography. It has revealed a man untroubled by those boundary experiences—feelings of guilt, insignificance, and dread—that afflict many who turn to religion, and he therefore had no understanding of the longing for a word from beyond. But, somewhat to his own surprise, he did come to appreciate Kant's sense of a moral imperative, and he tried to understand it within the total system of the critical philosophy. He wanted to be, unlike Reinhold, a sound interpreter of Kant; he also wanted to improve on Kant, though in a way quite different from the path taken by Fichte. What does such a person make of religion? The answer lies in Forberg's controversial essay, "Development of the Concept of Religion," published in 1798. Regrettably, the answer is not unambiguous. But I can turn for further help to Forberg's own commentary: the apology for his alleged atheism, published the following year.

Religion as Practical Belief

In an earlier paper, I conceded the ambiguities in Forberg's article but tried to show that his argument, though slippery, was not hopelessly confused.[14] He himself, it must be admitted, did little to encourage the reader to exercise charity, or even to take him seriously. At the end of the article, he added a series of what he called "captious questions," written, as he confessed in his autobiography, out of youthful devilry. The last question asks in effect: Are you kidding? And Forberg's answer is that he will leave it to the reader to decide. In his *Apology,* he noted that anyone who wished to keep some things sacred and safe from humor had better forsake philosophy and go to church and pray. But there was, of course, a serious motive

13. Fred. Chas. Forberg, *Manual of Classical Erotology* (*De figuris Veneris*), Latin text and Eng. trans. by Julian Smithson (1884; facsimile ed., 2 vols. in 1, New York: Grove, 1966), 5.

14. The earlier paper has not been published, but it has had a limited circulation and will eventually become—with revisions—part of an as-yet unfinished study I am engaged in, to be titled *Anima Mundi: The Debate about God in the Time of Goethe.*

behind all the mischief: he wanted to jolt his readers, if possible, into actually *thinking* about the assumptions of conventional piety. The charitable course is to oblige him by trying to follow his argument.

The aim of the article is clear enough: Forberg wants a new concept of religion that will preserve continuity with the old and yet be free from all the problems of belief in supernatural beings.[15] His task invites confusion, because the old connotations of the words "religion" and "belief" continually return. But the main drift of his argument is by no means unclear. His fundamental definitions of "religion" and "God" sound simple enough: "religion" is "a practical belief in a moral world government," and by "God" he means "the exalted Spirit who governs the world according to moral laws." Forberg explains that if the way the world goes is calculated to procure the final success of goodness, then there is a moral world government; otherwise, there is not. Hence he has no difficulty appropriating the hallowed biblical language of a "kingdom of God" that is to come on earth.

The difficulties begin when Forberg asks: But *will* the kingdom come? Is it a possible goal, or is it an illusion? He has so set up the question that if the kingdom will not come, it follows that there is no moral world government. But his attempt to answer his own question generates three formulas that do not at first seem to be identical in meaning. He variously says that the good person ought either (1) to *believe* that virtue will triumph, or (2) to *act as if* virtue will triumph, or (3) to *act as if he or she had decided* that virtue will triumph. The ambiguity can be resolved, or almost resolved, if we notice that for Forberg *practical* belief *is* "acting as if." *Theoretical,* or (as we might say) "factual," belief is simply immaterial to this purely practical belief, which is the content of the new religion. As practical belief, religion is commitment to the good, whatever the prospect. Moral commitment is not (theoretically) *believing that* the kingdom will come but (practically) *acting as if* the kingdom were coming. Such indications as Forberg gives suggest that he held an eventual triumph of goodness to be uncertain, even unlikely. But factual belief and factual disbelief in the coming of the kingdom are idle speculation anyhow: they just do not matter to genuine religion. That is the essential point. Forberg saves religion for the educated classes by making it logically independent of claims about the coming of the kingdom, or even claims about the existence of God.

I had to admit, however, in my earlier paper, that even the consistency obtained by taking "practical belief" and "acting as if" to be synonymous

15. Forberg's article, "Entwickelung des Begriffs der Religion," first published in *Philosophisches Journal* 8 (1798): 21–46, is most conveniently accessible in Hans Lindau, ed., *Die Schriften zu J. G. Fichte's Atheismus-Streit* (Munich: Georg Müller, 1912), 37–58.

is jeopardized by the occasional intrusion of what looks like a factual residuum in Forberg's religion. In one place, for instance, he asserts that belief is "the maxim to work for the promotion of good *at least as long as* the impossibility of success has not been clearly proved."[16] Quite what such a proof would look like, he does not say. But it certainly appears that at this point Forberg's practical belief entails a genuine, if very timid, factual claim.

Does the *Apology* dispose of this last vestige of theoretical belief in Forberg's religion? I think it does, although it is not totally free from conceptual problems of its own. At least it reinforces Forberg's basic Kantian strategy of locating religious discourse in the language of morals. And it does something more that is equally Kantian: having shown that morals cannot *rest on* religious belief as usually understood, Forberg shows how naturally, indeed inevitably (so he thinks), the moral disposition *gives rise to* factual religious beliefs. In his opinion, the assured result of philosophical discussions over the previous two decades is that belief in God cannot be the foundation of morality; rather must morality be the foundation of belief in God.[17] It is this twofold movement of thought that I want to draw out.

First, then, Forberg insists that duty is something absolute, unconditioned, grounded wholly in itself. "One ought because one ought, not because one wants something else, nor because God wants it."[18] A good man, he says, can do his duty as husband, father, or friend just as conscientiously if he holds another explanation of phenomena to be more probable than theism, or even if he prefers not to commit himself to any explanation at all. Forberg had been accused of undermining the morals of students by teaching atheism. His accusers had argued that the only sure way to keep young people virtuous is by holding before them the picture of the divine Judge, who will one day reward the good and punish the wicked. He rejects the charge of atheism, but thinks that an attack of atheism is no bad thing if it helps us to see whether we really are moral. He writes: "A mild attack of theoretical atheism is accordingly something everyone should actually wish to have at least once in his lifetime, to make an experiment on his own heart: to see whether it wills the good for its own sake, as it should, or solely for the sake of some advantage to be expected—if not in this world, then in another."[19] In short, if we cannot act rightly without the factual claims of conventional religion, then religion (in this sense) is the

16. Ibid., 55 (my emphasis).

17. *Friedrich Carl Forbergs der Philosophie Doctors und des Lyceums zu Saalfeld Rectors Apologie seines angeblichen Atheismus* (Gotha: Justus Perthes, 1799), 8.

18. Ibid., 22, 25.

19. Ibid., 35–36.

clearest proof of human corruption: it is powerless to create a genuinely moral disposition.

Conversely, the moral imperative shines most brightly when we do what we ought even if convinced that the world will remain eternally a world of utter rogues and idiots, as hitherto. And if some misanthrope, his gloomy disposition confirmed by experience of human falsehood and stupidity, were to ridicule all hope of a golden age to come *and yet* still acted consistently for the common good, his would be a true and genuine religious disposition. "Religion is not (theoretical) belief that a kingdom of God is coming. The endeavor to make it come *even if* one believes that it will never come—this, and this alone, is religion."[20]

In sum: Forberg's first argument is that because genuine religion is heeding the moral imperative, religion, like the imperative itself, is autonomous. There is nothing more to be said than simply, "I ought because I ought." Nothing at all is added to the moral imperative by asserting that there is a moral order, that its foundation is the will of God, or that virtue will triumph in the end. The point is a strictly logical one: Factual assertions belong in a different class than moral demands. It is therefore a matter of total indifference, as far as the moral imperative itself is concerned, whether or not one adopts a theistic worldview: whether one thinks the ultimate success of goodness likely, unlikely, barely possible, or an utter illusion. For, Forberg asks in an eloquent passage:

> What if there were no goal to attain, or—and for the athlete this is the same thing—only a goal at an infinite distance? What if the race were not for the goal, but a goal were supposed for the sake of the race . . . ? What if the commandment of reason by no means had the sense of running *in order to* reach the goal (which is the common good), but only *as if* one wanted to reach it?[21]

That, however, is only the first cadence in Forberg's movement of thought. Second, he recognizes in the *Apology* (though not in his original article) that genuine religion, while not itself theoretical belief, invites or even logically *demands* theoretical belief. The strictly practical belief of Kantian religion is then transformed into *theology*, something that religion as such has not the slightest need to bother itself with.[22] We can fairly paraphrase his point, I think, if we say that while the immediate deliverances of conscience can only be stated as "maxims" or rules of conduct, not as factual assertions, the deliverances of conscience are themselves quite remarkable facts, and as such they invite reflection.

20. Ibid., 160–63 (my emphasis); cf. 105.
21. Ibid., 141–43.
22. Ibid., 91–92, 133; cf. 119–20, 134–35, 164.

Perhaps Forberg makes the point best when he suggests that acknowledgment of the moral law *appears,* in reflection, as acknowledgment of a deity. Morally disposed individuals do not need to become explicitly conscious of the concept of deity, but they would be if they stopped to think about it. Hence Forberg rests his case in these words:

> I do not understand how I would have to express myself to escape the reproach of atheism. I teach that at a certain point of speculation the moral disposition unavoidably appears as belief in a moral world order, hence also as a belief in a *principle* of this moral world order. I conceive of this principle as a *supreme intelligence,* as an almighty, omniscient, holy being. My God is the God of the Christians.[23]

By way of commentary on this interesting defense, let me go back for a moment to Forberg's misanthrope. On the one hand, the misanthrope's total cynicism about his fellow humans is exactly what enables his moral disposition to shine so brightly, because he is resolved to do what is right anyway, even in a world full of rogues and idiots. His morals are impeccable. But there now appears to be some question about his intelligence, if he does not stop to think about his astonishing commitment to virtue. If he did, the grounds for his cynicism ought to vanish. Whatever the present appearance of human wickedness around him, reflection on the moral imperative within should convince him that he is not just doing his duty but affirming a moral order, the condition for the possibility of which is what is meant by "God." The moral disposition, it seems, is most clearly revealed in doubt, but the moral disposition itself tends to generate (theoretical) belief. This, I admit, is not expressly how Forberg puts it; he leaves his misanthrope doubting and grimly doing his duty. But I think I am only drawing out Forberg's own argument.

"Theology"—or, as he sometimes says, "*moral* theology"—is Forberg's word for reflection on genuine religion, or practical belief, or the moral disposition (these three being understood as identical). It is the theologian's task to draw out the concept of God implicit in the concept of morality and to find appropriate ways of representing it. Like Kant, Forberg will not admit that we can (strictly speaking) have knowledge of God. We can, however, find suitable analogies or symbols, not for picturing God, but for representing the relationship of the Unknown to its effects. And since the Unknown is the principle of *moral* effects, no other analogies are open to us than those taken from human life. All theology is therefore bound to be anthropomorphism, and we should not deceive ourselves

23. Ibid., 127–30, 136. The expression "appears as" may be considered another example of Forberg's elusiveness, perhaps even evasiveness. But he certainly must mean *theoretical* belief in this passage; and it is speculation he is talking about, not just wishful thinking. The "appearing as" is purely the result of conceptual analysis (157).

with the hope of removing everything human from the concept of God. "This, by the way," Forberg adds, "is no new doctrine. . . . I admit that we receive only a *symbol* of a principle, unknown in itself, of the moral course of the world. But have not all theologians, from time immemorial, admitted this?"[24] Well, it is hard to see how Calvin, at least, could disagree with Forberg here, since Calvin states it as a fundamental principle that we should not ask what God is in himself, but what he is like, or how he is disposed, to us.[25]

Toward a Moral Theology

My reading of Forberg's *Apology* has left out some intricate features of his argument, such as the interesting distinction he draws between logical and real possibility. But I believe I have shown, without oversimplification (or willful suppression of any pertinent evidence), that his essential case is fairly represented as twofold, and it is this that justifies my own twofold thesis. His practical, as-if belief denies not the existence of a moral order or God, but only the moral pertinence of theoretical belief in them. Hence it was still possible for him, having blocked the route from factual to practical belief, to concede that there is a one-way path in the other direction. Forberg, I conclude, was not a fictionalist in Vaihinger's sense, using modes of thought known to be false; he left the door open to theological hypotheses that may possibly be true.

Vaihinger, of course, noted the many passages in which Forberg's thought sounded agnostic rather than atheistic. But there is no need to infer that Forberg's thinking must therefore have fallen apart into two incompatible doctrines. Two versions of the as-if doctrine, Vaihinger held, lay side by side unreconciled in Forberg's article and defense: a moderate or weaker version, which was agnostic, and a radical version, which—like Vaihinger's own philosophy—was positivistic and pessimistic. The inconsistency was present, he thought, in both the original article and the subsequent apology, but on the whole he saw Forberg making good progress from the weaker to the more radical doctrine: that is, from agnosticism to the fictionalism that knows its fictions are untrue.

In actual fact, it seems to me, Forberg's case is fundamentally consistent throughout, but becomes more clearly nonfictionalist in the later work. What I have characterized as his second logical move emerges only in the defense. In the article, factual belief was said to arise from the *wish* of the good heart; in the apology, it arises also out of *reflection*. But in neither of the two sources is theoretical belief said to be false. Nowhere have I been

24. Ibid., 132–58; quotations on 154, 156. On the difference between a picture and a symbol, see 168–69.

25. Calvin, *Inst.*, 1.2.2, 10.2; 3.2.6.

able to discover evidence for Vaihinger's blunt assertion that "Forberg unequivocally denies the existence of a moral world order."[26] Forberg's point, in the first part of his argument, is that *even if* there is no moral order, that makes no difference to the moral obligation in which genuine religion consists. Vaihinger, by contrast, wanted Forberg to say that I should act as if there were a moral order *although,* in fact, there is not.[27] He transformed the "even if" (*selbst wenn*) into an "although" (*obgleich*). Consequently, he had no interest in the second part of Forberg's argument but thought that for him the concept of a moral order was a mere "accidental way of looking at things" (*eine zufällige Betrachtungsweise*).[28] "Only . . . morality," he says, "is certain, not the moral world order."[29] But Forberg says rather, much more strongly, that the concept of morality *appears as* the concept of a moral order in reflection—inevitably.

It remains entirely possible that in his heart Forberg was a devious atheist. But the historian has only the texts to go by, and what Forberg actually says points toward what he called a "moral theology": not a casuistic theology that tells us *what we ought to do,* but a philosophical theology that reflects on the interesting fact that to be human is, among other things, to feel *that one ought.* If Forberg was right, so to feel is tantamount to believing that humans live in a moral order, and he was therefore willing to admit that we should acknowledge moral order as our distinctively human element.[30] This is the factual or theoretical belief that practical belief leads to, but in no sense needs. And the problem of anthropomorphism is solved in this moral theology by the argument that God-talk is talk about the moral order, or about the principle of its possibility. For there is no other way in which we can conceive of the activity of this unknown principle than by analogy with human moral agency like our own.

His conception of moral theology, borrowed from Kant, was cer-

26. Vaihinger, *Die Philosophie des Als Ob,* 751. Vaihinger understands Forberg's use of the expression *als ob* to mean that for him the moral world order was only a fiction (ibid.; cf. 748). But that is not what Forberg said. He did think that theology could deduce from the moral consciousness only the *thought* of God (*Apologie,* 157), or the *idea* of a kingdom of God (138–39), and he certainly wanted to guard against the illusion that symbolic language about God is literal (149–50). That, however, is not to deny the existence of the moral order or its principle, nor does it follow that for him symbolic language was nonreferential—as the fictionalist position maintains.

27. Ibid., 751.

28. Ibid., 752. What is "accidental," according to Forberg, is *whether* the morally disposed individual decides to reflect or speculate; *if* he or she does, theoretical belief follows infallibly (*Apologie,* 130). This, of course, does not make any particular speculation infallibly correct; speculation is "accidental" also in the sense that systems come and go like fashions in clothing (20, 91). Nevertheless, speculation is answerable before the forum of logic (111–12). Forberg takes it seriously as an intellectual enterprise.

29. Vaihinger, *Die Philosophie des Als Ob,* 746.

30. Forberg, *Apologie,* 145.

tainly not the main burden of Forberg's writing. The fact that he devotes a large section of his *Apology* to it is, in a way, ironic. The reason why he first wrote about Kant's notion of practical belief (in his article on the concept of religion) was that it seemed to provide comfort for those who wished to claim theoretic knowledge of God even after the collapse of the traditional proofs of God's existence. They wanted, as Forberg puts it, to bring back all kinds of nonsense through the back door. His aim was to insulate Kant's notion of practical belief from the abuse to which it was liable.[31] It is all the more remarkable, then, that—on second thought—he found the notion of a moral theology at least viable. Obviously, however, one has to be careful to stress his insistence that moral theology cannot strictly give knowledge of God, and that it belongs to the domain of speculation rather than religion. Indeed, he remained skeptical whether *any* speculative explanations ever really explain things.[32] He remained, in short, an agnostic who looked through the doorway of moral theology but was not much interested in going in.

To criticize, or to correct, or to defend Forberg's conception of a moral theology would require another essay—in the constructive, rather than the historical, mode. It is enough to have shown it as part of a philosophical scheme that has the merit of greater coherence than has previously been recognized and, to this extent, may help in the identification of perennial issues in philosophical theology. I may as well admit that the theologian in me does think that the idea of a moral theology still has possibilities. But the task calls for historical circumspection as well as philosophical wit. I have been at pains to show how the idea arose out of a particular stage in the history of Western philosophy. Forberg's confidence in the assured results of two decades of philosophical discussion proved, like everything else in history, to be transient. The moral law would have to be defended, these days, against subjectivist interpretations of moral experience. In 1943, C. S. Lewis (1898–1963) could still end a talk on right and wrong as a clue to the meaning of the universe with this expansive conclusion:

> These, then, are the two points I wanted to make. First, that human beings, all over the earth, have this curious idea that they ought to behave in a certain way, and cannot really get rid of it. Secondly, that they do not in fact behave in that way. They know the Law of Nature; they break it. These two facts are the foundation of all clear thinking about ourselves and the universe we live in.[33]

31. Ibid., 175–77; cf. 95–98, 110–11.

32. Ibid., 26–27, 96–97, 112.

33. C[live] S. Lewis, *Mere Christianity* (New York: Macmillan, 1954), 7. The talk was first published in 1943.

Too expansive, perhaps! Still, Lewis's remarks reflect part of the permanent legacy of the Kantian philosophy: the recognition that the sense of moral obligation is at least *one* clue to the remarkable cosmic experiment going on in *one* small corner of the universe.[34]

34. See the famous conclusion to Kant, *Critique of Practical Reason,* trans. Lewis White Beck (New York: Liberal Arts, 1956), 166–68. See further B. A. Gerrish, "Toward a Moral Theology: Forberg on Practical Belief," *Criterion* 29 (1990): 10–13.

Part Three

SCHLEIERMACHER

7

Friedrich Schleiermacher (1768–1834)

THE PUBLICATION of Schleiermacher's anonymous book *On Religion: Speeches to Its Cultured Despisers* (1799) has been hailed as the birth of a new theological era. But even his friends found it, in some respects, a puzzling work. Friedrich Schlegel (1772–1829), for instance, as we know from an amusing letter of Schleiermacher to Henriette Herz (19 June 1799), demanded to know where the new author's "center" was. Over the years, as the first book grew into the collected works, the answer to Schlegel's question did not become any easier. And yet it is obviously crucial for any attempt to sum up Schleiermacher's lifetime achievement. The task calls, not for an inventory of all his writings and ideas, but for the courage to single out dominant motifs that seem to determine, if by no means to exhaust, the thoughts that have to be left out.

A Pietist of a Higher Order

As the first division of the collected works indicates (it was planned in thirteen volumes, of which eleven were published), Schleiermacher concerned himself with virtually every branch of theological studies except Old Testament. There are titles on philosophy of religion, systematic theology, New Testament, church history, Christian ethics, and practical theology. He was, besides, a busy preacher, and the entire second division of the works consists of ten further volumes of sermons. The third division, titled "Philosophy" (in nine volumes), embraces studies in the history of philosophy; in dialectic (epistemology and metaphysics), ethics, politics, psychology, aesthetics; in philology and education. In addition, Schleiermacher was an amazingly prolific letter-writer and—through his labors on Plato's dialogues—one of Germany's most eminent classical scholars. Although much more still remains in unpublished manuscripts, it is a formidable corpus; and it is not difficult to understand why he was accused of carrying on his private education in public. Even so, to represent him only as a preacher and a professor would still be to miss his full significance as a public figure in church, academy, and nation.

If, however, one's interest is not in the man as such but in his contribution to religious studies, there can hardly be any doubt where his significance is to be sought: in the determination and skill with which he took up again the specifically *dogmatic* task. He lavished immense care on the publication of his dogmatics, whereas his philosophy survives largely in the form of unpublished lectures; and the manuscripts of his *Dialectic* betray the fact that philosophically he had difficulty in making up his mind. His dogmatics remained, in his own estimate at least, independent of philosophical influences. True, it can be fully understood only from its place in a total theory of the sciences, and the content he gave to it brought the subject closer to what we should today call the "humanistic study of religion." Indeed, Schleiermacher's theology exercised a powerful influence on the development of self-consciously nontheological ways of studying religion that do not always admit their parentage. His dogmatics was neither narrow nor conventional. But it *was* dogmatics. He took up once more an enterprise that had languished in the Age of Reason, and he developed it in ways that quietly acknowledged the impossibility of older models.

The result was a reconstruction of the theological tradition so brilliant and subtle that one does not know which to marvel at more: the startling creativeness of his innovations or the ingenuity of his carefully forged links with the past. For sustained systematic power and intellectual penetration, his dogmatic masterpiece *The Christian Faith* (1821–22; 2d ed., 1830–31) is unsurpassed in Christian theological literature. Anyone sufficiently familiar with both will be struck by the parallels between Schleiermacher's *Glaubenslehre* (as he liked to call it) and Calvin's 1559 *Institutio*. But the classical Reformation system is more loosely organized; and if Calvin's rigor is sometimes sacrificed to his rhetoric, it must also be admitted that the artistry of his design suffered from his inability to ignore his opponents. Perhaps it is only with the much earlier masterpiece of Western theology, the *Summa Theologiae* of Thomas Aquinas, that the *Glaubenslehre* can be justly compared. At any rate, this—from the other side, so to say—was the verdict pronounced by Johannes Evangelist von Kuhn (1806–87), of the Catholic Tübingen School, who wrote: "Among all the later and present-day theologians, only Schleiermacher can be compared with him [Thomas] as far as scientific force and power are concerned."[1]

No summary account of a work so densely packed as *The Christian Faith* can possibly do it justice. But I may take my bearings from Schleiermacher's own remarks in his oft-cited letter to F. H. Jacobi (30 March 1818). The philosopher had described himself as a pagan in intellect but a

1. Quoted from the *Tübinger theologische Quartalschrift* (1839) by Robert Stalder, whose *Grundlinien der Theologie Schleiermachers* has been undertaken to justify "in some measure" von Kuhn's estimate. See vol. 1, Veröffentlichungen des Instituts für Europäische Geschichte Mainz, vol. 53 (Wiesbaden: Franz Steiner, 1969), ix. Translations in this chapter are mine unless otherwise stated.

Christian in feeling. To Schleiermacher, this was a confusion of categories. Paganism and Christianity, he insists, can run into conflict only in the same sphere, the sphere of religion; and religion (or, better, "religiousness") is a matter of feeling. All the intellect can do is to reflect on this feeling and interpret it. If Jacobi's feeling is Christian, how can his intellect put a pagan interpretation on it? Rather than any such conflict of feeling and intellect, Schleiermacher wants to speak of nothing more than a "polarity." Jacobi's metaphor for his predicament was of two bodies of water that never come together. Schleiermacher cheerfully accepts the separation but changes the metaphor, for the things that are here separated belong indispensably together in a "galvanic pile," in the operation of which the innermost life of the human spirit consists.[2] In Schleiermacher's own experience, the religious feeling remained relatively constant; what changed was his explication of it. Consequently, if conflict is plainly to be read in his early biography, it can in principle have been only a conflict between old interpretations and new as he sought to attune two sides of his personality.

The contrast drawn in Schleiermacher's response to Jacobi was correctly specified by A. E. Biedermann (1819–85). What one might expect as the companion of deep religious feeling (*Gefühl*), he points out, is speculative profundity; but what one finds in Schleiermacher is keenness of intellect (*Verstand*), turned in critical inquiry precisely upon the center of his feeling. Biedermann is again exactly right when he says that, if religion was the center of Schleiermacher's feeling, it took the quite specific form of a *Heilandsliebe* ("love of the Savior"), given to him from beyond anything the human spirit could generate for itself. At least, that was Schleiermacher's own judgment: the fact that he took the unusual risk of subjecting so delicate an experience to critical scrutiny was what made him, as he said of himself, a "pietist (*Herrnhuter*) of a higher order." Or, as Biedermann puts it, it was the union in him of two strikingly different characteristics, commonly encountered separately in sharply antithetical individuals, that made Schleiermacher the "regenerator of modern theology."[3]

Perhaps the mystery of Schleiermacher's center is not incorrectly resolved, then, if one locates it in a distinctive type of Christian sensibility—but only if one immediately adds that this center stands in a kind of dialectical tension with his critical intellect. It is easy to see why Schleiermacher writes to Jacobi, not about his "center," but about "the two foci of my own ellipse." Furthermore, the Christian sensibility itself, as he sees it, is not

2. The original text of the letter has been reissued by Martin Cordes in "Der Brief Schleiermachers an Jacobi: Ein Beitrag zu seiner Enstehung und Überlieferung," *Zeitschrift für Theologie und Kirche* 68 (1971): 195–212.

3. Alois Emanuel Biedermann, "Schleiermacher," *Ausgewählte Vorträge und Aufsätze*, ed. J. Kradolfer (Berlin: Georg Reimer, 1885), 188–91, 197–98.

simple but compounded of two elements. It is clear that for Schleiermacher an awareness of God is a datum of human consciousness as such: all it takes to recognize it is "a little introspection."[4] What remains axiomatic for him, on the other hand, is that in the specifically Christian awareness of God everything is related to the redemption accomplished by Jesus of Nazareth (*Gl.*, § 11). Whatever may be the exigencies of abstract exposition, in the actual life of the Christian there is a mutual penetration of two moments, a "general God-consciousness" and a "relation to Christ," neither of which is reducible to the other (*Gl.*, § 62.3). Hence I may fairly concentrate my exposition on these two themes. And this will once again have the merit of corresponding closely with Schleiermacher's own remarks to Jacobi.

His goal, he remarks, though never finally attainable, is simply to comprehend the deliverances of the Christian consciousness and to find their place alongside other regions of human experience.

> If, then, my Christian feeling is conscious of a Divine Spirit in me that is something other than my reason, I will never give up searching for it in the deepest depths of the nature of the soul. And if my Christian feeling becomes conscious of a Son of God who differs from the best of us otherwise than by a "better still," I will never cease to search for the begetting of this Son of God in the deepest depths of nature and to tell myself I shall as soon comprehend the Second Adam as the first Adam, or first Adams, whom I must likewise accept without comprehending them.[5]

To a quite remarkable degree, this confession summarizes the theological quest of a lifetime. The reflective activity of the intellect upon religiousness Schleiermacher calls, in the same passage, "dogmatics"; what it seeks to interpret, if it is a Christian dogmatics, is Christian feeling. And he clearly picks out the two principal objects that he seeks to grasp as the content of the Christian consciousness: the Divine Spirit and the Second Adam. Even what is perhaps the main difficulty for his dogmatic task is at least touched on: how the contents of the Christian consciousness are to be related to the concept of "nature," which the intellect acquires partly from other sources. He acknowledges that the two functions of feeling and intellect give rise to an oscillation, a constant effort to attune the two never-completed activities of philosophy and dogmatics. Finally, he goes on, in the same paragraph, to indicate that his enterprise maintains continuity with the language of tradition, but is not tied to the letter. The dogmatic

4. He uses this expression in the midst of his analysis of immediate self-consciousness (*Gl.*, § 4.1), and there is no reason to suppose that the method changes when he goes on to speak of the consciousness of God. In the present chapter, references to the *Glaubenslehre* (abbreviated as *Gl.* or, for the first edition, *Gl.*[1]) will usually be given hereafter in the text.

5. Translated from the text in Cordes, "Der Brief Schleiermachers," 209.

language shaped by Augustine is rich and deep enough to be still serviceable if handled with discretion. But the original and in this sense "fixed" interpretation of Christian feeling is the Bible, which may only be better understood—and developed. "As a Protestant theologian, I shall let no one curtail my right of development."

Schleiermacher was convinced that his link with the Protestant Reformers lay not only in the right of development that he claimed for himself but also in the experiential nature of his entire procedure. As he asks his friend, Friedrich Lücke (1791–1855), "Was it not the case with our Luther . . . that his theology was manifestly a daughter of his religion?"[6] He could equally well have appealed to John Calvin, the principal doctor of his own Reformed tradition, for whom the only knowledge of God with which theology was to concern itself was given in "piety," much else being firmly excluded as "speculation." A characteristically Protestant style of descriptive theologizing lay behind both of the two determinative themes of Schleiermacher's dogmatics. He himself spoke of it as "empirical."

GLAUBENSLEHRE: DOGMATICS FOR A NEW AGE

The task Schleiermacher set himself in his dogmatics can be stated readily enough: he intended to give a disciplined account of the distinctively Christian way of being religious, more particularly as it appears in the "evangelical" (Protestant) church. Concerning the first edition of *The Christian Faith,* he wrote to Lücke that "the presentation of the peculiarly Christian consciousness was . . . the actual aim of the book" (*Sendschr.,* 33). He was fully aware that such a program, however secure its links with the past, betokened a new direction in Christian theology; it even invited a new designation, *Glaubenslehre* or "the doctrine of faith." In practice, Schleiermacher found it convenient still to use the old term "dogmatics," but he knew he was venturing on something different from orthodox and rationalist theologies alike. Against the orthodox Protestant tradition, the enterprise of *Glaubenslehre* is not defined as essentially exegetical; further, the determination is announced at the outset rigorously to exclude the philosophical elements that had intruded even into orthodoxy, but still more into the rational theologies of the eighteenth century. "The fundamental thought of the inquiry before us," Schleiermacher writes, "is that the philosophical and the dogmatic are not to be mixed" (*Gl.*[1], § 2, note b). Dogmatic science has an "empirical" character that distinguishes it both from a biblical theology and from philosophical speculation; and it is this same empirical character that lies behind the requisite ordering of the dogmatic materials.

6. *Sendschr.,* 16. The open letters, which first appeared in the journal *Theologische Studien und Kritiken* (1829), will be cited hereafter in the text.

Theology as Science

Schleiermacher furnished a general guidebook to the theological terrain in his remarkable *Brief Outline on the Study of Theology* (1811; 2d ed., 1830), still perhaps the best work of its kind.[7] In the *Outline,* dogmatics is not identical with theology but is only a part of it. Christian theology is the sum total of the scientific studies and rules without which church leadership would be impossible. It is constituted as a distinct field, not simply by its content (although all the parts do have a common relationship to a particular way of believing), nor by a uniform method, but precisely by its practical goal of equipping Christian leaders. Its main divisions are philosophical, historical, and practical theology; and dogmatics—surprisingly, at first glance—is assigned to the second division along with exegetical theology and church history.

The divisions Schleiermacher makes within the total field of Christian theology are only to be fully understood by their place in his general scheme of the sciences, which is simply presupposed in the theological writings but can readily be extracted from the lectures on philosophical ethics, dialectic, and aesthetics. First of all, theological studies belong to the general *domain* of "ethics," by which Schleiermacher means the science of reason—of all that pertains to the human spirit, its history and culture. Next, within ethics so defined, two *kinds* of knowing are distinguished: the "speculative" kind is directed to essence and works with concepts, while the "empirical" kind is directed to existence and works with judgments.[8] But the individual sciences do not all belong wholly to one or the other of these two kinds: some sciences combine the two, or combine their results. Third, then, Schleiermacher distinguishes these hybrid disciplines by their respective *goals* as either "critical," if they issue in knowledge, or "technical," if they issue in rules of action.

In this overall scheme, the place of the three main divisions of theology can be roughly determined if we say that philosophical theology is a critical discipline, historical theology is empirical, and practical theology is technical. Only it must immediately be added, by way of qualification, that the three theological disciplines are not to be isolated from one another but coexist in a continuous exchange. So, for instance, a genuinely historical view of Christianity presupposes the findings of philosophical theology (*KD,* § 65, § 252). Exactly what it is that historical theology owes to philosophical theology is a question that can be postponed. For now, we

7. *Kurze Darstellung des theologischen Studiums,* hereafter abbreviated *KD* and cited in the text.

8. The second of the two domains to which the total body of knowledge is assigned Schleiermacher calls "physics," the science of nature; and in physics, too, a distinction is made between "speculative" and "empirical" kinds of knowing.

have the epistemological location of dogmatics: it belongs to historical theology in the sense that its concern is with a particular aspect of concrete human existence—namely, a specific, historically given way of believing (a *Glaubensweise*). It is, in short, "ethical" knowledge of the "empirical" kind; and, so understood, it plainly has the same general subject matter as church history, from which it is distinguished simply as historical knowledge of how the church and its faith are now, in the present. If allowances are made for eccentricities of terminology, Schleiermacher's placement of dogmatics on the scientific tree is clear enough, and it has some important methodological consequences.

As a historical-empirical discipline, dogmatics does not have to establish its object of inquiry; it takes it as given (a *datum*) and seeks only to explicate its content. In this sense, *Glaubenslehre* "presupposes" faith, and there is no need to inflate the discipline with attempted proofs of, for instance, the existence of God (*Gl.*, § 33.3). Christian piety is a fact: dogmatic inquiry exfoliates as it seeks to trace the ways in which this fundamental fact enters into relation with other facts of consciousness. To be sure, the fundamental fact (*Grundtatsache*) of dogmatics must be described as an *inward* fact; and in this respect dogmatics differs, not only from deductive sciences that begin with a fundamental *principle* (*Grundsatz*), but also from those disciplines that are historical in the sense of embracing a definite field of *outward* perception (*Gl.*, § 28.2).

Schleiermacher's recognition that dogmatics is not history as ordinarily construed did not incline him to abandon its classification as historical theology. But the inwardness of the fundamental fact does mean, so he believed, that dogmatics can be pursued only from the inside, by one who has had the inner experience. This, of course, has nothing to do with any special miracle of grace: it is simply a general epistemological principle (*Gl.*, § 13, postscript). In particular, the way the church's teaching "hangs together" (its *Zusammenhang*) can be convincingly presented only by someone who starts from personal conviction. Dogmatics is historical theology by reason of its historical *datum;* yet a dogmatic treatment of doctrines is not a purely historical *report* such as anyone with the requisite information could give of any system whatever (*KD*, § 196; cf. *Gl.*, § 19.1).

Nowadays, we would be less likely to call the analysis of self-consciousness "empirical" (*Sendschr.*, 20–21), or to classify dogmatics as "historical theology" on the grounds that its data belong to historical existence. In some of its stages, as we shall see, Schleiermacher's procedure has plain affinities with what we would rather call "phenomenological" method. But, despite the terminological obstacles, the general character of the approach he adopted need not be unclear to us, especially when contrasted with the alternatives. To begin with, if dogmatic propositions arise solely out of "logically ordered reflection on the immediate utterances of the devout self-consciousness" (*Gl.*, § 16, postscript), and if it is specifically the Protestant self-consciousness that is made the datum of dogmatic inquiry (*Gl.*, § 23), then the task plainly cannot be carried out through direct scriptural exegesis. The more immediately pertinent texts are in fact the Protestant creeds or confessions (*Gl.*, § 27.1–2).

It would be a total misunderstanding of Schleiermacher, however, if one were to infer either that he was a Protestant confessionalist (an unlikely inference!) or that he was indifferent to the Scriptures. The point is a strictly methodological one. Of the three types of dogmatics that he mentions—scriptural, scientific, and confessionalist (*Gl.*, § 27.4)—he was naturally attracted to the second by his strong systematic drives. But he did not believe that a scientific dogmatics should diverge too far from the other two types, nor that dogmatics of *any* kind could relegate the autonomous task of exegetical theology to a merely subordinate role (*Gl.*, § 19, postscript; *Gl.*, § 27.3). More important, the specific mode of being religious that constitutes the subject of his discipline, and of which the confessions are simply historical expressions, is a consciousness of being under the word of God. If Schleiermacher found no place for the proclamation of the word or the unparalleled authority of Scripture, then it would not be the evangelical consciousness that he was talking about. In actual fact, while he can see the point of the old dogmatic preambles on Scripture as the norm of authentic Christian piety, he sets his doctrine of Holy Scripture where the Reformers had in part already placed it: under ecclesiology. There the New Testament acquires the primary character of a preaching by and about Christ that generates faith (*Gl.*, § 128.2–3), and one should not be surprised to find in this segment of *The Christian Faith* the plainest affirmations of scriptural authority and sufficiency (*Gl.*, § 129.2, § 131.2) or of the absolute centrality of the ministry of the word (*Gl.*, § 134.2, § 135.1; cf. *Gl.*, § 15.2).

Theology and Philosophy

Schleiermacher's theoretical veto of speculative intrusions into dogmatics should not be taken as antimetaphysical; nor, on the other side, does his actual use of speculative categories betray an inconsistency. Once again, as with his views on the appeal to Scripture, it is all a question of methodological uniformity (*Gleichförmigkeit des Verfahrens: Gl.*, § 33.3). Speculation has its own legitimacy, but it belongs on the scientific tree at another point than dogmatics. And if the dogmatic theologians find it useful to appropriate speculative categories, they may do so only insofar as the content of the categories is determined by their own science, not by that of the philosophers.

The fundamental question concerns the way in which talk about God is *generated*. The dogmatician's sole concern is with statements that arise out of the immediate religious consciousness (in a manner to be specified more exactly in due course). It may well be that the path of speculation also leads to statements about a Supreme Being that look very like dogmatic statements. But precisely because they arise from a different activity of the human spirit, it is imperative not to confuse them with genuine dogmatic statements; otherwise, the consistency of the dogmatic method will be impaired. If, then, dogmatic theologians choose to borrow the language of some philosophical school, they take it in freedom to shape only the *form* of their propositions. The extraordinary question whether a proposition can be true in philosophy and false in theology, or vice versa, cannot properly arise: the proposition, despite similarities of form, simply could not have the same meaning in the two different contexts (*Gl.*, § 16, postscript).[9] By "scholasticism," a term he uses as pejoratively as did the Protestant Reformers, Schleiermacher means exactly the confusion of dogmatics and speculative philosophy (*Gl.*, § 28.3).

It does not follow, of course, that dogmatics and philosophy are mutually opposed, only that they are different. Each has its roots in human nature, and an actual conflict between them would have to presuppose an unthinkable disharmony in human nature itself (*Gl.*, § 28.3). Besides, as we have noted, dogmatics is not the whole of Schleiermacher's theology: it is expressly linked with ethics (in his peculiar sense) and with the philosophy of religion by the critical discipline of philosophical theology, which serves to locate the language of evangelical faith on the language map. For if we are to talk coherently about the distinctive faith of the Christian church, we must be able to specify in general what is a "church" (i.e., a religious community) and what is a "faith" (i.e., what is religion). Hence the introduction to the *Glaubenslehre* proceeds, first of all, to anchor the language of dogmatics in a definition of the essence (or determining characteristics) of Christianity. The closely woven argument, culminating in proposition 11, first decides what a religious community is (with propositions borrowed from *ethics*); second, how the various religious communities may be related to one another (propositions borrowed from *philosophy of religion*); and third, what is the Christian religious community's distinctive essence (propositions borrowed from *philosophical theology*). In this manner, Schleiermacher's preamble to dogmatics sets out, not to demonstrate anything (seeing that the discipline begins with actual facts of experience), but simply to find the place of evangelical faith among other modes of being religious and the place of religiousness itself among the diverse functions of the human spirit (*Sendschr.*, 20–21, 54–55; *KD*, § 21). And this, naturally, can be accomplished only with the assistance of

9. See also *Gl.*, § 2.1; the handwritten note to *Gl.*, § 4.4, cited in Redeker's edition; and the postscripts to *Gl.*, § 19 and § 33.

speculative and critical disciplines that work with general concepts, not exclusively with concrete individuals. "Philosophy," in Schleiermacher's usage, covers the activity of just these disciplines, along with the epistemological inquiry of what he calls "dialectic."

The Shape of the New Dogmatics

If Christian doctrines are individually accounts of Christian religious affections (*Gl.*, § 15), dogmatic theology is the science that explores the coherence of the total doctrine prevalent in a particular church at a given time (*Gl.*, § 19; *KD*, § 195). But *how* exactly is the mass of doctrinal material to be shown as a systematic whole? Schleiermacher bestowed special care on the architectonics of his *Glaubenslehre* because he recognized that the meaning of a proposition is determined in part by its context or location; indeed, he held that the arrangement, along with the precision of its language, is what gives a dogmatics "scientific form." It is not sufficient to move the immediate utterances of religious feeling out of their original poetic and rhetorical form into technically correct ("dialectical") language, unless the resulting propositions are brought into a definite relationship with one another (*Gl.*, § 28.1–2). Schleiermacher's own arrangement was an ingenious combination of a traditional twofold division of "parts" and a threefold division of "sections" that was uniquely his own.

Since Calvin, Reformed dogmatics had commonly moved from the knowledge of God as Creator to the knowledge of God as Redeemer; and in Calvin himself, at least, Adam's fall meant that the second kind of knowledge, though treated later, must in actual experience now come first. Schleiermacher adopts the inherited two-part scheme, drawing out its plain implication that the doctrine of God is given in the system as a whole, not in a single *locus de Deo* that can be disposed of early in the presentation (see *Gl.*, § 31.2). And in him, too, the order of exposition reverses the order of experience, but not quite for Calvin's reason. The logical movement of Schleiermacher's system is from the abstract to the concrete. Everything in a Christian dogmatics turns strictly on the fact of redemption, and his thinking is therefore wholly misconstrued if it is not recognized that the explication of the consciousness of grace in part 2 of *The Christian Faith* is the determinative point of reference for the entire system (*Gl.*, § 84.4; cf. *Gl.*, § 90.2). "Piety," isolated in the introduction for separate consideration, is the irreducible abstraction that places religious language on the language map. The doctrines of creation and preservation in part 1 present next, not the full Christian consciousness, but the religious consciousness still in abstraction from the antithesis of sin and grace (*Gl.*, § 50.4, § 62.1, § 64.2), or, as Schleiermacher puts it in his heading, "that religious self-consciousness which is always both presupposed by and contained in every Christian religious affection." Only in the doctrine of redemption in part 2 does he turn to the fully concrete evangelical consciousness. And even within part 2 the passage from the abstract to the concrete is invoked to explain the separate treatment of sin: if we consider the consciousness of sin per se, we are still moving in the region of the abstract, since the full Christian understanding of sin, as of everything else, is given only by reference to the decisive fact of redemption (*Gl.*, § 66.2, § 79.1).

The originality of Schleiermacher's order lay still more in his combining the inherited twofold scheme with a threefold distinction between different "forms" that dogmatic propositions may take (*Gl.*, § 30). In the primary and strict form, they are *descriptions of human states:* that is, they are about the religious consciousness, which we may consider either abstractly in itself (part 1) or concretely as subject to fluctuation (part 2). If we take account of the subdivision of part 2, which considers sin and grace separately as two aspects of a single antithesis, we shall then find ourselves speaking of the religious consciousness under three headings: as a consciousness of the general relationship between self, world, and God (part 1), as a consciousness of sin (part 2, first aspect), and as the full Christian consciousness of grace (part 2, second aspect). Under each heading, the dogmatic inquiry is turned directly to certain "human states." But if the religious consciousness is of the self in relation to God and the world, it is entirely possible to shift the focus from the self-consciousness as such to one of these two elements disclosed in it. If we focus our attention on the presence of God to the religious consciousness, our dogmatic propositions will be formed as *concepts of divine attributes and modes of action.* Similarly, if we focus on the self's awareness of the world, they will become *assertions about characteristics of the world.* And since propositions of the second and third forms can likewise be developed under the three headings already mentioned, the structure that emerges may appropriately be pictured as a three-by-three grid.[10]

Here, then, is the shape of the new dogmatics: After the introduction, it falls into two parts, one of which is subdivided and each of which contains separately grouped propositions in three forms. The arrangement is not obscure, but it is certainly complex and perhaps strikes the reader as even a little artificial. Yet the methodological principle behind it is crucial. The "empirical" procedure that Schleiermacher proposes requires everything in the system to be presented as a modification of the immediate self-consciousness. Now this immediate self-consciousness, analyzed in his introduction (as we shall see), discloses the self as coexistent with the

10. See Horst Stephan, *Geschichte der deutschen evangelischen Theologie seit dem deutschen Idealismus,* 2d ed., revised by Martin Schmidt (Berlin: Alfred Töpelmann, 1960), 103. A similar diagram will be found in Claude Welch, *Protestant Thought in the Nineteenth Century,* vol. 1 (New Haven: Yale University Press, 1972), 74–75.

world, and both as co-posited by God. But if the analysis thus provides a warrant for distinguishing three forms of proposition, it is not difficult to see that all three forms cannot possibly have the same status: the second and third are expressly distinguished as "secondary." And even in the secondary forms, which could in principle be dispensed with, nothing is to be asserted that cannot be "developed out of propositions of the first form" (*Gl.*, § 30.2). Dogmatic statements about the world and God emphatically do not pretend to offer either a natural science or a theistic metaphysics. Rather, they express the way in which the religious consciousness—or, more specifically, the sinful consciousness or the redeemed consciousness respectively—*perceives* the world and God. The intrusion of additional matter that originates either in natural science or in metaphysical speculation would only dilute the purely dogmatic method.

It does not follow that a system of Christian dogmatics says nothing at all about the kind of world we live in, or that Christian faith is compatible with any state of affairs whatever. Schleiermacher certainly admits that not every view of the world is compatible with the religious consciousness (*Gl.*, § 28.1) and that the dogmatician has a responsibility so to express the content of the Christian consciousness that no conflict with natural or historical science will arise (*Sendschr.*, 40). His *Glaubenslehre* is dogmatics for a new age, not only by reason of its affinity with the subjective and historical turn in modern thinking, but also because it fully accepts the obligation to adjust its formulas to the current state of knowledge. And just there, of course, lie many of the problems with respect to our two determinative themes: the Divine Spirit and the Second Adam.

The Divine Spirit and Natural Causality

In his brilliant apology *On Religion,* Schleiermacher, then a Reformed chaplain in a Berlin hospital, tried to induce his cultured friends to take a second look at the religion they despised. They were accustomed to the view that religion means, above all, the beliefs in a personal deity and a personal immortality, together with the prudent behavior these beliefs recommend; and they found that they were more interested in other things. Schleiermacher's strategy was to show them that religion is in actual fact a "sense and taste for the infinite" that gives a deeper worth to the things they valued most. It is reducible neither to beliefs nor to morals, yet it inspires the quest for knowledge and accompanies morality like sacred music. It ought, besides, never to have been missed by those who cherish art, imagination, individuality, and spontaneity.

However astute, the argument pleased hardly anyone. The cultured despisers were disappointed to find, in the final address, that it was the

Christian religion they were supposed to embrace. And yet Schleiermacher's fellow churchmen and churchwomen had already decided, by the time they had finished the second address, that what he commended was not Christianity at all. In *The Christian Faith,* written after he had returned to Berlin and had been appointed to a theological chair at the new university, he perhaps tried harder to reconcile church people than to appease the despisers. At least, he sought to remove the suspicion of pantheism that had hovered over his talk about God and uncompromisingly heightened—indeed, absolutized—the redemptive activity of Christ.

God and the Feeling of Absolute Dependence

Schleiermacher was convinced that many who think themselves opposed to belief in God are only repelled by the standard presentations of the subject and are by no means strangers to the affections of the God-consciousness (*Gl.,* § 172.2). The task he set himself was to develop his own concept of God solely by analysis of the religious self-consciousness, moving (in the manner we have noted) from the most abstract to the fully concrete. As in the *Speeches,* so also in *The Christian Faith* he held that the *essence* of "piety," the irreducible element in every religion, must be sought neither in beliefs nor in behavior but in "feeling," by which he meant the immediate self-consciousness underlying all our knowing and doing. It is "immediate," and so assigned to "feeling," in the sense that the self has not yet made itself the object of its own contemplation (*Gl.,* § 3.2, § 3.4).

A little introspection, Schleiermacher holds, can catch the original polar structure (*Duplizität*) of self-consciousness as a consciousness of self and other together. It is a consciousness, as he puts it, of the "being of the subject for itself" and "its coexistence with an other," which in its totality is "the world." The relation of self and other revealed in self-consciousness is one of reciprocal influence: Introspection discloses the self both acting upon the other and being acted upon by it, or, what is the same thing, as conscious of its partial freedom and partial dependence. In short: "Our self-consciousness, as a consciousness of our being in the world or of our being together with the world, is a series divided between the feeling of freedom and the feeling of dependence" (*Gl.,* § 4.1–2). But look again, Schleiermacher bids us, and you will find in addition a feeling of *absolute* dependence—unqualified, that is, by any reciprocal influence from the self. And *this* feeling cannot arise from the influence upon us of anything presented to us in the world, nor from the influence of the world as a whole (in the sense of the totality of temporal being); for on any such object we would in fact exercise a counterinfluence. The feeling of absolute dependence is the consciousness that even the entirety of our *activity* is "from somewhere else." And this is what is meant by "piety" (*Gl.,* § 4.3–4).

Observation of immediate self-consciousness thus shows it to have a necessarily religious determination. Plainly, it is misleading when Schleiermacher's term "feeling" is taken for the emotional side or faculty of human life. For what appears to observation, he thinks, is something fundamental about the structure of our personal life as such. Piety is not relegated to one department of life but is understood to pervade life in its entirety and in each moment. In response to the critics of the first edition of his *Glaubenslehre,* Schleiermacher stressed that he had meant our consciousness of the actual way in which our being is determined. But because this consciousness does not depend on any previously grasped ideas, he did not like to term it a "knowing." "What I understand by 'pious feeling' by no means proceeds from conceptions (*von der Vorstellung*)," he explained, "but is the original attestation (*Aussage*) of an immediate existential relationship" (*Sendschr.*, 13, 15). Not that there cannot be an original concept of God, arrived at by another route (i.e., philosophically): it is simply that such a concept would be of no concern to dogmatics, which must begin from piety (*Gl.*, § 4.4).

For dogmatics, the original use of the term "God" is to denote the "whence," given in self-consciousness, of our receptive and active existence. And the *most* original conception (*Vorstellung*) with which we are concerned can be nothing more than articulation of the feeling of absolute dependence. Made into the object of reflection, the feeling of absolute dependence "becomes," as Schleiermacher has it, a consciousness of *God.* And whatever more is put into the conception of God must be developed out of the fundamental content given in immediate self-consciousness. In this sense, dogmatics starts not from a rationally established *idea* but from an original *revelation* of God (*Gl.*, § 4.4).

God-Talk and World-Talk

In a striking departure from the dogmatic tradition, Schleiermacher turns immediately from his prolegomena to the doctrines of creation and preservation; he simply passes over the doctrine of the Trinity, which appears only in the famous conclusion to the work as a whole. The reason for postponing his remarks on the Trinity is made transparently clear, and it once again expresses the cardinal dogmatic rule. As ordinarily understood, the term "Trinity" has reference to eternal distinctions in the Godhead (*Gl.*, § 170.2); but in dogmatics,

> since we have to do only with the consciousness of God that is given in our self-consciousness along with the consciousness of the world, we have no formula for the being of God in itself as distinct from the being of God in the world. We should have to borrow any such for-

> mula from the province of speculation, and so become unfaithful to the nature of our discipline [*Gl.*, § 172.1].

It is easy to see for ourselves, without any explicit guidance from the author, that the doctrines of creation and preservation, by contrast, follow naturally enough upon the introduction: as Schleiermacher understands them, they are simply explications of our feeling of absolute dependence.

To begin with, it may seem as if he has laid a quite insufficient foundation for a doctrine of God. For what, after all, can be said of God on the slender basis of the feeling of absolute dependence, especially if, as he insists, the feeling is something simple and unchanging? The problem is resolved by further analysis of self-consciousness. Our language about God does not simply assert that self-consciousness points to a "whence" of the feeling of absolute dependence. Rather, it is about the ways in which this fundamental feeling coexists with what Schleiermacher calls the "sensible self-consciousness"—that is, with our experience of nature and of other selves (*Gl.*, § 5.3; cf. *Gl.*, § 5.1). The feeling of absolute dependence never fills a moment of consciousness but accompanies our entire existence as the consciousness that all of our "self-activity" comes from somewhere else (*Gl.*, § 4.3). And this consciousness, while always there for deliberate observation to uncover, varies in strength precisely because of its union with the sensible self-consciousness, which does not uniformly encourage the emergence of the "higher" consciousness (*Gl.*, § 5.5)—although we must obviously avoid any suggestion that awareness of God is compatible only with moments of pleasure in our perception of the world (*Gl.*, § 5.4).

If for the moment, however, we set aside the fluctuations of the God-consciousness and inquire only about its relation to the sensible self-consciousness as such, what we have is nothing other than the doctrines (in part 1) of creation and preservation, both of which are about the feeling of absolute dependence or about the divine causality disclosed in it. But in taking his stand on his usual methodological point, Schleiermacher now has something more than procedural purity in mind: the ideas of God and nature are also at stake. In the first place, he wants so to interpret "creation" that nothing is said about a supposed temporal beginning of the world and of humans, since any such notion would make the divine causality too much like a human work in the realm of reciprocity (*Gl.*, § 36.2, § 39.1, § 40.2, § 41). What we must rather assert, on the basis of our feeling of absolute dependence, is that the realm of reciprocity itself (including ourselves) has a "whence" that is *not* subject to reciprocity. Similarly, in the second place, Schleiermacher wants so to interpret "preservation" (the term he prefers to "providence") that nothing is said about God's intervening in the closed causal system of nature, but that God is identified as nature's timeless and spaceless ground (*Gl.*, § 34.2, § 47.2, § 54). To his way of thinking, there is therefore a close connection between the consciousness of God and our consciousness of being placed in an all-embracing system of nature (*Gl.*, § 34, § 46.1); and he can conclude that the divine causality, though not identical with natural causality, must be equated with it *in scope* (*Gl.*, § 51). The only God-talk possible for the dogmatician is a particular kind of world-talk.

That these are not exactly the traditional Christian doctrines of creation and providence, needs no emphasis. True, Schleiermacher leaves no room for the cry of "pantheism" thrown at the earlier *Speeches*. Given his analysis of the feeling of absolute dependence (in his introduction) and his characterization of divine causality as the world's eternal ground (in part 1), there is simply no way in which God-consciousness and world-consciousness could be logically confused; his annoyance with the critics on this point was fully justified.[11] But in at least three respects his conception of God's relation to the world remained unconventional, not to say heretical. First, the object of providential care is for him the system, not directly the individual, and any thought of God's making ad hoc decisions or performing isolated acts for anyone's benefit is firmly excluded (see, e.g., *Gl.*, § 46.1). Though he spoke freely of divine "preservation" (*Erhaltung*), Schleiermacher disliked the very term "providence" (*Vorsehung*), which seemed to him, in comparison with the biblical term "foreordination" (*Vorherversehung*), to give inadequate expression to the connection of the part with the whole (*Gl.*, § 164.3). Second, while in a sense he did set "God" and "nature" over against each other as antithetical concepts (*Gl.*, § 96.1), he also treated them as correlative (*Gl.*, § 46.2, § 54). In *The Christian Faith,* as in his *Dialectic,* the world is not without God, nor is God without the world. Third, he resisted any attempt to include personality among the dogmatic attributes of the world's ground. The divine causality may be termed "spirit," and it is said to be "omniscient," but in order to deny that it is a lifeless mechanical force rather than to assert that God has a consciousness like ours (*Gl.*, § 51.2, § 55).

To many of Schleiermacher's contemporaries, it was astonishing that anyone who had so transformed the traditional picture of God could fulfill the office of an evangelical preacher. D. F. Strauss (1808–74), for instance, in his reflections on prayer and the personal God,[12] asserted that for Schleiermacher prayer could be only the expression of a conscious illusion, retained partly out of habit and partly for the sake of his congregation. About this, however, Strauss was entirely mistaken. In the very first collection of his printed sermons, Schleiermacher included one titled "The

11. See the handwritten comment on *Gl.*, § 4.4, mentioned already (in n. 9 above).

12. David Friedrich Strauss, *The Old Faith and the New: A Confession,* trans. from the 6th ed. by Mathilde Blind (New York: Henry Holt & Co., 1873), sec. 35.

Power of Prayer in Relation to Outward Circumstances,"[13] which is the exact homiletical counterpart to what was later asserted, as a forthright doctrinal conclusion, in *The Christian Faith:* "Our proposition sets prayer, too, under divine preservation, so that prayer and its fulfillment or non-fulfillment are only parts of the same original divine order; consequently, that something might otherwise [i.e., in the absence of prayer] have turned out differently is only an empty thought" (*Gl.,* § 47.1). As a pastor, Schleiermacher did not conceal this conclusion from his flock, although he naturally set it in the context of a more naive and direct religious discourse. In the sermon, he remarks that of course children may tell their father what it is they desire. In Gethsemane Christ himself laid his longing before his heavenly Father. (Anthropomorphism, we infer, is entirely proper at the immediate religious level.) But just there, in the experience of Christ, lies an important admonition: what he wanted was not granted him, but his wishes had to be bent to the will of God. (So the text itself invites dogmatic controls on naive anthropomorphism.) It is a rule of prayer that God is to be approached as the Unchangeable Being,

> in whose mind no new thought and no new decision can arise since God said to Godself, "All that I have made is good" [Gen. 1:31]. What was decreed then will come to pass. . . . If, because of the way God has ordained the tissue of events, you must do without what you wish for, you have your compensation in all the goodness that you see in the world. . . . But the Wise One is also kind. God will not let you suffer and do without solely for the sake of others. God's will is that for the justified everything should work together for their own good [Rom. 8:28]. So arises trust that, within the whole, notice has been taken of us, too, however small a part we may be.

What strikes one most about this homiletical exercise is perhaps the ease with which Schleiermacher can avail himself of the inherited Reformed or Calvinistic vocabulary (with its strong sense of an elaborate divine "plan" in which individuals must seek their place). Very little adjustment seems to be needed, to say nothing of any dissembling. Of course, "translation" takes place, but Schleiermacher was perfectly open about that, too. In a moment of gratuitous candor he admits what must be obvious to any reader of *The Christian Faith:* that dogmatic language, though expressly pointed toward ministry, is not immediately available for preaching but has to be thought through and reworded (*Sendschr.,* 59). In his sermon on prayer, what is reworded is in part a theme already contained in his first book. To be religious and to pray, says the preacher, are one and the same thing; but the prayer without ceasing that the Apostle commends (1

13. Reproduced in KS 1:167–78. The collection first appeared in 1806 and does not claim to report the spoken word exactly.

Thess. 5:17) consists in the art of combining every thought of any importance with thought about God. In other words, as the apologist had said already, it is to have the sense of the infinite in every moment of one's finite existence. This the Christian consciousness certainly presupposes. But it is not, of course, the specific content of the Christian consciousness.

The Second Adam and the Consciousness of Grace

Sent to school with the Moravian Brethren at Niesky (in 1783), the young Schleiermacher had brought happiness to his family with his letters home about the love, the peace, and the mercy of the Savior. Although there is plain evidence of earlier spiritual disquiet, his troubles reached the turning point only after he had transferred to the seminary at Barby (1785). In the short autobiographical sketch he later prepared for the church authorities (1794), he spoke of "companionship with Jesus," commended to him by his teachers, as something he longed for rather than had. No doubt, its cultivation was inhibited partly by the questioning spirit that had begun to awaken in him (no thanks to his environment). Finally, in a letter of 21 January 1787, he shattered his father's illusions about him: he had lost his faith and could no longer believe in the deity of Christ or his vicarious sacrifice. And yet anyone who looks back on the letter from the vantage point of *The Christian Faith* will be bound to feel that what Schleiermacher lost was not (or not for long) his faith but his first interpretation of it—if, indeed, he ever did appropriate for himself the lessons he was taught in the Brethren's classroom. Although estrangement from the orthodox doctrines, begun even before he entered the seminary, culminated in a systematic critique of dogma, everything in the *Glaubenslehre* still hung on the picture of the Savior and its compelling attraction. And one can well understand Strauss's nettling remark that "Schleiermacher's Christology is a last attempt to make the churchly Christ acceptable to the modern mind."[14]

The Ideal Made Historical

By postponing his discussion of the Trinity, Schleiermacher hoped he might avoid some of the wrong turnings taken on the road to Nicaea (cf. *Gl.*, § 172.3). But he did not simply ignore the differences between his own christological doctrines and the inherited dogmas: the central division on the person and work of Christ in *The Christian Faith* was interlaced with some vigorous polemic. He was able to appropriate a tradition of criticism going back from the Enlightenment Neologists to the Socinians of the Reformation period. More important, he was also a debtor to more positive attempts at reformulating the christological problem, among which

14. Strauss, *The Christ of Faith and the Jesus of History: A Critique of Schleiermacher's Life of Jesus*, trans. Leander E. Keck (Philadelphia: Fortress Press, 1977), 4.

Kant's *Religion within the Limits of Reason Alone* (1793) had been a penetrating and influential example. For Kant, the question was not: How could two whole natures, the one human and the other divine, have been united in the person of the incarnate Son? but rather: What is the religious idea (or ideal), and how was it related to the historical individual, Jesus of Nazareth? And the problem so formulated was made all the more urgent by developments in historical criticism that raised doubts about the nature of the New Testament documents: whether they could be trusted as sources of genuine information about the historical Jesus.

Whatever he learned from others, however, Schleiermacher's approach to the problem was entirely his own, rooted in the distinctive methodological principles we have already explored. The first clear traces of the fresh approach made their appearance not in the *Speeches* but in a relatively minor product of his tenure at the University of Halle: the little dialogue *Christmas Eve* (1806). Partly perhaps for apologetic reasons, the fifth speech had remained tentative and even ambiguous in its statements about Christ; and the uncertainties were not entirely resolved by the explanations added to the third edition (1821). The significance of Christ had certainly been located in the idea he embodied, the idea of mediation; but he had not been presented as the only mediator, nor had finality been claimed either for his person or for his idea. In other words, the defense of Christianity in the *Speeches* falls short of traditional Christian sentiments, despite one or two more generous phrases that do not seem quite to harmonize with the rest.

The *Christmas Eve* dialogue, on the other hand, plainly indicates that the Christian consciousness is where christological reflection must actually *begin*. Leonard's cynical opinion is that nothing more can be discovered in the historical documents than conflicting christologies. The counterarguments of Ernest and Edward do not deny the historical difficulties, but they suggest that it is not with the Gospels that we have to begin—unless perhaps we turn (with Edward) straight to the mystical evangelist, John, who was the least interested in particular events. We take our point of departure preferably from the actual Christmas joy of the Christian community, its experience of a heightened sense of existence that can only be traced back to the appearance of the Redeemer.

The christological assignment for *The Christian Faith,* then, is this: so to speak of Christ that we can account for his perceived effects on the consciousness of the Christian community. Only within this frame, we may say, can Kant's question be answered. And criticism of church dogma immediately takes on a quite different significance than it had for the Neologists: its role is to conform the trinitarian and christological formulas to the Christian self-consciousness, a task which the Protestant Reformers unfortunately neglected (*Gl.,* § 95.2, § 96.3, § 172.3). The formulas required for an adequate christology will be the results of arguing back from the observed effect to its sufficient cause. It must be admitted that, as time was to show, the structure of this christological argument landed Schleiermacher in difficulties that even his closest disciples found embarrassing: Alexander Schweizer, for instance, pointed out that a Roman Catholic dogmatics could establish, by an exactly parallel argument, the Roman Church's belief in Mary as the Sinless Queen of Heaven.[15] Others less sympathetic to Schleiermacher's christology, such as Wilhelm Dilthey, pointed out that the alleged historical cause seemed *more than* sufficient to account for the religious consciousness observable in the Christian church. In view of the difficulties, it is hardly surprising when the attempt is made (by Martin Redeker, for example)[16] to deny that Schleiermacher's procedure really did follow an effect-to-cause pattern. For the moment, I am not concerned to evaluate the soundness of the procedure but only to state what I think it was. And I am bound to conclude that, if allowance is made for the un-Kantian, putatively historical content of Schleiermacher's "postulate," Strauss understood him correctly: Just as the existence of God was for Kant a postulate of the practical reason, so the dogma of Christ was for Schleiermacher a postulate of Christian experience.[17]

It was not, however, the *old* dogma that Schleiermacher wanted to reestablish by this route, though one is surprised to find just how close, in the end, he came to it. Beginning with the approximations to blessedness that occur in Christian experience, he first establishes that these are always associated with a new "collective life" (*Gesamtleben*) that works against the collective life of sin. And since this consciousness of grace is always referred to the redemption accomplished by Jesus of Nazareth, we must affirm that the new collective life of the Christian community goes back to the influence of Jesus, who effects redemption by the communication of his own God-consciousness (see esp. *Gl.*, §§ 87–88).[18] The train of argument then culminates in proposition 93:

> If the spontaneous activity of the new collective life is taken to be originally in the Redeemer and to proceed from him alone, then as an

15. Alexander Schweizer, *Die Glaubenslehre der evangelisch-reformirten Kirche dargestellt und aus den Quellen belegt*, 2 vols. (Zurich: Orell, Füssli, 1844–47), 1:94.

16. Martin Redeker, *Schleiermacher: Life and Thought*, trans. John Wallhausser (Philadelphia: Fortress Press, 1973), 131–32.

17. Strauss, *Charakteristiken und Kritiken: Eine Sammlung zerstreuten Aufsätze aus den Gebieten der Theologie, Anthropologie und Aesthetik*, 2d impression (Leipzig: Otto Wigand, 1844), 41.

18. Schleiermacher assumes rather than demonstrates that, through the picture of Jesus transmitted in the Christian community, the impartation of redemption works today just as it did in the days of Jesus' earthly existence, by the impression of his personality. See, e.g., *Gl.*, § 29.3, § 88.2.

> individual historical being he must have been at the same time ideal (*urbildlich*): that is, the ideal must have become fully historical in him, and his every historical moment must at the same time have carried in it the ideal.

In short, that "the Word became flesh" (probably Schleiermacher's favorite text) means that in Christ the ideal became historical. For Kant, by contrast, who in this respect was a forerunner of the Hegelians, the ideal was always immanent in human reason as such, and the historical Jesus could at most have given it a public foothold; it is, besides, quite unlike the God-consciousness of the *Glaubenslehre,* a purely moral ideal.[19] It hardly needs to be pointed out that Schleiermacher was much better able than Kant (as well as more eager) to preserve the link with orthodox Christian tradition: his Christ is perfect, sinless, utterly unsurpassable, and precisely because of his perfect God-consciousness there was an actual being of God in him (*Gl.*, § 93.2, § 94.2).

Such a generous claim on the Redeemer's behalf, even if not quite the orthodox *vere Deus,* immediately poses again the problem of the natural. For how can the perfect realization of the ideal in Jesus possibly be compatible with the *vere homo,* his genuine humanity? Schleiermacher's ingenious reasoning has here two sides to it. On the one hand, since the God-consciousness is something human, even the perfect God-consciousness of Jesus cannot as such be termed supernatural; it is, after all, nothing other than the *human* ideal (*Gl.*, § 13.1, § 14 [postscript], § 22.2). And the God-consciousness of Jesus both developed naturally in him and is transmitted naturally to others (*Gl.*, § 89.2, § 93.3). (As far as the miracles reportedly worked by Jesus are concerned, Schleiermacher sets them aside as a merely historical or scientific problem of no pertinence to dogmatics: *Gl.*, § 47.3, § 103.4). On the other hand, the *appearance* of the perfect God-consciousness in history, Schleiermacher thinks, was certainly supernatural, if only in the carefully circumscribed sense that we cannot explain it by its environment in the collective life of sin but must assume a creative divine act (*Gl.*, § 88.4, § 89.1, § 93.3). And even the emergence of such novelties in nature is not without scientifically attested analogues (*Sendschr.*, 40). The important thing, as Schleiermacher remarked to Jacobi, is not to let anyone prescribe the limits of nature.

The World as Theater of Redemption

Even the historical novelty of a unique revelation cannot, *sub specie aeternitatis,* be construed as an arbitrary divine intervention: if it is a divine

19. Immanuel Kant, *Religion within the Limits of Reason Alone,* trans. Theodore M. Greene and Hoyt H. Hudson (1934; reprint, New York: Harper & Brothers, 1960), 113, 143–44.

act, it must be eternal (*Gl.*, § 13.1). And so the doctrine of timeless causality lies behind the doctrine of Christ, too. Conversely, christology completes what part 1 has taught us about the divine causality. For what is omnipotence to me if I do not know its goal (*Ziel*)? All the propositions of part 1 are empty frames until filled with the content of part 2 (*Sendschr.*, 32; cf. *Gl.*, § 167.2, where the equivalent term is *Motiv*). To be sure, it cannot be said that one event is any more or any less the effect of omnipotence than another (*Gl.*, § 57.1); even sin cannot have been smuggled into the world by some accident that escaped the divine causality. But what can and must now be said is that the total unbroken fabric of events has a pattern. With complete logical consistency, Schleiermacher embraces (carefully qualified) the formula thrown at the old Reformed divines as the supposed reductio ad absurdum of their belief in the sovereignty of God: That God is "the author of sin" can be given an acceptable sense once it has been understood that God ordains sin, like everything else, for the sake of redemption (*Gl.*, §§ 79–81). All the divine activities in the old ecclesiastical mythology—with its narrative of a temporal creation, a temporal fall, an incarnation to restore humankind, and so on—are collapsed into a single divine "decree" to raise humanity to a higher level of consciousness:

> There is only *one* eternal and general decree to justify humans for Christ's sake. It is the same as the decree to send Christ; otherwise, the sending of Christ must have been conceived and determined in God without its outcome. This decree, once more, is *one and the same* with the decree to create the human race, inasmuch as in Christ first is human nature completed [*Gl.*, § 109.3].

The proper title for *Christ* in this scheme is "the Second Adam" precisely because in him the creation of humanity is perfected: in the unity of the divine decree everything, from the beginning, has pointed toward the appearance of the Redeemer (*Gl.*, § 89.1, § 89.3, § 94.3, § 97.2, § 164.1–2). And Schleiermacher can unroll a historical tapestry as remarkable as any in the more conventional Christian theologies: Christ is the absolute center of history; all humanity is related to him, though many do not know it; and all religions are destined to pass over into Christianity (*Gl.*, § 13.1, § 86.1, § 93.1; cf. *Speeches*, fifth speech, explanation 16). The church, in which Schleiermacher detects a being of God analogous to the being of God in Christ, is the locus of Christ's continuing influence and the historical means by which the kingdom of God must be extended and the divine election consummated (*Gl.*, §§ 123–25, §§ 119–20; cf. *Gl.*, § 87.3).

Similarly, the only attribute of *God* that answers to the experience of redemption is love. For the work of redemption has been shown to turn upon the union of the divine essence (*Wesen*) with human nature in Christ, and by God's "love" is meant that in God which corresponds with the human inclination to want union with another; it is the underlying divine disposition (*Gl.*, § 165.1, § 166.1). Now, everything that is truly predicated of God as a divine attribute must be an expression for the divine essence. And yet neither in Scripture nor in the teaching of the church do we in fact find propositions that are parallel to "God is love": love alone is equated with the being or essence of God (*Gl.*, § 167.1). Of course, the divine love may not be so construed that it negates the attributes already specified. Yet all the attributes pertaining to creation and preservation and even those related to the consciousness of sin are no more than provisional and preparatory, finally gaining their full significance only in relation to the love of God (*Gl.*, § 56 [postscript], § 64.2, § 167.2, § 169.3). Nevertheless, Schleiermacher finds that he has one last attribute to discuss.

Accompanying the divine love, but not quite of equal status with it, is the wisdom of God, which is "the art of (so to say) perfectly realizing the divine love" (*Gl.*, § 165.1). That wisdom does not fully share the favored rank of love is clear, Schleiermacher thinks, from the fact that we do not say "God is wisdom," and he offers an explanation on the basis of his distinctive method. The forgiven person is directly conscious of *himself* or *herself* as the object of the divine disposition of love; only by an extension of self-consciousness does the experience of redemption lead one to affirm the perfect harmony of *all* things (*Gl.*, § 167.2, with the parallel passage in *Gl.*[1], § 183.3, cited in Redeker's edition). But it is with the divine wisdom that Schleiermacher's dogmatics concludes. *The Christian Faith* culminates in an essentially aesthetic vision of the world as the theater of redemption.[20] In other words, it ends on a note much loved by the old Reformed divines: the world is *manifestatio gloriae Dei*.

> What follows from the fact that we take the divine love to be also wisdom is first of all this: that, whatever else we think of in the term "world," we cannot possibly view the totality of finite being in its relation to our consciousness of God as anything other than the absolutely harmonious work of divine art [*Gl.*, § 168.1].

> The divine wisdom is the ground by virtue of which the world, as the theater of redemption, is also the absolute revelation of the Supreme Being—and therefore *good* [*Gl.*, § 169].

All that remains is the epilogue on the need to rethink the doctrine of the Trinity as an affirmation of the being of God in Christ and the church, so making it what in intention it originally was: the actual keystone of Christian doctrine (*Gl.*, § 170.1).

20. See further chapter 9 below.

The Reference of Christian Language

The leading criticisms that have been brought against Schleiermacher have always tended to cluster around the two major themes I have singled out. It has been alleged, first, that he loses the *divine* referent of Christian language in a subjective theory of religion as feeling; second, that he sacrifices the *historical* referent of Christian language to his subjective Christ of faith. At first it was the speculative theology of the Hegelians that was the chief, though by no means only, rival to Schleiermacher's system. But the dominance of a very different variety of Protestant liberalism at the other end of the century—the school of Ritschl—did not entirely break the original lines of criticism. Neither did the dialectical theology's assault on Schleiermacher in the early twentieth century. The explanation for this surprising continuity lies partly in the critics' propensity, seemingly incurable, to read him as a speculative thinker; one can then oppose him either with a more satisfactory system of speculation or else with the call to return to a more purely biblical and Reformation faith. Writing in 1933, Wobbermin identified as the fundamental error (the *proton pseudos*) of Schleiermacher criticism the assumption that his theology must be approached from the perspective of his philosophy; and he found this tradition of interpretation going back to the influential work of Wilhelm Bender (1845–1901), written under Ritschlian auspices, and even beyond—to Schleiermacher's first Hegelian critics. "One can bluntly describe Brunner's Schleiermacher book," he remarked, "as a modernized new edition of Bender's work."[21]

Schleiermacher and the Speculative Theology

In actual practice, perhaps, Schleiermacher's procedure of moving from figurative to scientifically exact language resembled the Hegelian program of transposing representations into concepts. But there was a significant difference of principle. For the Hegelians there was always the temptation to presume that philosophical reflection superseded religion by grasping its conceptual core, whereas for Schleiermacher the core of religion was not conceptual, and reflection could never be more to him than interpretation of what is original in the figurative form (*Gl.*, § 17.2).

The fact is that the followers of Hegel and the followers of Schleier-

21. Georg Wobbermin, "Methodenfragen der heutigen Schleiermacher-Forschung," *Nachrichten von der Gesellschaft der Wissenschaften zu Göttingen aus dem Jahre 1933*, philologisch-historische Klasse (Berlin: Weidmann, 1933), 34, referring to Wilhelm Bender, *Schleiermachers Theologie mit ihren philosophischen Grundlagen dargestellt*, 2 vols. (Nördlingen: C. H. Beck, 1876–78), and Emil Brunner, *Die Mystik und das Wort* (Tübingen: J. C. B. Mohr [Paul Siebeck], 1924).

macher started from two quite different intellectual visions. The *ewiger Vertrag* (usually translated "eternal covenant") of which Schleiermacher wrote to Lücke was a kind of nonaggression pact: not, that is, a unification of Christian faith with scientific inquiry, but an agreement on the part of each to let the other go its own way unhindered. Where Jacobi saw only conflict, Schleiermacher discovered at most an oscillation—and the Hegelians looked for a synthesis. Biedermann, for instance, insofar as he was critical of Schleiermacher, followed the Hegelian line. He admitted that religion and philosophy are autonomous domains of the human spirit, yet not in such fashion that they simply lie outside each other, to be related only as polar opposites. The interpretation of piety in doctrines does not pass out of the domain of religion proper, as though religious feeling itself remained wholly unaffected; the relation to God, mistakenly held to be pure feeling, already has one foot, as Biedermann puts it, in thinking. His own aspiration was after a consistent philosophical penetration of religion. Hence, although he resisted the common Hegelian tendency to dissolve religion in thinking, he could only deplore Schleiermacher's cheerful philosophical eclecticism.[22] Even the theologian, so the Hegelians insisted (Biedermann among them), had to take a firm philosophical stand. Obviously, insofar as Schleiermacher the theologian seemed in practice to be more deeply engaged in speculation than his dogmatic principles allowed, the Hegelians could regard the inconsistency as a happy one (even if he did not seem to speculate very well). Strauss, for example, did not object to the Spinozism he detected in part 1 of the *Glaubenslehre,* but only to a certain lack of candor about it: the author, he remarked, threw a cloak of piety over the backs of his philosophical troops, but during the more vigorous maneuvers their true colors peeked out.[23]

The specific differences between Schleiermacher and the speculative theologians were often concentrated on the concept of God. Symptomatic is the fact that while *he* downgraded the doctrine of the Trinity in its inherited form as an obsolete mixture of dogmatics with speculation, the Hegelians found themselves nowhere more at home than in trinitarian speculation (although their thoughts on the subject were unconventional). But the philosophy of Hegel, if preeminently speculative, was also emphatically historical, and it is not surprising that christology became a second focus of disagreement. F. C. Baur (1792–1860), who found Schleiermacher's concept of God excessively abstract,[24] also argued that

22. Biedermann, "Schleiermacher," 201–4.

23. Strauss, *Charakteristiken,* 171–72.

24. See, for example, Baur's letter to his brother (26 July 1821) reproduced in Heinz Liebing, "Ferdinand Christian Baurs Kritik an Schleiermachers *Glaubenslehre,*" *Zeitschrift für Theologie und Kirche* 54 (1957): 225–43, esp. 238.

he failed to establish the identity of his religious ideal with the historical Christ.[25] True, Schleiermacher did not argue for the sinless historical Redeemer solely by a dogmatic deduction from the church's consciousness; he accepted the obligation to look at the Gospel sources, launching in 1819 what is said to have been the first course of academic lectures ever devoted to the life of Jesus. But there the problems were, if anything, still more acute. Strauss, who exposed the logical structure of Schleiermacher's *dogmatic* argument, also subjected his *historical* lectures to ruthless criticism and showed convincingly that what Schleiermacher found in the Gospels was exactly what he was looking for: the "Savior" of his Moravian religious experience.[26]

Criticism of Schleiermacher from the standpoint of historical thinking proved more durable than the Hegelian philosophy that first produced it. We now have access, for instance, to Dilthey's interesting argument that he unjustifiably tied the universality of the ethical-religious ideal (the "kingdom of God") to the historical particularity of Jesus, whom he burdened with greatly inflated predicates.[27] During the first quarter of the present century, the signs were nonetheless favorable for a fresh development of Schleiermacher's revolutionary insights. The flaws exposed in the Ritschlian theology seemed to invite a return to the enterprise of the *Glaubenslehre,* at least insofar as its philosophical foundations had apparently been made secure. And, interestingly, some of the most historically minded thinkers were among the new admirers of Schleiermacher, including Ernst Troeltsch, who came to view the dominant Ritschlianism as a reactionary form of biblical positivism. Although Troeltsch associated himself with the History of Religions School, it was to Schleiermacher that he appealed in 1908 as the master of modern dogmatics—if only by reason of his program and not his doctrinal formulations.[28] And Troeltsch was only one of several theologians and scholars who contributed to what was greeted as a Schleiermacher renaissance.[29] Then came the Barthian deluge.

25. See esp. Baur's *Die christliche Gnosis, oder die christliche Religionsphilosophie in ihrer geschichtlichen Entwicklung* (Tübingen: C. F. Osiander, 1835), 637–56.

26. Strauss, *Christ of Faith,* 35.

27. Wilhelm Dilthey, *Leben Schleiermachers,* vol. 2 (in two part-vols.), ed. Martin Redeker (Berlin: Walter de Gruyter, 1966), also published as vol. 14 of Dilthey's *Gesammelte Schriften* (Göttingen: Vandenhoeck & Ruprecht, 1966), 473–507.

28. Ernst Troeltsch, "Half a Century of Theology: A Review," in *Ernst Troeltsch: Writings on Theology and Religion,* trans. and ed. Robert Morgan and Michael Pye (Atlanta, Georgia: John Knox Press, 1977), 79–81. See further chapter 12 below.

29. See Johannes Wendland, "Neuere Literatur über Schleiermacher," *Theologische Rundschau* 17 (1914): 133–43.

Schleiermacher and the Dialectical Theology

With the rise of the dialectical theology in the present century, Dilthey's criticism was turned upside down. Something very like the dualism he had detected in Schleiermacher's theology reappeared as the main object of disapproval in Emil Brunner's (1889–1966) *Mysticism and the Word*(1924); only now the universally religious was rejected in favor of the uniquely Christian, and it was flatly denied that Christianity could properly be treated as one of the religions of the world. Brunner granted that faith in Christ determined Schleiermacher's personal *piety.* His point was, however, that this faith could only be considered an alien intrusion in Schleiermacher's dogmatic *system,* which made the initial blunder of not starting from the Christian revelation but from a general theory of religion as mystical union with the All. Once Schleiermacher was trapped in the little garden of the pious, Brunner tells us, there was no way out: mystical religious experience lacks reference to Another. Against this mysticism, clearly documented in the *Speeches* and supported by the identity philosophy of the *Dialectic,* the word about Christ could only be spoken in contradiction.[30]

In his review of Brunner's vigorous indictment, Karl Barth found some features of his associate's critique to be objectionable, but he fully shared the verdict that the defendant's theology subjected the word of God to an intolerable bondage. And in a number of essays he suggested that the reason for the root methodological error lay in Schleiermacher's apologetic stance: at the very beginning, he subordinated the positive dogmatic task to the role of the apologist who is not a servant of Christianity but a master of it—a virtuoso. It took two "Assyrians" to call Jerusalem to order by exposing the fatal consequences of the initial flaw. Ludwig Feuerbach (1804–72) showed how the transcendent reality of the theologians could now be viewed as an illusion, and Strauss showed what happens if you venture to read the New Testament as history. In sum, from merely human religious experience, Barth argued, you cannot get either to God or to the real Christ, and in the middle third of our century the theological world was widely, though by no means universally, dominated by his reading of Protestant history.[31]

30. I have given a critical appraisal of Brunner's *Die Mystik und das Wort* in my *Tradition and the Modern World: Reformed Theology in the Nineteenth Century* (Chicago: University of Chicago Press, 1978), chap. 1.

31. See, in particular, the following writings of Barth (in English translation): *Protestant Theology in the Nineteenth Century: Its Background and History* (Valley Forge, Pennsylvania: Judson Press, 1973), chapters on Schleiermacher, Feuerbach, and Strauss; "The Word in Theology from Schleiermacher to Ritschl," in Barth, *Theology and Church: Shorter Writings, 1920–1928* (London: SCM Press, 1962); "Evangelical Theology in the Nineteenth Century," in Barth, *God, Grace and Gospel,* Scottish Journal of Theology Occasional Papers, no. 8 (Edin-

The dialectical theology's estimate of Schleiermacher and Protestant liberalism no longer carries immediate assent. I hope my exposition will have made clear, without the further argument I have attempted elsewhere, at least that what Schleiermacher *intended to do* and what Brunner *says he did* are two utterly antithetical operations. And I do not myself believe that Brunner took his adversary's programmatic statements seriously enough. Neither can I see sufficient reason to hold that Schleiermacher's undoubted concern to avoid conflict with science led him, as Barth thought, to relegate the dogmatic task to a secondary rank. There can, of course, be no question of just setting the neoorthodox criticisms aside; and if there are occasional signs at the present day that it has become possible in some quarters to dismiss them without engaging in detailed argument, that is cause for regret—just as, not so many years ago, one could only regret the dissemination of poorly substantiated, ritualistically repeated stereotypes about Schleiermacher. This does not alter the fact, however, that there is a real need to rediscover the theological generation that was swamped in the deluge. Thinkers like Hermann Mulert (1879–1950) and Wobbermin were not only sophisticated Schleiermacher scholars who immediately perceived the flaws in the dialectical theology's historiography, but also astute theologians in their own right who had strong reasons for believing that Protestant theology was on the verge of taking a wrong step.

The first line of Schleiermacher criticism had become, in Brunner, the accusation of "psychologism" or "agnostic expressionism." But Wobbermin, at least, recognized the possibility of a fresh defense that would draw out the affinities between Schleiermacher and Edmund Husserl (1859–1938). The basic aim of the *Glaubenslehre,* he suggested, was to develop a phenomenological theology in line with Luther's existential thinking, but also in anticipation of Husserl's notion of the intentionality of consciousness. And the givenness of God in the feeling of absolute dependence, Wobbermin pointed out, is something quite other than the inferential proof of God's existence that it has often been mistaken for.[32] The double comparison suggested by these remarks—with the Reformation (or at least Luther) and with phenomenological philosophy—is, I think, a program worthy of further exploration; I would myself insist, however, that

burgh: Oliver & Boyd, 1959); Barth, *The Theology of Schleiermacher* (Grand Rapids, Michigan: Eerdmans, 1982). The review of Brunner's book appeared in *Zwischen den Zeiten* (1924).

32. Wobbermin, "Schleiermacher," *Die Religion in Geschichte und Gegenwart,* 2d ed., 6 vols. (Tübingen: J. C. B. Mohr [Paul Siebeck], 1927–32), 5:176–77, 172–73. For Schleiermacher, of course, God is never given as an object; and this leads him to deny (in *Gl.,* § 4.4) any *Gegebensein Gottes,* although he does permit the expression that God is "given to us in feeling." See further chapter 2 above.

the Reformation comparison must be made more with Calvin than with Luther,[33] and I am not persuaded that the feeling of absolute dependence is the only or the best point at which to anchor our talk about God.

On the second line of criticism, Wobbermin's theological generation may have seen the way, not to defend Schleiermacher's christology (in the final analysis it may not be defensible), but to develop it and to pare off its objectionable features. If the history prerequisite to the occurrence or survival of evangelical faith had to consist of verifiable conclusions from life-of-Jesus research, Schleiermacher's christology would indeed be in serious trouble (and he would have a lot of company). But if we are to follow his own method consistently, then the directly pertinent history can only be the event in which Christ is proclaimed. Recognition of the need to relocate the fact on which faith depends lay behind the attempt to differentiate between *Historie* and *Geschichte.* On this discussion, too, Wobbermin made some exceptionally discerning remarks.[34] Although he was not entirely liberated from the temptation to move back from confidence in the proclaimed Christ to confidence in the historicity of the Synoptic Jesus, he did affirm the point—fundamental to Schleiermacher's theology—that the hallmark of the historical (i.e., of *Geschichte*) is not pastness but the reference to human existence in its "becoming." And he proposed that by *Historie* we should understand nothing other than researched *Geschichte,* this human existence made into the object of inquiry. Something like this lay behind Schleiermacher's conception of dogmatics as *historische Theologie.* The christological section of dogmatics, if its object is the impression made by the portrayal of Christ in the Christian proclamation, should be so conceived (to echo Schleiermacher's phrase) as not to get us entangled with science—in this instance, historical science.

Finally, the liberal rearguard was entirely capable of some countersallies of its own. As Mulert prophetically observed in 1934, it remained open to question whether Schleiermacher's critics would have any greater success in grasping the objective reality of God without being led astray by subjective presuppositions of their own. Some of what they characterized as "psychologism" and "historicism," Mulert suggested, might simply prove attributable to the fact that we can grasp nothing at all except with our psychological faculties and must incorporate everything that happens into the web of history.[35]

33. See chapter 8 below.

34. See Wobbermin's masterly and for the most part convincing study, *Geschichte und Historie in der Religionswissenschaft,* etc. (Tübingen: J. C. B. Mohr [Paul Siebeck], 1911), published as a supplement to the *Zeitschrift für Theologie und Kirche.*

35. Hermann Mulert, "Neuere deutsche Schleiermacher-Literatur," *Zeitschrift für Theologie und Kirche,* n.s., 15 (1934): 84.

A reappraisal of Schleiermacher is called for. In particular, a second look is needed at just those basic methodological moves of his that have been most fiercely contested. For all Brunner's determination to oppose him with "biblical-Reformation faith," Schleiermacher's experiential approach actually gave him a strong link with the heritage of Luther and Calvin; it was not simply an accommodation to modern habits of thought. Further, the subtle interweaving of *two* experiential motifs in his dogmatics, the universal awareness of God and the particular influence of Jesus, already transcended in some measure one of the most bitter theological debates of our century. Schleiermacher appears, rightly interpreted, to have worked from a point of view that neither rested on a "natural theology" (as commonly understood) nor yet hewed to a strictly "christocentric" line. The "word about Christ" was not, for him, the exclusive source of knowledge of God; but in the Christian it so determined the universally human awareness of God that Christians, he held, must be said to bear their entire consciousness of God only as something brought about in them by Christ (*Sendschr.*, 31). In the apt expression of Richard R. Niebuhr, Schleiermacher's manner of theological thinking was "Christomorphic," not in the Barthian sense "Christo-centric." And insofar as this makes Christ the "reformer" of human knowledge of God, Niebuhr rightly claims that Schleiermacher was more faithful to Calvin than was Barth.[36]

Equally important, Schleiermacher's approach does not isolate theology from other ways of studying religion, and yet does not dissolve it into nontheological disciplines either. Questions remain, of course, some of them forcefully posed by the neoorthodox critics, about the connection between his distinctively theological study of religion and other parts of his own intellectual system: the *Dialectic*, for instance, in which a philosophical doctrine of God is advanced, or the *Hermeneutic*, in which the interpretation of religious texts is subsumed under a general theory of understanding.[37] But here, too, the neoorthodox critique, notably Emil Brunner's, set the interpretation of Schleiermacher on a wrong track by exaggerating the importance of the *Dialectic* for understanding his dogmatics. A more fruitful inquiry is clearly suggested by the introduction to *The Christian Faith:* To what extent does the relationship of dogmatics to *ethics* (in Schleiermacher's sense) predetermine the interpretation of Christianity? Indeed, it should not be overlooked that Schleiermacher's own intended companion to the *Glaubenslehre* was the *Christliche Sittenlehre,* an

36. Richard R. Niebuhr, *Schleiermacher on Christ and Religion: A New Introduction* (New York: Charles Scribner's Sons, 1964), 161–62, 211–12. Cf. Redeker, who states that Schleiermacher thought "christocentrically" but not "christomonistically" (*Schleiermacher,* 149).

37. The pioneering work on hermeneutics was misleadingly included in the theological division of the *Sämmtliche Werke,* vol. 7.

unfinished work on Christian "ethics" in something like our sense of the word. It could well be argued that apart from the Christian ethics even his theology remains truncated; in his recognition of this Barth provided an important corrective to Brunner's *Mysticism and the Word*.[38] Even so, it is unlikely that one would wish to locate Schleiermacher's actual achievement—or his greatest contribution to religious studies—anywhere else but in his dogmatics.

38. Barth, *Protestant Theology*, 436. Unfortunately, the English translation misses Barth's allusion to Schleiermacher's notion of a "teleological" (not "theological"!) religion. See also Hans-Joachim Birkner, *Schleiermachers Christliche Sittenlehre im Zusammenhang seines philosophisch-theologischen Systems*, Theologische Bibliothek Töpelmann, vol. 8 (Berlin: Alfred Töpelmann, 1964), 27.

8

From Calvin to Schleiermacher: The Theme and the Shape of Christian Dogmatics

[The sense of the divine] is not a doctrine that must first be learned in school, but one of which every man is master from his mother's womb.
—JOHN CALVIN

Religion was the mother's womb in whose sacred darkness my young life was nurtured.
—FRIEDRICH SCHLEIERMACHER

THE RISE OF the Barthian theology after World War I occasioned an interesting debate on Schleiermacher and the Reformation. The literature devoted directly to the subject did not become extensive, and it established no consensus of interpretation or appraisal. But one can surely discover in it a common tendency, usually tacit but sometimes avowed, to assume that "Schleiermacher and the Reformation" means "Schleiermacher and Luther." My purpose is to examine this assumption and to show cause why the inquiry should be expanded to include Schleiermacher's relation to Calvin. In part, I shall be gathering up and developing some points that I have made elsewhere.[1] But I am also registering a plea on behalf of a neglected area of Schleiermacher research on which a great deal more remains to be done. It cannot be said, of course, that the issue of *Luther* and Schleiermacher has yet been extensively or definitively treated. But a scholarly interest in it and a literature on it do exist. The same can hardly be said for the theme "*Calvin* and Schleiermacher," although the beginnings have been made—with very diverse results—in the older, neglected works of Matthias Schneckenburger (1804–48) and Alexander Schweizer, and in more recent contributions by Wilhelm Niesel and Richard R. Niebuhr.[2]

1. See, in particular, B. A. Gerrish, *The Old Protestantism and the New: Essays on the Reformation Heritage* (Chicago: University of Chicago Press; Edinburgh: T. & T. Clark, 1982), chaps. 11–12.

2. Matthias Schneckenburger, *Vergleichende Darstellung des lutherischen und reformirten Lehrbegriffs*, ed. Eduard Güder, 2 vols. (Stuttgart: J. B. Metzler, 1855); Alexander Schweizer,

The State of the Question

One of the most perceptive of Schleiermacher's defenders who took up the question of his relation to the Protestant Reformation was Georg Wobbermin, as I have already suggested.[3] In an essay of 1931, he identified it as the question whether the turn to the subjective in the Reformation necessarily leads to subjectivism; and he maintained that it could finally be settled only by reference to Luther, since viewed as a whole the Reformation was Luther's work. For Wobbermin, plainly, the question of Schleiermacher and the Reformation was shaped by the assault of the dialectical theology on subjectivism, and he looked to Luther for the answer.[4]

The equating of the Reformation with Luther evokes misgivings when one reads, to take another example, Emanuel Hirsch's brilliant but more critical address, "Fichte's, Schleiermacher's, and Hegel's Relation to the Reformation," which appeared about the same time (in 1930).[5] From a footnote in Schleiermacher's essay on election (1819) Hirsch retrieves a lonely Luther citation, one of the "very few sayings of Luther that [Schleiermacher] used." He does not mention that the essay is rich in Calvin citations, or that it was conceived as a defense of Calvin's doctrine of election against the strictures of the Lutheran rationalist Karl Gottlieb Bretschneider (1776–1848). Since Hirsch's theme was Fichte's, Schleiermacher's, and Hegel's relation to the Reformation, did it not occur to him that Schleiermacher's apology for Calvin was pertinent to the discussion? And is it possible that the contrast he proceeds to draw between Schleiermacher's tranquil faith and the precarious faith of "the Reformers" might need to be modified if, along with his references to Luther's notion of faith as a risk, he had furnished references to Calvin's notion of faith as sure and certain knowledge of God's goodwill? Calvin's faith was not *unangefochten,* wholly unassailed by doubt, but it was not exactly suspended over "the abyss of despair" either.[6]

Hirsch goes on to offer an acute Kierkegaardian critique of Schleiermacher's idealistic-romantic transformation of justification by faith. Ac-

---

Die Glaubenslehre der evangelisch-reformirten Kirche dargestellt und aus den Quellen belegt, 2 vols. (Zurich: Orell, Füssli, 1844–47); Wilhelm Niesel, "Schleiermachers Verhältnis zur reformierten Tradition," *Zwischen den Zeiten* 8 (1930): 511–25; Richard R. Niebuhr, *Schleiermacher on Christ and Religion: A New Introduction* (New York: Charles Scribner's Sons, 1964).

3. See chapters 2 and 7 above.

4. Georg Wobbermin, "Gibt es eine Linie Luther-Schleiermacher?" *Zeitschrift für Theologie und Kirche* 39 [n.s. 12] (1931): 250–60.

5. Cf. chapter 2 above.

6. Emanuel Hirsch, "Fichtes, Schleiermachers und Hegels Verhältnis zur Reformation" (1930) in Hirsch, *Lutherstudien,* 2 vols. (Gütersloh: C. Bertelsmann, 1954), 2:121–68; see 140, 154–57. For Calvin's concept of faith, see especially *Inst.,* 3.2.7, 15, 21.

cording to Schleiermacher, the justifying verdict is truthful (not a legal fiction) because the Christian already bears the new life within and lives by it. Hirsch's critique is suggestive. In a footnote, he affirms a correspondence between Schleiermacher's doctrine of justification in the *Glaubenslehre* and Schneckenburger's portrayal of the same doctrine in Reformed "school theology."[7] But Hirsch does not pursue the point, nor does he raise the question of Schleiermacher's relation to Calvin himself, although Calvin's notion of a *duplex gratia* imparted through union with Christ might very well be pertinent.[8] As it is, the direction Hirsch's critique takes invites questions about his interpretation of Schleiermacher himself and, implicitly, Luther, and it is not my intention to pursue them here.[9] My point is simply that once again "Reformation" is being taken as synonymous with "Luther," only this time it is a Kierkegaardian Luther with whom we have to do.

Closer to our own day, in an article published in 1969, Paul Seifert—well known for his earlier study on the theology of the young Schleiermacher (1960)—rightly points out that the relation of Schleiermacher to the Reformation cannot be determined by his actual citations from the Reformers (or the confessions), and that this accounts for the relative neglect of the subject. But he discovers a formal parallel between Schleiermacher and Luther in that each initiated a new epoch by addressing the distinctive challenge of his own day: Luther asked how he could get a gracious God, and Schleiermacher how—without the authority of Bible or church—a person could become religious again. Further, Seifert argues for a more material parallel in that Schleiermacher's theology was christocentric and in this respect *gut lutherisch*. Schleiermacher did not only *want* to be (Barth), but actually *was,* a christocentric theologian.[10]

Once more, one notes that the question of Schleiermacher and the Reformation is shaped by criticisms from the side of the dialectical theology, and that Luther (or what is *lutherisch*) is the point of reference for framing an answer. And once more the reader may have some misgivings. It was certainly a monstrous interpretation when Karl Barth spoke of

7. Hirsch, 162 n. 1.

8. *Inst.*, 3.11.1.

9. Is it true, for instance, that Schleiermacher simply does not know sin as guilt (Hirsch, 163)? And has Hirsch taken note of Luther's insistence that the faith that justifies is a formal righteousness, or that our deliverance is through the "inherence" of Christ's righteousness? (See Gerrish, *The Old Protestantism*, 82–85.) Finally, is the difference between the revelation of God's love in my own history and an objective historical revelation *whose effect has to be personally appropriated* really as sharp as Hirsch makes out (166–68)?

10. Paul Seifert, "Schleiermacher und Luther," *Luther: Zeitschrift der Luther-Gesellschaft* 40 (1969): 51–68; see 54–59. Seifert's book on the young Schleiermacher was titled *Die Theologie des jungen Schleiermacher* (Gütersloh: Gütersloher Verlagshaus G. Mohn, 1960).

christology as a "great disturbance" in Schleiermacher's dogmatics.[11] And yet it can hardly be established that Schleiermacher was really a christocentric theologian in the strictest sense merely by referring, as Seifert does, to what is said in the celebrated eleventh proposition of *The Christian Faith* (second edition): that everything in Christianity is "related to the redemption accomplished by Jesus of Nazareth." It all depends on the meaning assigned to the term "christocentric." But this much, at least, may be said with assurance: According to Schleiermacher, the religiousness of Christians, like everyone else's, is as such constituted by their humanity, not by their relation to Christ, who is rather the source of its Christianness and its peculiar strength. And since Calvin, like Schleiermacher, found that he needed to talk about *homo religiosus* before he could expound faith in Christ, might it be useful to ask if Schleiermacher's theology is perhaps *not* christocentric—and therefore *gut calvinistisch?*[12] That this possibility is not considered by Seifert may have been partly due to Wilhelm Niesel's lecture, which he quotes, on Schleiermacher's relation to the Reformed tradition; since its publication in 1930, the lecture has frequently been cited as a sufficient reason to dismiss Schleiermacher's profession of loyalty to the "Reformed school."

These three essays—by Wobbermin, Hirsch, and Seifert, respectively—may suffice to justify my question. Although each of them has made important contributions to the theme of Schleiermacher and the Reformation, and I have not attempted to explore these contributions here, do they perhaps exemplify one of those misleading academic presuppositions that shut off a potentially fruitful avenue of inquiry? The naturalness of a comparison between Luther and Schleiermacher is plain enough: The one stood related to classical Protestant theology much as the other stood related to liberal Protestant theology, and they have every claim to be ranked as German Protestantism's most eminent theologians. Calvin must appear as something of an outsider in their company. But there may nevertheless be sound reasons for not prematurely closing the question of Schleiermacher and the Reformation with a comparison between him and

11. Karl Barth, *Protestant Theology in the Nineteenth Century: Its Background and History,* Eng. trans. (Valley Forge, Pennsylvania: Judson Press, 1973), 431–32.

12. Schleiermacher, *Gl.,* § 32.1, § 62.3. The notion that two elements are combined in the Christian consciousness—a general awareness of God and a specific relationship to Christ—makes it difficult to classify Schleiermacher's dogmatics as strictly "christocentric." And the term fits his thinking even less if taken, as it often is, to deny any genuine (i.e., non-idolatrous) awareness of God apart from Christ. Calvin's doctrine of sin enables him, unlike Schleiermacher, both to affirm a universal consciousness of God and to deny an actual knowledge of God outside Christ. The difference between Calvin and Schleiermacher in this respect is plain, but, as I hope to show, there is more to the agreement between them than has commonly been noticed. See further nn. 40, 65 below.

Luther alone. Naturally, the most convincing reasons would arise out of a detailed comparison between Schleiermacher and the Reformers on such individual doctrines as election, faith, justification, and the sacraments. This cannot be attempted here. Instead, I confine myself to pointing out that simply to identify the Reformation with Luther is to assign to Luther a status he did not have in Schleiermacher's own eyes and, at the same time, to miss the distinctive role he did assign to Calvin. In this way, a case may be made for venturing on the more challenging task of detailed comparison.

Schleiermacher and the Protestant Reformers

Some of those who have written incidentally on Schleiermacher and the Reformation have been struck by the paucity and coolness of his references to Luther.[13] But Schleiermacher was not a Lutheran, and even after the union of 1817 he continued to profess his allegiance to what he called the "Reformed school."[14] He held a conception of history as the collective work of a "common spirit" and was unwilling to attribute too much to individuals.[15] Granted this reserve, he was by no means grudging in his praise for Luther, whom he characteristically thought of as "our hero in the faith,"[16] and he remarked that the Reformed, too, acknowledged Luther as a singular and chosen instrument of God. But a gentle note of protest shines unmistakably through Schleiermacher's generous praise. He hoped that when the dividing names "Lutheran" and "Reformed" disappeared in the Church of the Union, it would no longer seem as if the Reformed were less respectful of the man after whom the Lutherans were named, nor yet as if the Lutherans were less concerned than the Reformed to avoid glorifying any one man too much.[17] He viewed Luther's achievement as part of a larger, unfinished Reformation that could not be the work of any single individual.[18] Interestingly, that is how Calvin, too, thought of Luther's achievement.[19]

It would be a manifest error, therefore, if one looked for very much *more* warmth in Schleiermacher's references to his own Reformers, Zwingli

13. See chapter 2, nn. 24, 25, above.

14. See, e.g., Schleiermacher, *An Herrn Oberhofprediger Dr. Ammon über seine Prüfung der Harmsischen Sätze* (1818), SW 1,5:341.

15. In the works cited above (chap. 2, nn. 24, 25), Bornkamm and Stephan both comment on Schleiermacher's notion of a collective spirit.

16. Schleiermacher, *Gespräch zweier selbst überlegender evangelischer Christen*, etc. (1827), SW 1,5:547.

17. *An Ammon*, SW 1,5:396–97.

18. *Gespräch zweier Christen*, SW 1,5:542–48, 625.

19. For documentation, see Gerrish, *The Old Protestantism*, chap. 2.

and Calvin, than he displayed in his references to Luther. It should not be overlooked that in his little-read lectures on church history Schleiermacher reserved some of his highest praise for the humanist Erasmus, who, he thought, held the purest, most truly evangelical idea of reformation. For Erasmus recognized that once practical abuses had been stemmed, and once a sounder instruction had gradually spread, diversity of doctrine could be left to disappear of its own accord. In other words, it would be a mistake to ask, Whose doctrines does Schleiermacher come closest to? as though that were the real question of Schleiermacher and the Reformation. He felt a certain kinship precisely with a reformer whose freedom of spirit, despite all that could be said against him, set him apart from those on both sides of the confessional split who wanted instant uniformity of doctrine.[20]

On one occasion, it is true, Schleiermacher did appear to rank another reformer's doctrine above Luther's. He began his Reformation address of 1817, delivered at the University of Berlin, by seeming to align himself with Zwingli: he expressed the hope that no one would be surprised to hear him, of all people, speak on that occasion as one "more addicted to Zwingli's doctrine than Luther's."[21] A rhetorical stratagem, perhaps, more than a confession of faith? Or perhaps no more than an allusion to his reputation? But in that case one must wonder to what Zwinglian doctrine he was reputedly addicted. The address itself does not suffice for an answer. A plausible case could be made, however, for asserting an affinity between Schleiermacher and Zwingli on the doctrine of God. In his *Commentary on True and False Religion,* Zwingli's stress on the immanence of God (*Hoc est deus in mundo, quod ratio in homine!*), his close identification of natural and divine causality, his conception of God as the life and motion of all that lives and moves, the abundant goodness that loves to impart itself—all of these characteristically Zwinglian thoughts find an echo in Schleiermacher.[22] Commenting on some of Zwingli's ideas in the sermon *On the Providence of God* (1530), Alexander Schweizer remarked that

20. Schleiermacher, *Geschichte der christlichen Kirche* (1840), SW 1,11:582. Nobody should infer from my remarks in this paragraph the "thesis" attributed to me by one reader of the original paper: that in Schleiermacher's eyes Erasmus was the *Hauptfigur der Reformationszeit.* My language was and is, I hope, more circumspect. The alleged thesis would contradict my actual thesis about Schleiermacher and Calvin! See Martin Ohst, *Schleiermacher und die Bekenntnisschriften: Eine Untersuchung zu seiner Reformations- und Protestantismusdeutung,* Beiträge zur historischen Theologie, vol. 77 (Tübingen: J. C. B. Mohr [Paul Siebeck], 1989), 71n., a work that in many other respects may be commended for its discussion of Schleiermacher and the Reformation.

21. Schleiermacher, *Oratio . . . A. MDCCCXVII. habita* (1817), SW 1,5:311.

22. Ulrich Zwingli, *De vera et falsa religione commentarius* (1525), CR 90.842.25, 641.16, 646.25, 650.36, 651.12. Cf., for instance, Schleiermacher, *Gl.,* § 52.2, § 46.2, § 55.1, § 166.1.

Zwingli, too, had he lived after Spinoza, would have been accused of Spinozism; all Zwingli lacked was the more precise terminology of *natura naturans* and *natura naturata*.[23]

In other respects, however, Schleiermacher displays little or no affinity with Zwingli. He does not echo Zwingli's conception of church and state, and on the sacraments he clearly understands the Reformed position to be Calvinistic. He finds Zwingli's sacramental ideas "rather meager and dry," and he assumes that the Lutherans and the Reformed alike hold to a partaking of the body and blood of Christ in the Eucharist and differ only concerning the mode of partaking: whether along with the bread and wine, or by a heavenly elevation of the soul. In short, "Zwingli is not the Reformed church."[24]

Calvin is not the Reformed church either. But he does seem to have been the Reformer whom Schleiermacher regarded most highly *as a theologian*. He did not claim to be a Calvin scholar, but he knew Calvin's *Institutes* thoroughly. (Like the English, he treated the title *Institutio* as though it were plural, *Institutionen*.) When a theological opponent attributed a dubious sentiment to Calvin, Schleiermacher's reaction was confident: "I cannot find this principle anywhere in my Calvin; rather, as I consider the matter more closely, I find grounds enough in my slight knowledge of Calvin to assert that he cannot have written that." His confidence was vindicated. When his opponent came up with a reference, it turned out that he had misrepresented a passage from the third book of the *Institutes*, and Schleiermacher was perfectly well acquainted with it. The phrase "my slight knowledge of Calvin" has more than a touch of irony in it. "I thought the proof would come," Schleiermacher says, "from who knows what more seldom read commentary of Calvin!" But the alleged reference was to a section of the *Institutes* that the author of the essay on election knew very well.[25] He also knew well the chapters on the sacraments in book 4, that is, on the other main point at issue between Lutherans and Reformed. But he refers in his *Glaubenslehre* to all four books of the *Institutes*, whether or not he ever looked into the "seldom read" commentaries.

Schleiermacher admired the *Institutes* for two main reasons, neither of which comes as any surprise. First, the *Institutes* is a priceless work because it never loses touch with the religious affections, not even in the most intricate material. It is presumably this same point that Schleiermacher is mak-

23. Schweizer, *Glaubenslehre der evangelisch-reformirten Kirche*, 1:92. Cf. Barth's discussion of the concept of divine *concursus* in his *Church Dogmatics* III, 3, § 49, Eng. trans. (Edinburgh: T. & T. Clark, 1960), 96, 117.

24. *An Ammon*, SW 1,5:381, 386; *Zugabe zu meinem Schreiben an Herrn Ammon*, SW 1,5:409–10.

25. *Zugabe*, SW 1,5:409–10.

ing when he speaks of Calvin's strict combination of rigorous criticism and the properly religious element. In other words, Calvin, we may say, never lost sight of the fact that theology really *is* about the actual Christian religion. Second, Schleiermacher ranked the *Institutes* highly for sharpness of method and systematic compass. He commended the work also for a third reason, because of its agreeable Latin style. But, clearly, what Schleiermacher admired most in Calvin's *Institutes* was exactly what he himself strove to achieve in his own *Glaubenslehre:* a dogmatics that has at once a churchly character, given by its consistent reference to the Christian religious affections, and a scientific character, given by the exactness and mutual coherence of its concepts.[26]

It is true that Schleiermacher found the *Institutes,* when judged by these two criteria, not without defects. For while it has, unlike Melanchthon's *Loci communes,* a genuinely systematic character, the systematic impulse is hindered by a polemical tendency, behind which Schleiermacher detected the false assumption that the religious impulse itself can be captured in the letter of particular doctrinal formulas. The lively development of a genuine systematic form must arise directly out of evangelical principles; a polemical dogmatics, by contrast, more naturally assumes the scholastic form of questions, theses, and antitheses, and the connection between doctrine and the religious principle itself becomes a matter of secondary interest. Lutheran dogmatics in particular came to be dominated, in Schleiermacher's opinion, by polemic—against the Catholics and the Swiss. And even Calvin's *Institutes,* though much more strictly systematic, is not free of this defect.[27] However, this criticism only makes all the more visible the points at which we should compare Schleiermacher and Calvin, if the comparison is not to be arbitrary but to have some basis in Schleiermacher's own judgments about his predecessors. Accordingly, we need to look more closely, first, at Calvin's notion that piety is the actual theme of Christian theology; second, at his attempt to give his *Institutes* an overall shape or structure. In each respect it will be shown that there are instructive parallels with Schleiermacher's *Glaubenslehre* that invite a comparison between the two great classics of Protestant theology.[28]

26. *An Ammon,* SW 1,5:345; *Geschichte der Kirche,* SW 1,11:602. The principal criteria Schleiermacher is employing in his judgments on the *Institutio* are simply the two tests of ecclesial and scientific value specified in *Gl.,* § 17; cf. §§ 27–28.

27. *Geschichte der Kirche,* SW 1,11:615–16.

28. In what follows, I have not taken up the "definiteness of concepts" that Schleiermacher combines with systematic coherence in his second, scientific test of dogmatics. But here, too, one could point to the obvious parallel between Schleiermacher's *Leitsätze* and Calvin's definitions (e.g., his definition of "faith" in *Inst.,* 3.2.7). There is an interesting stylistic difference in Calvin's preference for leading up to his definitions rather than beginning with them (as Schleiermacher does).

The Theme of Christian Theology

Schleiermacher himself drew attention to a formal resemblance between his theology and Luther's: for both, theology was reflection on the religiousness shared by the theologian with other believers in Christ. Whereas the rationalist holds that piety is generated from concepts, and that the study of theology may therefore be expected to make one pious, the truth is, according to Schleiermacher, that theology arises as the already religious subject turns back in thought upon its own religiousness. This, he believed, was clearly the way in which Luther's theology arose.[29] Luther did not, of course, like Schleiermacher, characterize his theological procedure as "empirical."[30] He might sooner have described it as biblical and exegetical. But what he looked for in the Scriptures was light on the experience of faith, which the Scriptures not only described but mediated to him. The Bible is the criterion of the experience, but the Bible read without faith is a closed book. Hence Luther could say: "Not Scripture alone . . . but experience also. . . . I have the matter itself [*rem*] and experience together with Scripture."[31] He could even venture to say: "Experience alone [*experientia sola!*] makes a theologian."[32] It seems entirely appropriate, then, to call his theology a "theology of experience" and to find in this expression a genuine point of contact with liberal Protestantism. The affinity is plain. It goes without saying that differences are not thereby excluded.

If the likenesses and differences between Luther's conception of theology and Schleiermacher's are not to be misstated, refinements of the expression "theology of experience" are no doubt called for.[33] But I must move on and face the question: Do we not have to do here precisely with a distinctively Lutheran theological style, a style of which Calvin and the Calvinists could hardly approve? Schweizer, at any rate, who wanted to establish Schleiermacher as the reviver of a distinctively Reformed theology, found himself obliged to admit that the "empirical-historical-anthropological" approach of his hero was Lutheranizing: in his view, a sound Reformed dogmatics should be theocentric and deductive, proceeding from the idea of God.[34] Others have held the view that Reformed dogmatics is properly deductive in the sense that it proceeds not from experience but from Scripture.[35] Though different, these two views of

29. *Sendschr.*, 15–16.
30. Ibid., 20–21.
31. Martin Luther, WAT, 1.340.30 (no. 701).
32. WAT, 1.16.13 (no. 46).
33. I have made some suggestions toward this end in chapter 2 above.
34. Cited in chapter 2, n. 33, above.
35. Hans Lassen Martensen, for instance; cited in chapter 2, n. 32, above.

Calvinistic dogmatics are not totally exclusive, and they agree in regarding the experiential-anthropological approach as more characteristic of Lutheranism.

The issues are much too complex to be settled, or even discussed, here. The sole point I need to stress, for now, is beyond controversy: After the famous opening chapter on the two parts of wisdom (knowledge of God and knowledge of self), Calvin actually begins his *Institutes* neither with the idea of God, nor with the authority of Scripture, but with a discussion of religion. Mainly on the basis of common human experience, he offers what we might call a description of the religious consciousness as that which distinguishes humanity from the rest of the animal kingdom.[36] The controversies that have raged over the introductory chapters of the *Institutes* must raise doubts about the clarity of Calvin's thoughts and their place in his overall argument. What exactly *is* the innate "sense of the divine"? And *why* does Calvin need to establish its existence in every human person? But the introductory chapters are, after all, there; and they make it quite impossible to classify the empirical-historical-anthropological approach as peculiarly Lutheran, as though Schleiermacher, in adopting it, had somehow deviated from his own Reformed tradition.[37]

Indeed, the fact that Calvin's theme in these chapters is religion rather than faith actually aligns Schleiermacher, at this point, more closely with Calvin than with Luther. The anthropological point of entry in the *Institutes* is not Christian existence but the universal phenomenon of human religiousness. Of course, Luther's thematizing of existence in faith was sometimes carried out through an explicit contrast with the religion of the "natural man";[38] and Calvin, for his part, intended to move on to what he called "full faith" or the *propria fidei doctrina* (*Glaubenslehre* properly so-

36. *Inst.*, 1.2–5.

37. Calvin seems, at times, to assign no other function to the *divinitatis sensus* than to establish the common guilt of all, none of whom, though they knew God, have honored God as God. Hence Calvin distinguishes sharply between natural and saving knowledge of God. (In addition to the discussion in the 1559 *Institutio,* see Comm. Rom. 1:20–21; cf. the "argument" to Comm. Gen., also Comm. Ps. 19:7.) But it seems clear that the saving knowledge, when it comes, attaches itself to a remnant of the natural knowledge; otherwise, Calvin's famous comparison of Scripture to a pair of spectacles, which brings to clear focus a *confusa alioqui Dei notitia,* would make no sense (*Inst.*, 1.6.1; cf. 14.1). Consequently, I do not see how those for whom a "christocentric" theology entails denial of a point of contact for the gospel can cite Calvin in their support. The resemblance between Calvin and Schleiermacher will naturally seem closest to those who share my reading of Calvin. But I cannot enter any further into the debate here, and I do not need to. The structural parallel is there—that is, the historical-anthropological starting point in a discourse on human religiousness—however differently the argument may be worked out in each of the two dogmatic systems.

38. See Gerrish, *Grace and Reason: A Study in the Theology of Luther* (1962; reprint, Chicago: University of Chicago Press, 1979), chap. 7.

called!).[39] But the logical order of Calvin's presentation throws a distinctive emphasis on the concept of natural religion. Moreover, right at the beginning another word, "piety," has been introduced: it stands for *true* religion, which is the proper fruit of the innate sense of God. "Faith," in Calvin's vocabulary, is simply the restoration of the original relationship of piety that existed between Adam and God. In content, *fides* and *pietas* are identical insofar as both denote the right human response to the paternal goodwill of God. They differ in that *fides* is directed to the assurance of God's goodwill in Christ. *Pietas,* true religion, and its restoration as *fides*—this is the actual theme of Calvin's *pietatis summa.*[40]

Paul Seifert, as we have had occasion to notice, observes that the new situation in which Schleiermacher found himself at the turn of the nineteenth century demanded a shift in the formulation of the religious question, from "How do I get a gracious God?" to "How do we become religious [*fromm*] again?" It might well be said that in actual fact Calvin already introduced this "new" question in the sixteenth century. For him, it was mainly a question of sin, whereas for Schleiermacher it had become mainly a question of secularization. But the parallel is striking, and the difference is by no means absolute. It follows that there is no need to argue, as Van Harvey does in an interesting essay on Schleiermacher's method, that although Schleiermacher, like the Reformers, intends theological affirmations to be descriptions of God not in Godself but as given to faith, he is nevertheless separated from them by an important difference of vocabulary.[41] Harvey is of course right in saying that Schleiermacher's terms "consciousness," "piety," and "feeling" "cannot be easily substituted for what the Reformers meant by 'faith.'"[42] But Calvin, at least, also used the terms *religio, sensus,* and *pietas;* and while there are undoubted differences between his psychology of the religious consciousness and Schleiermacher's, it is exactly the parallels of vocabulary that alert us to a possible similarity of method.[43]

It may be added that on the understanding of human religiousness there was a difference between Calvin and Zwingli, and it once again suggests that Schleiermacher's closest affinity among the Reformers was with Calvin. Zwingli, too, began his systematic work with reflections on reli-

39. *Inst.,* 1.6.1; cf. 6.2. The French version of 1560 states (in 1.6.1, OS 3:61n.) that the saving knowledge *emporte pleine foy avec soy.*

40. *Inst.,* 1.2.1, 3.2, 4.1; 2.6.4; 3.2.16. From the passages in book 1, it may be inferred that *pietas* is the proper attitude that should issue from the *divinitatis sensus,* and *religio* in turn is the outward form or expression of *pietas.* The title to the first edition describes Calvin's work as a *pietatis summa* (see OS 1:19).

41. Van A. Harvey, "A Word in Defense of Schleiermacher's Theological Method," JR 42 (1962): 151–70; see 153–54.

42. Ibid., 154.

43. See further Gerrish, *The Old Protestantism,* 203–4, 379 n. 35.

gion; indeed, Zwingli's *Commentary on True and False Religion,* his gift of healing ointment from Germany to France,[44] must be considered in this respect, as in others, the pioneer work of Reformed dogmatics. But, as J. Samuel Preus has pointed out, Zwingli's approach was more historical and empirical, Calvin's more natural and essentialist. That is to say, whereas Calvin sought the origins of religion in a universal endowment of human nature, Zwingli saw religion, even outside the sphere of Christian revelation, as a response to specific divine activity on particular occasions (which he conceived of after the pattern of God's quest for "man" in Genesis 3:9). One would not wish to exaggerate this contrast, since for Calvin the *divinitatis sensus* is of course implanted by God and stirred by God's self-disclosure in nature. But Preus does, I think, establish that the contrast is there. In a word, Calvin's approach was more anthropological than Zwingli's. As Preus says: "For Zwingli, the 'seeds' [of religion] were not a universal or permanent human endowment or potentiality as they were for classical authors and for Calvin."[45] And, we may add, for Schleiermacher! If we bring Preus's contrast to our present discussion, it unmistakably confirms our contention that there is a striking resemblance between Schleiermacher's approach and Calvin's. We could in fact hardly do better than borrow a concept from Schleiermacher and say that what Calvin was talking about in the introductory chapters of the *Institutes* was an *Uroffenbarung,* a revelation not simply at the beginning of human history but in the depths of every human consciousness.[46]

The theme of Calvin's dogmatics was *pietas,*[47] as the theme of Schleiermacher's dogmatics was *die Frömmigkeit.* For both of them, this theme had to be protected against the incursions of "speculation," which is the attempt to speak of God *apart from* the devout consciousness. Here, too, as soon as the comparison is suggested, both similarities and differences come to mind, and I have tried to sort them out elsewhere. Schleiermacher did not, like Calvin, consider speculation useless or presumptuous, but simply as another enterprise of the human spirit, alongside dogmatics and not to be methodologically confused with it. Hence he thought that even the dogmatic theologian might speculate when off duty. In his very last days, on his deathbed, Schleiermacher testified that he was constrained to think the profoundest speculative thoughts along with his deepest reli-

44. This is Zwingli's own description of his book (*Commentarius,* CR 90.629.15).

45. J. Samuel Preus, "Zwingli, Calvin and the Origin of Religion," *Church History* 46 (1977): 186–202; quotation on 193.

46. Schleiermacher's actual expression is *eine ursprüngliche Offenbarung* (*Gl.,* § 4.4). Cf. Calvin's *prima et simplex Dei notitia* (*Inst.,* 1.2.1).

47. Of course, the theme of the *Institutio* is *cognitio Dei.* But it is *pietas* that defines the exact kind of knowledge with which theology has to do. "Neque enim Deum, proprie loquendo, cognosci dicemus ubi nulla est religio nec pietas" (*Inst.,* 1.2.1).

gious feelings. It must be admitted that he was under the benign influence of opium at the time. But the testimony was entirely consistent with his lifelong determination, so like Calvin's, to do theology within the limits of piety alone.[48]

In sum, while it can be said that Calvin's understanding of the theme of dogmatics was no different from Luther's insofar as theology had become for both of them reflection on the actual existence of the Christian, nevertheless Calvin's language is closer than Luther's to Schleiermacher's language, and his thought is closer than Zwingli's to Schleiermacher's thought. In Calvin, as in Schleiermacher, the theme of *pietas,* broadened into an account of *homo religiosus,* has become the first item on a carefully structured dogmatic agenda, and it continues to regulate the agenda by its exclusion of speculation from beginning to end.

The Shape of Christian Theology

Calvin's very first book, his commentary on Seneca's *De Clementia* (1532), extols orderly arrangement as not the least among the ornaments of speech. He thought Seneca deficient in it.[49] But his own assiduous cultivation of it made Calvin himself, in due course, the preeminent systematician of the Protestant Reformation. No doubt, the contrast between Luther the occasional writer and Calvin the system-builder has often been overdrawn. Structural principles, such as the two-kingdoms doctrine, are not lacking in Luther's theology; and if a system had to have a center, Luther's constant reference to his chief article might qualify his thinking as *more* systematic than Calvin's, which had no one center or first principle, whether forgiveness, predestination, or anything else. But Luther never ventured to write a *pietatis summa;* Calvin did.

Were it not for the final revision of the *Institutes,* however, there would be no compelling reason to name Calvin the preeminent systematician among the Reformers. The first edition (1536) was designed to be a simple catechism. The revision of 1539 only brought the work closer to the pattern of Melanchthon's *Loci Communes* (first published in 1521), Zwingli's *Commentary on True and False Religion,* and even, on a much smaller scale, William Farel's (1489–1565) *Summary and Brief Declaration* (1525).[50] As

48. For documentation and further discussion, see Gerrish, *The Old Protestantism,* 201–3.

49. "Dispositionem etiam desidero, non postremam orationis lucem" (*Calvin's Commentary on Seneca's De Clementia,* ed. Ford Lewis Battles and André Malan Hugo, Renaissance Text Series, vol. 8 [Leiden: E. J. Brill, 1969], 10).

50. Guillaume Farel, *Sommaire et briefve declaration,* ed. Arthur Piaget (Paris: E. Droz, 1935). This is a facsimile of the original edition (1525), a solitary copy of which was discovered in the British Museum. The original title indicates that Farel, too, thought in terms of *loci communes:* the work is a summary and declaration *daulcuns lieux fort necessaires,* etc.

Calvin himself indicated in a preface to the 1545 French edition of his *Institutes,* his purpose was simply to treat inclusively the principal matters comprised in the Christian philosophy.[51] And it could be said that Melanchthon had just done that very ably in the third and last edition of his *Loci* (1543–44), in which he skillfully wove into the order followed by the articles of the creed a narrative motif drawn from Scripture.[52] By this time, Melanchthon had come to exhibit a strong sense of the dogmatician's need to see how the pieces fit together in the total design. However, he is still thinking of order in terms of due sequence; and what is relatively new to Protestant dogmatics in Calvin's final *Institutes* of 1559 is a sense of order as logical or organic connection.

In his preface to the final edition, Calvin wrote: "Although I did not regret the labor spent [on earlier versions], I was never satisfied until [the work] was arranged in this order that is now set out."[53] Two things, in particular, are distinctively Calvin's own by the time he was able to write those words. First, there is what we may call the "introduction" to the work as a whole: the discourse (already mentioned) on piety and the common religious consciousness of humanity. It was probably suggested to Calvin by Zwingli; and it was amplified from Zwingli's own major source, the *De natura deorum* of the pagan philosopher—*Ethnicus ille*—Cicero (106–43 B.C.E.).[54] We have noted how the introductory remarks on piety serve to define the boundaries of a *pietatis summa.*

Second, there is Calvin's important notion of the twofold knowledge of God as Creator and Redeemer, which seems to have been very much his own conception.[55] He could have found the expression *duplex cognitio dei,* with a somewhat similar meaning, in Luther.[56] But the way in which he conceived of the relationship between the two knowledges is distinctive. It even appears to reverse a judgment made by his Reformed predecessor, Zwingli, who had written in his *Commentary:* "Knowledge of God in the

51. ". . . en traictant les matieres principales et de consequence, lesquelles sont comprinses en la Philosophie Chrestienne" (CR 31:xxiii). Here, too, the divisions of Christian dogmatics are thought of as *loci communes.* The phrase quoted appeared already in the French version of 1541.

52. Philip Melanchthon, *Loci praecipui theologici* (1543), preface, CR 21:603–7. Melanchthon's conception of dogmatic order is particularly clear in his preface to his own German translation of the *Loci: Heubtartikel Christlicher Lere* (1558), CR 22:51–58. Calvin, of course, knew the *Loci* well (in Latin); he wrote a preface for the French translation published at Geneva in 1546 (CR 37:847).

53. *Inst.,* OS 3:5.

54. *Inst.,* 1.3.1. See further Egil Grislis, "Calvin's Use of Cicero in the *Institutes* I:1–5: A Case Study in Theological Method," *Archive for Reformation History* 62 (1971): 5–37. See further n. 71 below.

55. *Inst.,* 1.2.1, 6.1, 6.2, 10.1.

56. Luther, *In epistolam S. Pauli ad Galatas commentarius* (1535), WA 40^{1}.607.28: "Duplex est cognitio Dei, Generalis et propria. Generalem habent omnes homines," etc.

nature of the case precedes knowledge of Christ."[57] For Calvin, all right knowledge of God is born of obedience: no one has the slightest taste of sound teaching who does not first become a pupil of Scripture, which is the school of God's children. Zwingli could say that, too. But Calvin believes that obedience to the word is inseparable from faith in Christ and the preaching of the cross. It follows that for him, quite otherwise than for Zwingli, redemption through Christ precedes the knowledge of God, or, to put it in Calvin's own terms, the knowledge of God the Redeemer is antecedent to the knowledge of God the Creator.[58]

Calvin does say in one place that first in order came the knowledge of God as founder and governor of the universe, then the other knowledge that is given in the person of the Redeemer. But that is intended as a historical judgment about the story of the human race.[59] He makes it clear that in the order of individual experience, since the fall, knowing God as Redeemer must come before knowing him as Creator; it is by faith that we understand the world to have been created by the word of God (Heb. 11:3), and faith has its own peculiar way of understanding creation to include the divine preservation of the world.[60] Hence the doctrine of redemption, strictly speaking, has dogmatic priority over the doctrine of creation, which entirely depends upon it. The fact that Calvin nevertheless decided to follow the conventional, quasi-historical order and to present creation first, before redemption, should not be permitted to obscure his conviction that in the order of experience a genuine awareness of God as Creator is strictly a function of being redeemed.[61]

It follows that there is a strong prima facie resemblance in structure between the *Institutes* and Schleiermacher's *The Christian Faith,* which also presents a two-part system of doctrine, introduced by a discussion of religion in general, and understands the relationship of the parts in somewhat the same way. Both parts assert no more about God than concerns piety; and while Schleiermacher, like Calvin, places creation before redemption, he expressly points out that the reverse order would be entirely proper and

57. CR 90.675.33.

58. *Inst.,* 1.6.2, 4; 2.6.1.

59. Ibid., 1.6.1. Calvin can also speak of this order as the *naturae ordo* (1.2.1, 14.20; 2.6.1). But it has been disrupted by sin. "Certe post lapsum primi hominis nulla ad salutem valuit Dei cognitio absque Mediatore" (2.6.1).

60. Ibid., 1.5.14, 16.1; cf. 1.14.21. It is astonishing how close Calvin is in these passages to Schleiermacher's characteristic thoughts that every event may be deemed a "miracle" (in the second of the *Reden über die Religion*), and that for the devout consciousness "preservation" is the actual content of the doctrine of creation (*Gl.,* § 39.1, etc.).

61. Without redemption, there is no *vera [Dei] notitia* or *recta pietas* (*Inst.,* 1.4.1). The point could be further illustrated from Calvin's use of the parallel conception of a *duplex cognitio hominis,* since he holds that the created condition of humanity can be clearly known only through contemplation of the Second Adam (*Inst.,* 1.15.1, 4).

in some ways more appropriate. For, as he puts it, "Christians bear their entire consciousness of God in themselves only as something brought about in them through Christ."[62] Why, then, does Schleiermacher not begin directly with redemption? One reason he gives (not the only one) is that an academic book is not like a banquet in which the inferior wine is served last, when the guests are too drunk to care. Schleiermacher saves his best—redemption through Christ—until last.[63]

What results is a dogmatic connection between creation (or preservation) and redemption exactly conveyed in the heading to part 1 of the *Glaubenslehre* (second edition): as far as Christian dogmatics is concerned, the awareness of God as Creator is *presupposed by and contained in* the Christian religious affections, which, in their essential nature, are a consciousness of redemption. Even the universal consciousness of God, though its presence can be verified by anyone who has acquired the art of introspection, becomes what Schleiermacher calls an *actual* consciousness in Christians only through their relation to Christ.[64] And the presentation of it in dogmatics is not an autonomous natural theology but strictly a part of the analysis of Christian consciousness—the best part being still to come.[65]

How close these reflections are to articulating the shape of Calvin's *Institutes,* whatever differences there may be between him and Schleiermacher, is surely evident. Both of them presuppose an original revelation, which the doctrine of creation elaborates, and both think of the doctrine of preservation as the distinctive way in which faith grasps creation. But both hold that the doctrine of creation, as far as Christian dogmatics goes, can only be seen in the light of redemption, not presented as a natural theology.[66] Even the crucial role of the fall and sin in Calvin's presentation of the *divinitatis sensus* is not without its counterpart in Schleiermacher. For Schleiermacher's explanation that part 1 of the *Glaubenslehre* considers the

62. *Sendschr.,* 31. Even this striking and important assertion does not meet the most stringent criteria of "christocentricity" (see n. 12 above). It is strictly a judgment about the *Christian* consciousness, and it insists that the Christian's consciousness of God is what it is, in *all* of its expressions (the doctrine of preservation as well as the doctrine of redemption), because of the Christian's relation to Christ. It says nothing about the general consciousness of God *apart from* Christ; much less does it deny that there can be an authentic awareness of God without Christ.

63. Ibid., 32; cf. 35.

64. *Gl.,* § 4.1, § 32.1. Cf. *Gl.*[1], § 39: "Das ursprüngliche ein höchstes Wesen mitsezende Abhängigkeitsgefühl wird in uns Christen nicht anders zum wirklichen Bewusstsein als mit der Beziehung auf Christum."

65. *Gl.,* § 29.2, § 62.3. I return to the relationship between creation and redemption in my next chapter (9).

66. See nn. 46, 58, 60, and 65 above. While the doctrine of creation, for both Calvin and Schleiermacher, explicates a relationship between God and humans that is already implicit in the *original* revelation, for neither of them can the doctrine be written without the perspective of the *special* (or historical) revelation in Christ.

feeling of absolute dependence *abstractly* in itself, apart from the antithesis of sin and grace, corresponds to Calvin's announced intention to inquire *hypothetically* about the primal knowledge of God to which nature would have led had Adam not fallen.[67] Finally, it may be pointed out that the distribution of the doctrine of God over the whole *Glaubenslehre*—a procedure in which Gerhard Ebeling sees a complete departure from the traditional order of dogmatics—turns out to have a clear antecedent in Calvin's apparent intention to make the entire *Institutes* (not just book 1) a presentation of the *duplex cognitio dei* as Creator and Redeemer.[68]

My conclusion in this brief chapter is simply that the question of Schleiermacher and the Reformation should not be reduced to the question of Schleiermacher and Luther, but should at least include some attention to Calvin's *Institutes*. I have not ventured to move beyond this claim and to argue for a literary dependence of Schleiermacher on Calvin. A remark in the preface to the second edition of the *Glaubenslehre* makes a conscious and deliberate dependence on the dogmatic structure of the *Institutes* hard to suppose. "I have invented nothing, so far as I remember," Schleiermacher writes, "except the arrangement and here or there a descriptive phrase."[69] His arrangement of the material was the one thing for which he was willing to claim originality. This, of course, by no means rules out the possibility of a greater debt to the shape of the *Institutes* than Schleiermacher either acknowledged or realized.[70] But there is little point in trying to argue for such a dependence if the pertinent evidence is not available. I

67. Schleiermacher, *Gl.*, § 50.4, § 64.2; Calvin, *Inst.*, 1.2.1 ("si integer stetisset Adam"). It makes a difference, however, that Calvin's remark is found before he turns directly to the doctrine of creation: it belongs to what Schleiermacher would term *Einleitung*.

68. Gerhard Ebeling, "Schleiermachers Lehre von den göttlichen Eigenschaften," in *Wort und Glaube*, vol. 2: *Beiträge zur Fundamentaltheologie und zur Lehre von Gott* (Tübingen: J. C. B. Mohr [Paul Siebeck], 1969), 305–42. Ebeling's important essay was originally published in *Zeitschrift für Theologie und Kirche* 65 (1968): 459–94; English in *Schleiermacher as Contemporary*, ed. Robert W. Funk, *Journal for Theology and the Church*, vol. 7 (New York: Herder and Herder, 1970), 125–62.

69. ". . . ausgenommen die Anordnung und hie und da die Bezeichnung."

70. The possibility is strengthened by the difficulty of identifying any other model that might have influenced Schleiermacher. We know from one of his letters to Gass (11 May 1811) that he made a close study of Quenstedt and Gerhard when preparing his lectures on dogmatics: "Zur Dogmatik verglich ich, als ich sie das erstemal gründlich las, den Quenstedt, jetzt den Gerhard; die Einleitung war ganz neu, indem ich alles hierhergehörige aus der philosophischen Theologie hier beigebracht habe" (*Fr. Schleiermacher's Briefwechsel mit J. Chr. Gass*, ed. Wilhelm Gass [Berlin: Georg Reimer, 1852], 94). But I cannot see anything in Quenstedt or Gerhard that might suggest a two-part system of doctrine with an introduction on dogmatics and the religious consciousness, much less Schleiermacher's distinctive conception of how the parts are related. See Johannes Andreas Quenstedt (1617–88), *Theologia didactico-polemica sive systema theologicum* (1685; 3d ed., Wittenberg, 1696); Johann Gerhard (1582–1637), *Ioannis Gerhardi Loci theologici*, 9 vols. (and index volume) in 3 (1610–22; Leipzig, 1885).

am content with the more cautious suggestion that a purely systematic comparison of the *Institutes* and the *Glaubenslehre* is a much more natural undertaking than has generally been assumed, and that the comparison should cast some light on our understanding both of Calvin and Schleiermacher and of the theological relationship between the Reformation and modern Protestantism. The first step is to recognize that a detailed material comparison between the two systems is invited, and facilitated, by the close structural parallels between them, only some of which I have attempted to point out.[71]

71. Any further agenda ought, I think, to take up the question of propositions borrowed from philosophy—a question that is currently moving to the forefront of Calvin research and has always been central to the interpretation of Schleiermacher.

9

Nature and the Theater of Redemption: Schleiermacher on Christian Dogmatics and the Creation Story

Quite simply, I have interrogated the feeling common to all devout Christians and have only tried to describe it.

Any dogma that represents an actual element in our Christian consciousness can be so conceived as not to get us mixed up with science.
—FRIEDRICH SCHLEIERMACHER

THE QUESTION I want to address in this chapter is what one does with the creation story in dogmatic, as distinct from biblical, theology. More exactly: What is the *place* of "creation" within a dogmatic system? The answer will of course turn around the answer to a prior question: What is dogmatic theology, and how does it differ from biblical theology? As my title indicates, I propose to take my bearings from Friedrich Schleiermacher's understanding of Christian dogmatics, although, as is my habit, I shall also mention John Calvin by way of comparison and contrast with Schleiermacher. I shall not try to give a detailed, prudently qualified account of either one, or of all the likenesses and differences I find between them on our theme. A great deal will have to be left unspoken, some of it obvious enough, some perhaps not so obvious. My limited aim is to indicate briefly what I take to be the pertinent features of Schleiermacher's dogmatics and the corresponding treatment of creation that they lead him to; then, after putting in a good word for him against his latest critics, to conclude with a suggested revision of his approach. It seems to me to be a modest revision. But I should admit in advance that Schleiermacher himself might possibly consider it a surrender of one of his fundamental claims: that the essence of piety lies neither in knowing nor in doing, but in feeling or immediate self-consciousness. Moreover, the dogmatic revision I am proposing is two-sided and carries with it a historical corollary he certainly would not have liked: that the New Testament must be understood as far more deeply rooted in the Hebrew Scriptures than he was willing to admit. It is precisely here, I believe, in his attitude to the "Old Testament," that we find one of his most far-reaching departures from the Reformed school to which he professed allegiance.

The Task of Christian Dogmatics

Calvin's *Institutes* and Schleiermacher's *Christian Faith* have both won a secure place among the masterpieces of theological literature, and it seems natural to compare them as classics of dogmatic theology. And yet, so striking are the differences of style and approach between them, that one may finally wonder whether they really belong in the same literary genre. Comparison, though natural, could be misleading. In the interval between Calvin and Schleiermacher, theology divided into fields, and the fields into subfields. Hence, the fact that Schleiermacher's work is not as full of biblical texts as Calvin's is obvious, but it is beside the point if one forgets to add that by Schleiermacher's day dogmatic theology and biblical (or exegetical) theology had become two separate fields. Schleiermacher had to ask: What are the dogmatic theologians doing, if they are *not* expounding the oracles of God?

This is not to suggest that in Calvin's day biblical theology and dogmatic theology were indistinguishable. One might wish to argue that Calvin's biblical commentaries are just as much "theology" as the various editions of his *Institutes,* and yet that the commentaries and the *Institutes* represent different kinds of theological literature. True enough. But the point is that the *Institutes,* though something other than a collection of commentaries, nonetheless proceeds largely by marshaling biblical evidence, and Calvin believed that the soundness of his "dogmatics" (if we may so call it) was to be judged by the correctness of his exegesis. In this sense, dogmatics remained for him biblical theology. Indeed, the *Institutes* became even more explicitly a biblical theology in its later editions. By the time he published the second edition (1539), Calvin had moved away from the catechetical model of the first (1536) toward something much closer to the *Loci Communes* ("theological topics"; first edition, 1521) of Philip Melanchthon. The serious student of the Bible meets with certain constantly recurring theological themes: sin, law, grace, and so on. Calvin had come to view his *Institutes* as a useful companion for such students to read along with his commentaries. The discussion of recurring themes could be kept much briefer in the commentaries if the reader had the wisdom to keep the *Institutes* close at hand.[1]

But then, of course, the question arises: How does one arrange the

1. John Calvin, *Epistola ad lectorem* (preface to the *Institutes*), OS 3:5–7. The editors give the 1559 version of the preface and indicate variations from the earlier text in their notes.

topics? Calvin evidently devoted a great deal more thought to this question than did his friend Melanchthon, whose topics were initially suggested to him by his lectures on Paul's Letter to the Romans. Calvin's systematic instincts called for a tighter organization, and when the definitive edition of the *Institutes* finally appeared (1559), he had given the work its familiar arrangement under the two main themes "The Knowledge of God the Creator" and "The Knowledge of God the Redeemer in Christ."[2] The new arrangement, however, did not indicate any change in the purpose of the work; the *Institutes* remained a companion to Bible studies, and Calvin accordingly kept the preface to the earlier, second edition, although with a number of changes.

Schleiermacher also worked with a two-part system of dogmatics, which dealt in turn with creation and redemption, and like Calvin he devoted a great deal of thought to the arrangement of his material. The very first proposition of his *Christian Faith,* in the first edition (1821–22), defined dogmatics as "the science of the coherence (*dem Zusammenhange*) of the doctrine current in a Christian church at a given time."[3] Both Calvin and Schleiermacher, then, aimed at a comprehensive, logically ordered presentation of the Christian religion (or Christian faith), and at point after point the overall structure of their respective works really does invite comparison between them. Nevertheless, with respect to the data, the status, and the use of dogmatics, Schleiermacher departed significantly from Calvin's model.

In the first place, Schleiermacher understood dogmatics to be a descriptive, rather than an exegetical, field of study. Like Calvin, he wanted a comprehensive statement of Christian faith, and to this extent they held a common view of their subject matter. But whereas Calvin tried to get at the subject through interpretation of the Bible as the authoritative statement of what Christian belief should be, Schleiermacher thought of dogmatics as empirical understanding of an actual, present way of believing (a *Glaubensweise*).[4] He did acknowledge the possibility of what he called a "scriptural dogmatics," and he never claimed that his was the only way to practice dogmatic theology, or even that any system had to follow one model exclusively. It is just that he himself preferred to regard exegetical

2. See Edward A. Dowey, Jr., *The Knowledge of God in Calvin's Theology,* 2d ed. (New York: Columbia University Press, 1965).

3. This became proposition 19 in the second, revised version (1830–31). The "propositions" (*Leitsätze*) of *Gl.*[1] are included in Redeker's edition as an appendix.

4. *Sendschr.,* 20–21, 25–26, 28, 33; *KD* §§ 1, 26, 97, 188, 195. The procedure of dogmatics is "empirical" in that it describes actual facts of experience (*Sendschr.,* 20–21). Cf. *Gl.,* § 28.2, § 33.3, § 64.1–2, § 100.3.

theology and dogmatic theology as two distinct, coordinate fields.[5] One reason he gave for his preference is that he wrote his dogmatics expressly for the church of the Prussian Union between Lutherans and Reformed, and while the Scriptures are the norm of what is Christian, a Protestant dogmatics has to ask, more specifically, what is evangelical. For this purpose, the most immediate data will be the Reformation confessions of faith, used less as tests of orthodox belief than as the primary expressions of the evangelical Christian "spirit." Schleiermacher's method, too, like Calvin's, is inescapably hermeneutical insofar as it works with texts, albeit different texts. But it is also, as has often been said, psychologizing: what he is after is a description of a particular variety of religious affections or a specific religious consciousness. The method is not individualistic, however, as is sometimes further supposed, since it is a collective consciousness that occupies his attention. And it cannot be a merely statistical method either, but remains, in its own manner, normative. Dogmaticians do not distribute questionnaires; they turn to the earliest sources of the evangelical faith, where the waters presumably flowed most purely.[6]

In the second place, precisely because he understood dogmatics to be descriptive, Schleiermacher was more modest than Calvin about the status of dogmatic assertions. Calvin took it for granted that Christian truth was the whole of sound religion. Schleiermacher acknowledged that those for whom a Christian dogmatics is written, being Christians, will presuppose the truth of Christianity; that is the nature of the faith being described, and it is the task of dogmatics to explicate faith, not to defend or to doubt it. But it does not follow that truth is wholly lacking in other religions.[7] There are many faiths. In his introduction Schleiermacher tries, as a preliminary task, to locate Christianity among them—to define Christianity's distinctive essence—and at the same time to indicate the place of dogmatics among the empirical sciences. He proceeds, as everyone knows, by arguing that each historical religion is a particular modifica-

5. *Gl.*, § 19 (postscript), § 27.3, § 27.4. Dogmatic theology strives for completeness (*Gl.*, § 18.3, § 20.1, § 29.2), but completeness can be attained in more than one way (*Sendschr.*, 46–49; cf. 41).

6. *Gl.*, § 27.1–2; *Gl.*, § 15, § 16 (postscript), § 31; *KD* § 83. For Schleiermacher's view of the Reformation confessions, see further his "Über den eigenthümlichen Werth und das bindende Ansehen symbolischer Bücher" (1819), KS 2:141–66, esp. 143–44, 159–62. His intention to do the science of a *collective* religious consciousness is plainly conveyed in his ecclesial norm (*Gl.*, § 17.1)—indeed, in the very title he gave to his dogmatic work (*Der christliche Glaube nach den Grundsätzen der evangelischen Kirche . . .*).

7. Schleiermacher asserts that his presentation is relative to dogmatics, and that dogmatics is only for Christians (*Gl.*, § 11.5). But presumably a descriptive Islamic dogmatics could be written on Schleiermacher's principles by a Muslim, who, of course, would write for Muslims and would presuppose the truth of Islam.

tion of the feeling of absolute dependence; Christianity is distinguished from other monotheistic faiths (*Glaubensweisen*) by the fact that everything in it is related to the redemption accomplished by Jesus of Nazareth. The task of Schleiermacher's dogmatics is to describe this faith in its Protestant form.[8] He does not have to deny the authenticity of other forms of Christianity, or even of other religions. As a dogmatic theologian of the evangelical church, he believed Christianity to be the highest form of monotheistic faith. But as at least an amateur philosopher of religion, he recognized that what dogmatic theology does—and so, the status of the discipline as a science—can only be understood from a neutral point "above" the various religions.[9]

In the third place, while both Calvin and Schleiermacher wrote dogmatics mainly to educate pastors, Schleiermacher did not think of his work as a companion to Bible study (although it could conceivably be so used), but rather as a treatise on what we might call "the dynamics of faith." Pastors need a firm grasp on how the faith they are to nurture actually functions. Of course, they need *biblical* theology for that, too, which is why exegetical theology must be regarded as a coordinate field of theological study along with dogmatics. The primary usefulness of *dogmatic* theology is that it shows how the Christian way of believing "hangs together" (its *Zusammenhang*), and this in turn makes it easier for the pastor to sort out the great wealth of biblical images—an abundance that, without the discipline of dogmatic training, might occasion one-sided teaching, false teaching, or conflicting teachings in the church.[10] The times also called for pastors who clearly understood how to relate the dynamics of faith to the

8. Schleiermacher's definition of the essence of Christianity is given in *Gl.*, § 11. The connection with Jesus brings about a modification of the feeling of absolute dependence: the fundamental *Christian* feeling is of the need for redemption and its satisfaction in Christ (*Sendschr.*, 31, 47), and these are facts of experience (*erfahrungsmässige Tatsachen*), not facts of consciousness antecedent to experience (ibid., 21–22). On the notion of a "placement" (*Ortsbestimmung*) of Christianity, see *Sendschr.*, 53–56.

9. *Gl.*, § 7.3, § 8.4, § 10 (postscript), § 11.5. That the argument of the introduction was intended to define the place of dogmatics among the sciences, as well as the place of Christianity among the religions, is clearly indicated in *Sendschr.*, 58–59. On the vantage point "above" Christianity, see *KD*, § 33, and *Gl.*[1], § 6. Schleiermacher makes it abundantly clear that this vantage point is only provisional; it is not the standpoint of the dogmatic theologian, since the entire introduction lies outside dogmatics proper (*Sendschr.*, 55–56; *Gl.*, § 1.1).

10. Dogmatics (*das dogmatische Verfahren*) exists only for the sake of preaching (*die Verkündigung: Gl.*, § 19.1). What is needed is a clear and stimulating description of a shared inward experience, and "doctrine" is simply a means to this end (*Sendschr.*, 16; cf. *Gl.*, § 18.3). Dogmatics has its usefulness as a guide to teaching in the pulpit (*Sendschr.*, 29), though the language of dogmatic theology is not designed to be carried over into the sermon without translation (ibid., 59). On the regulative and systematic function of dogmatics in sifting biblical imagery, see *Gl.*, § 16.3, § 17.2, § 20.1, § 28.2, § 50.1, § 61.4. Not dogmatics only, but every branch of theology serves the leadership of the church directly (*Gl.*, § 19 [postscript]).

rapid dissemination of knowledge from the natural sciences. The doctrine of creation provides us with an excellent test case for this conception of dogmatics. The double question the dogmatician asks is: Where does the belief in creation fit into a description of the Christian consciousness, and can that belief be so presented as not to get us mixed up with natural science?[11]

Creation and Redemption

In premodern Christian dogmatics, the place of "creation" was automatically dictated by the assumption that the creation was one act in a sequence of divine acts. The dogmatic order was supposedly historical or chronological: In accordance with the eternal decrees, God first created the world and humans; then, when Adam and Eve fell through their disobedience, God intervened in human history by the election of a chosen people; in the fullness of time, God became incarnate in Jesus of Nazareth; and now God continues to establish the kingdom through the spread of the church. If we remove the divine decrees beyond time, then creation appears as act one in a divine drama. Presumably Calvin, for instance, required no lengthy reflection to make "The Knowledge of God the Creator" the theme of the first book of his 1559 *Institutes*. In the temporal sequence of divine works, creation is where everything begins; redemption is where it is going, at any rate for the elect.

Already in Calvin, however, there is the possibility of an alternative order. If, as he argued, the knowledge of God the Creator was lost or at least suppressed and distorted by the fall, then in the order of Christian experience—as distinct from the order of divine works—redemption actually precedes a true knowledge of the Creator; or perhaps we could say that since the fall knowledge of God the Creator depends on, and is contained in, knowledge of God the Redeemer.[12] Calvin, to be sure, did not decide to follow the experiential order, or he would have written the four books of the *Institutes* backward, so to say, beginning with what is now the last book and ending with what is now the first. But the experiential perspective apparently leads him to make two distinct (though not incompatible) claims about creation and revelation.

On the one hand, Calvin thinks that the Scriptures, though given to counteract the effects of sin, actually provide such information about the beginning of the world as we could not possibly have had, without special

11. The two quotations that serve as my epigraphs at the beginning of this chapter will be found in *Sendschr.*, 25, 40. Cf. Calvin's interesting attempt to exclude from the doctrine of the Virgin Birth matters that belong not to theology but to philosophy and medicine (*Inst.*, 2.13.3).

12. *Inst.*, 1.5.14, 1.6.1, 2.6.1.

revelation, even if Adam had never fallen. The narrative of creation, to be sure, is not a strictly scientific account; nevertheless we are informed, for instance, that God created the world and humans over a period of six days, which we certainly could not know had God not chosen to reveal it to Moses. Notice what this implies about the nature of revelation: it is information, not otherwise available, imparted in a supernatural manner.[13] On the other hand, Calvin can also say that through the revelation of Scripture we are enabled to view nature with a clearer vision and to perceive what we should and would have known but for the fall: that nature is the handiwork of the Creator. The Scriptures are like reading glasses: they aid our weak vision and focus the otherwise confused knowledge of God in our minds. Of course, the Scriptures teach us to perceive God as Redeemer; but without the word, we would not even recognize God as artificer of the universe. Revelation, from this perspective, is not supernaturally conveyed information; it is divinely restored vision. And only those whose blindness has been healed by God the Redeemer can recognize God as Creator.[14]

Calvin provides us, in effect, with two quite different dogmatic approaches to creation. Schleiermacher was well aware of them both. He admits that Christians have commonly linked creation with the opening chapters of Genesis, understood as a factual narrative about the beginning of all spatial and temporal existence. But the Mosaic account of creation is mythical rather than proto-scientific; and Schleiermacher notes that many eminent Jewish and Christian thinkers, including Calvin, did not treat it as biblical science. The time has now come to turn over to the natural scientists the entire question of how the universe first took shape. Dogmatic theologians can await the results calmly, because it is not really their business.[15]

Naturally, Schleiermacher was apprehensive that the Mosaic narrative might lend itself to anthropomorphic images of the divine activity, as though God made the entire temporal and spatial universe the way a human artificer fashions some object within time and space.[16] But his fundamental objection to basing a doctrine of creation on the Mosaic narrative was more directly related to his preference for the second methodological option. Even if the Mosaic description *were* a historical account, it could

13. Ibid., 1.14.1–2. Calvin does not doubt that the history of creation is revealed truth, but because Moses presents it in language accommodated to the unlearned, anyone who wants to learn astronomy must look elsewhere. See Comm. Gen. 1:6; cf. *Inst.*, 1.14.3.

14. *Inst.*, 1.5.14, 1.6.1, 1.14.1. Cf. the "argument" to the commentary on Genesis.

15. *Gl.*, § 36.2, § 40.1–2. If the Genesis narrative is mythical and myth is the attempt to convey in story form a particular mode of human being in the world, then a proper exegesis might very well contribute to just such a doctrine of creation as Schleiermacher desired. But he was more concerned to exclude improper exegesis.

16. *Gl.*, § 41, § 46.1. Strictly speaking, there is only one divine activity: namely the creating, sustaining activity that forms the whole world (*Gl.*, § 100.2).

only give us natural science communicated in an extraordinary way; it would tell us little or nothing about the real content of faith in creation, and so would have little or no interest for dogmatics. Hence the development of a strictly dogmatic account of creation could not take the form of an exegesis of the Mosaic narrative. The crucial question must rather be: What does belief in creation mean as an element in the Christian religious consciousness?[17]

Now the most important consequence of this approach is not that the Genesis account of creation must not be taken literally, but that the doctrine of creation is not, strictly speaking, about how the world got started at all; rather, it is about the way the devout mind perceives the natural order. This is Schleiermacher's first major contribution to our theme. He turns our attention from the creation "in the beginning" to the creature-consciousness that every Christian has in the present. Hence, as he expressly points out, there is no essential reason for distinguishing an act of creation from the activity of providence (or, as he prefers to say, "preservation"). He thinks there is even a strictly historical warrant for not separating creation from preservation as though they were two divine works or activities: the original creedal formula in the Roman Symbol was, "I believe in God the Ruler of all things (*theon pantocratora*)," and this is also the original, simple expression of the consciousness that the world exists only in absolute dependence on God.[18]

Given Schleiermacher's dogmatic method, creation tends to collapse into providence, providence being the more fitting of the two expressions for the feeling of absolute dependence. The problem with the idea of creation is not merely that in itself it affirms absolute dependence only for the beginning of things, but also that, insofar as it refers to a remote past, it cannot possibly represent anything immediately given in the present religious consciousness. If we say that it *is,* after all, an item of faith, that can only mean faith in the improper sense of assent to extraordinarily communicated items of information. It does not follow that curiosity about origins is wholly inappropriate, only that the origin of finite being is of no interest to Christian piety or Christian dogmatics and can safely be left in the hands of scientific theorists. Even the debate over eternal creation, as distinct from a temporal beginning, has no bearing on the content of the feeling of absolute dependence, and it is a matter of indifference how it is

17. *Gl.*, § 36.1, § 40.2. Unlike Calvin, Schleiermacher does not assert that *only* the Christian consciousness contains an awareness of creation; on the contrary, he thinks that the doctrines of part 1 of his *Glaubenslehre* will tend to coincide with those of other religions (see *Gl.*, § 29.1–2, § 34.3). However, monotheistic piety exists only concretely—in connection with the distinctive features of a positive religion (*Gl.*, § 32.3).

18. *Gl.*, § 36 (note). On the term "providence" (*Vorsehung*), see *Gl.*, § 164.3. Schleiermacher's preferred term throughout the discussion in §§ 46–49 is *Erhaltung*.

decided. If the correct dogmatic procedure is consistently followed, there will be no temptation for theology to lose itself in foreign territory or to pass from the distinctively religious domain to the speculative and the natural-scientific domains.[19]

So what *is* the content of what used to be called the "doctrine of creation"? It is quite simply our consciousness of being in the world as finite beings who are absolutely dependent on God. Here Schleiermacher makes a second contribution that is equally important. To be absolutely dependent upon God cannot be simply identical with our dependence on the world, and yet, he insists, these two relations are inseparable in our actual experience: we become aware of our total dependence on God precisely as we become conscious of ourselves as part of the world, understood as one causal system. The consciousness of God and consciousness of ourselves as part of a causal nexus tend to rise and fall together. Schleiermacher noted in the margin of his own copy of *The Christian Faith:* "Togetherness of the feeling of dependence and the consciousness of the world." In this way, he forged the crucial link between the religious doctrine of "creation" (as we may continue to call it) and the fundamental presupposition of natural-scientific inquiry: that the world constitutes an orderly whole. God and nature are not, so to say, in competition in the religious consciousness, as though what is assigned to natural causality must inevitably be taken away from God. Divine causality and natural causality, though different in kind, are coextensive; they belong together.[20]

Here Schleiermacher was perfectly aware that his exposition put him at loggerheads with much popular piety, and it may seem as if his entire dogmatic method is jeopardized. No Christian doubts the day-to-day preservation of the natural order by God's sustaining hand. But there is a common tendency among believers to picture God's *sustaining* activity as interrupted from time to time by special *creative* or *miraculous* acts. Indeed, there is even anxiety that the natural sciences, precisely by reducing the entire course of nature to regular, undeviating patterns ("laws"), constitute a threat to the pious expectation that God can and does intervene in nature when and where God wills. For it is exactly in such extraordinary acts of divine intervention that many devout souls chiefly see the hand of God. Piety thus seems to have a vested interest in opposing the advance of

19. *Gl.*, § 36.1–2, § 37.1–3, § 38.1–2, § 39.1, § 39.3; § 40.2, § 61.1; § 41.2; § 37.3, § 39.1–2. Cf. the discussions of the Devil and the origin of sin in § 45 (postscript) and § 72.1–2. In practice Schleiermacher did retain a distinction between "creation" and "preservation," but more for pedagogical than for substantive reasons (*Gl.*, § 39.3).

20. *Gl.*, § 32.2, § 34, § 46, § 47, § 51.1. Schleiermacher's handwritten note is given in Redeker's edition (1:180). Cf. *Gl.*, § 33: in the feeling of absolute dependence, our self-consciousness represents the finitude of our being.

scientific research; conversely, the better the scientists understand the working of the natural order, the less devout they are likely to be.[21]

Schleiermacher's response to this apparent dilemma is characteristic. To be sure, he opposes any thought of divine (or demonic) intervention in the course of nature as destructive of sound scientific procedure. The introduction of an element of irregularity into the natural order undermines the very concept of nature itself—and with it scientific inquiry.[22] But the essential question, he believes, is not whether interventions in the course of natural events are possible or scientifically conceivable but, as far as Christian dogmatics is concerned, what they would mean for the religious self-consciousness. And if the core of the religious consciousness is indeed total confidence in the reliability of the natural order that God sustains, then a suspension of the normal workings of nature can only be judged as much a threat to piety as it would be to science. It is simply wrong to imagine a creative divine activity that enters in at individual moments as *another* activity *besides* God's sustaining activity. Such a perverted notion has its roots not in Christian piety, but in a confused worldview that invokes dependence on God as the explanation for events only where the causal nexus is concealed. "We are clearly quite wrong," Schleiermacher concludes, "if we allege, as a general experience, that the incomprehensible as such is more conducive to the awakening of the religious feeling than that which is understood." His reason is plain: rightly interpreted, the heart of religion is the feeling of absolute dependence on God that the very regularity of nature evokes in us. We cannot, of course, draw in advance limits on what is or is not naturally possible; much that we now perceive as "miraculous" may one day yield to scientific explanation. Nevertheless, it can be stated as a general rule that the interests of religion and the interests of natural science coincide.[23]

Schleiermacher's attempt to rethink the doctrine of creation arose, then, from his determination to carry through a strictly dogmatic method—and from his unfailing confidence that the dogmatic method, as he understood it, could not possibly set faith and science against each other. Any appearance of conflict between religion and natural science must be ascribed to one of two causes: either that the nature of genuine piety is being misconstrued, or that the limits of the natural are being too narrowly drawn. Schleiermacher's fear was that if the church refused to undertake the needed reconstruction of the old doctrine of creation, then in the very near future

21. *Gl.*, § 34.2, § 38.2, § 46.1.
22. *Gl.*, § 46.1, § 47.2.
23. *Gl.*, § 47.1; § 38.2; § 46.1; § 47.3, § 49 (postscript).

religion would go with obscurantism, science with unbelief.[24] For this reason, he attached great importance to the themes of creation and preservation in the first part of his system of doctrine. But his careful distinction between the two parts of the system should rule out any suggestion that the doctrine of creation, or the feeling of absolute dependence itself, is the real heart of his Christian faith. In itself, the doctrine of creation is only an empty frame, to be filled in, as he puts it, by the subsequent discussion: that is, by his description of the full Christian consciousness of redemption. For what does the omnipotence of the Creator mean to me until I know its purpose, which is disclosed only in the consciousness of the *new* creation? Schleiermacher assumed that the readers of his introduction and first part would supply from their own Christian consciousness what his exposition held momentarily in abeyance.[25] From the critics' reception of his first edition, he realized that he had assumed too much.

Schleiermacher and His Critics

From his own day until ours, a succession of critics have been unwilling to take Schleiermacher's word for it when he claims to be simply describing how Christians believe, and there has been a surprising amount of continuity in the critical tradition. In the first half of our century, the assault came mainly from the side of neoorthodoxy. The most extensive neoorthodox critique to be published, Emil Brunner's *Mysticism and the Word* (1924), alleged that "mysticism" in Schleiermacher's theology supplanted the word of God. In Brunner's judgment, a general concept of religion, derived from the philosophy of religion, determined the entire content of Schleiermacher's imagined description of Christianity; all that was really Christian in his dogmatics belonged not to the essence of Christianity but merely to the mode of its historical manifestation. In other words, the feeling of absolute dependence, according to Brunner, was the actual essence of Schleiermacher's Christianity. The Christian has the feeling of absolute dependence accidentally in the form of a connection with Jesus Christ, whereas another monotheist—a Stoic, for instance—lacks this special Christian element without thereby missing anything essential in piety itself.[26]

Some fifteen years ago, in *Tradition and the Modern World,* I tried to show

24. *Sendschr.,* 37.

25. Ibid., 32–33.

26. Emil Brunner, *Die Mystik und das Wort: Der Gegensatz zwischen moderner Religionsauffassung und christlichem Glauben dargestellt an der Theologie Schleiermachers* (Tübingen: J. C. B. Mohr [Paul Siebeck], 1924); see esp. 129, 132. Karl Barth's lectures on the theology of Schleiermacher (1923–24) were not published until 1978: *Der Theologie Schleiermachers, Karl Barth Gesamtausgabe,* 2,11 (Zurich: Theologischer Verlag, 1978).

why Brunner's reading of Schleiermacher's dogmatics would not do.[27] I suppose it could be said that the argument I made there was fifty years late as a response to neoorthodoxy. In any case, it was ten years *too early* to serve as a reply to the present wave of "antifoundationalist" criticisms of Schleiermacher, although, as a matter of fact, the issues remain largely the same. There is no need to repeat my case in detail. But I cannot afford to let the newer critiques pass unquestioned, because if they were right, then my interpretation of where the doctrine of creation belongs in Schleiermacher's dogmatics would be mistaken: "creation," as a thematization of the feeling of absolute dependence, would not be so much a formal presupposition of Christian faith as its essential content.

One of the most vigorous and detailed antifoundationalist critiques of Schleiermacher, which we may fairly take as representative, has come from Ronald Thiemann. In an article titled "Piety, Narrative, and Christian Identity," Thiemann argues that Schleiermacher made philosophical theology the key theological discipline, and that he assigned it the pivotal role of justifying Christian faith by uncovering its universal religious content. The price Schleiermacher allegedly paid for this *foundational* method is twofold: the distinctiveness of Christian identity becomes secondary to the universal form of religion, and Christian theology becomes correspondingly abstract and remote from the concrete expressions of Christian faith and life.[28] In his book *Revelation and Theology,* Thiemann's interpretation of Schleiermacher is in some respects more cautious. He refers expressly to Schleiermacher's own statement of what the introduction to his dogmatics was all about, and he recognizes at least the possibility that Schleiermacher's method might well, on a charitable reading, be taken to support just such a *descriptive* theology as Thiemann himself prefers.[2929] Nevertheless, in the book, too, Schleiermacher is presented as one of the foundationalists for whom the central theological task is apologetic: to justify Christian claims, and especially the claim

27. B. A. Gerrish, *Tradition and the Modern World: Reformed Theology in the Nineteenth Century* (Chicago: University of Chicago Press, 1978), chap. 1, esp. 22–39.

28. Ronald F. Thiemann, "Piety, Narrative, and Christian Identity," *Word and World* 3 (1983): 148–59. Thiemann assigns to Schleiermacher's philosophical theology the task of disclosing the "self-identical essence of piety" (151). Subsequently, he states that foundational theology claims to "discern the unchanging essence of Christianity" (156). But unless the essence of Christianity is taken to be identical with the essence of piety (which is certainly not Schleiermacher's view), these two tasks should in fact be carefully differentiated.

29. Thiemann, *Revelation and Theology: The Gospel as Narrated Promise* (Notre Dame, Indiana: University of Notre Dame Press, 1985); see esp. 28, 172 n. 5. Thiemann also grants that "demonstration of the essential religiousness of human nature . . . may well be part of an overall apologetic strategy" (ibid., 155), and he does not see narrative theology as a *substitute* for a discursive dogmatic theology: theologians are not storytellers ("Piety, Narrative, and Christian Identity," 159 n. 25).

to a prevenient divine revelation, by grounding them in a self-evident, noninferential belief or set of beliefs, or in a universal religious experience.[30]

It is, of course, what Schleiermacher himself calls the "dangerous introduction"[31] to his dogmatics that gives rise to the antifoundationalist critique. He does indeed seek, in the opening paragraphs of *The Christian Faith,* to isolate a self-identical element that underlies all religions and is an essential constituent in human consciousness. But he does not do so in order to offer, as Thiemann asserts of foundationalists in general, a "theoretical justification for Christian belief in God's prevenience." The quest for a "full-scale justification of belief in God's prevenience"[32] is not Schleiermacher's. If one insists on looking for such a justification in *The Christian Faith,* one would do better to look at his doctrine of election: Schleiermacher was a supralapsarian Calvinist, and justifications of divine prevenience do not come any more "full-scale" than that.[33] But as far as the introduction to his dogmatics is concerned, I see no reason for doubting that he was doing there exactly what he claimed to be doing.

Schleiermacher insists repeatedly that in his introduction he is not trying to justify Christian beliefs or to provide a philosophical foundation for dogmatics. The function of his propositions borrowed from philosophical theology is not to defend Christianity by grounding it in a universal religious consciousness, but, quite the contrary, to show what is special to Christianity—to define its essence and so to draw the boundaries within which appropriate expressions of distinctively Christian faith must be contained. And he tells us expressly that there is no way to justify Christianity (or any other positive religion) by philosophical means, even if we wanted to; he simply assumes that Christian dogmatics is written for those who need no such justification because they are already believers in Christ.[34]

When, therefore, Thiemann writes that for foundationalism "apologetics inevitably emerges as the *primary* theological task" and that "the two most

30. Thiemann, *Revelation,* 7, 24–31, 73–75, 158–59 (n. 20). The feeling of absolute dependence is not strictly a belief at all (as Thiemann implies on 31); and the reason why it must be a consciousness of *God* is not that it is immediate or precognitive (29) but that our dependence on anything less than God, or even on the sum total of finite existents, is never absolute (*Gl.,* § 4.4, § 32.3).

31. *Sendschr.,* 33.

32. Thiemann, *Revelation,* 7, 69.

33. *Gl.,* § 120.3; cf. § 79.1.

34. *Sendschr.,* 17–18, 31–32, 38–40, 54–56; *Gl.,* § 10 (esp. the postscript), § 11.5, § 22.2. On the other hand, see *Gl.,* § 8.4. In the context of the present discussion of foundationalism, it is particularly interesting to find Schleiermacher describing piety as *das Unbegründete* and saying: "Von einem Begründen ist gar nicht die Rede bei mir" (*Sendschr.,* 17, 20). Cf. *Gl.,* § 2.1, § 34.3. Thiemann writes of a shift from assumption to argument as theology moves into the post-Cartesian world (*Revelation,* 11–12). But a case could be made for holding that Calvin, at least, was more concerned than Schleiermacher to *argue* for the universality of the religious sense and the divine origin of the Christian revelation (see *Inst.,* 1.3 and 1.8).

important theological activities—the development of a universal justificatory argument and the defense of Christian claims before the bar of rationality—are carried on independent of the internal logic of Christian belief and practice and with little reference to criteria of judgment internal to the Christian tradition," his remarks scarcely fit Schleiermacher.[35] Throughout his dogmatics, Schleiermacher rests his argument chiefly on the Lutheran and Reformed confessions—norms specific to Protestant Christianity. And I think he would be fully justified in asking again, as he did in 1829, that any who doubt whether his method can fairly represent a specific Christian doctrine should at least consider how he actually explicates Christian doctrines in the second, main part of his system. Few of his early critics seem to have troubled themselves with the second part at all; of those who did, some, to his obvious amusement, were annoyed to see that he could still wear his churchly mantle with a certain natural ease.[36]

Against what he takes to be the foundationalist misconception of the theological task, Thiemann calls for a "conception of theology as primarily a descriptive activity, a second-order mode of reflection which displays the logic inherent in Christian belief and practice"; or again, "an interpretive activity which seeks to illuminate the structures embedded in beliefs and practices," eschewing theoretical defenses of Christian doctrine.[37] But that, it seems to me, is a perfect statement of Schleiermacher's own dogmatic aims. Thiemann further calls for a theology that allows for the thoroughly historical character of theological thinking and hence for diverse expressions of Christian faith at any given time. And the nonfoundationalists, he insists, speak from within the religious community, their theology being an exercise of the Anselmian *fides quaerens intellectum*—a quest to understand faith, not to justify it.[38] But these, too, are cardinal points in Schleiermacher's theological program.

Surprisingly enough, then, or so it seems to me, Thiemann's antidote to foundationalism resembles Schleiermacher's theological program much more closely than does the malady he diagnoses. His prescriptions for a healthy theology were expressly proposed a century and a half ago by Schleiermacher. And this ought to promise well for a much better accommodation between Schleiermacherians and the antifoundationalist "narrative theologians" than we seem to have managed in the last few years. Schleiermacher

35. Thiemann, *Revelation,* 74. For Schleiermacher the only possible "foundation" for a dogmatic assertion is to establish that it is the *correct* expression of the Christian self-consciousness (*Sendschr.,* 56). In his own terminology, the task of "apologetics" is to defend the *distinctiveness* of Christianity (*KD,* § 39, §§ 44–46; *Sendschr.,* 57; *Gl.,* § 2.2, § 19.1, § 28.3).

36. *Sendschr.,* 62–63; 33. Some readers treated the introduction as though it were the real kernel of the whole book (31).

37. Thiemann, *Revelation,* 72.

38. "Piety, Narrative, and Christian Identity," 155–56.

was a pioneer in his recognition that theology is a thoroughly historical discipline and that there will always be a diversity of ways of expressing the common faith. Dogmatics can never be more than the science of the system of doctrine current in *a* church at *a* particular time, and that is why he classified dogmatics as a branch of historical theology. The subject matter of dogmatics is not static but in constant movement and change.[39] And precisely because he could not conceive of anyone doing theology save in the believing community, he wrote boldly on the title page of his great dogmatic system his two epigraphs from Anselm: "I do not seek to understand in order that I may believe, but I believe in order that I may understand. . . . For anyone who has not believed will not experience, and anyone who has not experienced will not understand."[40]

Although it never occurred to Schleiermacher, as it did to the neo-orthodox, to deny that Christianity is one religion among others, the accent in his dogmatics falls unmistakably on the particularity of Christian faith. His instincts were against what he called "the tendency to regard Christianity simply as a means of advancing and propagating religion in general," as though its own distinctive nature were merely accidental and secondary. One critic charged Schleiermacher in his own day with trying to absorb what is distinctively Christian into a universal religious knowledge, and he replied that any such knowledge could only be an *abstraction from* what is Christian. It was not *his* theology but rationalism's that would have surrendered the particularity of Christian faith to a common religion of humanity, which he considered no religion at all but a Teutonic mishmash of morals and metaphysics; and he thought that this travesty of religion went far to explain why French atheism had made incursions into Germany.[41]

Schleiermacher's distinctive contribution to the doctrine of creation will be appreciated only where he is seen for what he was: a church dogmatician whose main concern was to explicate the peculiarly Christian consciousness of sin and grace. The idea of absolute dependence, articulated in the doctrines of creation and preservation, cannot ground or justify Christian faith. It is not "an atemporal essence which is prior to all historical and cultural particu-

39. *Sendschr.*, 31; *Gl.*, § 19.2. Cf. *Friedrich Schleiermachers Weihnachtsfeier* (1806), critical ed., ed. Hermann Mulert, Philosophische Bibliothek, vol. 117 (Leipzig: Dürr, 1908), pref. to the 2d ed. (1826), 57–58; *KD*, § 195 (cf. § 33 from the 1st ed., cited in Scholz's footnote 1 on page 11).

40. Anselm, *Proslogium*, chap. 1; *De fide trinitatis et de incarnatione verbi*, chap. 2. On the role of conviction in dogmatics, see also *Gl.*, § 13 (postscript), § 19.1, § 33.3, § 100.3, § 114.1; *KD*, § 196. It is not dogmatics but philosophical theology that takes its point of departure from "above" Christianity (*KD*, § 33; cf. *Gl.*[1], § 6). Schleiermacher did think that dogmatics had the right to borrow concepts from philosophy, but only on the same condition that Thiemann finds in Barth (*Revelation*, 173 n. 7): that their meaning must then be given by the new linguistic context (*Sendschr.*, 60; *Gl.*, § 16 [postscript]).

41. *Gl.*, § 11.4, § 24.3; *Sendschr.*, 17, 28–29; cf. *Reden*, 244, 246–47.

lars";[42] it is rather an *abstraction from* historical and cultural particulars. If one is to speak at all of a "foundation" or "grounding" of Schleiermacher's faith, then it is the particular that grounds the universal, not the other way around. The actual foundation of the Christian's confidence in the divinely governed world order is faith in Christ. This is why Schleiermacher can only assign the doctrine of creation to the religious consciousness presupposed by and contained in the Christian religious affections. If this is "foundationalism," it is a kind of inverted foundationalism, in which the universal religious consciousness or feeling of absolute dependence emerges in connection with the particular form of a historical faith. This was already Schleiermacher's standpoint in the famous *Speeches on Religion,* in which, after saying a great deal about religion in the abstract, he finally admonished the cultured despisers that only those can finally hope to know religion who are willing to pitch their tent *somewhere.* Why not in Christianity?[43]

Creation and the Moral World Order

The connection Schleiermacher makes between the universal and the particular elements in Christian faith turns out to be anything but reductive. Christians receive their entire consciousness of God from Christ. Their sense of dependence on God is awakened by Christ. But they also receive from him the awareness that the world is more than a law-governed causal nexus ("nature"); it is, as Schleiermacher puts it, a "theater of redemption." In the order of exposition, the last word goes to redemption, but it is actually the first word in the order of Christian experience: faith in creation, although it brings them closer to other monotheists, is awakened in Christians by the Redeemer.[44]

The way the "feeling of absolute dependence" functions as a concept in Schleiermacher's dogmatics—the way it relates to the doctrines of creation and redemption—thus seems to be free of the difficulties most commonly attributed to it. It is another question, however, whether the concept itself can be sustained. "Feeling," in the sense of "immediate self-consciousness," is by definition elusive: a living movement that stops when you stop to look at it.

42. Thiemann, "Piety, Narrative, and Christian Identity," 155.

43. *Reden,* 257, 275, 287. Oman translates the first passage: "Only those who . . . pitch their camp [*sich niederläßt*] in some such positive form, have . . . any well-earned right of citizenship in the religious world." Schleiermacher, *On Religion: Speeches to Its Cultured Despisers,* trans. from the 3d German ed. (1821) by John Oman (1894; reprint, New York: Harper and Row, 1958), 223–24.

44. *Gl.*[1], § 39; *Sendschr.,* 31; *Gl.,* § 29.2, § 32.1, § 169. The efficacy of redemption enables us to assert that the purpose of the divine government of the world is the planting and extension of the Christian church; from the very beginning, the natural order would have been quite different had not the human race been destined for redemption through Christ (*Gl.,* § 164).

But as long as you leave it alone, it remains indeterminate and you cannot say what it is. In Schleiermacher's own lifetime, it was argued against him that religious feelings must be by-products of religious ideas. I think he defended himself successfully against the argument that piety presupposes the idea of *God*. That the feeling of absolute dependence rather gives rise to the idea of God seems to me a defensible analysis. But can you have a feeling of absolute dependence without the idea of *dependence?* And if not, how can it be maintained that the feeling belongs purely to the domain of immediate self-consciousness—unmediated, that is, by reflection? Schleiermacher would patiently reply, I expect, that what he is talking about is something always latent in human consciousness as pure feeling, but it only comes to expression in thought as a feeling of absolute dependence. Indeed, in itself it is an actual existential relationship; piety is its most primitive expression.[45]

A "little introspection" is supposed to reveal all of this to us.[46] But perhaps it is not merely frivolous when one recent author gives us this report: "Now I have described the feeling of absolute dependence to a colleague of mine who is thirty years old, lucid of memory, more than astute enough to follow the description, and an enthusiastic member of a developed Protestant community. He stoutly denies that he has ever had the feeling."[47] I would not myself be inclined to take this for a conclusive refutation of Schleiermacher. Immediate self-consciousness—a field of consciousness beyond whatever it is that engages our attention at any given moment—is a perennially fascinating notion, and it may have a great deal to do with the specifically human way of being in the world. But the problems are enough to make me doubt the wisdom of beginning Christian dogmatics with it or making the thematization of it the content of the doctrine of creation. If one is still willing to try Schleiermacher's *approach*, one may need another *starting point*. And what intrigues me here is something else that he himself frequently says in speaking of creation and preservation: that piety has to do with our sense of being part of a

45. *Sendschr.*, 13–15; cf. *Reden*, 53–56 (2d ed.); *Gl.*, §§ 3–4. That the feeling of absolute dependence presupposes the concept of dependence has been argued recently by Wayne Proudfoot in *Religious Experience* (Berkeley and Los Angeles: University of California Press, 1985); see esp. 18–19. Of course, Schleiermacher himself asserts that the feeling of absolute dependence emerges only in conjunction with the feeling of partial dependence on the world (e.g., *Gl.*, § 5.3, § 60.1). The question is what this means for the notion of immediate self-consciousness.

46. *Gl.*, § 4.1. Presumably, "introspection" (*Selbstbeobachtung*) is the method for the entire section, not just for § 4.1. Indeed, Schleiermacher constantly appeals to the reader's introspection also in dealing with the specifically Christian facts from which the feeling of absolute dependence is only a logical abstraction. A similar appeal is occasionally made by Calvin (e.g., *Inst.*, 1.7.5).

47. Robert Roberts, "The Feeling of Absolute Dependence," JR 57 (1977): 252–66; quotation on 260.

stable, orderly whole.[48] Could the doctrine of creation be more suitably taken to articulate, not the elusive feeling of absolute dependence, but our sense that we exist in an ordered and therefore meaningful world?

Perhaps this invites the objection that some of our colleagues never have *this* feeling either. But the problem then is not, I think, conceptual, as though the notion as such were too elusive for us even to know what it means. The problem has to do rather with alienation; we know what a "sense of order" means, but the thing itself sometimes runs away from us. Hence it seems exactly right to assert that the sense of order is *contained in* the Christian's faith in Christ as Redeemer, though others may have it in other ways, and still others may lose it or not have it securely at all. And I would also wish to argue that there is in fact a conceptual fit between faith in Christ and the sense of order, because the sense of order too is a kind of faith—a confidence by which we live, but which we cannot prove.

Christian dogmatics is not required to demonstrate that this more general faith is the underlying content of every empirical religion (though it *may* be) but only to explicate its content as an actual presupposition of faith in Christ. No more is asked of the dogmatician than to ensure that all the pieces of the Christian way of believing are there, and in a logical arrangement that makes sense. If the subject matter of Christian dogmatics is indeed Christian faith as a way of believing, then it surely does make good sense to begin with the question: What is believing? Schleiermacher already hovered on the brink of so phrasing the first question of dogmatics when he wrote that "there is something common to all ways of believing (*Glaubensweisen*) by virtue of which we put them together as kin, and something peculiar in each by virtue of which we separate it from the rest."[49] He no doubt had in mind the historical religions. But to communicate what Christian dogmatics is about, it seems to me a natural enough move to go back to less explicitly religious ways of believing, and finally to that "inevitable belief," as A. J. Balfour called it, that we inhabit an orderly world.[50] While not a religious belief as we commonly use the word "religious," it is the presupposition of every scientific experiment and seems to underlie human existence as such. We should try the experiment of putting this "existential faith" (as we may call it) in the place that the feeling of absolute dependence presently occupies in Schleiermacher's dogmatics.[51]

It will not be expected of me to say much more here about the notion of existential faith, which I have explored in greater detail in the chapter on F. H. Jacobi, the philosopher of faith to whom Schleiermacher would have dedi-

48. See n. 20 above.

49. *Gl.*[1], § 6.

50. See chapter 4, n. 6, above.

51. Cf. Gerrish, *Tradition and the Modern World,* 36–38, 211–12 n. 77.

cated *The Christian Faith* but for his (Jacobi's) death in 1819. But I must at least indicate why (in my opening remarks) I described the proposed dogmatic revision as "two-sided." It seems to me that, for all his emphasis on the teleological (or ethical) character of Christian monotheism, Schleiermacher's cosmic vision in his dogmatics, or at least in his doctrine of creation, remained one-sidedly aesthetic, and it was perhaps (for understandable reasons) more dominated by the theoretical problems of religion and natural science than a present-day doctrine of creation can afford to be. At any rate, I should think that if the Christian consciousness presupposes a stable world order at all, it surely presupposes its moral character, perceiving it as a source not only of security but also of responsibility; and this, too, is something it holds in common with the monotheistic faiths of Judaism and Islam.[52] Schleiermacher includes no ethical moment either in his definition of piety or in his doctrine of creation. This is perhaps the price he had to pay for his determination not to *reduce* religion to ethics but to differentiate it from science and morals alike. And the anti-Kantian strain in his religious thought seems to have been reinforced by his failure to appreciate the religion of the Hebrew Scriptures, which he always saw in terms of a legalistic and anthropomorphic piety that was wholly distasteful to him.[53]

If we say, as is said often enough, that the concluding propositions on the Trinity constitute a feeble appendix to Schleiermacher's dogmatics, even though he intended them to provide the keystone, then it is with the magnificent vision of the world as the theater of redemption that *The Christian Faith* achieves its actual climax. His vision represents an interesting variation on the old Calvinistic theme of the manifestation of God's glory. He writes in the very last proposition on redemption: "The divine wisdom is the ground by virtue of which the world, as theater of redemption, is also the absolute revelation of the Supreme Being, and therefore *good*." In effect, this makes the goodness of the world an eschatological concept, lying more in the future consummation of redemption than in a divine creative work of the past. The goodness of the world becomes, in fact, a moral task, and Schleiermacher leaves his dogmatics on the threshold of Christian ethics: "For we are now confronted [he writes] with the task of more and more securing recognition for the world as a good world, as also of forming all things into an organ of the divine Spirit in harmony with the divine idea originally underlying the world order, thus bringing all into unity with the system of redemption."[54] I

52. For Schleiermacher's own classification of Islam as an aesthetic, rather than a teleological, faith, see *Gl.*, § 9.2. It is significant that he apparently did not consider the distinction between the aesthetic and the teleological types of monotheism to be important for the doctrine of creation (cf. *Gl.*, § 29.2).

53. See, e.g., *Reden*, 275–78; *Sendschr.*, 28–29, 41–42; *Gl.*, § 8.4, § 9.2, § 12.2, § 27.3, § 77.2, § 94.2, § 132.2.

54. *Gl.*, § 169.3; trans. in Mackintosh and Stewart, 736–37.

have no quarrel with this eloquent confession. My point is simply that it surely presupposes not just a world order but (to borrow one of Fichte's favorite expressions) a "*moral* world order,"[55] and I cannot see why Schleiermacher did not carry the ethical moment back into his doctrine of creation, unless it was because his definition of piety as the feeling of absolute dependence stood in the way.[56]

With the revision proposed, Schleiermacher's doctrine of creation still seems to me a sound model for Christian dogmatics. "Creation" is not about the way the world first got started, but about the kind of world that is presupposed by the Christian drama of redemption. The adequacy of this way of presenting the doctrine must be judged precisely by the double test of correctly describing the Christian consciousness while avoiding conflict with natural science. And while I do not think dogmatics is apologetics, it does seem to me that to interpret the doctrine of creation as an attempt to thematize existential faith puts the apologist in a position of strength. No apologetic can be the ground or foundation on which Christians repose their faith, which is, by definition, faith in Christ. An attempt to rest Christian faith on arguments would be to misconstrue the phenomenon of faith, and for just this reason it would be poor dogmatics. But this is merely to make the common distinction between the context of discovery and the context of justification, and not by any means to deny that there is a place for apologetics.

True, there are Christians who may find it hard to recognize in such a doctrine of creation their actual Christian faith. If their belief is assent to supernaturally imparted information, then for them creation will be about how the world began—one item in a list of Christian credenda. I can only judge their approach to be wrong. But at least the approach I am recommending instead has no need to deny the genuineness of a *faith* in creation that is conveyed by a largely erroneous *doctrine* of creation, such as, for instance, most of us would take creationism to be. Someone who clings tenaciously to belief in the six-day work of Genesis may be mistaken about the status of the biblical story, but nonetheless nurtured by it in a sound confidence in the world order and a sense of responsibility for stewardship of its resources. Moreover, is it

55. See, e.g., J. G. Fichte, "Über den Grund unsers Glaubens an eine göttliche Weltregierung" (1798), in *Die Schriften zu J. G. Fichte's Atheismus-Streit* (Munich: Georg Müller, 1912), 26, 34–35. For Fichte, the world is constituted by the ego as a *stage* for moral action (30–31).

56. This is by no means to imply that Schleiermacher neglected ethics. For him Christian ethics, like exegetical theology, was a distinct theological field and not a part of dogmatics. He thought that the teleological character of Christianity was better expressed in Christian ethics than in dogmatics (*Gl.*, § 29.2). The existential relationship that piety attests gives rise, precisely through the recognition of it in piety, to specific volitions as well as thought (*Sendschr.*, 15, 19). My question, however, is whether Schleiermacher's ethical emphasis ought not to be reflected also in the *dogmatic* propositions that express the presuppositions of Christian faith concerning the constitution of the world.

not the case that the weight of theological opinion since Schleiermacher's time has moved over to his side of the boat? He anticipated that Christians would have to learn to do without much that many of them still thought to be inextricably tied up with the essence of Christianity, including the very *concept* of creation as usually construed, and not just the Mosaic *account* of it. Even while admitting that orthodoxy was not then on his side, he ventured to predict that some day it would be: "I am firmly persuaded that my discussion is an inspired heterodoxy, which in its own good time—if not just because of my book and not until long after my death—will become orthodox."[57]

57. *Sendschr.*, 29.

Part Four

ERNST TROELTSCH

10

Protestantism and Progress: An Anglo-Saxon View of Troeltsch

IT IS HARDLY possible to speak of a personal exchange of ideas between Ernst Troeltsch and the "Anglo-Saxons."[1] His correspondence with Friedrich von Hügel (1852–1925) seems to have been his most regular point of contact with Britain. Death prevented what was to have been his first visit to England and Scotland in March 1923; the lectures he was to have given at Oxford, London, and Edinburgh had to be read for him, as a kind of memorial tribute, by others. In his introduction to the lectures, von Hügel commented on some oddities in Troeltsch's knowledge, and estimate, of the English mentality. Troeltsch, he wrote, was able to contrast the German mind and the Western European mind only by taking John Stuart Mill (1806–73) and Herbert Spencer (1820–1903) as the most recent English thinkers and wholly ignoring British idealism.[2] But it could be argued that since the death of von Hügel himself, two years later, British philosophy has reverted to type, and it is a type not far removed from Troeltsch's image of the British mind as cast in an empirical and libertarian mold.

Some years earlier, in 1904, Troeltsch had paid a visit to the United States, in the company of Max Weber (1864–1920), to take part in the grandiose Congress of Arts and Science held at St. Louis, Missouri, in connection with the St. Louis World's Fair. The occasion was to be used in part as a data-gathering excursion for Weber's thesis on the relationship between the Calvinist ethic and the spirit of capitalism. Their host in Tonawanda, New York, a German-born pastor named Hans Haupt, was asked to prepare for their visit by collecting information about the American denominations and their moral attitudes, especially on economic practices. Haupt reported that during their stay his visitors argued with each other

1. It should be noted at the outset that the expression "Anglo-Saxons" is used here simply because Troeltsch used it, not because I find it a very apt one.

2. Friedrich von Hügel, introduction to Ernst Troeltsch, *Christian Thought: Its History and Application* (1923; reprint, New York: Meridian Books, 1957), 19–20. The German version was published with the title *Der Historismus und seine Überwindung* (1924; reprint, Aalen: Scientia Verlag, 1966).

the whole time, except when making the mandatory tours of such places as Niagara Falls; they did not discuss his material with him, although they did take it with them. "Haupt had the impression," says Wilhelm Pauck, to whom I owe this report, "that the professors knew all that could be known without having to weigh empirical evidence." Possibly we should make allowances for Pastor Haupt's bruised self-esteem; and Pauck adds that, whatever grounds Haupt may have had for his complaint, Troeltsch and Weber did in fact make extensive use of factual data and statistics in their work on Calvinist economic ethics. In any case, as far as I know, we have already exhausted the list of Troeltsch's first-hand encounters—one actual and one only planned—with the Anglo-Saxon world.[3]

It is entirely fitting that his paper at the congress was "Psychology and Epistemology in the Science of Religion." Empirical psychology was the field in which he believed he had most to learn from America, in particular from William James (1842–1910), although he was convinced that an exclusively empirical method in psychology would remain barren without the rational element contributed by German thinking.[4] While he certainly recognized the historical importance of some of the movements in Anglo-Saxon intellectual history (English deism, for example), there is only one other area, besides the psychology of religion, in which he might be said to have been a debtor, and that is in his belated adaptation of English democratic ideals to the conditions of the postwar Weimar Republic. In religious thought generally, he seems always to have remained self-consciously the spokesman of the German spirit, which he contrasted with the essentially practical spirit of Anglo-American religion.

Naturally enough, then, my task is not to speak of what the Anglo-Saxons may have given to Troeltsch, but rather of how Troeltsch's ideas have been received in Britain and America. I ask, first, what was the relation of the "Chicago School" to his work. And last, after reviewing the British and American literature on him, I offer my own opinion of his continuing worth for the present-day theological enterprise in the Anglo-Saxon world and beyond.

3. Wilhelm Pauck, *Harnack and Troeltsch: Two Historical Theologians* (New York: Oxford University Press, 1968), 72. It remains to be seen whether the continuing quest for biographical materials will in due course yield a fuller picture of Troeltsch's personal connections with Britain and America and his actual experiences in the United States.

4. Ernst Troeltsch, "Main Problems of the Philosophy of Religion: Psychology and Theory of Knowledge in the Science of Religion," in *Congress of Arts and Science: Universal Exposition, St. Louis, 1904*, vol. 1, ed. Howard J. Rogers (Boston and New York: Houghton, Mifflin and Company, 1905), 275–88. See also Troeltsch, "Empiricism and Platonism in the Philosophy of Religion: To the Memory of William James," *Harvard Theological Review* 5 (1912): 401–22 (German in GS 2:364–85).

Troeltsch and the Chicago School

In the work translated into English as *Protestantism and Progress,* Troeltsch remarked that "an essentially practical Protestantism, conservative in doctrine but not intensely dogmatic, forms the backbone of the great Anglo-Saxon portion of our modern world."[5] A few years later, in his lectures on Christian doctrine (*Glaubenslehre*), he noted that old-style dogmatics in the sense of a systematizing of biblical doctrines had become rare but survived in America, where the old European works of dogmatics still found a ready market.[6] Both these judgments were made at the time of the fundamentalist controversy, in which Chicago played a leading role on the side of the modernists. In the years 1909 to 1915, twelve pamphlets titled *The Fundamentals* were produced through the cooperation of Old School Calvinists and the dispensationalists. Roughly speaking, the controversy that resulted may be said to confirm one of Troeltsch's judgments, about the practical bent of Anglo-Saxon religion, but not the other. The supposed theological conservatism of American Protestants was partly dissolved in a radicalism that its advocates would not even call "liberal," because they were conscious of having moved beyond the limits even of liberal Protestantism. In some respects, the views of the Chicago "modernists," as they came to be called, strikingly resembled Troeltsch's position, and it is natural to ask whether Chicago had become an outpost of Troeltschian enlightenment in the New World.

In response to the editors' invitation, Troeltsch wrote his article "The Dogmatics of the '*Religionsgeschichtliche Schule*'" for the *American Journal of Theology,* since 1897 the theological quarterly of the University of Chicago Divinity School. (Later, in 1921, the quarterly was combined with *The Biblical World* and renamed *The Journal of Religion.*) In a footnote, Troeltsch expressed his sense of kinship with Chicago theologian G. B. Foster (1858–1918). Referring to his own book on the absoluteness of Christianity, Troeltsch added: "A similar point of view was worked out in Professor George Burman Foster's *The Finality of the Christian Religion,* Chicago,

5. Troeltsch, *Protestantism and Progress: A Historical Study of the Relation of Protestantism to the Modern World,* trans. W. Montgomery (1912; reprint, Boston: Beacon Press, 1958), 185; cf. ix–x, 162–64. German: *Die Bedeutung des Protestantismus für die Entstehung der modernen Welt,* 2d ed. (Munich and Berlin: R. Oldenbourg, 1911), 92. Hereafter the pages in the second German edition are given in parentheses after citation of the English. The first edition of the original lecture (1906) appeared in the *Historische Zeitschrift.* The English translation has been reissued in the Fortress Texts in Modern Theology series as *Protestantism and Progress: The Significance of Protestantism for the Rise of the Modern World* (Philadelphia: Fortress Press, 1986), but my references follow the pagination of the earlier printings.

6. Troeltsch, *Glaubenslehre: Nach Heidelberger Vorlesungen aus den Jahren 1911 und 1912,* ed. Gertrud von le Fort (1925; reprint, Aalen: Scientia Verlag, 1981), 7. See n. 26 below.

1909."[7] Just a compliment to the host journal perhaps? Or does it invite the question of Troeltsch's relations with the so-called Chicago School?

The question is complicated because it naturally presupposes an answer to the prior question: What was the Chicago School? There have been a Chicago School of architects and a Chicago School of political theorists, to say nothing of a group of Chicago literary critics and a Chicago style of jazz. Even if we confine our attention, as we shall, to the Chicago School in theology, there is disagreement about its membership and chronological limits. For now, I must simply assert without argument that the name "Chicago School" is properly applied to the advocates of a particular approach to history, which came to be called "the socio-historical method." I therefore take the question of Troeltsch and the Chicago School to be this: What was the relation of the socio-historical method to the historical approach of Troeltsch?

Foster is not the best representative of Chicago for providing an answer to this question; his philosophical interests set him somewhat apart from the socio-historical method, which is linked rather with the names of his colleagues, Shailer Mathews (1863–1941) and Shirley Jackson Case (1872–1947).[8] The creed of the socio-historical school, it has been said, was that there is no history but social history, and Case is its prophet.[9] Al-

7. Troeltsch, "The Dogmatics of the 'Religionsgeschichtliche Schule,'" AJT 17 (1913): 1–21, esp. 11, n. 1 (German in GS 2:510). He refers to the second edition of Foster's book; the first appeared in 1906.

8. Charles Harvey Arnold, in his *Near the Edge of Battle: A Short History of the Divinity School and the "Chicago School of Theology" 1866–1966* (Chicago: Divinity School Association, University of Chicago, 1966), takes Foster as the first representative of the Chicago School. Bernard E. Meland, by contrast, regards Foster as "more of a dissident voice within the School." See Meland, "The Empirical Tradition in Theology at Chicago," introduction to *The Future of Empirical Theology,* ed. Meland, Essays in Divinity, vol. 7 (Chicago: University of Chicago Press, 1969), 14, n. 20. The explanation for this initially surprising disagreement is partly that Arnold tends to view the history of the Chicago School and the history of the University of Chicago Divinity School as, at least since 1906, virtually coextensive, whereas Meland is more inclined to identify the Chicago School with Mathews, Case, and the socio-historical method. Arnold does, of course, note the opposition between the anti-speculative socio-historical method and the "religio-philosophical method" of Foster, whose work pointed toward what Arnold presents as the second and third periods of the one school (see especially *Near the Edge,* 32). Outside the United States it is "process theology" rather than the earlier historical approach it came to overshadow that is most commonly associated with Chicago. But whichever way the story is divided, or the labels applied, it may perhaps be said that there is general agreement both about the difference between the Chicago church historians and the Chicago philosophical theologians and about the underlying continuity of a common empirical emphasis that united them.

9. Ernest Cadman Colwell, unpublished paper delivered at the Vanderbilt University Consultation on the Chicago School; cited by William J. Hynes, *Shirley Jackson Case and the Chicago School: The Socio-Historical Method,* Biblical Scholarship in North America, no. 5 (Chico, California: Scholars Press [for the Society of Biblical Literature], 1981), 14.

though Mathews was actually the senior member of the team, we may, for our present purposes, take our information from the mouth of the prophet.

One of Case's best statements of his method formed the introductory chapter to his book *The Social Origins of Christianity* (1923). There he used the expression "*socio*-historical" to bring out what he perceived as the decisive move New Testament scholarship was taking beyond *literary*-historical inquiry. Literary criticism, he points out, has already replaced the old doctrinal use of the Bible, especially by Protestants, for the purpose of extracting normative solutions to the problems of a later age. As part of the church's canon, the New Testament could once be viewed, without regard for its original setting, as a static and unified body of sacred literature. But historical work on the formation of the canon and on the text, language, date, and authorship of the individual writings has discredited the old approach by demonstrating the composite character of the New Testament and even of some of its particular books. And *now,* a further step is being taken.

The social experience of the Christian community, Case goes on, is being more and more recognized as a key to understanding the early history of the Christian movement and the genesis of its sacred literature, and it has become essential to view the Christians as part of a larger social whole, first Jewish and later Gentile. "When study of the New Testament is undertaken from this point of view and fashioned in accordance with this new interest, it ceases to be merely literary-historical in type, and takes on a form that may be described more distinctively as social-historical." And the same socio-historical approach must be consistently applied not only to New Testament exegesis but to the entire history of ancient Christianity.[10]

Other, comparable statements on the socio-historical method could be cited. Especially interesting is Case's theological autobiography, in which he traced his own pilgrimage from Albrecht Ritschl's (1822–89) modified doctrinal use of Scripture and Adolf von Harnack's (1851–1930) essentialism to the frank acknowledgment that the theologians were projecting their own modern faith onto the Scriptures. Historical study led him to the inescapable conviction that the truth of dogma is always relative; the theological quest could not be a search after doctrines normative

10. Shirley Jackson Case, *The Social Origins of Christianity* (Chicago: University of Chicago Press, 1923), 1–37; quotation on 24. "In childhood [the new religion] was rocked in a Jewish cradle and . . . it grew to maturity in a gentile home" (Case, *The Evolution of Early Christianity: A Genetic Study of First-Century Christianity in Relation to Its Religious Environment* [Chicago: University of Chicago Press, 1942], 32). A more strictly linguistic-literary approach to New Testament studies was represented at Chicago by Ernest DeWitt Burton (1856–1925) and Edgar J. Goodspeed (1871–1962).

for all time. "From concentration upon reduction and simplicity," he says, "we turned to the study of variety and complexity."[11] But enough has been said, without the need for further documentation, to establish a plain affinity between the respective aims of the Chicago School and the History of Religions School in general, Troeltsch in particular. Is it proper to conclude that Chicago had indeed become a Troeltschian outpost in the New World?

It is true that Mathews and Case, like Foster, had both studied in Germany (Mathews at Berlin, albeit not in theology, and Case at Marburg and Berlin), and they kept abreast of German scholarship. But three considerations make it unlikely that they could be classified as *Troeltsch-Schüler.* First, those who have made a close study of the Chicago School, or have been directly associated with it, have expressed surprise at the scarcity of the references Mathews and Case made to Troeltsch. Especially noteworthy is the testimony of German-born and German-educated Wilhelm Pauck (1901–81), who studied at Chicago for a year (1925–26) and later, after declining an invitation from Göttingen University, returned to teach in Chicago for more than a quarter of a century (1926–53).[12] Reminiscing about the Chicago years, Pauck confessed his astonishment that Mathews, Case, and his other Chicago colleagues "did not study Troeltsch more closely and . . . made no use of his Sozial-Lehren." His question therefore was: "Why was Troeltsch not a more important figure among the Chicago School? Troeltsch was really their man . . . and the socio-historical method . . . would have been supported by Troeltsch."[13]

Second, however, it must be asked how far the apparent methodological resemblances between Case and Troeltsch can in fact be pressed. Both of them, it is true, spoke of a reciprocal relationship between Christianity and society. But Case was so fascinated by the impact of the environment

11. Case, "Education in Liberalism," in *Contemporary American Theology: Theological Autobiographies,* ed. Vergilius Ferm, first series (New York: Round Table Press, 1932), 105–25; quotation on 112. See also the essay with which Case launched JR as successor to AJT and *The Biblical World:* "The Historical Study of Religion," JR 1 (1921): 1–17, reprinted in JR 29 (1949): 5–14 as a memorial tribute to Case. It is ironic that the newly named journal soon afterward became again a theological quarterly—largely the organ of the process theologians—and that there was talk of changing its name once more.

12. Marion Hausner Pauck, "Wilhelm Pauck: A Biographical Essay," in *Interpreters of Luther: Essays in Honor of Wilhelm Pauck,* ed. Jaroslav Pelikan (Philadelphia: Fortress Press, 1968), 345–46. The position at Göttingen was for an instructor in the church history of Hanover, and Pauck felt he had outgrown the confines of local history; he indicated that he would prefer to teach American church history, but there was no immediate demand for it in Göttingen.

13. I owe these Pauck citations to Hynes, who quotes them from a private letter and the unpublished record of a conference respectively (*Case and the Chicago School,* 102). Hynes furnishes more exact data on Case's references to Troeltsch and concludes in essential agreement with Pauck: "It must at the very least remain an irony of history that no direct, one-on-one exchange occurred between [Case and Troeltsch]" (ibid., 104).

on Christianity that he appears at times to have resolved the dialectic. The contrast with Troeltsch must not be exaggerated. Case did not regard the rise of Christianity as a mere by-product of social forces; rather, he discovered in primitive Christianity a new religious impulse, proceeding from Jesus, which used theological notions and outward forms as the media of its self-expression. He writes that "the personal influence of Jesus' own life is . . . the key to the origin of the new religion," and that "only a historical Jesus, whose personality impressed itself vividly upon his followers, explains the vital element in the new religion."[14] Like Troeltsch, Case assigned a major role in Christian history to the activity of forceful personalities, whom he thought of as reacting *on,* not merely reacting *to,* their environment.[15] But one is often at a loss for words to describe what exactly, for Case, the religious impulse contributes. Troeltsch, too, identified "productive force" as the elusive essence of Christianity;[16] but he kept a firm hold on the gospel of Jesus as the initial, irreducible, and still unexhausted source of the ceaseless exchange between protest and compromise in the history of the church.[17] In Case's presentation, by contrast, the two-way traffic—the reciprocal interaction between ideas and environment—often seems to have become one-way only.

Third, the distinctive language of the socio-historical method invites another comparison: with native American pragmatism, behind which lies a biological image of humans seeking fulfillment of their needs through adaptation to their environment.[18] As one writer on the Chicago School remarks, in addition to the stimulus it received from new approaches to the study of history, the school's endeavor "partook also, if only by a process of osmosis, of the philosophy of pragmatism which, at that time, had come into prominence in the department of philosophy at the University of Chicago under John Dewey."[19] What characterizes pragmatism is its strictly *functional* approach, and one could just as accurately

14. Case, "The Historicity of Jesus: An Estimate of the Negative Argument," AJT 15 (1911): 20–42, quotation on 42; "Is Jesus a Historical Character? Evidence for an Affirmative Opinion," AJT 15 (1911): 205–27, quotation on 227.

15. Case, *Evolution of Early Christianity,* 27–28, 39–40; "Education in Liberalism," 115. Cf. Troeltsch, *Glaubenslehre,* 20–21.

16. Troeltsch, "Was heisst 'Wesen des Christentums'?" GS 2:418; "Dogmatics of the 'Religionsgeschichtliche Schule,'" 12 (GS 2:510–11).

17. Troeltsch, *The Social Teaching of the Christian Churches,* trans. Olive Wyon, 2 vols. (1931; reprint, Chicago: University of Chicago Press, 1981), 1:34, 39, 43, 48–50; 2:1002–4 (cf. GS 1:14–15, 15–16, 25–26, 31–33; 2:975–77). Olive Wyon's translation has been reissued in the Library of Theological Ethics series (Louisville, Kentucky: Westminster/John Knox Press, 1992).

18. See, e.g., Case, *Evolution of Early Christianity,* preface and chapters 1–2. In this work Case criticizes Troeltsch, whom he sees as not entirely emancipated from unhistorical modes of thought but simply relocating the absolute religion in the future (13–14).

19. Meland, "The Empirical Tradition," 18.

term Case's method "functional" as "socio-historical."[20] He was inclined to regard beliefs and doctrines as secondary products of the evolutionary adaptation of Christianity to its environment, and he repeatedly asserted that "functional significance" is the actual criterion by which the value of a religious idea or practice must be judged: the test is "the measure of satisfaction and assistance which it renders."[21] Once again, though the opposition is not to be overstated, we seem to have a very different viewpoint here than we find in Weber and Troeltsch, who were fascinated by the potency of at least some religious ideas and viewed religion as an independent variable in the total fabric of society. Case's writings, on the other hand, hover at the brink of a kind of reductionism that one does not normally expect to find in a divinity school.

As a way of doing history, the socio-historical method represents some permanent methodological gains. Its fruitfulness is attested by the fact that several of the most important historical works by Mathews and Case have been reprinted from time to time and are still available. It has been argued that with its socio-historical method the Chicago School arrived independently at an approach to the New Testament that paralleled German form criticism (*Formgeschichte*), in which the specific needs of the early Christian communities are presumed to have shaped the units of oral tradition that lie behind the canonical Gospels.[22]

As an approach to theology, however, Chicago functionalism ended with a dilemma more serious than any Troeltsch is alleged to have fallen into in his final years. At first, Case thought it appropriate to judge christologies in part by their fidelity to the Jesus recovered by historical scholarship. But he never held that this was a sufficient criterion for a present-day estimate of Christ; everything in religion had to pass the test of whether it met the needs of the day. And the historical criterion gradually receded into the background. Even the social nature of religion seemed to get mislaid in the transition from history to present-day belief, and Case left individual believers to their individual resources. Each is to believe whatever he or she thinks ought to be believed in the light of personal experience and knowledge; all that matters is that one's set of beliefs must be "genuinely the precipitate of one's own true self." The recounting

20. Ibid., 26. Similarly, Hynes writes: "Perhaps the most distinctive factor in Case's socio-historical method is its radical functionalism" (*Case and the Chicago School*, 83; cf. 138).

21. Case, "Education in Liberalism," 113–14; cf. *Evolution of Early Christianity*, 24–25, 43–44.

22. "The Chicago school's emphasis on 'environmental factors' was an independent parallel to form criticism" (Henry J. Cadbury, "New Testament Scholarship: Fifty Years in Retrospect," *Journal of Bible and Religion* 28 [1960]: 194). I am not qualified to endorse this judgment, or to reject it; but it does seem to me that one might do well to look for Chicago parallels to—or dependence upon—European biblical scholarship rather than Troeltsch's *Social Teachings*.

of the past is only exemplary: it serves to show how our predecessors went about the same task for themselves.[23]

No doubt, there was a strongly subjective element in the accounts Troeltsch gave of how a value is made. But Case's viewpoint still seems to have been different: he lacked, or perhaps lost, anything like Troeltsch's powerful sense of tradition and community. For Case, the problem was not how to lift values out of the past; he ended with a past and a Christ that served only as a formal, contentless inspiration, inciting each of us to create a private religious world. The evidence, in short, does not warrant the hypothesis that the Chicago School was much influenced by *The Social Teachings*. One may wish to argue, however, that there were features in the native American mentality that provided a fertile soil for Troeltsch's approach; for the fact is that *The Social Teachings* eventually came to enjoy a remarkable authority in America at large, whatever Mathews and Case thought—or knew—of Troeltsch in Chicago.

Troeltsch's Anglo-Saxon Interpreters

Intellectuals of Troeltsch's eminence scatter the good seed widely, and their tracks are not always easy to make out. Much of his influence in America has been mediated personally—in the classrooms of scholars like James Luther Adams, who has won the highest respect as an interpreter of Troeltsch (and Tillich), first at Chicago, later at Harvard. Adams is of course an original thinker in his own right, not simply a *Troeltschforscher.* And in general Troeltsch's ideas have been disseminated by some of the most creative minds in recent American history, including Reinhold Niebuhr and his brother, H. Richard Niebuhr (1894–1962), who in his youth wrote a doctoral dissertation on Troeltsch's philosophy of religion (Yale University, 1924). Paul Tillich, we may add, carried with him to America a strong interest in Troeltsch's thought.

One is not likely to encounter dissent if one suggests that the dominant Troeltschian theme for all of these distinguished thinkers has been, in one form or another, "religion and culture." This is certainly the theme that has spread Troeltsch's influence in the United States beyond the limits of the theological world. It may well be that Protestant modernism in America, even if it belied his image of Anglo-Saxon conservatism, indicated a certain receptivity to his ideas insofar as he stood for closer relations between theology (or the study of religion) and the social sciences. The Chicago School probably developed independently of *The Social Teach-*

23. Case, "Education in Liberalism," 117–18. Cf. Case, *Jesus through the Centuries* (Chicago: University of Chicago Press, 1932), chap. 13, esp. 351–63, 370–71, 375–76; *The Christian Philosophy of History* (Chicago: University of Chicago Press, 1943), 161–63, 168–73, 182–87.

ings, whether wholly or partly, but it was surely *The Social Teachings* that found the most receptive readership in the United States, even among the theologians. When the Society for the Scientific Study of Religion launched its own journal (in 1961), the first volume contained a series of seven articles on the writings of Troeltsch. Between them, they touched on every aspect of his work, but it is significant that his name was more particularly linked with the scientific study of religion. One might say that the new *Journal for the Scientific Study of Religion* fulfilled somewhat the role Case had in mind for the *Journal of Religion,* which, ironically enough, even with its new title had again become a theological journal (closely associated for a time with the Chicago process theologians). In short, it was the theme of *The Social Teachings* that found, or won, attentive American ears—all the more so when Olive Wyon's English translation was published.

The first book by Troeltsch to appear in English was *Die Bedeutung des Protestantismus für die Entstehung der modernen Welt* (1906; 2d ed., 1911), which likewise was concerned with the theme of religion and culture. The English version appeared in 1912 with the catchy title *Protestantism and Progress,* although "Protestantism and Regress" might have fit the thesis of the book equally well. It was followed in 1923 by *Christian Thought: Its History and Application,* and in 1931 by Wyon's translation of *Die Soziallehren* under the title *The Social Teaching of the Christian Churches.* (The plural "teachings" perhaps sounds a little unnatural to British ears, but why *die Gruppen* were dropped from the title remains less clear.) When *The Social Teaching* was reprinted in 1949, American church historian Roland Bainton (1894–1984) drew attention to the interesting fact that while Troeltsch's reputation had declined in Europe, his influence in the United States had mounted to the point where "in many quarters he [was] treated as a veritable gospel, and his conclusions [were] accepted with an uncritical devotion wholly alien to his own spirit." Bainton proceeded to furnish some of the requisite criticisms, assessing Troeltsch's interpretations over the whole course of church history. He found it necessary to fault him on several points and judged that the work should be canonized for its method rather than its conclusions: Troeltsch, he maintained, had "introduced a new method of writing church history" and in so doing had produced "a great pioneer work."[24] Since the publication of the interesting study by Manfred Wichelhaus,[25] the novelty of Troeltsch's method can no

24. Roland H. Bainton, "Ernst Troeltsch—Thirty Years Later," *Theology Today* 8 (1951–52): 70–96. The article was reprinted in the third series of Bainton's collected papers, *Christian Unity and Religion in New England* (Boston: Beacon Press, 1964).

25. Manfred Wichelhaus, *Kirchengeschichtsschreibung und Soziologie im neunzehnten Jahrhundert und bei Ernst Troeltsch,* Heidelberger Forschungen, vol. 9 (Heidelberg: Carl Winter, 1965).

longer be taken for granted, but method was no doubt the right thing for Bainton to emphasize. As far as material criticisms are concerned, it is unfortunate that while he found Troeltsch mistaken about Luther, outdated on the sects and mysticism, and thin on America, Bainton endorsed Troeltsch's defective understanding of the God of John Calvin. There can be no doubt that on all these themes *The Social Teachings* has exercised a powerful influence in the English-speaking world.

The large number of recent translations of Troeltsch will certainly help to broaden Anglo-Saxon interest in him.[26] But it seems evident that up to the present *The Social Teachings* is the work through which he has been best known in both Britain and America. For this reason, it is curious that book-length studies of him in English have been the work of theologians rather than historians or social scientists. There are, to be sure, a great number of references to him in numerous works that are not about him alone, and not all by theologians. One thinks of the familiar volumes by Friedrich von Hügel (1921), H. R. Mackintosh (1937), H. Stuart Hughes (1958), and Georg Iggers (1968).[27] But if we confine ourselves to Troeltsch studies in the strict sense, and if we set aside unpublished dissertations, only five books come to mind, all more or less theological in character. The earliest was R. S. Sleigh's *The Sufficiency of Christianity* (1923), written as a Ph.D. dissertation at the University of Aberdeen. Not intended merely as a study of Troeltsch but as an attempt at theological construction in conversation with him, it focused on questions of dogmatics and philosophy of religion. Sleigh had spent a year in Heidelberg before Troeltsch moved to Berlin, and he had studied Troeltsch's writings with evident appreciation. His book must have taken him several years to write; even so, it was finished too soon for him to offer more than a couple of inserted notes on *Historicism and Its Problems* (1922), or to take any account at all of the posthumous lectures, *Christian Thought: Its History and*

26. For translations already published when this chapter was first written, see *Ernst Troeltsch: Writings on Theology and Religion,* trans. and ed. Robert Morgan and Michael Pye (1977; reprint, Louisville, Kentucky: Westminster/John Knox Press, 1990), 253–55. Two further volumes that I spoke of as "forthcoming" have now appeared, both of them in the Fortress Texts in Modern Theology series: Troeltsch, *Religion in History,* essays translated by James Luther Adams and Walter F. Bense (Minneapolis: Fortress Press, 1991), and *The Christian Faith,* translation of the lectures on *Glaubenslehre,* trans. Garrett E. Paul (ibid.). The first of these two volumes is published in the United Kingdom by T. & T. Clark, Edinburgh.

27. Baron Friedrich von Hügel, *Essays and Addresses on the Philosophy of Religion,* first series (1921; reprint, London and Toronto: J. M. Dent & Sons, New York: E. P. Dutton & Co., 1931); Hugh Ross Mackintosh, *Types of Modern Theology: Schleiermacher to Barth* (1937; reprint, London: Nisbet & Co., 1949); H. Stuart Hughes, *Consciousness and Society: The Reorientation of European Social Thought 1890–1930* (New York: Alfred A. Knopf, 1958); Georg G. Iggers, *The German Conception of History: The National Tradition of Historical Thought from Herder to the Present* (Middletown, Connecticut: Wesleyan University Press, 1968).

Application. It was dedicated "with reverent affection" partly to the memory of the recently deceased Troeltsch. But it is also a monument to the folly of writing a dissertation on a creative thinker *before* he is deceased: it was already out of date the day it was published.[28]

No further book on Troeltsch appeared in Britain until more than fifty years had passed. Meanwhile, in the 1960s, three pertinent volumes appeared in quick succession on the other side of the Atlantic. One of them, Pauck's lively biographical sketch of Harnack and Troeltsch (1968), I have mentioned already. Pauck had been a student in Berlin (1920–21) and vividly recalled the profound impression Troeltsch had made on him. Not so much concerned as Sleigh with Troeltsch's ventures into dogmatics and philosophy of history, Pauck characterized his two subjects as "historical theologians." He was intrigued by Troeltsch's historical interpretation of Christianity—with universal historical methods and in the wider context of religious and social history—and he insisted that Troeltsch himself did not attach much importance to his work in systematic theology. In an appendix, he translated the brilliant tribute Troeltsch paid to Harnack on the occasion of Harnack's seventieth birthday: it indicates clearly and forcefully how church history might become a sufficient substitute for the old dogmatics.[29]

Like Pauck's book, the slightly earlier study by Thomas Ogletree, *Christian Faith and History* (1965), was about two thinkers and not about Troeltsch only. Indeed, the dissertation in which Ogletree's book had its origin (Ph.D. diss., Vanderbilt University, 1963) was titled "Christology and History in the Theology of Karl Barth: A Critical Exposition in Light of the Historicism of Ernst Troeltsch." Although he thought a comparison of Barth and Troeltsch could be fruitful, Ogletree was mainly concerned to present the contrast between two mutually exclusive answers to the problem of faith and history. One interprets Christian faith by its wider setting in history—and especially in a pluralistic history of religions—while the other reads all history in the light of Christian faith. Hence the comparison aims, in the end, not at a synthesis but a choice: "One either gives controlling place to the methods and conclusions of historical thinking or to the methods and conclusions of dogmatic thinking. Between these two there does not seem to be any middle ground." The two alternatives are cogently presented, without oversimplification. Ogletree's sympathies were finally with Barth, who understood the significance of history to be constituted by the history of Jesus Christ. My own sympa-

28. R. S. Sleigh, *The Sufficiency of Christianity: An Enquiry concerning the Nature and the Modern Possibilities of the Christian Religion, with Special Reference to the Religious Philosophy of Dr Ernst Troeltsch* (London: James Clarke & Co., 1923).

29. See n. 3 above. Pauck returned to Berlin in 1923 and received his doctorate two years later under Karl Holl.

thies, I must confess, are more with Troeltsch. Christianity is christocentric, but when christocentrism is made the yardstick for judging every religion, it appears to become, as Troeltsch said, the dogmatic counterpart of geocentrism in cosmology and anthropocentrism in metaphysics—an absolutizing of our own location in history. I cannot imagine Troeltsch being persuaded by Barth's artful claim that the church's confession of Jesus Christ as the one word of God is a purely christological statement, which as such relativizes even Christianity and the church.[30]

The book that more than any other has introduced Troeltsch's thought to British and American students is Benjamin Reist's *Toward a Theology of Involvement,* which was published on both sides of the Atlantic (1966). Though it began as a doctoral thesis (Th.D., Princeton Theological Seminary, 1958), its scope was uncommonly broad for a dissertation. "The problem in the English-speaking world," Reist explained, "is that the thought of Troeltsch is simply not considered on the broad spectrum across which it moves."[31] Hence the subtitle of the original dissertation described it as "an introduction to the thought of Ernst Troeltsch." Nevertheless, though it ranges widely and ably over Troeltsch's writings, a single line of argument runs throughout the book.

Reist approves the program of reformulating Christian ideas "with unreserved involvement [*Eingehen*] in the modern world," and he has the highest regard for *The Social Teachings.* But the Troeltsch of the *Glaubenslehre,* who tried his own hand at reformulating Christian doctrines, does not fare so well: the attempt, according to Reist, simply collapsed. Partly, the problem lay in the subjective element in Troeltsch's procedure, so that he could offer only "a theology for the third type" (that is, for religious individualism or mysticism). But the main reason for the collapse was that in his philosophy of history "individuality" finally overwhelmed "development"; which means, in the domain of theology, that the supreme validity of Christianity dissolved into the plurality of the world religions. Troeltsch could not overcome historical relativism on the only ground he would admit, history itself. "The implication," Reist concludes, "is that no one can."[32]

As with Ogletree, so with Reist: We end with a critical verdict strongly colored by what the English-speaking world calls "neo-orthodoxy." In the light of the theological revolution of the 1920s, Reist warns us, to repeat Troeltsch's errors would be "unpardonably stu-

30. Thomas W. Ogletree, *Christian Faith and History: A Critical Comparison of Ernst Troeltsch and Karl Barth* (New York and Nashville, Tennessee: Abingdon Press, 1965), esp. 13, 37, 44, 132, 230.

31. Benjamin A. Reist, *Toward a Theology of Involvement: The Thought of Ernst Troeltsch* (Philadelphia: Westminster Press, London: SCM Press, 1966), 10.

32. Ibid., 17, 178, 83.

pid."[33] Up to a point, *Toward a Theology of Involvement* follows Troeltsch's own account of his development in the first of the lectures he was to have given in Britain. But I cannot see any evidence that the second thoughts he there described were very traumatic for him: he wrote not of the collapse of his theology, but of its modification. Christianity, as one manifestation of the divine life, becomes valid *for us*. "The practical bearing of this new manner of thinking," Troeltsch wrote, "differs but little from that of my earlier view." Instead of proclaiming the collapse of his theology, then, we might better ask ourselves the reason why his calm relativism so alarms us. He himself would no doubt ascribe it to self-will and the spirit of domination.[34]

Finally, there is the publication that emerged from the international Troeltsch Colloquium, held in 1974 at Lancaster University. Titled *Ernst Troeltsch and the Future of Theology* (1976), the volume documents once again the theological character of Anglo-Saxon books on Troeltsch. In this instance, the concentration on problems of constructive theology is partly accidental, since the colloquium itself was divided into two sections, "The Future of Theology" and "Religion and Social Change." Only the papers of the theology section were published. All of them were by British scholars, if I count myself as at least partly British, but with the addition of an introductory essay by Hans-Georg Drescher on Troeltsch's intellectual development.

It is not possible to take up the individual contributions to *Troeltsch and the Future of Theology* here. They ranged widely over the dialectical theology, theological method, the essence of Christianity, and the so-called other religions. Suffice it to say that one will not find in these essays any "canonization" of Troeltsch's theology (to borrow a word from Bainton); indeed, one finds some sharp criticisms of him. Nevertheless, taken as a whole, the volume conveys the sense that he has not been disposed of, and that he therefore needs to be heard again on his favorite themes, which have not been definitively solved since his death. And in contrast to the criticisms made by Ogletree and Reist, the criticisms from the Lancaster Colloquium cannot be placed under the aegis of neoorthodoxy.[35]

33. Ibid., 202.

34. Troeltsch, *Christian Thought*, 57, 62.

35. John Powell Clayton, ed., *Ernst Troeltsch and the Future of Theology* (Cambridge: Cambridge University Press, 1976). For sample criticisms of Troeltsch, see 68, 96, 157. A little surprisingly, perhaps, the editor remarks in his preface: "Troeltsch's importance for the study of church history, the sociology of religion and the philosophy of history and culture is generally acknowledged and well covered in the secondary literature. It was felt, however, that his contribution to theology in particular has not received sufficient attention" (x). But this is not intended as a remark exclusively about books in English, and Clayton has partly in

Troeltsch and Theology Today

The conclusion toward which these reflections have led us is twofold: While the most influential of Troeltsch's writings in the Anglo-Saxon world has been *The Social Teachings,* the Troeltsch literature has been largely the work of theologians; and much of it has been negative and critical, finding in his thought unresolved problems rather than a theological paradigm. Even the most warmly appreciative book about him in English, Sleigh's *Sufficiency of Christianity,* was peppered with critical remarks; and the appreciative comments in Pauck's mostly descriptive study were not directed to Troeltsch's attempts at strictly *systematic* theology. A cautious shift in the direction of a more evenly balanced appraisal can be detected in the last of the five volumes mentioned. But the negative verdict of Ogletree and Reist in the 1960s has by no means been lifted. Anyone who ventures to look for something more in Troeltsch's theology than an instructive failure is still exposed to the risk of being thought (in Reist's damning phrase) "unpardonably stupid."

Nevertheless, I have to admit that my own principal interest in Troeltsch has always been, and still is, prompted by the question: What should Christian theology look like if it permits itself to be shaped from beginning to end by the kind of historical thinking that Troeltsch both analyzed and stood for? What should be the shape, the procedure, and the content of a theology of historicism or, in Schleiermacher's sense of the

mind the need for a more sympathetic *reappraisal* of Troeltsch's theological questions. Rubanowice's study of Troeltsch did not reach me, unfortunately, until after my reflections on the state of the literature had already been written and presented: Robert J. Rubanowice, *Crisis in Consciousness: The Thought of Ernst Troeltsch* (Tallahassee: University Presses of Florida, 1982). The author, a historian of ideas, sets out precisely to compensate for the heavily theological interest of previous British and American books on Troeltsch by offering an introductory survey of his writings in their full range. Particularly welcome is the chapter devoted to Troeltsch's political writings. Like Ogletree and Reist, however, Rubanowice does not move beyond the estimate of Troeltsch as a great questioner who represents, rather than overcomes, a crisis of consciousness. Additions to Troeltsch studies in English since the present chapter was first published (1984) confirm, on the whole, the dominant interest in his theological ideas: Wendell S. Dietrich, *Cohen and Troeltsch: Ethical Monotheistic Religion and Theory of Culture,* Brown Judaic Studies, no. 120 (Atlanta, Georgia: Scholars Press, 1986); Sarah Coakley, *Christ without Absolutes: A Study of the Christology of Ernst Troeltsch* (Oxford: Oxford University Press, 1988); George E. Griener, Jr., *Ernst Troeltsch and Herman Schell: Christianity and the World Religions, An Ecumenical Contribution to the History of Apologetics,* European University Studies, series 23, vol. 375 (Frankfurt am Main: Peter Lang, 1990). I have reviewed Coakley's admirable study in JR 71 (1991): 270–72. Though he does not speak for the Anglo-Saxons, I should mention also, among the English-language studies of Troeltsch, Toshimasa Yasukata, *Ernst Troeltsch: Systematic Theologian of Radical Historicality,* AAR Academy Series, no. 55 (Atlanta, Georgia: Scholars Press, 1986).

term, a *historical* theology? And my interest in the question would not have survived had I been convinced by the critics that such a theology is impossible—cannot be done.

This, at any rate, was the line of questioning that I pursued in my own contribution to the Lancaster Colloquium by means of a reappraisal of Troeltsch's *Glaubenslehre.* I tried to specify the several ways in which theology, for him, had to be historical. I was not so much concerned to defend him or to reject him as to hear him in a work that had commonly been ignored or dismissed. However, I was not interested in mere reporting, and I did point out what seemed to me both the promise and the embarrassment of a historical theology.[36] The inquiry was carried out at the formal level of methodology; but earlier, in another address, I ventured to explore one of Troeltsch's most important material themes, arguing that in his lecture on the significance of the historicity of Jesus for faith he pegged more on knowledge of the historical Jesus than his own historicist principles required.[37]

There is no point in rehearsing the content of these two addresses, both of which have been reprinted in slightly revised versions. I should certainly mention, however, that Walter Wyman has carried the discussion an important step further in his University of Chicago dissertation (Ph.D., 1980). Wyman seeks, as I had done on a much smaller scale, to specify the defining characteristics of *Glaubenslehre* as a theological genre distinct from the old *Dogmatik.*[38] He carried out some of his research in Germany, and he reports that when he presented the argument of the dissertation in a seminar, one astonished comment was: "Eine tolle Fragestellung!" That, of course, was not said in a Troeltschian stronghold. Troeltsch in fact perceived the entire contrast between the old dogmatics and the new signaled in the change of nomenclature that Schleiermacher occasioned. And yet, at the same time, he held that the theological shift from *Dogmatik* to *Glaubenslehre* was already latent in the achievement of Martin Luther. As a postscript to what I have written elsewhere, then, I will venture a brief comment on each side of Troeltsch's twofold appeal, to Schleiermacher and to Luther.

36. Gerrish, "Ernst Troeltsch and the Possibility of a Historical Theology," in *Ernst Troeltsch and the Future of Theology,* ed. Clayton, 100–135; reprinted in Gerrish, *The Old Protestantism and the New: Essays on the Reformation Heritage* (Chicago: University of Chicago Press; Edinburgh: T. & T. Clark, 1982), 208–29.

37. Gerrish, "Jesus, Myth, and History: Troeltsch's Stand in the 'Christ-Myth' Debate," JR 55 (1975): 13–35; reprinted in *The Old Protestantism,* 230–47.

38. Walter E. Wyman, Jr., *The Concept of Glaubenslehre: Ernst Troeltsch and the Theological Heritage of Schleiermacher,* AAR Academy Series, no. 44 (Chico, California: Scholars Press, 1983).

As far as Schleiermacher's theological enterprise is concerned, the critical difficulty is certainly the one raised by Benjamin Reist with respect to Troeltsch: If the superiority of Christianity among the religions of the world is surrendered, is not the heart cut out of Christian theology, so that it must simply collapse?[39] And if the answer is affirmative, does that not establish the impossibility of a "dogmatics of the *religionsgeschichtliche Schule*"? The early, "Heidelberg" Troeltsch, followed by Hermann Süskind (1879–1914), believed that Schleiermacher could rest his dogmatics on the immediate assurance of Christian faith only because he assumed that the philosophy of religion could demonstrate what faith takes for granted: the superiority of its own religion.[40] There are some obstacles in the way of accepting this notion as a correct interpretation of Schleiermacher. But it plainly indicates that Troeltsch made doubly difficult what he took to be the first task of dogmatics; he built his theology not only on *belief* in the "supreme validity" of Christianity, but on the possibility of *proving* it. Reist's case is therefore a very plausible one: When the absoluteness of Christianity is surrendered, must not the entire dogmatic edifice collapse? And is this not in fact what happened with the move, so to say, from Heidelberg to Berlin?

These questions are by no means easily mastered. They cannot be localized within dogmatic prolegomena but are bound to resurface throughout the entire dogmatic system: most obviously in christology and eschatology, because one must eventually ask about the unsurpassability of Christ and the possibility of a single goal of human history. Moreover, since Troeltsch was not granted length of life to return to his "first love," the philosophy of religion, we are forced in some measure to speculate about the answers he might have proposed.[41] However, from his posthumously published lecture "The Place of Christianity," it seems reasonable to deduce at least one thing: it would not have been difficult for him to reconceive the task of Christian theology as simply to furnish an account of how the divine life is manifested in Christian faith, no inferences being drawn about the inferiority of other religions, much less about the need to

39. Plainly, the same question is being raised in another form when Ogletree sides with Barth's christocentric reading of history.

40. See Süskind, *Christentum und Geschichte bei Schleiermacher: Die geschichtsphilosophischen Grundlagen der Schleiermacherschen Theologie,* part 1: *Die Absolutheit des Christentums und die Religionsphilosophie* (Tübingen: J. C. B. Mohr [Paul Siebeck], 1911). Süskind took his inspiration from two of Troeltsch's publications: his essay "Rückblick auf ein halbes Jahrhundert der theologischen Wissenschaft" (1908; reprinted in GS 2:193–226) and his review (in the *Theologische Literaturzeitung,* 1909) of Hermann Mulert's book on Schleiermacher's philosophy of history. See also Troeltsch, "Dogmatics of the 'Religionsgeschichtliche Schule,'" 10–11 (GS 2:509–10).

41. Troeltsch, "Meine Bücher," GS 4:15.

demonstrate the superiority of Christianity.[42] Perhaps the way would then be open for enlarging those occasional signs of willingness in his *Glaubenslehre* to listen to the other religions, not merely to underscore their differences from Christianity. As Michael Pye has pointed out, the logic of Troeltsch's presuppositions suggests that the other religions should not be disposed of in the introduction to a Christian dogmatics, where discussion of them can hardly avoid being apologetic, but rather moved out into the dogmatics proper, where they may become theological resources and not competitors. "Everything of value in all the [religious] traditions," Pye says, "is available for modern man."[43]

To this I would only wish to add that Süskind's pursuit of what he held to be the logic of Troeltsch's and Schleiermacher's principles led, in my opinion, in exactly the wrong direction. He feared that without a demonstration of the truth of Christianity *Glaubenslehre* would be left standing in the air.[44] Schleiermacher did not care for the term *begründen* that Süskind so freely employed. But if we admit it at all as a description of Schleiermacher's procedure, it must surely be said that what "grounds" his dogmatic enterprise is its anchorage in common human experience, not his ability to prove the truth of peculiarly Christian claims. The limited use to which he actually puts his comparison of religions (in the introduction to his *Glaubenslehre*) is to provide him with a definition *per genus et differentiam* of the distinctive essence of Christianity. A *ranking* of religions is not really needed for this purpose. It remains true, no doubt, that a historian of religion, or the adherent of another religion, could only read Schleiermacher's classification as Christian apologetics—a tacit ranking. For this reason, it might be worth considering whether even a *comparison* of the religions is required for dogmatic prolegomena: the nature of Christian faith could be described without it. The problem of Christian absolutism would still emerge later, but it would not be present to mislead at the very threshold. To this extent, Schleiermacher's dogmatic heritage could surely be made compatible with Troeltsch's final surrender of absolutism, whereas the direction in which Süskind wanted to lead it would indeed have ended in "collapse."[45]

42. Troeltsch, "The Place of Christianity among the World Religions," in *Christian Thought*, 33–63.

43. Pye, "Ernst Troeltsch and the End of the Problem about 'Other' Religions," in *Ernst Troeltsch and the Future of Theology*, ed. Clayton, 194.

44. Süskind, *Christentum und Geschichte*, 104, 116.

45. Since Schleiermacher himself so expressly rejected the language of grounding, proving, providing foundations in dogmatics, it invites confusion to import it into the interpretation of his theology. If it is to be heuristically useful at all, a clear distinction must in any case be maintained between the foundation of a dogmatic system and the foundation of Christian faith itself. (On the foundation of Christian faith, see chapter 9, nn. 43, 44, above.)

All of which may seem to be a long way from Martin Luther.[46] But Troeltsch found in the religiousness of the reformer a turn to the subject, and it was this above all that he rightly took to be a link between the two Protestantisms. Since his day, religious subjectivity has been the theme of more than one theological debate. On the one side, developments within Protestant theology have raised doubts about the virtue of the religious subjectivity that gains a foothold in Luther. On the other side, subjectivism has continued to be identified by Roman Catholic critics as the main flaw not in Luther alone, or in modern Protestantism alone, but in Protestantism generally. We have seen that even the irenic image of Luther presented by Joseph Lortz still pictured him as a reformer limited by his own subjectivity, which prevented him from being a *Vollhörer* of the word of God. And while some Roman Catholic scholars since Lortz have excluded Luther's personal limitations as irrelevant to his witness for the gospel, in the work of Paul Hacker we have perhaps the most extreme version of the old polemical theme: Luther's religion becomes faith in faith itself.

If, for a moment, we can bracket these other conceptions of Luther's subjectivity and ask only about Troeltsch's interpretation of it, the heart of the matter may be seen in his twofold thesis: first, that Luther moved religion into the domain of the psychologically intelligible; and second, that the religion of personal conviction, which had its source in Luther, bases itself on history without petrifying history into dogma.[47] The key to this twofold shift in religiousness lay, as Troeltsch clearly recognized, in the substitution of the word of God for the medieval sacraments as the actual means of grace. The dissolution of the concept of the sacraments he held to be the central religious idea of Protestantism, and he informed von Hügel that he could not recognize in the church and its sacraments a legitimate development of the mind of Jesus.[48]

Troeltsch's twofold thesis about Luther and the modern religious consciousness will be taken up in more detail in my next chapter. Of course,

---

Schleiermacher does begin his dogmatic system by situating the language of Christian faith in the wider context of human experience and discourse, but such a "placement" is by no means a proof: it serves the interests of understanding rather than demonstration. For my own understanding of the logic of Schleiermacher's argument in the introduction to the *Glaubenslehre,* see my *Tradition and the Modern World: Reformed Theology in the Nineteenth Century* (Chicago: University of Chicago Press, 1978), 29–39.

46. The original address on which this chapter is based was given in the year of the Luther anniversary (1983), and I was expressly asked to take Troeltsch's Luther interpretation into account.

47. Troeltsch, *Protestantism and Progress,* 193, 203 (96, 101).

48. Troeltsch, "Protestantisches Christentum und Kirche in der Neuzeit," in *Geschichte der christlichen Religion,* ed. Paul Hinneberg (*Die Kultur der Gegenwart: Ihre Entwickelung und ihre Ziele,* II, 4, 1), 2d ed. (Berlin and Leipzig: B. G. Teubner, 1909), 439–40, 456–59, 470; *Christian Thought,* 18.

he knew perfectly well that the Luther who looks toward modernity is not the whole Luther: the assertion of continuity is framed by the fundamental contrast between the old Protestantism and the new that unprejudiced historical inquiry discovers. But Troeltsch insisted that the continuity, too, was just as much a discovery of historical inquiry and not a judgment of value.[49] With the qualifications that accompany it, his thesis has by no means been set aside by historical scholarship. What has happened, rather, is that the problem of Luther and the modern world has received less attention than that of Luther and the medieval world. It is entirely possible, no doubt, to deplore Troeltsch's sketch of Protestantism and progress on theological grounds, but historically it remains an astute and perceptive account of how theology moved on from the old Protestantism to the new. The dogmatics of the new Protestantism could indeed, as Troeltsch says, appeal to Luther, and it often did. Nevertheless, he added that this "dogmatics" is dogmatics no more, because it knows no dogmas but only the ideas latent in Christian believing. These it draws from the total resources of the Christian heritage, and it adjusts them to modern conceptions of the world. That, he believed, was why Schleiermacher renamed the task *Glaubenslehre*.[50]

49. Troeltsch, "Protestantisches Christentum," 742; *Protestantism and Progress,* 204 (101–2).

50. Troeltsch, "Dogmatik," RGG 2:106–9. Like Alexander Schweizer before him, Troeltsch actually makes much more of the contrast between *Dogmatik* and *Glaubenslehre* than Schleiermacher himself did; he gave it, in fact, a sharply polemical turn. But he did not misread Schleiermacher in this respect. See my next chapter.

11

From Dogmatik to Glaubenslehre: A Paradigm Change in Modern Theology?

IN AN EARLY essay on history and metaphysics, Ernst Troeltsch declared that the historical-critical method, once it gains an entrance, brooks no limits. Developed to deal with natural events, it is bound, if applied to the supernatural, to dissolve it into the natural and to interpret it as analogous to everything else. A separation between the natural and the supernatural, the humanly conditioned and the directly divine, becomes impossible.[1] In another essay, published the same year, Troeltsch compared the historical-critical method to leaven: it transforms everything and finally bursts the entire mold of previous theological methods.[2]This, clearly, sounds like a promising candidate for the title of what Kuhn has taught us to call a "paradigm change."[3] So impressed was Troeltsch with the radicalness of the transformation that he believed it required a new name for the constructive theological enterprise: no longer *Dogmatik,* but *Glaubenslehre.*

In what follows, I do not claim that *Glaubenslehre* really *is* the new theological paradigm, though I do not deny it either. The claim, or the denial, would require not only a close analysis of the language of paradigm change but also an extensive attempt to locate Troeltsch in the history of modern theology. Instead, I merely sketch what I take to be the heart of the transformation that Troeltsch proclaimed, and then go on to show, in agreement with him, that the new by no means severed all continuity with the old but brought to fruition a possibility latent in Reformation theology. I recognize that even on these two themes, or rather subthemes, a great deal more could be said. But I have attempted to hold on firmly, as far as possible, to the thread of a single argument.

1. Troeltsch, "Geschichte und Metaphysik," *Zeitschrift für Theologie und Kirche* 8 (1898): 5–6.

2. Troeltsch, "Über historische und dogmatische Methode in der Theologie" (1898), GS 2:730.

3. See Thomas S. Kuhn, *The Structure of Scientific Revolutions* (1962; 2d ed., Chicago: University of Chicago Press, 1970). On the occasion for writing the present chapter, see Introduction, n. 11, above.

Dogma and History

Another Troeltschian aphorism opens up the heart of the matter: The new dogmatics "is dogmatics no longer, because it knows no dogmas."[4] The concept of church dogma was an early casualty in the invasion of historical thinking. In Troeltsch's mind, at least, "dogma" stood for something that historical thought must deny: the possibility of fixed and final points (*Lehrfestsetzungen*) in the ceaseless flux of the history of doctrine. Although the old Protestantism took over the ancient trinitarian and christological dogmas, strictly speaking it had no dogmas; but in their place it put the propositions of the Bible similarly understood as doctrinal definitions. Modern Protestantism, by contrast, discovers in Scripture "representations of faith," mutable products of the imagination that express a practical religious attitude. The task of *Glaubenslehre* is to reduce both these and subsequent Christian representations to their conceptual content.[5] It is a task that never ends: there is a plasticity to the concepts of faith that makes them always newly adaptable to the natural and historical sciences of the present day.[6] Plainly, this is an understanding of theology as far removed from Protestant orthodoxy as from Roman Catholicism. If we still venture to speak of "the faith that was once for all entrusted to the saints" (Jude 3), it cannot be any definitive *forms* of faith that we are to contend for.

Troeltsch discovered the pioneer of the new dogmatics in Friedrich Schleiermacher. In this he was undoubtedly correct. "The Christian church," Schleiermacher had written, " . . . is a phenomenon of change [*ein Werdendes*], in which at every moment the present must be grasped as the product of the past and the germ of the future."[7] The concern of theological studies generally is with something in ceaseless motion, an ever-changing community; dogmatics is the part of theological studies that concerns itself with the changing community on its believing, thinking side. In short, a modern dogmatics—that is, a dogmatics that takes historical consciousness in earnest—is, as Schleiermacher put it, a part of *historical* theology, and it can never claim to yield more than an account of "the doctrine prevalent in a Christian church at a particular time."[8]

Schleiermacher took the recognition of change to be a defining mark of distinctively Protestant thought. "The Protestant view of the Christian church," he said, "includes this essential characteristic: that we think of it

4. Troeltsch, "Dogmatik," RGG 2:109.
5. Troeltsch, "Dogma," RGG 2:105–6.
6. "Dogmatik," col. 108.
7. Schleiermacher, *KD¹*, § 33.
8. Ibid., § 97, § 195; *Gl.*, § 19.

as a totality in movement, as something capable of progress and development."[9] Hence he claimed the "right of development" in dogmatics strictly as a Protestant theologian.[10] In the Roman Church, on the other hand, he could see only immutable norms, so that there the question of doctrinal development could not arise. The passage of time may have proved the mutability of this verdict on Roman Catholicism, too. But there remains an apparent difference between Schleiermacher's notion of development and, say, the notion later put forward by John Henry Newman (1801–90), who had no thought of discarding dogmas but only of showing how they came to be. If for Schleiermacher the datum of reflection was *ein Werdendes,* for Newman it was, so to say, *ein Gewordenes*. The cycle of growth in Newman's idea of development achieves its finality—its fruition or maturity—in dogma; in Schleiermacher's idea, the cycle continues to the senility and dissolution of dogma. And this means that the dogmatic task must include the critique of dogmas and, where necessary, the discarding of them as obsolete.[11]

Historical thinking calls for a similar reappraisal of the Reformation confessions. In part, Schleiermacher affirmed the confessions as legitimate protests against errors and abuses that had crept into the church. What it means to affirm the "symbolic books" in this way is indicated in the curious formula of subscription that he proposed: "I declare that I find wholly consonant with the Holy Scripture and the original teaching of the church everything that is taught in our symbolic books against the errors and abuses of the Roman Church."[12] From this somewhat negative point of view, the Protestant confessions are an affirmation of the biblical norm only against certain deviations from it. But Schleiermacher also understood them more positively as a distinctive expression of the Christian idea, jointly necessary with Roman Catholicism to the historical manifestation of Christianity. The Reformation was a relatively new beginning, and its symbolic books still have their unique value as the first public embodiment of the Protestant spirit. Historical understanding thus provided Schleiermacher with a middle way between confessionalism, which lacked a sense of historical distance between the nineteenth century and the sixteenth, and rationalism, which could see no present usefulness for the documents of another day. No confession of faith, he maintained, has the power of excommunication; and yet, even as products of human au-

9. Schleiermacher, *Die christliche Sitte nach den Grundsätzen der evangelischen Kirche im Zusammenhange dargestellt* (1884), SW 1,12:72.

10. Schleiermacher to F. H. Jacobi, 30 March 1818. See chapter 7, n. 2, above.

11. *KD,* § 205; *Gl.*, § 95, etc.

12. Schleiermacher, "Über den eigenthümlichen Wert und das bindende Ansehen symbolischer Bücher" (1819), KS 2:164.

thorship in a human context, the symbolic books do have a relative permanence as ecclesiastical norms.[13]

But what of the Holy Scriptures? Schleiermacher did not exempt them from the relativities of history. He denied that reformation could ever mean simply the restitution of the apostolic age: what has once been can never be brought back again. But, as he pointed out in his remarks on the Protestant confessions, there is a difference between the first decisive moments and the subsequent course of a historical development. And it is this historical principle that makes it possible, and necessary, to take the New Testament as the norm of what is authentically Christian, just as the confessions are the norm of what is authentically Protestant. The parallel is not exact, because the Protestant spirit is not wholly new but rather a new expression of the Christian spirit. The historical point of view, however, is the same. It follows that the scriptural norm is not to be simply identified with the letter of the New Testament, and that no exclusive appeal can be made to the Bible (no *scriptura sola!*). The development of doctrine arises out of a critical use of Scripture and constant attention to the current state of knowledge in other fields.[14]

Schleiermacher apparently recognized that the shift in theological method he proposed made a change of name desirable. He did not coin the word *Glaubenslehre,* which is the German equivalent of *doctrina fidei,* an expression that goes all the way back to the Latin fathers. Philipp Jakob Spener (1635–1705) seems to have been the first to use *Glaubenslehre* in the title of a book on Protestant theology (*Evangelische Glaubenslehre,* 1688), but *Dogmatik* was the preferred term throughout the eighteenth century. Schleiermacher never abandoned the dominant term, but he did like to speak of his own great systematic work as his *Glaubenslehre,* notably in the open letters to his friend Friedrich Lücke. Further, he tells us in the introduction to *The Christian Faith* (second edition) that the title, in which he avoided the name *Dogmatik,* contains elements for a definition of the subject. A handwritten note explains that *Glaubenslehre* means a description or presentation of faith: "Darstellung des Glaubens ist Glaubenslehre."[15] One may hazard the guess that Schleiermacher may have been prevented from surrendering the name *Dogmatik* not only by the weight of custom, but also by the inflexibility of the other name, *Glaubenslehre,* which lacks usable cognates.

The contrast between *Dogmatik* and *Glaubenslehre,* only hinted at by

13. Schleiermacher, *Reden,* 301–2; *Gl.,* § 24; *Christliche Sitte,* 212; "Das Ansehen symbolischer Bücher," 143–44, 159–62; *Gl.,* § 27.

14. *Gl.,* § 24.1, § 27.1; *KD,* § 83, § 103, § 167, § 177, § 181. Cf. the letter to Jacobi (n. 10 above).

15. Redeker's edition, 1:9. The full title, *Der christliche Glaube nach den Grundsätzen der evangelischen Kirche im Zusammenhange dargestellt,* was truncated in the English translation.

Schleiermacher, was sharpened by his pupil, Alexander Schweizer, who chose *Glaubenslehre* as the actual title for his own systematic work and expressed astonishment that his colleague, the speculative theologian A. E. Biedermann, would wish to call "dogmatics" the end product of his ruthless critique of ecclesiastical dogma.[16] At the same time, the recognition that theological studies as a whole, including dogmatics, bear an ineradicably historical stamp—by reason of their historical datum—led to the programmatic historicizing movement in German Protestant thought. In the work of both F. C. Baur and Adolf von Harnack, despite their very different estimates of church dogma, the movement threatened to dissolve dogmatics altogether as an independent discipline. Troeltsch, on the other hand, at any rate during his Heidelberg period (1894–1914), followed Schleiermacher's model more closely and avowedly, though it must be admitted that he weakened the scientific claims of *Glaubenslehre* even while asserting its place as an independent field of theological study. Still more than Schweizer, Troeltsch stated the antithesis between *Glaubenslehre* and *Dogmatik* in sharply polemical tones;[17] and more than Harnack, though scarcely more than Baur, he presented historical method as a working procedure inextricably interwoven with a comprehensive historical mode of thought, which, he believed, held the key to understanding everything concerned with the products of human existence and culture.

We find in Troeltsch another way of speaking about dogmatics, which also had its roots in Schleiermacher but may seem, at first sight, to diverge from the emphasis on history: the content of *Glaubenslehre* is a "theology of consciousness" (a *Bewusstseinstheologie*).[18] This, of course, corresponds to Schleiermacher's definition of Christian doctrines (*Glaubenssätze*) as interpretations of the Christian religious affections presented in speech.[19] And there is in fact no disharmony here with the turn to history; for the mutable historical forms are precisely expressions of the Christian consciousness, or the specifically Christian way of believing.[20] Schleiermacher, as we have seen,[21] could describe his dogmatic method as "empirical" in the sense that it dealt with actual facts of experience. He proceeded by an interrogation of the Christian consciousness, and what he discovered by this procedure gave him the test for weighing old dogmatic

16. Alexander Schweizer, *Die christliche Glaubenslehre nach protestantischen Grundsätzen,* 1st ed., 2 vols. (Leipzig: S. Hirzel, 1863–72), 2:v.

17. Besides the article on "Dogmatik" (n. 4 above), see Troeltsch, *Glaubenslehre* (see chapter 10, n. 6, above, § 1 [10]); "The Dogmatics of the 'Religionsgeschichtliche Schule,'" AJT 17 (1913): 17 (German in GS 2:516).

18. Troeltsch, *Glaubenslehre,* § 11 (132).

19. *Gl.,* § 15.

20. For the term *Glaubensweise,* see *KD,* § 1.

21. *Sendschr.,* 20–21, 25; *Gl.,* § 95, etc.

forms. That in Troeltsch's mind, at least, this entire approach combines the historical and the psychological viewpoints in perfect harmony, is strikingly indicated by his use of the compound expression "the historical-psychological view."[22] And it was here, in the psychologizing of faith, that he thought he detected a line of continuity going back through Schleiermacher to Martin Luther.

Word and Faith

Once again, we can take our point of departure from a Troeltsch quotation (cited earlier): The effect of Luther's *sola fide,* he suggests, is that "religion is drawn entirely . . . into the domain of the psychologically transparent." There it becomes the affirmation of a particular way of perceiving God and God's grace.[23] Troeltsch goes on to make the interesting remark that, as a consequence of Luther's faith, the new path to the old destination becomes more important than the destination itself. Indeed, the way *contains* the goal: faith, as a way of perceiving God, now *is* redemption, not the way to attain it. The subjective assurance of believing becomes religion itself.[24]

Though always intriguing and illuminating, Troeltsch's formulations are not always self-evidently right. Can one, for instance, really advance as smoothly as he does from Luther to the very modern proposition that the idea of faith has triumphed over the content of faith?[25] But he was right, I believe, when he claimed to discover in Luther's *faith* the crucial link between the old Protestantism and the new; and he never made the mistake of inferring that this link must therefore represent the whole Luther, or even the essential Luther. Neither did he somehow fail to notice the importance of the word of God in Lutheran theology, although he may have failed to appreciate fully the sacramental power of the word. It was, in fact, precisely in Luther's discovery of the word that Troeltsch found the clue to the significance of Luther's faith. In this he was surely on the right lines. In the Lutheran gospel a linguistic change takes place that calls for reappraisal of the entire religious vocabulary inherited from the Middle Ages. The ripples of change really do, as Troeltsch perceived, radiate out from the concept of the word; and it can be shown that the effect of the change was indeed to move religion toward psychological transparency.

In the Roman Catholic view (or views), justification was held to be effected by the supernatural infusion of sacramental grace. This grace, to be sure, does move the will to accept it in faith, and what is imparted by it is something analogous to a human "virtue" in the Aristotelian sense: it is a

22. Troeltsch, *Gl.*, § 8 (103).
23. *Protestantism and Progress* (see chapter 10, n. 5, above), 193 (96).
24. Ibid., 194 (96), 197–98 (99).
25. Ibid., 199 (99).

donum habituale (the gift of a new habit or disposition). To this extent, the gift of grace is made intelligible. The process, however, by which the gift is given and the proper nature of the gift itself are not presented as transparent, but as supernatural; and that the process happens at all is known only by an authoritative revelation. As Thomas Aquinas put it: Although justification is not in every respect miraculous, it is utterly mysterious in that it is brought about by a hidden divine power.[26] The movement of the free will is not, in any case, an unconditional requirement, since in the sacrament of baptism justification is normally bestowed on infants, who cannot exercise free will. (The same holds good for the justification of lunatics and morons.)[27] And the movement of faith perfected by love, where it does occur, is likewise said to be "infused": that is, not acquired but imparted supernaturally.[28]

Luther's conception is strikingly different. Once the word of God is identified as the definitive vehicle of grace, it no longer makes sense to describe the efficacy of the means of grace in terms of an *opus operatum,* or to define the corresponding subjectivity as the absence of impediment.[29] A word is a means of communication. Unheard, it is spoken in vain, loses its character as word; it attains its finality only as it awakens attention, discernment, and commitment. For Luther, word and faith are correlative. He who believes, has! As the Augsburg Confession says: "The gospel teaches that we have a gracious God . . . provided we believe it" (article 5). Here the form of grace as spoken word has changed the meaning of grace. In terms of scholastic theology, the accent has moved from habitual grace to *gratia increata.* In Luther's own terms: "I take grace in the proper sense of the favor of God—not a quality of the soul."[30] Not "entirely," but up to a point, the process of justification has been moved into the domain of the psychologically transparent.

It would be absurd to suggest that the Reformers were out to eliminate the mystery from justification. But they did reduce the mystery by the fundamental thought that faith in God, as trust, is not brought about by a miraculous infusion but by God's showing Godself trustworthy. Philip Melanchthon makes the point especially clear in his *Apology of the Augsburg Confession.* As long as sinners perceive God as angry, or vengeful, or exacting, they cannot love God. But it takes a sure word of God to convince them that God is not in fact angry; and the perception of God as not angry

26. ST I–II, q. 113, art. 10.

27. Ibid., art. 3.

28. Ibid., art. 4.

29. "Si vis gratiam consequi, id age, ut verbum dei vel audias intente vel recorderis diligenter; verbum, inquam, et solum verbum est vehiculum gratiae dei" (Luther, *In epistolam Pauli ad Galatas commentarius* [1519], WA 2.509.13–15; LW 27:249).

30. *Rationis Latomianae confutatio* (1521), WA 8.106.10; LW 32:227.

but merciful in Christ is just what is meant by faith, which hears and heeds the word—and so, which justifies. Grace comes as a word, a promise of mercy, proclaimed in the sermon and depicted in the sacraments; and the form of grace as spoken or visible word determines the form of the response as faith. While, then, faith and love for God are inseparable, faith must precede and love must follow.[31]

The drive toward psychological transparency in Reformation thought could also be illustrated many times over from John Calvin, despite the care with which he affirms the mysterious activity of the Spirit as an invariable ingredient in every operation of grace. Take, for instance, his acute analysis of the process of repentance. Whereas Melanchthon spoke of faith as a part of penitence,[32] Calvin reversed the order, asserting that repentance is born of faith, and he gave a psychological reason: None can apply themselves seriously to repentance unless they know that they belong to God, and none are really persuaded that they belong to God unless they have first recognized God's grace.[33] But I must dispense with further instances. Recent objections to religious "subjectivism" require me next to reaffirm a distinction I made before.

In making salvation depend on believing that one is saved, Luther, it has been argued, threw the religious subject back upon itself, precluding the self-abandonment to God in which genuine faith consists. This, surely, is a serious misrepresentation of Luther's faith, which was faith precisely in the word—single-minded contemplation of Christ (*intuitus Christi*). But although Luther's *faith* was not anthropocentric, he did present an early type of anthropocentric *theology* insofar as he made the believing subject the object of thought. And this is exactly what Schleiermacher held to be the task of *Glaubenslehre:* dogmatic propositions, in his view, arise out of logically ordered reflection on the utterances of the devout self-consciousness.[34] Such a conception of the theological task naturally accompanies, perhaps even is occasioned by, a highly personal variety of faith. But it remains a matter of methodological importance to recognize that one may make the religious subject the object of inquiry without making either the inquiry or the religion "subjective" (in a pejorative sense). It is just such a theology that is a latent possibility in Luther and becomes an explicit program in Schleiermacher.

In Schleiermacher's dogmatics, faith turns back upon itself *in reflection,* makes its own believing an object of thought: Christian existence, viewed from the inside, becomes the actual datum of theology. When a disputed point of doctrine lies before him, Schleiermacher can do no more

31. See esp. *Apol.*, 4.110, 129, 295; 4.262, 337; 4.67, 174, 275–76; 4.141.
32. Ibid., 4.398.
33. *Inst.*, 3.3.1–2.
34. *Gl.*, § 16 (postscript). Cf. chapter 2 above.

than to appeal to the actual facts of the Christian consciousness—which means, in effect, the consciousness of the reader. At the same time, however, his constant endeavor is to make Christian experience intelligible as a matter of historical existence. Once the Redeemer has made his appearance in history, his influence is disseminated in a purely natural way; and this means that his "work" can be understood through comparison with the psychological impact of one person on another.[35] The supernatural has become a natural fact of history.[36] The entire process of conversion can accordingly be laid out on essentially psychological lines, the "word" exercising the decisive role, as it did for the Reformers.[37]

A Historical Theology

The relationship between the old Protestantism and the new remains elusive. On the one hand, the lines of continuity cannot be restricted to the one theme (with two sides) that we have taken up from Troeltsch. Others have urged the kindred point, no less pertinent to the subject of historicizing, that Luther's faith in the word of God alone gave him a sovereign freedom over against every attempt to objectivize the gospel in doctrines and institutions, and so opened the way to historical reappraisals of them as products of time and circumstance. Still other lines of continuity have been missed, I believe, in the common failure to look at Schleiermacher's relation to Calvin, which is no less interesting and important than his relation to Luther.[38]

On the other hand, the elements of discontinuity need to be uncovered, too. Perhaps most obvious, as far as theological method is concerned, is the distinction Schleiermacher drew between dogmatics and exegetical theology, which he did not regard as the substance of dogmatics, or even a part of it, but rather as an independent and coordinate discipline.[39] For now, however, all these further questions, important though they are, must be set aside and a suitably modest conclusion attempted.

Perhaps the right conclusion should be that the history of Protestantism discloses not one, but two "paradigm changes" in Western theology: one that enthroned history, and another that enthroned the word. Troeltsch, however, perceived them as fundamentally one. Despite far-reaching changes that he discovered in the transition from *Alt-* to *Neuprotestantismus,* he believed that *Glaubenslehre,* the new dogmatics, could

35. See esp. ibid., § 100.2–3.
36. Ibid., § 88.4.
37. Ibid., § 108.5–6.
38. See chapter 8.
39. *Gl.,* § 19 (postscript).

justly appeal to the subjectivizing of the ideas of faith and revelation brought about, at least in principle, by Luther.[40] His belief turns out to be by no means fanciful. Schleiermacher himself, we have seen, was already persuaded that, in making dogmatics a matter of reflection on the data of Christian religiousness, he had Luther for his forerunner. But whether or not the pedigree of *Glaubenslehre* can be so written that two changes are seen as one development, the profile of a distinctively modern approach to Christian theology begins to emerge.

Variations of the approach are possible, and distinctions within it are required if dogmatics is to be differentiated from other kinds of theological and religious inquiry. The course of theology in the twentieth century has exposed some of its weaknesses or perils. But it no longer belongs to one church or one party. It has become, in some quarters, so much the commonly accepted approach that it is easy to forget how sharply it differs from conceptions of theology before the rise of the historical consciousness. In a word, it is not the explication of authoritative dogmas, nor the exegesis and systematizing of Scripture, but disciplined reflection on a historically given, historically mobile way of believing.

40. "Dogmatik," col. 109.

12

Ubi theologia, ibi ecclesia? Schleiermacher, Troeltsch, and the Prospect for an Academic Theology

How precisely everything fits and locks together in the realm of knowledge! You can say that the more a subject is dealt with in isolation, the more incomprehensible and confused it appears.
—FRIEDRICH SCHLEIERMACHER

Schleiermacher believed vigorously in the oneness of the world of the mind and delighted in it. . . . Anyone who does not see him in this light will never quite understand him.
—HEINRICH SCHOLZ

The problem is the lack of any unity of the sciences and the loss of the will or the means even to discuss the issue.
—ALLAN BLOOM

THE TERM "academic theology" is often used scornfully, to mean a theology that has lost touch with the life of the church and the duties of working ministers and is therefore good for nothing, like salt that has lost its savor. But I use it here, without prejudice, simply to mean theology done in a university, not in a seminary or theological college. The university, no less than the church, is an institution with its own set of aims and values; an "academic theology" considers itself answerable to these aims and values, whether or not the results are useful to the churches or help to make good clergy.[1] Perhaps the German term *wissenschaftliche Theologie* ("scientific theology") would do as well. For whether theology has a legitimate place in the universities depends, in large part, on the scientific respectability of its method: that is, on how well theologians can state and justify the rules by which they profess to

1. In one educator's words, the university's only excuse for existence is "to provide a haven where the search for truth may go on unhampered by utility or pressure for 'results.'" Robert Maynard Hutchins, *The Higher Learning in America,* Storr Lectures (New Haven: Yale University Press, 1936), 43. On the two hindrances, "vocationalism" and "empiricism" (the mere piling up of information), see further ibid., 111, 117–18.

attain knowledge. But I have preferred the institutional to the methodological term—"academic" rather than "scientific"—because I want to avoid any odious suggestion that a scientific theology (in the sense given) could be pursued only in a university, not in a seminary or a monastery. It is arguable in any case that in English the word "scientific" has been preempted by the *natural* sciences, and that even the *social* sciences employ it only by license. For this reason, too, "academic theology" is usually my preferred term.

How one thinks of the university-based divinity school is bound to reflect one's estimate of the distinctively theological task. The linguistic, literary, and historical activities of the theologian's immediate neighbors in the divinity school are not usually felt to be problematic in themselves, although their location in the divinity school, rather than in the humanities, may be judged compromising precisely because of the theological company they keep. Colleagues outside the divinity school, and sometimes even colleagues inside, are inclined to view the theologian as like some agent of a foreign power: because the theologian's ultimate loyalty lies elsewhere, she or he cannot be trusted to keep the law of the land or to contribute to the common good.[2] Whether what is done under the rubric of "academic theology" is salutary to the churches, then, is not here the issue. Is it salutary to the universities?

An enormous literature in several languages has addressed the question in the last two hundred years; if we posed it in terms of the scientific status of theology, we would have to add that it already engaged some acute minds in the Middle Ages. Unfortunately, however, the discussion these days is often queered by ambiguity, so that instead of answering it one may end in confusion over what the question really is. In particular, the word "theology" is commonly used as though everyone knew what it meant, whereas in fact theologies come in several varieties, and the question might better be phrased: *What* theology, if any, has a legitimate place in the academy?

My purpose in this essay is accordingly to check the academic credentials of just one way of doing theology: Friedrich Schleiermacher's. Naturally, I choose the model that, in my opinion, still has the strongest claims to potential fruitfulness in the American universities, although it was developed not in America but in Germany. My own theological interest at present is, in fact, in the historical development and continued viability of this mode of theologizing. Here I simply ask about its institutional home,

2. The image is suggested by Sir Walter Moberly on behalf of the critics of designing Christians: "However high-minded your intentions, you are like government servants who use their position to further the interests of a foreign power. . . . [Y]ou are not serving the university but are seeking to use it as an instrument for purposes which are not its own" (*The Crisis in the University* [London: SCM Press, 1949], 28).

and I am convinced that Schleiermacher's thoughts on this question have been widely misrepresented, not least by Ernst Troeltsch. I recognize, of course, that there are varieties of university, too, as well as varieties of theology. But, for now, I intend to approach the problem of theology and the university from the standpoint of one concept of theology. To begin with, I want to explore the reasons why there is a problem at all.

The Problem of an Academic Theology

It goes without saying, I assume, that the place of theology in the modern university can be defended only where its abdication as queen of the sciences is presupposed. Granted that Christian theology can no longer provide, as it did in the Middle Ages, the unifying principles of the entire system of human knowledge, can it nonetheless claim a legitimate, if humbler, place in the university? It may be that theology has its own small niche, along with other arts and sciences, in an academy that has become in principle more egalitarian. But it may also be that the academy should remain vigilant even after the ancient crown of theology has been quietly encased in the museum of history.

Take, for instance, John Henry Newman's plea for theology in his classic study *The Idea of a University* (1852), the literary product of his association with the new Catholic University of Ireland.[3] The university, he says, is "a place of *teaching* universal *knowledge*."[4] It is not a place where truth is simply discovered, which would not require students. Nor is it a place where assorted truths are mechanically acquired. The requisite knowledge is "philosophical": not a mere pile of information, it calls for actively organizing what is learned, a systematizing of it to assign things their value in relation to one another.[5] Hence, the communication of

3. The book has been through several editions. My page references are to John Henry Cardinal Newman, *The Idea of a University Defined and Illustrated, I: In Nine Discourses Delivered to the Catholics of Dublin, II: In Occasional Lectures and Essays Addressed to the Members of the Catholic University,* new impression (Westminster, Maryland: Christian Classics, Inc., 1973), which follows Newman's second revision, published in 1873, and accordingly includes the lectures and essays he added at that time to the 1852 discourses. I shall also refer to the important original fifth discourse, "General Knowledge Viewed as One Philosophy," which Newman excised when he made the first main revision in 1859. My page references for the fifth discourse (1852) are to Newman, *The Idea of a University,* etc., new ed., ed. Charles Frederick Harrold (New York: Longmans, Green, 1947), appendix, 389–406.

4. *Idea,* ix. In his essay "What Is a University?" (first published in 1854), Newman defines the university as "a place for the communication and circulation *of thought* [my emphasis], by means of personal intercourse." See "Rise and Progress of Universities," chap. 2, in Newman, *Historical Sketches,* vol. 3, new ed. (London: Longmans, Green, 1889), 6.

5. *Idea,* 111, 125, 130, 134, 137. In the original fifth discourse Newman said: "The assemblage of Sciences, which together make up Universal Knowledge, is not an accidental or

knowledge belongs to the formation of the *person:* it imparts a virtue, a habit of mind, to be esteemed for its own sake and not as an instrument for acquiring or doing anything else, although the cultivated intellect does, as a matter of fact, help equip us for many kinds of activity.[6]

Now the system of universal or organized knowledge would of course be broken if any domain of inquiry were omitted. The circle, Newman insists, is an undivided whole from which each science is only an abstraction, a portion of truth.[7] And that is why there must be theology in the university. Theology is a branch of knowledge with as much right as astronomy to have a place in the university; it is the science of God, the truths we know about God put into system.[8] University teaching without theology would accordingly be unphilosophical, lacking in wholeness. This could indeed be said of the absence of any portion of knowledge. But Newman cannot resist claiming a little more for theology. Its exclusion would not only break the circle in the sense of leaving it incomplete; it would disrupt the unity of learning for the further reason that the science of God touches on so many other sciences. He concludes that religious truth is not only a portion, but a condition, of general knowledge, and that theology is therefore the highest and widest branch of knowledge—though it does not interfere with the freedom of any secular science in its own department.[9] And the special need for theology suggests to him the need for the beneficent presence of the church.

Newman's theme, to be sure, at any rate in the first eight discourses, is not the Catholic university but simply the university. In this sense, his discourses are only, as he says, preliminary.[10] But the ultimate goal—a truly Catholic university—is already reflected proleptically in his idea of a university in general, and the argument threatens to fall apart. For, on the one hand, the university is certainly not a convent or a seminary: its purpose is to fit persons for *this* world, not for the next. And what goes with this purpose is not so much the Catholic faith as a religion or philosophy of reason, or of civilization, which is ambivalent from the Catholic point of view. Partly present alongside the Catholic faith, partly in conflict with it, the religion of reason contains elements of truth, which are nonetheless false

a varying heap of acquisitions, but a system, and may be said to be *in equilibrio,* as long as all its portions are secured to it" ("General Knowledge," 389). This conveys as well as any of his utterances what Newman meant by the idea or form that gives the university unity (cf. ibid., 394, 396).

6. *Idea,* ix, 101, 114, 121, 125–26, 165–67, 177–78.

7. Ibid., 50, 60, 72.

8. Ibid., 19–20, 42, 61.

9. Ibid., 66–67, 70; "General Knowledge," 399.

10. *Idea,* 214.

because they are not the whole truth.[11] On the other hand, however, the university *as such* ought to teach revealed or Catholic theology, since it is, after all, truth.[12] And it would be absurd not to recognize that the church has an interest in such an activity. "The Church has no call to watch over and protect Science: but towards Theology she has a distinct duty. . . . Where Theology is, there she must be."[13]

Ubi theologia, ibi ecclesia! That is the problem in a nutshell, though Newman hardly recognized it as such. The surrender of her crown has not quite left theology to struggle alone in a competitive, democratic environment. The church is still there to assist from above, and the idea of a university passes over gently into the idea of a Catholic university.[14] It is easy to see why the citizens of a secular and pluralistic university would still be anxious about the possibility of a divided loyalty. History has taught them that the church, when weary of argument, will reach for a stick. And they may begin to suspect that from a common-or-garden university, as distinct from a Catholic or other sectarian one, theology had best be excluded; at most they could make room for an objective description of theology, not for doing it, and there seems to be no reason why such description would require a theological faculty. Besides, can it seriously be maintained that theology is a science? How can it be if it is subject to the church's well-meant, but wholly inappropriate, supervision?[15]

Not every champion of theology sees the church in Newman's authoritarian terms. But their dilemma, I suspect, *mutatis mutandis,* remains essentially the same: either a bloodless religion of reason that fits comfortably into the academy, or else a frankly Christian theology that awakens the suspicion of a divided loyalty. Newman grasped the second horn of the dilemma; others have found themselves impaled on the first. An instructive example can be found in the exchange between Robert Maynard Hutchins (1899–1977) and William Adams Brown (1865–1943). In reply to the thesis put forward by Hutchins, that the ordering of knowledge in the university calls not for Christian theology but for Greek meta-

11. Ibid., 232; 182, 200, 214.

12. The conclusion to the original fifth discourse states bluntly: "A University, so called, which refuses to profess the Catholic Creed, is, from the nature of the case, hostile both to the Church and to Philosophy" ("General Knowledge," 406). For this reason, Newman opposed not only the absence of religion in education but also the introduction of a "general religion": that is, a deliberately nonsectarian Christianity or a natural religion that would embrace Judaism and Islam as well (ibid., 400–401).

13. *Idea,* 214, 215, 227.

14. Ibid., ix.

15. In *The Idea of a University,* at least, Newman does not seriously entertain the possibility that the minor premise of his argument—that theology is a science—could be questioned. See 19–20, 67.

physics,[16] Brown took up the cause of theology. He meant a theology that uses Christian faith as at once a clue to understanding the universe and a religious basis for the democratic tradition.[17] But his argument carried him so far away from everything distinctively Christian that Hutchins could retort, in effect: *Your* theology is *my* metaphysics. "Everything that Mr. Brown puts in the category of theology," he said, "I should call natural theology."[18]

Similar, it seems to me, was the dilemma Sir Walter Moberly (1881–1974) fell into in his winsome book *The Crisis of the University* (1949). He started from a muscular Christian viewpoint, expressed in bold talk of "Christianization," but was driven to the lame conclusion that Christians will have to settle for the principle of the half-loaf. Half a loaf is better than none: the Christian can at least work for rational reforms in the university that are not incompatible with Christianity.[19] But this implies, surely, that they are at home in the university just insofar as they set aside their ecclesiastical commitments and work with the same rational and humanistic assumptions as the non-Christians—even, indeed, the nontheists. Moberly did believe that the theological faculty, as the custodian of Revelation (with a capital *R*), still had its special mission: not only to educate clergy but to confront the entire student body with the Christian challenge. But theology, so conceived, is inevitably isolated and embattled, and Moberly expressly rejected any attempt to assimilate it to other academic studies.[20] His image of the Christians in the university as "government servants who use their position to further the interests of a foreign power" seems only too apt.

The question, then, has now become this: Is the connection of an explicitly Christian theology with the claims of the church such that it must necessarily march out of step with everyone else in the academy, or else be honorably retired? Hutchins, for one, gave an unfavorable verdict with all his usual forthrightness: "Theology is banned by law from some universities. It might as well be from the rest. Theology is based on revealed truth and on articles of faith. We are a faithless generation and take no stock in revelation. Theology implies orthodoxy and an orthodox church. We have neither."[21] And we are back with the rule (or the warning): *Ubi theo-*

16. Hutchins, *Higher Learning*, chap. 4.

17. Brown, *The Case for Theology in the University* (Chicago: University of Chicago Press, 1938), 13, 112.

18. Hutchins, preface to Brown, *Case for Theology*, vii.

19. *Crisis*, 310.

20. Ibid., 278–92, 306–8.

21. *Higher Learning*, 97. Note that it is specifically a dogmatic theology that Hutchins disapproves of: "When . . . I said that theology could not assist us, I was thinking only of dogmatic theology, which rests upon faith, or supernatural knowledge" (preface to Brown, *Case for Theology*, vi).

logia, ibi ecclesia.[22] Whether or not we agree with Hutchins will depend, or should depend, on what theology we have in mind.

Schleiermacher on the Theological Faculty

At first glance, Schleiermacher appears to afford very little help. Though not quite in Newman's manner, he too subordinates theology to the church, and, quite *unlike* Newman, he seems uncertain of theology's right to a place among the sciences. While plans were being drawn up for the new University of Berlin, he put together his *Occasional Thoughts on Universities in the German Sense* (1808), in which he directly addressed the question of the theological faculty and its place in the academic community. Taken together with his sketch of the theological curriculum in his *Brief Outline of the Study of Theology* (1811; 2d ed., 1830), his remarks seem to permit theology at best a lower rank among the university disciplines and to justify its existence purely on the grounds of its service to the church. It is easy to see why later German theologians found his position to be objectionable in itself and an open door to still more objectionable theologies that came after him—without sufficient reason, as I shall try to show.

For Schleiermacher, "science" (*Wissenschaft*) was not, as it has become for us, one of several divisions of human knowledge. As he explained it in his thoughts on universities, science is the collective enterprise in which every researcher, in every field of inquiry, is engaged, and the fragments of knowledge that each contributes can be fully appreciated only in their relation to the whole.[23] External pressures, such as the immediate needs of the state, or competition between one state and another, may impose limits on the ideal of a single community of learning. But true scholars and scientists everywhere, whatever the demands of specialization, understand themselves to be mutually dependent in one inclusive enterprise, and they are bound to concern themselves intensely with the general principles that define knowledge in every department of inquiry. The state, no doubt, is inclined to dismiss such a concern as fruitless speculation and to demand instead new discoveries and the spread of factual information in fields pre-

22. I do not mean to imply that this formula conveys the *only* problem with theology; it is a *root* problem in the sense that others grow out of it. Two additional objections, that theology talks about nonempirical objects and that it isolates Christianity from other religions, will be touched on along the way. Still others (theology rationalizes religion, privatizes religion, and so on) are ignored here but would call for the same approach, which asks: *What* theology?

23. Schleiermacher, *Gelegentliche Gedanken über Universitäten in deutschem Sinn, nebst einem Anhang über eine neu zu errichtende* (1808), in Ernst Anrich, ed., *Die Idee der deutschen Universität: Die fünf Grundschriften aus der Zeit ihrer Neubegründung durch klassichen Idealismus und romantischen Realismus* (Darmstadt: Hermann Gentner, 1956), 223–24. This is the passage from which my first epigraph is taken at the beginning of this essay.

sumed to be useful. The scientific spirit, however, is by its very nature systematic: it cannot grow to full consciousness where there is no conception of one whole domain of knowledge, at least in outline.[24]

By a *university* Schleiermacher understood precisely the institutional home for the awareness of science as a single activity powered by a common interest in the unity and form of knowledge. A *school,* by contrast, exists for education—to impart the elements of knowledge in certain basic fields—and can only strike the initial spark of the scientific spirit in a few naturally gifted youths. And the *academy,* or learned society, the third main type of institution for the pursuit of learning, exists for the advancement of knowledge in a particular discipline by masters, who already have the scientific spirit. The burden of maintaining the idea of a common scientific enterprise therefore falls squarely on the university, which stands between the school and the academy (in Schleiermacher's sense); and it would be disastrous, Schleiermacher thought, if the university became either an advanced school or a cluster of academies and specialized institutes. The true scientific spirit requires that every field of knowledge must be cultivated, and each only as a part of the whole.[25] It was this recognition, he believed, that had given birth to the distinctively German university, and in effect it made the faculty of philosophy ("arts and sciences," as we would say) the new queen of the sciences (*in der Tat Herrin*). For in the faculty of philosophy the sciences are bound together as one and made the object of an all-inclusive critical scrutiny.[26] Philosophical instruction is the basis for all other pursuits in the university; indeed, the actual university is contained in the faculty of philosophy alone—or would be if the university were purely the creation of the scientific community.[27]

Where, then, does theology fit in? The problem is that it finds its home *outside* the faculty of philosophy, in one of three "special schools" (*Spezialschulen*), or "positive faculties," that owe their existence to certain social needs sponsored by the state. The faculties of law, medicine, and theology—"professional schools," as we now call them—do not spring naturally out of the scientific impulse; each arises from the necessity to ground an indispensable practice or profession securely in an explicit theory and in the transmission of accumulated knowledge (*Tradition von Kenntnissen*). Thus the theological faculty

> took shape in the church to preserve the wisdom of the fathers; to prevent the future loss of what was already done in former times to

24. Ibid., 226–32, 238, 246.

25. Ibid., 233–45. It is interesting to note how closely agreed Schleiermacher and Newman were at this point—for all their obvious differences in other respects.

26. Ibid., 258, 260.

27. Ibid., 240, 250, 257. Clearly, Schleiermacher uses the adjective "philosophical" sometimes to refer to a faculty, sometimes to a department within the faculty.

> separate truth from error; to give a historical basis, a secure and definite direction, and a common spirit to the further development of doctrine (*der weiteren Fortbildung der Lehre*) and of the church. And as the state became more closely tied to the church, it had to sanction these provisions too and take them under its care.[28]

Now what professional education in theology, law, or medicine requires, according to Schleiermacher, is not so much a single academic discipline as a mixture of several disciplines that have their natural home in the faculty of philosophy. This is what he means by a "positive science": an assemblage of sciences, or fragments of sciences, brought together to equip practitioners in one of the professions. "Theology," as he uses the word, is just such a positive science, so that the theological faculty does not find its unity directly in the nature of knowledge but brings it in from the outside, so to say, to meet the complex needs of church leadership. Theology as a whole, then, manifests the scientific spirit imperfectly because its parts are put together accidentally—for a strictly practical end. Take away the practical end, and the parts will naturally revert to whatever departments of the philosophical faculty they were taken from; there alone, in the faculty of philosophy, is the sense for the inner connection of all knowledge maintained and the natural drive and organization of the scientific enterprise fully expressed.[29] In this sense, the discipline of theology and so the theological faculty itself lead a kind of parasitical existence in the academic community.

It is undeniable that this line of argument implies a marginalization not only of the theological faculty but of the schools of law and medicine as well; the center of the university lies elsewhere. Schleiermacher even admits the risk that the "professional schools" (to use our term) may come to resemble mere trade schools and fall into unscientific superficiality. But if the creative advancement of science finds its proper home in the faculty of philosophy, the remedy, he thinks, is for those who teach in the professional schools to establish their credentials in the field of pure science. Unless they hold simultaneous appointments in the faculty of philosophy, they should be required at least to give occasional lectures in one of the disciplines the faculty of philosophy embraces, without worrying about the relevance of the lectures to the work of their own school. Only in this way can the vital connection of law, medicine, and theology with pure science, and so the place of professional education in the university, be made secure. In short, the scientific standing of a professional school and its teaching staff is externally accredited, and any teacher of law or theology who lacks the inner drive to achieve success in some department of pure

28. Ibid., 258. Translations from the German in this chapter are mine.
29. Ibid., 259; *KD*, §§ 1, 5, 6.

science deserves to be laughed out of the university.[30] The vocation of the theologian certainly appears to bear the burden of a divided loyalty. In the eyes of some interpreters, notably Troeltsch, Schleiermacher must be held responsible for the fact that after him an actual antagonism between ecclesiastical and scientific interests threatened to split the theological faculty itself.

Historical Theology and Dogmatic Theology according to Troeltsch

It is often said that in nineteenth-century Germany the Protestant theological faculties became polarized into two factions; sometimes the explanation is added that it was Schleiermacher who at least opened the door to the conflict between them. Advocates of a strictly scientific theology had to distance themselves from his view of theology as a practical and churchly discipline. Even so sympathetic an interpreter as Heinrich Scholz (1884–1956), who hailed the return to Schleiermacher after the passing of Albrecht Ritschl and reissued the *Brief Outline* in 1910, looked back to what he admitted to be at least an apparent flaw in the book's theological program. By deriving theology from church leadership, Schleiermacher seemed to have moved into the center a merely external, practical motif: alien to science and a danger to pure inquiry, it threatened to ruin theology by reducing it to a higher technology.[31] Scholz exonerated Schleiermacher by arguing that another strand in the *Brief Outline* makes the understanding of Christianity, rather than the need for church leadership, the actual goal and organizing principle of theological studies.[32] But it is unquestionably the practical, churchly strand that has dominated the secondary literature. Troeltsch's opinion is particularly interesting because he professed himself to be Schleiermacher's disciple.[33]

Writing at about the same time as Scholz, in the *Journal for Scientific Theology* (1908), Troeltsch noted that much Protestant theology in the

30. *Gelegentliche Gedanken,* 261–62.

31. *KD,* pp. ix, xxviii.

32. Ibid., pp. xxx–xxxi. I think myself that an even more important point is the one Scholz makes in the passage from which I have taken my second epigraph (pp. xxxvi–xxxvii). Cf. Newman's remark that "a truly great intellect . . . is one which takes a connected view of old and new, past and present, far and near, and which has an insight into the influence of all these one on another." (*Idea,* 134).

33. See my essay "The Possibility of a Historical Theology: An Appraisal of Troeltsch's Dogmatics" (1976), in Gerrish, *The Old Protestantism and the New: Essays on the Reformation Heritage* (Chicago: University of Chicago Press, Edinburgh: T. & T. Clark, 1982), 208–29; further, Walter E. Wyman, Jr., *The Concept of Glaubenslehre: Ernst Troeltsch and the Theological Heritage of Schleiermacher,* AAR Academy Series, vol. 44 (Chico, California: Scholars Press, 1983).

second half of the nineteenth century had become largely indifferent to the problems of the church. Since the theological faculties were state institutions, they were relatively independent of the churches. There was no necessity for the biblical scholars or the church historians, at least, to relate their work to the needs of the church; they shared the presuppositions and methods of cognate disciplines located elsewhere in the university and remained unconcerned with the latest ecclesiastical causes. This, of course, Troeltsch points out, placed the burden of churchly concerns all the more heavily on the systematic and practical theologians, and dogmatics came to be perceived as merely a matter of personal conviction. A frightful gap had opened up between dogmatic theology and scientific, historical theology.[34]

The theoretical basis for this frightful gap, Troeltsch believed, could be traced back to none other than Schleiermacher, who conceded the impossibility of strict, scientific knowledge of the transcendent and assigned dogmatics to practical theology.[35] Dogmatics is then a discipline that makes use of the methods and findings of science but is not itself a science.[36] And if theology exists simply to influence practical life, the way is cleared for theologians who take science much less seriously than Schleiermacher did. Troeltsch's favorite example was Ritschl, who lifted out of the normal, profane course of history just as much as his Lutheran piety required—notably, the personality of Jesus, which he proclaimed a miracle of revelation—and calmly continued to affirm the anthropocentric view of the world as made for humanity, not troubling himself one bit about the theory of evolution.[37]

Like Scholz, Troeltsch was willing to absolve Schleiermacher from some of the blame for this unhappy turn, though he did not doubt that it was the *Brief Outline* that prepared the way with its basic theological type.[38] For Schleiermacher did at least see the necessity to link dogmatics

34. Troeltsch, "Rückblick auf ein halbes Jahrhundert der theologischen Wissenschaft" (1908), GS 2:194–99; cf. 221.

35. "Die Dogmatik wurde . . . von Schleiermacher geradezu der praktischen (er selbst sagt freilich 'historischen') Theologie zugewiesen" (ibid., 201). The significance of Troeltsch's departure from Schleiermacher's actual language will become apparent below. It is in fact the character of dogmatics as *historical* theology that, in Schleiermacher's view, makes it the science it is: what it knows is the Christian way of believing as a historical phenomenon. Troeltsch's terminological shift, innocent though he makes it sound, conceals a confusion between piety, which is *not* knowledge (i.e., of God), and dogmatic science, which *is* knowledge (i.e., of piety). See the references given in n. 71 below.

36. Ibid., 207.

37. Ibid., 204–5, 211, 218. On *theologische Scheinhistorie,* see also 221–22.

38. Schleiermacher was the man "der mit der Trennung der wissenschaftlich-historischen und der praktisch-vermittelnden Disziplinen die ganze Situation geschaffen und erkannt hat" (ibid., 225; cf. 205–6, 208, 210).

with *philosophical* theology. In Troeltsch's mind, that set the agenda for the present. What we need is a philosophy of religion, or *Religionswissenschaft*, that will justify religious symbols as a genuine, if inadequate, form of knowledge and will demonstrate the supreme validity (*Höchstgeltung*) of Christianity among the religions of the world. Apart from such philosophical support, the very existence of our Christian theological faculties cannot be defended, unless we are prepared to say that we have them for purely accidental and cultural reasons—because we happen to be Christians. A philosophy of religion is the common presupposition for the work of both the historical and the dogmatic theologians, and Schleiermacher's program remains the unfinished program of all scientific theology.[39]

In his later years, as is well known, Troeltsch himself undermined his own grand design for Christian theology as his confidence in the supreme validity of Christianity faded.[40] But I do not believe it follows that Schleiermacher's concept of theology has no future. It is hard, perhaps impossible, to claim that Troeltsch's program ever was, in the respect indicated, an authentic development of Schleiermacher's.[41] Despite a few puzzling ambiguities, it seems clear to me that in the end Schleiermacher thought a proof of the superiority of Christianity to be as impossible for the philosophy of religion as it is unnecessary for dogmatics.[42] But be that as it may, what, we must ask, was the consequence of Troeltsch's program for dogmatics itself? The answer is that dogmatics remained in his eyes—though without disapprobation—purely an expression of personal conviction, undertaken for the ends of preaching and teaching in a church; it was not a science in the true sense but a part of practical theology.[43] If, then, Schleiermacher's conception of the practical goal of theology was a problem, Troeltsch hardly solved it. He made it worse.

Perhaps one moral to be gleaned from the story of German theology from Schleiermacher to Troeltsch is that dutiful professions of allegiance to scientific theology or the science of religion (*Religionswissenschaft*) have not automatically proved to be a safe prophylactic against personal reli-

39. Ibid., 219, 223–26.

40. See, in particular, "The Place of Christianity among the World Religions," one of the lectures he was to have delivered in England in 1923: Troeltsch, *Christian Thought: Its History and Application*, ed. F[riedrich] von Hügel (1923; reprint, New York: Meridian Books, 1957), 33–63, esp. 51–57. The lectures appeared in German the following year with the title *Der Historismus und seine Überwindung: Fünf Vorträge*, ed. Friedrich von Hügel (1924; reprint, Aalen: Scientia Verlag, 1966); see 74–79.

41. In *other* respects, it certainly *was*. See the literature cited in n. 33 above.

42. The point is a controversial one, but see, in particular, Schleiermacher, *Gl.*, § 11.5; cf. § 7.3, § 33.3.

43. Troeltsch, "Die Dogmatik der 'religionsgeschichtlichen Schule'" (1913), GS, 2:500–524, esp. 514–15. The article first appeared in English in *AJT* 17 (1913): 1–21.

gious commitments. The same moral could be drawn from Adolf von Harnack's famous resistance to the introduction of chairs for the "general history of religion" into the German theological faculties. He marshaled several arguments for his position, but the decisive one was that Christianity is not one religion, Jesus Christ not one master, among others.[44] A lingering Christian absolutism, it seems, may cling to the thought even of a historical scholar who can virtuously assert that "in our historical work we cannot and must not consider the doctrines of the churches."[45] For the moment, however, I wish to keep the focus on Schleiermacher, who held unequivocally that not only the systematic theologian but the church historian, too, *should* think about the needs of the church.

One final testimony, closer to our own day, may be cited concerning the alleged problematic consequences of his stand; it demonstrates that Troeltsch's line of interpretation is still very much alive. In his informative study *Theology and the Theory of Science* (1973), Wolfhart Pannenberg writes:

> The result of Schleiermacher's attempt to base theology on the requirements of church leadership was that a confessional and ecclesiastical standpoint (*eine konfessionelle Kirchlichkeit*) functioned as the unquestioned foundation of theology and could therefore be immunized against criticism. That, of course, was not Schleiermacher's intention, but it clearly shows up a limitation in the way he defined theology.[46]

It is difficult to see how such an ecclesiastical complacency could ever appeal to any pertinent "limitation" in Schleiermacher's definition of theology. His understanding of the ecclesiastical *goal* of theological studies never implied that the interests of the church might control the actual *content* of the theologian's work. On the contrary, he took care to prevent any such implication. What he said of the study of church history can surely be generalized to every branch of theological study, as he understood it: the interests of the church and the interests of scholarship (*das wissenschaftliche Interesse*) cannot contradict each other for the very good reason that absolute impartiality is in the church's best interests.

44. Adolf von Harnack, "Die Aufgabe der theologischen Fakultäten und die allgemeine Religionsgeschichte, nebst einem Nachwort" (1901), *Reden und Aufsätze,* 2d ed., 2 vols. (Giessen: Alfred Töpelmann [J. Ricker], 1906), 2:159–87, esp. 172–73.

45. Ibid., 176.

46. Pannenberg, *Wissenschaftstheorie und Theologie* (Frankfurt am Main: Suhrkamp Verlag, 1973), 255. Like Heinrich Scholz, Pannenberg recognizes (a little grudgingly) the other strand in the *Brief Outline,* according to which the *material* unity of theology is derived from its overall concern with the nature or essence of Christianity; it is the science of Christianity or of the Christian religion (253–54, 430).

> Hence even the liveliest interest of the evangelical theologian in his church must not prejudice either his research or his presentation of it. And it is just as little to be feared that the results of this research will weaken his interest in the church; at worst, they can only give him the impulse to work with others for the removal of recognized defects.[47]

No one can seriously doubt that this was Schleiermacher's procedure in his own labors. It is not the theologian's task merely to preserve, or to produce on demand, whatever the church currently thinks it needs, but to help bring the language of the church into closer conformity with the authentic essence of Christian faith.[48] Such a conception of the task was possible for Schleiermacher only because he derived the scientific character of the several parts of theology not from their practical end but from their place in a carefully articulated theory of science.[49] He would not in fact disagree when Pannenberg says that "the science of Christianity is surely not *constituted* by the church's and society's interest in it."[50]

Schleiermacher on the Science of Dogmatics

The practical, professional, and ecclesiastical organization of theology, so much in evidence in the *Thoughts on Universities* and the *Brief Outline*, gives us one side of Schleiermacher's thinking on the nature of the discipline, not the whole. It by no means tells us all he has to say about an "academic theology" in the sense in which I am using the term: roughly, for what he himself calls "dogmatic theology" or *Glaubenslehre*.[51] "Theology" (without further qualification) is his word for the entire theological curriculum. Dogmatics is one of the pieces that make up the whole.[52] The pieces are put together from sciences that have their natural home in the faculty of philosophy. It follows that the scientific status of dogmatics cannot be settled simply from its place in the theological curriculum, or its institutional lo-

47. *KD*, § 193.

48. *Gl.*, §§ 21–22; *KD*, §§ 60, 84.

49. Schleiermacher's *Wissenschaftslehre* is less readily accessible than the thoughts on universities and brief outline; it has to be put together chiefly from lectures that he himself never published. An admirable sketch, particularly helpful in showing the location of theology in Schleiermacher's organization of the sciences, is given by Hans-Joachim Birkner, *Schleiermachers Christliche Sittenlehre im Zusammenhang seines philosophisch-theologischen Systems*, Theologische Bibliothek Töpelmann, vol. 8 (Berlin: Alfred Töpelmann, 1964), esp. 30–87. For further discussion, with a wealth of references to the secondary literature, see Gunter Scholtz, *Die Philosophie Schleiermachers*, Erträge der Forschung, vol. 217 (Darmstadt: Wissenschaftliche Buchgesellschaft, 1984), esp. 64–78, 127–40.

50. *Wissenschaftstheorie*, 254.

51. See chapter 11 above.

52. *KD*, §§ 97, 195–231.

cation in the theological faculty; it depends more properly on its *theoretical* location in the system of sciences.[53]

There are admittedly some tensions in Schleiermacher's pertinent utterances on dogmatics. In one place, for instance, he asserts that dogmatics (*das dogmatische Verfahren*) exists only for the sake of the Christian proclamation.[54] But I see no reason to doubt that if there were no practical need for ministers to proclaim the Christian message, dogmatics must be one of the fragments of theological study that could in principle, with whatever modifications, revert to the philosophical faculty—that is, to what we would call "the humanities." In Schleiermacher's theory of the sciences, as we have seen, dogmatics is an *empirical* science: its data are facts of human experience, since it attempts to give an account of a particular way of believing or being religious.[55] More exactly, dogmatics is classified as *historical* theology: it is a part of the scientific treatment of a historical phenomenon—the part, namely, that deals with the present state of the Christian community's beliefs. The past state of those beliefs is assigned to church history, which is also, in Schleiermacher's scheme, a part of historical theology.[56] Hence it would hardly have been possible for him to drive such a wedge between dogmatic theology and history of Christianity as Troeltsch imagined—as though one were and the other were not a sci-

53. This is not the place to present Schleiermacher's theory of science in general. It is intricate not only because of its ambitious scope but also because of what must seem to us to be an eccentric terminology. I have tried to state the main points very briefly in chapter 7. In the present chapter, I must be content simply to document Schleiermacher's classification of dogmatics as an empirical-historical science, although it is neither a *mindless* empiricism nor a mere historical *report* (see nn. 58 and 80 below).

54. *Gl.*, § 19.1. See also n. 65 below.

55. The entire positive science of theology is concerned with Christianity understood as a *Glaubensweise*, or a particular way of being conscious of God (*KD*, § 1). Accordingly, dogmatics has no other purpose than to give a description or elucidation of the Christian consciousness; its subject matter is actual facts of experience (see *Sendschr.*, 20–21, where Schleiermacher expressly uses the word *empirisch;* cf. ibid., 33–34, and *Gl.*, § 28.2).

56. *KD*, §§ 81, 97, 195, 252. In *KD*, § 195, doctrine is expressly taken to be simply one part of the church's social condition. Schleiermacher's language is (to us) confusing because we normally contrast empirical and historical sciences and apply the word "historical" only to past events or the study of past events. For him, by contrast, historical facts are just as much empirical data as are the objects of immediate sense perception (*Gl.*, § 28.2), and a discipline is historical not because its data are past events but because it deals with the flux of human existence—including its present, which can be understood only as the product of the past and the germ of the future (*KD*, § 26). A complication in Schleiermacher's position surfaces clearly in *Gl.*, § 28.2, where he points to a double distinction: Dogmatics differs not only from deductive-conceptual sciences (because it starts from a fact, not from an axiom) but also from those historical sciences that embrace a "definite field of *outward* perception" (because the fundamental fact of Christian piety, which dogmatics postulates, is an "inner fact").

ence.[57] Both are parts of historical theology, and when Schleiermacher says that historical theology "coheres (*zusammenhängt*) with science proper through philosophical theology," he cannot mean that church history and dogmatics are *not* sciences; he means that this is how they *are* sciences. They would lack scientific status if they confronted the mass of data without the organizing concepts that philosophical theology supplies; for that would be *mindless* traditioning (*geistlose Überlieferung*).[58]

Schleiermacher expressly states that by reason of its content historical theology, which includes dogmatics, is a part of the modern study of history (*neuere Geschichtskunde*).[59] Presumably, then, the dogmatic theologian would be required in Schleiermacher's order of things to give occasional lectures in the department of history; and if the theological faculty went out of business tomorrow, dogmaticians could seek employment in the faculty of philosophy, though it is not entirely clear how, or how far, they would have to adapt their discipline in making the move. Perhaps dogmatics in some form would become one of the special divisions of historical science that "are annexed to the philosophical faculty just so long as they are not dealt with pragmatically in the interests of some practical goal."[60]

Now, of course, Schleiermacher's terms (*Geschichtskunde, empirisch,* and so on) seldom, if ever, coincide exactly with our English equivalents, and the proliferation of divisions, departments, and professional schools in our present-day American universities complicates the picture still further. But the cardinal point, even if it is little more than a bare hint, remains: he thought it possible so to conceive of theology (dogmatics) that it could in principle have a place in the humanities. It may be replied that what belongs in the humanities is history of religions or *Religionswissenschaft,* not theology, and that history of religions can establish its legitimacy only insofar as it remains untarnished by any taint of theology. But what Schleiermacher in fact did was exactly to move *theology* a good step closer to what came to be called "the scientific study of religion." It is his conception of the theological *faculty* that has obscured this fundamental move.

Schleiermacher did not represent dogmatics as the science of supernaturally revealed truths or the science of God, but held it to be a strictly human science that deals with one variety of one fundamental aspect of

57. See, e.g., Troeltsch, GS 2:514–15.

58. *KD,* §§ 28–29, 65. A *merely* empirical treatment, or *mindless* empiricism, is insufficient (ibid., §§ 21, 59, 256). History is not chronicle (ibid., §§ 153, 252).

59. Ibid., § 69.

60. *Gelegentliche Gedanken,* 259. The examples Schleiermacher gives of scientific areas in which professors of law and theology should want to distinguish themselves are *reine Philosophie, Sittenlehre, philosophische Geschichtsbetrachtung,* and *Philologie* (ibid., 261–62).

human experience. For precisely this reason, he could launch his dogmatic project only by placing the Christian way of believing in the context of other religious faiths and bringing religion in general into relation with other types of human experience.[61] And while he followed tradition in giving dogmatic propositions also in the form of statements about God's activities and attributes, as well as in the form of statements about human experience, he could envision a future theology that would confine itself wholly to the description of the religious affections, as befits a consistently empirical discipline.[62]

Naturally, this vision of the theology of the future has been greeted with horror by many other theologians, and their objections need much more careful attention than I can possibly hope to give them here. Even so judicious a theologian as Pannenberg asserts that Schleiermacher contributed unintentionally to the discrediting of talk about God: he treated religion only as a form of subjective experience, not as the self-manifestation of divine reality.[63] I do not myself think the criticism is just: Schleiermacher held religion generally to be a revelation of the divine in the depths of every human consciousness, and the Christian religion to be the effect of the historical revelation in Jesus of Nazareth.[64] He thought that he had shown *how* to talk about God. But, for the moment, I am more interested in the fact that his anthropological dogmatics of the future does, in a sense, approach the methodological "bracketing" of reality claims that is recommended by historians of religions. The truth of dogmatic assertions is the correctness with which they describe the Christian way of believing; they do not strictly *assert* the Christian way of believing or claim that what Christians believe is true, even if the dogmatician, as a Christian, *thinks* it is true.[65]

61. The twofold placement (*Ortsbestimmung*) of the Christian way of believing was the main purpose of the opening sections of the *Glaubenslehre* (*Gl.*, §§ 2–11; *KD*, §§ 21–22; *Sendschr.*, 54–55).

62. *Gl.*, § 30; *Sendschr.*, 47–48.

63. *Wissenschaftstheorie*, 266, 374.

64. *Gl.*, § 4.4, § 10.

65. On bracketing reality claims, see, e.g., Joachim Wach, *Introduction to the History of Religions*, ed. Joseph M. Kitagawa et al. (New York: Macmillan, 1988), 22–27. Cf. Ninian Smart on methodological agnosticism or neutralism (*The Science of Religion and the Sociology of Knowledge: Some Methodological Questions* [Princeton, New Jersey: Princeton University Press, 1973], 57, 66, 158–59) and Peter L. Berger on other worlds and human projections (*The Sacred Canopy: Elements of a Sociological Theory of Religion* [Garden City, New York: Doubleday, 1967], 88–89, 179–88). The varieties of truth claim that one finds made, or reported, in a work of theology need to be disentangled more carefully than they can be here. But I think Wach is too hasty when he writes: "[T]he assertion that a particular religion is true . . . will always be the first and last assertion of every dogmatics" (*Introduction*, 46). Schleiermacher, at least, thought that adherents of another religion could assent to his definition of Christianity without adopting Christianity as true for them (*Gl.*, § 11.5); perhaps he could

No doubt, what distinguishes Schleiermacher's dogmatics from *Religionswissenschaft,* as usually understood, is chiefly that he did not think a correct account of the Christian way of believing *could* be given by anyone who did *not* believe. He offered, not an outsider's reading of a historical tradition, but an insider's, and this entailed for him the attempt to put the best construction on it, to cast it in the most suitable form, and so to open up possibilities for its future. "Development of doctrine" is a key phrase in his understanding of theology. The dogmatic theologian does not reproduce a static system of beliefs, nor even chart the course of a living tradition, but is rather a conscious agent of a tradition's continuing vitality, adaptation, and change.[66] For while the essence of the dogmatic task is simply *describing* the religious affections correctly (which is what makes it an empirical task),[67] it can only be carried out by *developing* the inherited doctrinal forms—subjecting them to a critical appropriation that immerses itself as far as possible both in the particular tradition and in the current state of knowledge generally.[68]

Clearly, no such constructive task is normally undertaken by the practitioners of *Religionswissenschaft*. But the difference between *Religionswissenschaft* and *Glaubenslehre* is by no means that the latter has a less scientific, purely churchly and practical, intent. Even what Schleiermacher calls the "ecclesiastical value" of dogmatic propositions is strictly an empirical, and to this extent scientific, criterion: their fidelity to the Christian religious affections. The "scientific value" of the propositions only makes the reference to the religious affections more exact and systematic.[69] The necessity to do dogmatics from within the tradition—a necessity he expressly affirms[70]—did not require of him a surrender of his scientific principles (a point to which I shall return later). In his own intention at least, dogmatics was to be a science, part of the scientific treatment

have hoped for similar understanding for the rest of the *Glaubenslehre*. Unfortunately, however, he immediately goes on to say that dogmatics is "only for Christians" (cf. also *Gl.*, § 2).

66. *Gelegentliche Gedanken,* 258; *Gl.*, § 19.3–4, § 25.2, § 27.2. Cf. Schleiermacher's letter to F. H. Jacobi (30 March 1818): text in Martin Cordes, "Der Brief Schleiermachers an Jacobi: Ein Beitrag zu seiner Entstehung und Überlieferung," *Zeitschrift für Theologie und Kirche* 68 (1971): 195–212; see 209.

67. *Gl.*, §§ 15–16.

68. *Gl.*, § 16 (postscript), § 19 (postscript); *KD*, §§ 177, 180–81; *Sendschr.*, 64–66. Philosophical language is borrowed only to aid in giving the form of dogmatic propositions; their content is given by the religious affections themselves (*Gl.*, § 16 [postscript], § 19 [postscript]; *Sendschr.*, 59–61, 66).

69. *Gl.*, § 17; cf. *Gl.*, § 28.1.

70. It is already affirmed in the Anselmian motto on the title page of the *Glaubenslehre*. See also *Gl.*, § 13 (postscript), § 19.1; *KD*, § 196. Philosophical theology, on the other hand, adopts a neutral standpoint "above" Christianity (*KD*, § 33).

of the historical career of Christianity.[71] The prospect for an academic theology looks very different from Schleiermacher's perspective than it did later from Troeltsch's. If the theology of the future were reconceived as a humanistic discipline, the church's faith would be there not to control the inquiry but to provide the subject matter of a science that asks for no special favors.

Christian Theology and the Humanities

The picture of theology in Schleiermacher's *Thoughts on Universities* and *Brief Outline* inevitably strikes us as remote. It is not simply that theology, as he saw it, was in the service of the church (which, by and large, is how we still see it), but that in his world one church had a privileged social status; its clergy were in effect civil servants or, as Kant liked to say, tools and instruments of the government.[72] The theological faculty was there because the state had taken the education of the clergy under its wing. Pannenberg doubts if Schleiermacher ever realized just how dependent he left theology on the interests of the state as well as on the interests of the church.[73] In any case, whether or not he realized it, the theological faculty, as Schleiermacher conceived of it, was bound to be threatened if the social standing of the church took a turn for the worse. And that is clearly what has happened, at least in the eyes of our present-day intelligentsia.

Even though his actual *thoughts* on the subject are partly dated, it need not follow that Schleiermacher's *concern* for the relation of theology to church and society is of no interest anymore. It can be translated, up to a point, into the language of our own discussions on religion and public life, or the university and the common good. Perhaps in our situation the mission of the university-based divinity school will be less exclusively oriented toward church and ministry, more directly toward the social order, than Schleiermacher could have thought. Within the university, the divinity school may help nurture candid, self-critical appraisals of the social role of the academy itself. For while the free quest for truth is a good in itself, it is still pertinent to ask how it is related to other goods, especially since "truth for truth's sake" tends to coincide with the self-interest of university professors. But that is not my theme here. I am more interested in seeing that the *other* side of Schleiermacher's thoughts on theology as an academic discipline will not be overlooked.

71. *Gl.*, § 19, § 31.1; *KD*, § 252.

72. Immanuel Kant, *Der Streit der Fakultäten/The Conflict of the Faculties* (1798), trans. and ed. Mary J. Gregor, Janus Library (New York: Abaris Books, 1979), 24. The clergy administer a "statutory religion": a religion contained in writings authorized by the government, which accordingly have the force of law (32–34).

73. *Wissenschaftstheorie*, 250.

My thesis has been that anyone who turns to him for possible insight on the place of theology in the university will very likely learn more from what he says about the theoretical unity of science than from what he says about the pragmatic unity of theological studies. I do not of course suppose that in our world his dogmatics could pass as unproblematic, or that it could be adopted without further ado once the terminological eccentricities are removed; only that its possibilities as an academic theology have still not been exhausted, but rather obscured. Most of the objections leveled against theology as a university discipline either miss him completely or at least need to be reconsidered, and we have hardly begun to explore the possibilities of theology ("dogmatics," in his parlance) as a humanistic rather than a professional discipline. Naturally, such a change, if ever made, would shape the discipline even while providing it with a home. An academic theology would be motivated by "the scientific spirit": it would have to show its place on the scientific map, to share its methodological principles with other disciplines, and to relate its own findings as far as possible with theirs.[74] It should even have something to contribute to the common enterprise besides its actual findings, because the fact is that in the historicizing of knowledge theology was a pioneering discipline; other disciplines, which mistook theological reform for a discrediting of theology, have had to catch up.[75]

I realize, of course, that in the university it is easier to make a case for philosophical, or natural, theology than for an explicitly Christian, constructive theology. I am certainly in favor of a philosophical theology, though I doubt if it could ever do all that Troeltsch once expected of it.[76] If, with David Tracy, we distinguish the three communities to which theology is addressed as the academy, the church, and society, then I agree with him that the kind of theology that is *primarily* related to the academy will be philosophical or fundamental. But my question here has been whether there is *also* a place in the academy for what he calls a "systematic theology," the discipline to which he assigns the task Schleiermacher gave to *Glaubenslehre*—the task of reinterpreting the tradition for the pres-

74. See, in addition to the citations already given, the famous passage on the "eternal covenant" in *Sendschr.*, 40.

75. See Stephen Toulmin's interesting reflections, "The Historicization of Natural Science: Its Implications for Theology," in Hans Küng and David Tracy, eds., *Paradigm Change in Theology: A Symposium for the Future,* trans. Margaret Kohl (New York: Crossroad, 1989), 233–41.

76. If the question of the truth or validity of religious claims is in effect bracketed in dogmatic theology, the need for a philosophical theology to take it up becomes all the more urgent. But Troeltsch himself finally abandoned the attempt to prove the *highest* validity of Christianity (see n. 40 above).

ent.[77] The old names for this discipline, "dogmatic theology" or simply "dogmatics"—names Schleiermacher himself never gave up—are no longer very helpful, because "dogmatic" has acquired the pejorative sense of obstinate and overbearing insistence on a dogma. The association may not be entirely accidental. Theodor Reik has argued that the formation of a dogma in the church, such as the dogma of the Trinity, resembles psychologically the emergence of an obsessional idea in neurotic patients. "To such people," he says, "the dogma appears eternal and released from all temporal limitations."[78] Be that as it may, the label "dogmatics" is probably irretrievable in the academy and perhaps should be abandoned even in the church. For, as Troeltsch put it, dogmatics is no longer dogmatics when it knows no dogmas anymore.[79] What is left, however, according to Schleiermacher, is not a mere personal confession of faith for the inspiration of future clergy, as Troeltsch supposed, but a *scientific* description of a particular way of believing *as seen from the inside.* And there, perhaps, in the last phrase, are the grounds for a lingering suspicion on the part of the academy. Is the church—mediately, at least, in the form of an ecclesiastical commitment—still present, only better hidden?

Well, Schleiermacher was probably right in holding that dogmatics, in his sense, could be done only from the inside—by someone who shared the faith to be scrutinized. That followed from his definition of the dogmatic task. A *report* on what Christians say they believe could be undertaken by any outsider with sufficient information. But it is unlikely that an outsider could, or would even wish to, engage in bringing about a *development* of the doctrines in which the faith is expressed. The question is, then, whether such development—such an "act of traditioning," as we say—is out of line with what goes on in other university disciplines. Schleiermacher apparently did not think so. Although he freely used the Anselmian language of faith seeking understanding, he was not claiming to possess information supernaturally communicated to the elect, but rather affirming a hermeneutic principle: Inner facts cannot be simply observed but call for introspection, participation, and even commitment.[80] Presumably, the transmission of knowledge in the schools of law and medicine is

77. Tracy, *The Analogical Imagination: Christian Theology and the Culture of Pluralism* (New York: Crossroad, 1981), 56–57, 64, 68.

78. Reik, *Dogma and Compulsion: Psychoanalytic Studies of Religion and Myths* (New York: International Universities Press, 1951), 48, 69.

79. Troeltsch, "Dogmatik," RGG 2:109.

80. *Gl.*, § 13 (postscript). In *KD*, § 196, Schleiermacher makes the interesting observation that without personal conviction one could give a historical report but not a persuasive presentation of the *Zusammenhang* of doctrine—the way it hangs together (cf. *KD*, § 195). Dogmatic theology is *die Wissenschaft von dem Zusammenhange* and calls for an "apologetic" taking of sides (*Gl.*, § 19.1).

not subject to the same limitation. But is there perhaps at least an analogy to the theologian's commitment in the humanities?[81]

Even in the natural sciences, in which so high a premium is placed on fresh observation and novel discoveries, commitment to a tradition of inquiry and discovery is by no means out of place. But since I was myself a student of Greek and Latin before I turned to theology, it is more natural for me to try a comparison between theology and the classics (not, I hope, between one losing cause and another). In school, those of us who took the "classical side" (as we put it) were not merely taught the rudiments of the Greek and Latin languages. Even a journeyman philologist could have dragged us through Homer's Greek. But we learned to appreciate Homer from an exuberant master who found our labored efforts at word-by-word translation so painful that he would interrupt us—usually with the theological expletive, "Oh, *God!*"—and would then race through page after page translating for us, chuckling happily as he went. He wanted us not just to construe the *Iliad* correctly, but to love Homer and to let him shape our spirits.

But more than that, we were constantly plied with something like tracts on behalf of the gospel of Hellenism. In an address delivered at the annual meeting of the Classical Association in 1954, the then secretary frankly classified some of the association's publications as "protreptic" (a nicer word, he thought, than "propaganda").[82] Printed as handy booklets, small enough to slip into your pocket, these evangelistic tracts—mostly lectures or addresses in origin—could be distributed by schoolteachers to their eager pupils. Even more ambitious were whole volumes that raised the banner of a classical education. Sir Richard Livingstone (1880–1960) was perhaps the outstanding master of the genre. By means of a selective and highly idealized portrait of ancient Athens, he assured us that Greek ideals could help us with the chief weakness of our age: the lack of a definite view of life. He did not conceal from us the partial antagonism between Hellenism and Christianity but left us to make the choice for ourselves—or to follow the early church into a happy syncretism.[83]

I do not believe that we ever felt our minds were being violated; and

81. An analogy is *all* I am here looking for. The precise form in which Schleiermacher gives the Anselmian model of theologizing is, in my opinion, dubious. "[Q]ui expertus non fuerit, non intelliget" risks making theology esoteric. It is one thing to insist that the theologian needs to be *expertus* to give an adequate presentation of the Christian way of believing, quite another to infer that nobody else will understand what is said unless he or she is also *expertus* or *experta*.

82. L. J. D. Richardson, "The Classical Association: The First Fifty Years," *Proceedings of the Classical Association* 51 (1954): 23–41; see 32.

83. R. W. Livingstone, *Greek Ideals and Modern Life* (London: Oxford University Press [Geoffrey Cumberlege], 1935), 2–6, 37, 174–75; idem, *The Greek Genius and Its Meaning to Us*, 2d ed. (ibid., 1915), 123–24.

we did not all become true believers, as some of our essays on the benefits of a classical education made only too clear. (I recall one impudent schoolboy arguing that a classical education teaches us many things we would not even wish to know without the benefit of a classical education.) We were not offended. We smiled a bit. But there was, I think, a danger: we were convinced of our intellectual superiority to pupils in what C. P. Snow (1905–80) would call the *other* culture[84] and did not realize the deprivation our education actually entailed. Like the little band of Spartans at Thermopylae, we were delaying the advance of the barbarian hordes. The philosopher G. E. Moore, who sixty years earlier had sat in the same classroom I sat in afterward, told of the many hours he spent on his weekly quota of prose and verse composition in Greek and Latin, and wondered in retrospect: "Possibly it would have been better for me if some of those hours had been spent upon some of the Natural Sciences, of which I learned absolutely nothing at school."[85]

When those of us who were loyal to the classics moved on to the university, we were excited by E. R. Dodds's (1893–1979) brilliant study *The Greeks and the Irrational* (1951), not only because it offered a somewhat iconoclastic reinterpretation of the ancient Athenians (though that was appealing enough to the undergraduate mind) but also because he was plainly talking about the Dionysian passions that lurk behind the Apollonian smile of every reasonable, civilized man or woman. His work brought together the ancient texts and the newest anthropological and psychological theories, and we saw at once that his interpretation of Euripides as both the spokesman of the Greek enlightenment and its adversary was a comment on human nature. "Primitive," as Dodds remarked, is a fair enough description of most people's mental behavior most of the time. The Greeks were no exception: they illustrate the rule.[86]

My point then, if I dare generalize from these shamelessly personal recollections, is that in varying degrees the best humanistic scholarship arises out of a powerful sense of the abiding value and universal significance of some tradition of learning. It is never a cold autopsy on a dead body. As Newman says, a little effusively, the university is "the place where the professor becomes eloquent, and is a missionary and a preacher, displaying his science in its most complete and most winning form, pour-

84. C[harles] P[ercy] Snow, *The Two Cultures and the Scientific Revolution,* Rede Lecture (Cambridge: Cambridge University Press, 1959).

85. Moore, "An Autobiography," in Paul Arthur Schilpp, ed., *The Philosophy of G. E. Moore,* Library of Living Philosophers, 2d ed. (New York: Tudor Publishing Company, 1952), 6.

86. E[ric] R[obertson] Dodds, *The Greeks and the Irrational* (1951), 6th printing, Sather Classical Lectures, vol. 25 (Berkeley and Los Angeles: University of California Press, 1968), viii, 188.

ing it forth with the zeal of enthusiasm, and lighting up his own love of it in the breasts of his hearers."[87] It does not follow, of course, that *any* kind of advocacy, propaganda, or proselytism is justified, much less apocalyptic warnings of the wrath to come. But we can hardly demand of our theologians a more ascetic standard of detachment than we expect of their colleagues in other departments of the university. The Athanasian Creed claims too much for its obscure propositions when it promises eternal destruction to anyone who doubts them. In a secular university, at any rate, the theologian does not say, "This is the Catholic Faith, which except a man believe faithfully, he cannot be saved." She says rather: "Here is something of value that our world cannot afford to lose, something still alive that I cannot bring myself to treat as though it were dead." And then she proceeds to put the best construction on it.

Reinterpretation for the sake of transmitting something perceived to be of enduring worth lies at the heart of our humanistic enterprise. But so do the right and duty to test everything for oneself and the freedom to reject what is commended by one's teachers, however earnest and winsome they may be. Hence, although the academy does not need to exclude the creative development of a religious tradition by an insider (who else could develop it creatively?), it does have a responsibility not to give *absolute* precedence to one religion over another. Ideally, it should want to find room for theologians and philosophers who are working on, and within, other religious traditions than Christianity. This, too, is the logic of Schleiermacher's position—once the subordination of theological studies to the needs of church leadership is put in perspective. Within what he calls the "faculty of philosophy" only a *relative* precedence, at most, could be given to Christianity as the dominant religious tradition in our own culture.

Perhaps the future for the divinity schools, too, lies in the same genuinely ecumenical direction. But it has not been my purpose in this essay to justify university-based divinity schools, only to explore the main reason why they are often found to be problematic. My conviction is that the existence of divinity schools is a further question on which we have yet to learn all we could from Schleiermacher. Once again, the most important texts are not the *Thoughts on Universities* or the *Brief Outline;* there is more to learn from his epoch-making reflections on religion and the religions in his famous *Speeches* to the cultured despisers.[88] For, as far as I can see, a divinity school (or something like it under another name) is required in a secular and pluralistic university only if religion is an "independent vari-

87. "What Is a University?" 16.

88. Not least among Schleiermacher's pertinent insights is that if you want to know what it means to be religious, you have to settle *somewhere* (*Reden,* 257). This is a quite different justification for particularity than Harnack's claim that anyone who knows *this* religion (Christianity) knows them all (Harnack, "Die Aufgabe," 168).

able" (as the sociologists put it), worthy of exploration from every possible perspective, including the perspective of church leadership.

This, clearly, is another large question. But it is not unrelated to the question I have tried to explore: What kind of theology belongs in the academy? I do not pretend that Schleiermacher's is the only, or even the most widely accepted, view of theology at the present time. But I do think it is at least defensible as an academic theology. Anyone who believes that theology is possible and meaningful in the church alone, that it begins with God in his revelation in Jesus Christ, and that it is scientific just insofar as it corresponds to the word of God through the obedience of faith, will need to come up with a quite different account of theology's credentials as a university discipline, or may prefer to pursue it somewhere else.

Index